DYNAMIC ASSESSMENT IN PRACTICE

Dynamic assessment embeds interaction within the framework of a test–intervene–retest approach to psychoeducational assessment. This book offers an introduction to diagnostic assessors in psychology, education, and speech/language pathology to the basic ideas, principles, and practices of dynamic assessment. Most important, the book presents an array of specific procedures developed and used by the authors that can be applied to clients of all ages in both clinical and educational settings. The authors discuss their approach to report writing, providing a number of examples to demonstrate how they incorporate dynamic assessment into a comprehensive approach to assessment. The text concludes with a discussion of issues and questions that need to be considered and addressed. Two appendixes include descriptions of additional tests used by the authors that are adapted for dynamic assessment as well as information about dynamic assessment procedures developed by others and sources for additional information about this approach.

H. Carl Haywood is Professor of Psychology, Emeritus, at Vanderbilt University and was Professor of Neurology in the Vanderbilt University School of Medicine from 1971 until 1993. He was also founding Dean of the Graduate School of Education and Psychology at Touro College in New York, where he instituted graduate programs based heavily on cognitive development and cognitive education. He has published extensively on cognitive education and dynamic assessment as well as on mental retardation, intrinsic motivation, development of intelligence and cognitive abilities, and neuropsychology.

Carol S. Lidz has held faculty positions in psychology at Temple University and the Graduate School of Education of Touro College, where she designed and directed the school psychology program. In 2004, she joined Freidman Associates, where she provided school neuropsychological assessments of children with learning disorders. She is the author of books, chapters, and articles on dynamic assessment and assessment of preschool children. She lives in Philadelphia and is engaged in research and professional writing.

Dynamic Assessment in Practice

CLINICAL AND EDUCATIONAL APPLICATIONS

H. Carl Haywood

Vanderbilt University

Carol S. Lidz

Philadelphia, PA

CAMBRIDGE
UNIVERSITY PRESS

CAMBRIDGE UNIVERSITY PRESS
Cambridge, New York, Melbourne, Madrid, Cape Town, Singapore, São Paulo

Cambridge University Press
32 Avenue of the Americas, New York, NY 10013-2473, USA

www.cambridge.org
Information on this title: www.cambridge.org/9780521849357

First published 2007

Printed in the United States of America

A catalog record for this publication is available from the British Library.

Library of Congress Cataloging in Publication Data

Haywood, H. Carl, 1931–
Dynamic assessment in practice : clinical and educational applications /
H. Carl Haywood, Carol S. Lidz.
    p.   cm.
Includes bibliographical references and index.
ISBN-13: 978-0-521-84935-7 (hardback)
ISBN-10: 0-521-84935-7 (hardback)
ISBN-13: 978-0-521-61412-2 (pbk.)
ISBN-10: 0-521-61412-0 (pbk.)
1. Learning disabilities – Diagnosis.   2. Learning ability – Testing.
3. Dynamic assessment (Education)   I. Lidz, Carol Schneider.   II. Title.
RJ496.L4H39   2007
618.92'85889 – dc22   2006009176

ISBN   978-0-521-84935-7 hardback
ISBN   978-0-521-61412-2 paperback

Go straight to pine
Trees to learn pine
And to bamboo stalks
To know bamboo

    – Basho (1644–1694)

Contents

Preface

Dynamic assessment (DA), an interactive, test–intervene–retest model of psychological and psychoeducational assessment, is a rapidly developing approach of increasing interest to practicing psychologists. In one form or another, DA has been applied in psychological, neuropsychological, speech/language, and educational contexts. Several major texts now describe the various theories, models, and procedures of DA. These texts provide information primarily concerning the background, research, and descriptions of DA procedures; however, none of the texts puts these procedures into the hands of practitioners in a way that equips them to implement the approach. Furthermore, although trainers are often well informed about theoretical models and, in many cases introduce their students to the ideas and principles of DA, few trainers actually work with their students to develop and refine their professional application of these skills.

Seeking to fill this void, we describe in this book basic DA approaches and procedures and elaborate the full instructions, scoring approaches, and interpretation possibilities of DA procedures that we and others have developed and that we actually incorporate into our own practices. We use these procedures to extend, supplement, and enrich our assessments to bridge the gap between assessment and intervention and to deepen insight into the functioning of our clients. We present DA not as a substitute or replacement for existing approaches to assessment but as an extension of and addition to these more traditional procedures; DA provides important information that is simply not available from other sources.

This text is unique within the DA literature in that we conceptualize the assessment process in relation to a model of mental functioning to which the procedures are anchored. The model, derived from a developmental view of "normal" intellective and cognitive functioning, is a positive (not deficit-based) description of the functions involved in mental processing that relate to learning. The procedures address the assessment–intervention gap and help practitioners to identify the special needs of individuals being assessed as well as to generate plans for programming and instruction.

The book is organized, both physically and conceptually, to take account of the assessment needs and practices primarily in clinical psychology and school/educational psychology. It is in these two domains that dynamic assessment is most urgently needed. This book is relevant for either graduate students or practicing professionals in the fields of clinical, school, and counseling psychology and neuropsychology. It is appropriate as a text for graduate courses in advanced diagnostic assessment. Although designed primarily for use by psychologists, it would also be of interest to advanced practitioners and university educators in the fields of speech/language pathology and both special and regular education.

Readers might wonder why we have invited two distinguished scientist-practitioners to write forewords to the book. It is precisely because we have addressed the book principally to practitioners in the applied domains of clinical psychology and education, and we sought help in setting these two giant enterprises as application sites for the theories, approaches, and practices presented here.

Chapters 1 through 3 concern theory and basic principles, intended to introduce readers to dynamic assessment and to start out with a level playing field for both novice and veteran practitioners. Chapters 4 through 8 provide specific instructions for administration of dynamic assessment procedures that we have designed and used in our practices. Chapter 9 is addressed to one of the major concerns of DA trainers and newly trained practitioners: the reporting of the outcomes of DA. In our own experience training both graduate students and seasoned professionals to do DA, report writing has emerged as a strong concern; therefore, we have provided some guidelines as well as examples of such reports. Chapter 10 serves as a summary and discussion of special issues in dynamic assessment. There are two appendixes that provide readers with information about dynamic assessment procedures that are currently available from publishers as well as an array of dynamic resources such as Web sites and training sources. The book contains additional materials that readers can download and print for their own use, including some original tests as well as forms, scoring sheets, and guides. These materials are accessible at the Cambridge University Press Web site: **www.cambridge. org/9780521849357**. To access this material, the required username is **lecturer** and the password is **solutions05**. We have included this downloadable material in an effort to make DA materials and procedures more readily available and accessible to professionals who need them. We must insert two words of caution about use of these materials. First, it would be grossly incorrect to assume that these materials are the sum of DA tasks and materials, or even that they are representative of the field. They are what these two authors use and propose to other users. We happily acknowledge the existence and utility of many other sets of DA materials. Second, access to testing materials is no substitute for professional training in their use. Training in DA continues to be a large issue (see Chapter 10), but no matter what approach one takes to DA, specialized training in its theories, approaches, applications, materials, and interpretation is still essential.

Our major purpose in writing this book has been to put DA into the hands of practitioners and their trainers, or as close to that goal as we can get with the written word. We want readers to be able to move beyond passive expression of interest into actually doing DA. We are both of retirement age and have worked long and hard to enhance the continuing development of this approach. We have conducted research, trained practitioners, and designed procedures. We have talked and tested, but most of all we have listened and learned. We have tried to put what we have learned and what we have designed into these pages, hoping to pass our experiences on to the next generation.

We are grateful to those who have inspired us and to those on whose shoulders we stand. Reuven Feuerstein has of course been an important catalyst for much of the work that has been done in this area, and certainly for us he has been at various times both mentor and collaborator, and always friend. Both of us have learned a great deal from our graduate students and those psychological and educational professionals who have come to us for DA training in literally dozens of workshops in many countries. Most of all, we have learned extremely important lessons from the many individuals whom we have examined using the methods of DA. They have our sincere gratitude.

H. Carl Haywood
Carol S. Lidz
September 2006

Foreword

This text bucks a trend in clinical psychology. Much of modern-day assessment in the field has sadly become the formulaic application of computerized rules that unabashedly serve the singular goal of satisfying health insurers' mindless requirements for a psychiatric diagnosis. The practice of assessment has become restricted by those requirements. Technicians, or – even more frequently – computer programs, transform a client's responses to multiple-choice questions into numbers and categories that allow a clinical psychologist to begin intervention. In the best case, the intervention is "evidence-based" and grounded in empirical evaluation. But the divide between assessment and intervention has grown deeper, and the client's well-being has suffered.

Haywood and Lidz provide a much-needed antidote to this trend. They carry the torch of the rich tradition of transactional psychology and dynamic assessment in this novel text that brings these principles to life. This is a dynamic application of dynamic assessment.

The critical principle is that there is no divide between assessment and intervention. Intervention *is* assessment, and assessment *is* the intervention. The clinician learns about the client by testing the client's skill, knowledge, and ability to learn. The clinician asks a question, the client demonstrates, and the clinician aligns that response with an intricately structured, multi-dimensional schema and then asks another question. It is the relationship between clinician and client that is transactional, dynamic, and growing. The interaction is simultaneously an assessment of the client's current level of functioning and an intervention to boost that level. The recursiveness of the exchange between the clinician and the client is the engine for growth.

The concepts that guide dynamic assessment are steeped in the tradition of cognitive developmental theories of Vygotsky and Feuerstein, who recognized that human beings are not static entities but are always in states of transition and transactional relationships with the world. It is the transaction with the world that brings cognitive growth. These concepts have been kept alive with more recent revisions of cognitive developmental theory by Campione, Brown, and Bransford and with theories of multiple intelligences by Gardner and Sternberg.

The concepts are of obvious importance in the applied domain of intellectual assessment and intervention with problems of intellectual disability, learning disability, and reading failure. They are quite consistent with cutting-edge applications by other leading educational practitioner-theorists, including Mel Levine and Howard Gardner. But they are also of crucial importance to clinical psychological problems such as conduct disorder, oppositional defiant disorder, attention-deficit/hyperactivity disorder, depression, and even social disorientation in disorders of old age. The distinction between the cognitive and the social is an artificial one, and the dynamic assessor brings them together. For childhood externalizing problems, the child's "learning disability" is difficulty with focusing attention on specific tasks or recognizing others' emotions or intentions. The child's experience with the world is shaped by the world's contrary reaction to the child's difficulty, and the ensuing transaction escalates into conflict, fighting, and maladaptive behavior. The dynamic assessor's task in these cases is to understand the child's current level of "reading" the social world. When the clinician communicates different emotions, does the child grasp the distinction between sad and mad, or anger and fear? Does the child understand how to read his or her own emotional reactions? Does the complexity of these emotions overwhelm the child, leading to off-task behavior that is observed by others as inattention and hyperactivity? The clinical dynamic assessor will use the same principles of dynamic assessment to understand the child's way of experiencing the world, to suggest a slightly new way to the child, and to evaluate the child's response to this suggestion. The dynamic transaction between clinician and client is both assessment and intervention.

The concepts are consistent with the transactional nature of cognitive therapy for depressive disorder. The cognitive therapist asks questions to learn how the client thinks in social interactions and precisely where the client's cognitive distortions occur. Then the therapist suggests an alternative or suggests an activity that will enable the client to experience an alternative. The client's response to that activity drives the next intervention. Is this process assessment or intervention? It is both – it is transactional, and it is consistent with dynamic assessment principles as articulated in this text.

Expert dynamic assessment requires professional skill. Although this text provides the most hands-on applications to date, it is not a cookbook. Clinical expertise requires practice, experience, and feedback through supervision. These skills are developed through the same principles of dynamic assessment that Haywood and Lidz prescribe for clients. In this way, this text provides a dynamic assessment approach to teaching dynamic assessment. It is decidedly anti-cookbook and anti-computer.

The authors of this text are senior pioneers in the transformation of dynamic theory into clinical practice. They have been at it for decades. They live these principles, and they know firsthand how these principles really work. They bring their own experience to bear on these problems, and the result is a text that brings to life the principles of classic developmental theorists. This is a must-read for clinicians and educators, scholars and practitioners.

Kenneth A. Dodge, Ph.D., is the William McDougall Professor of Public Policy and Director of the Center for Child and Family Policy at Duke University. He leads an effort to bridge basic scientific research in children's development with public policy affecting children and families.

Foreword

Assessment specialists in the United States and Western Europe are fortunate to be able to select from hundreds of standardized norm-referenced tests. Test authors and test companies continue to provide a steady supply of additional excellent resources. Different assessment models and methods that supplement current resources also are needed, however.

This need was underscored in 1991 as I was preparing to direct the International Test Commission's conference on test use with children and youth at Oxford University. I reviewed then-current literature on desired changes in assessment practice (Oakland, 1995). Assessment specialists were requested to devote more attention to dynamic behaviors (e.g., problem-solving abilities) and less attention to static behaviors (e.g., general intelligence), to assess outcomes needed for the attainment of meaningful life activities, to identify temporary and improvable barriers to performance, and to emphasize formative evaluation methods.

Carol Lidz's book *Dynamic Assessment: An Interactional Approach for Evaluating Learning Potential* (1987) addressed many of these important issues. Her pioneering scholarship helped set the stage for other scholars and practitioners to become engaged in the use and development of what we now call dynamic assessment. Carl Haywood's early scholarship (e.g., 1992) also helped promote this important and emerging area.

Haywood and Lidz's current collaboration, *Dynamic Assessment in Practice: Clinical and Educational Applications*, synthesizes foundational scholarship (e.g., from Vygotsky and Feuerstein) and extends it in exemplary ways that enable assessment specialists to address issues I identified in 1991. Haywood and Lidz characterize dynamic assessment as an interactive process between the examiner and examinee with the goal of identifying pathways to the examinee's success. Processes central to dynamic assessment include identifying obstacles to more effective learning and performance, finding ways to remove or circumvent them, and assessing the effects of removing or circumventing obstacles on subsequent learning and performance.

Thus, the authors encourage examiners to focus on behaviors that are dynamic (i.e., changeable) – on problem-solving abilities, temporary and improvable barriers to performance, processes needed for the attainment of meaningful life activities – and to consider assessment and intervention to be linked inseparably and to be ongoing (e.g., using formative evaluation methods).

Haywood and Lidz describe dynamic assessment in ways that are complementary to other commonly used methods, including standardized testing, history taking, observing, and interviewing. Thus, dynamic assessment adds to and should not distract from well-honed assessment methods.

The ultimate goal of assessment should be an accurate description of behavior that helps promote development. The importance and currency of this goal are underscored by efforts to determine the degree to which students are benefiting from instruction and behavioral interventions (e.g., response to intervention). If students are not benefiting, professionals should focus on obstacles that can be circumvented or removed or behaviors that can be improved so as to better promote development. Thus, *Dynamic Assessment in Practice* is timely in that it provides methods to promote this goal.

In writing *Dynamic Assessment in Practice*, the authors intend to enable practitioners and instructors to acquire the knowledge and skills needed to use dynamic assessment. In part, this goal is achieved because both authors are excellent scholars and practitioners. These strengths are reflected in their command of literature (e.g., more than 300 references) as well as their ability to synthesize it in ways that promote practice. The addition of Web-based downloads that provide test forms and scoring sheets and guides practitioners and instructors further enhances the implementation of dynamic assessment.

Both authors have a distinguished history of devotion to finding pathways for children's success. Their interests and work have been on the cutting edge. Their passion for their work and persistence in its performance are important when undertaking a book of this magnitude and are reflected in the book's content and writing style.

The implementation of cardinal principles that form the foundation of dynamic assessment can be expected to have various unexpected positive consequences, one being the promotion of professionalism. Many assessment specialists work in systems that respect numbers more than professional judgment. The employment of principles advanced in *Dynamic Assessment in Practice* requires professionals to set aside numbers and to focus on dynamic behaviors. Professionals who are successful in implementing dynamic assessment methods are likely to be gifted in assessment (not just testing), to display instrumental knowledge of child and adolescent psychology, and to have a rich background in curriculum. In short, a high degree of professionalism is required to implement dynamic assessment successfully. Psychologists and other specialists, in an effort to enhance their knowledge and skills in ways that reinstate their importance as professionals rather than simply as psychometricians, can be expected to embrace the principles and methods described superbly in *Dynamic Assessment in Practice*.

Thomas Oakland, Ph.D., is Research Foundation Professor, Department of Educational Psychology, College of Education, at the University of Florida. His research has included children's temperament, test development and use, and legal, ethical, and professional issues in education and psychology.

REFERENCES

Haywood, H. C. (1992). Interactive assessment: A special issue. *Journal of Special Education, 26*, 233–234.

Lidz, C. S. (1987). *Dynamic assessment: An interactional approach for evaluating learning potential.* New York: Guilford Press.

Oakland, T. (1995). Test use in children and youth: Current status and future directions. In T. Oakland & R. Hambleton (Eds.), *International perspectives on academic assessment.* Boston: Kluwer Academic.

1 Dynamic Assessment: Introduction and Review

DEFINITIONS

Dynamic assessment (DA) is no longer a new approach to psychological and educational assessment; in fact, some of its current applications have been around for more than a half century (see, e.g., Feuerstein, Richelle, & Jeannet, 1953; Guthke & Wingenfeld, 1992). Despite such a relatively long history, it is still not widely practiced around the world (Elliott, 1993; Lidz, 1991, 1992). In April 2005, 588 literature citations relating to dynamic assessment were listed at the Web site www.dynamicassessment.com. The majority of those are of recent date, suggesting a rapid growth of interest in this topic in the last 10 to 15 years. A much broader search engine (www.google.com) produced 17,800,000 hits for this term; to be sure, the overwhelming majority of these did not relate to "dynamic assessment of learning potential."

At the dynamic assessment Web site, DA is defined as "an interactive approach to conducting assessments within the domains of psychology, speech/language, or education that focuses on the ability of the learner to respond to intervention." Others have defined it variously, but the constant aspect of the definition is active intervention by examiners and assessment of examinees' response to intervention. Haywood (1992b) suggested that dynamic assessment is a subset of the more generic concept of interactive assessment. He further suggested that "It might be useful to characterize as interactive any approach to psychological or psychoeducational assessment in which the examiner is inserted into an active relationship with a subject and does more than give instructions, pose questions, and record responses. 'Dynamic' should probably be reserved for those approaches in which the interaction is richer, in which there is actual teaching (not of answers but of cognitive tools), within the interaction and in which there is conscious, purposeful, and deliberate effort to produce change in the subject" (Haywood, 1992b, p. 233). Haywood and Tzuriel (2002) defined

1

dynamic assessment as "a subset of interactive assessment that includes deliberate and planned mediational teaching and the assessment of the effects of that teaching on subsequent performance" (p. 40). In current use, the two terms appear to be used interchangeably, together with such others as "dynamic testing" (e.g., Sternberg & Grigorenko, 2002; Wiedl, 2003) and "learning potential assessment" (e.g., Budoff, 1987; Hamers, Sijtsma, & Ruijssenaars, 1993). For further definition, see Carlson and Wiedl (1992a, 1992b), Feuerstein, Rand, and Hoffman (1979), Guthke and Wingenfeld (1992), Haywood and Tzuriel (1992), Lidz (1987), and Tzuriel (e.g., 2001). All of these approaches are in some sense "mediational," but there are other approaches to assessment that include intervention and response to intervention but that are not mediational. These would fit within the broad definition of DA.

Applicability of Dynamic Assessment

Although a few authors have suggested that dynamic assessment of learning potential should replace standardized, normative intelligence testing, our position does not come close to that. In fact, we insist that DA is not for everybody on all occasions but instead constitutes a valuable part of the assessment repertoire when used in conjunction with other forms of assessment, including standardized testing, social and developmental history taking, observation of performance in learning situations, and data gathered from clinical interview, parents, teachers, and others. The DA part of the repertoire is needed because it can add information about both present and potential performance that is not readily (or even at all) obtainable from other sources. Most dynamic assessment experts (e.g., Feuerstein, Haywood, Rand, Hoffman, & Jensen, 1982/1986; Haywood, 1997; Lidz, 1991) have suggested that this method is especially useful when

> *scores on standardized, normative tests are low,* and especially when they do not accord with information from other sources;
> *learning appears to be restrained* by apparent mental retardation, learning disability, emotional disturbance, personality disorder, or motivational deficit;
> *there are language problems,* such as impoverished vocabulary, difference between the maternal language and the language of the school (workplace), or delays in language development;
> *there are marked cultural differences* between those being examined and the majority or dominant culture, as, for example, in recent immigrants; and
> *classification is not the only or central issue, but the need to inform programming is important.*

In all of these situations, standardized, normative testing is likely to yield low scores and consequent pessimistic predictions of future learning effectiveness and school achievement. It is not the major role of DA to dispute those predictions; indeed, they are disastrously likely to prove accurate if nothing is done to overcome various obstacles to learning and performance. The role of DA is rather to identify obstacles to more effective learning and performance, to find ways to overcome those obstacles, and to assess the effects of removal of obstacles on subsequent learning and performance effectiveness. By extension of that role, a goal of DA is to suggest what can be done to defeat the pessimistic predictions that are often made on the basis of results of standardized, normative tests, including estimating the kinds and amount of intervention that will be necessary to produce significant improvement and the probable effects of such intervention. At the present stage of development of DA, those estimates are only rarely reducible to numbers. In fact, many adherents to DA resist precise quantification of estimates of learning potential or of ability to derive benefit from teaching because of fear that such quantification could lead to the use of DA data for the same purposes for which normative, standardized testing is generally used: classifying people, identifying those who are not expected to do well in school and other educational settings, and rank-ordering people with respect to presumed intellectual ability. One imagines with horror the development and use of a "modifiability index" or "learning potential quotient"!

Comparison of Dynamic and Normative/Standardized Assessment

A recurring theme in this volume is that the psychoeducational assessment process relies on data from diverse sources, of which DA is one. Because of that emphasis, it is useful to ask what it is that standardized tests do not do, or do not do well, and how DA can fill the gap left by these tests – or, indeed, to correct some of the errors of assessment that psychologists and others make when they rely exclusively on data from standardized tests.

Dynamic assessment has certain limitations, as well as some yet-unsolved problems, that make it important that the method be used appropriately, for specific purposes. First, because all approaches to dynamic assessment involve some effort to change examinees' performance, the data should not be used for classification and cannot be referred to normative tables for interpretation. Second, much of the interpretation of DA data depends on the skill and experience of the examiner. Third, the reliability of inferences regarding deficiencies in cognitive functioning has not been well established; that is, different examiners may reach different conclusions that reflect their own training and experience. In fact, the particular model that we present in this volume is not a deficit model; rather, it is one in which DA is used principally to identify areas of strength and potential strength, to discover what performance might be possible given optimal learning conditions and appropriate intervention, and to specify what those optimal conditions might be.

Standardized tests of intelligence are excellent instruments for the general purpose of classification, which is a useful activity when one is planning the allocation of limited resources or attempting to place individuals in groups where they can be served effectively. One such use is to identify gifted and talented children and youth so they can be educated in classes that require more investment of intellectual resources than do average public school classes. Another is to identify persons at the other end of the IQ distribution, that is, those who are likely to be mentally retarded and to require or benefit from special educational services.

By comparing each individual's score on standardized intelligence tests with the average score of persons of similar age and social background, that is, with the norms of the tests, one essentially rank-orders the tested person with respect to persons in the normative samples. One is then able to make such statements as, "This person's intellectual functioning is below that of 95% of children of his age." Even when tempered with a probability statement such as, "There is a 95% chance that his intellectual development lies between the 5th and 15th percentiles," it is still a rather confident statement that says there are severe limits on what can be expected by way of school learning. What is more, such an exercise tells us about an individual's performance compared with that of groups of others but nothing at all about how that performance could be enhanced.

The correlation between standardized intelligence test scores (IQ) and subsequent school achievement scores is between +.55 and +.80 – usually considered a strong correlation. Taking a value that is often cited, +.70, and squaring that coefficient, we find that IQ and subsequent school achievement share only 49% common variance, leaving roughly half of the variance in school achievement to be associated with other variables. For present purposes, what that means is that there is substantial error in using IQ to predict subsequent school achievement of individuals, and even of large groups; therefore, the usefulness of IQ even for classification is limited.

Returning to our illustration of "gifted and talented" and "mentally retarded" persons, a common observation is that the predictive errors are made in opposite directions. That is to say, relatively few people would be included in the "gifted and talented" group, so identified, who did not belong there, but there might well be a much larger number who would do well in special "gifted" classes but whose test scores do not qualify them for that category. On the other hand, overinclusion is the more common error when constituting groups of persons with mental retardation, resulting in the assignment of relatively many individuals to special classes for children with intellectual disability who might do better in regular, mainstreamed classes. In other words, standardized intelligence tests are more likely to make individuals appear to be less intelligent than they are capable of being than to make them appear to be more intelligent. How much difference that relatively constant error makes depends on whether one is working at the top or the bottom of the distribution of intelligence.

There are other important differences, and these are summarized in Table 1.1. It is important to note that our focus in this book is the presentation of our own approaches to DA. Because our DA roots are in mediational theory and practices, there is an inevitable bias in this direction.

Utley, Haywood, and Masters (1992), like Jensen (1980), found no convincing evidence to support the claim that standardized tests are inherently biased against certain subgroups in the population, such as ethnic minorities. Reviewing available literature on psychological assessment of minority children, they concluded

> that psycho-educational assessment instruments on which minority and majority groups score differently are valid according to a variety of criteria that are relevant to the tests' theoretical underpinnings. It might be said that such instruments actually have several kinds of validity, one of which is validity with respect to the use to which the tests [are] put. Tests that yield an intelligence quotient might possess strong validity in terms of being able to predict aspects of performance and achievement that can be linked to the concept of intelligence, but at the same time they might have poor validity in predicting responsiveness to a particular educational regimen that adapts teaching to meet certain needs. Put differently, a test that is used to assess how well or how rapidly a child learns may not predict how that child might best be taught. For such a purpose the best assessment might be one that targets how a child learns so that instruction may be tailored either to the child's manner of learning or toward changing how the child learns. In short, there is validity-for-a-given-purpose, and an instrument that is valid for one purpose (e.g., predicting correlates of intelligence) may not be valid for another (predicting the best sort of educational experience). (1992, p. 463)

Table 1.1. Comparison of "normative" and "dynamic" assessment approaches[a]

Comparison criterion what is compared	Normative assessment self with others	Dynamic assessment self with self
Major question	How much has this person already learned? What can he/she do or not do? How does this person's current level of performance compare with others of similar demographics?	How does this person learn in new situations? How, and how much, can learning and performance be improved? What are the primary obstacles to a more optimal level of competence?
Outcome	IQ as global estimate of ability *reflecting rank order in a reference (normative) group* Current level of independent functioning (ZOA)	Learning potential: What is possible with reduced obstacles to learning? How can such obstacles be reduced? How does the individual function with the support of a more experienced interventionist? (ZPD)
Examining process	Standardized; same for everybody Focus on products of past experience	Individualized; responsive to person's learning obstacles Focus on processes involved in intentional acquisition of new information or skills
Interpretation of results	Identification of limits on learning and performance; identification of differences across domains of ability Documentation of need for further assessment and possible intervention	Identification of obstacles to learning and performance; estimate of investment required to overcome them Hypotheses regarding what works to overcome obstacles to learning
Role of examiner	Poses problems, records responses; affectively neutral	Poses problems, identifies obstacles, teaches metacognitive strategies when necessary, promotes change; affectively involved

ZOA = zone of actual development; ZPD = zone of proximal development.
[a] Adapted from Feuerstein, Haywood, Rand, Hoffman, and Jensen (1982/1986), and from Haywood and Bransford (1984).

Utley, Haywood, and Masters (1992) further concluded that

> (a) standardized intelligence tests are not reasonably called upon to do jobs that we now see as important; (b) ethnic minorities may be especially subject to erroneous decisions and placements based upon standardized intelligence tests, not because of test bias or poor predictability but because ethnically and culturally different persons might often have need of different educational approaches that are not identified by standardized normative tests; (c) these are legitimate public policy issues; and (d) dynamic assessment has the potential to be an important adjunct to standardized intelligence tests, especially for use with ethnic minorities and other persons who are socially different, such as handicapped persons, culturally different persons, and persons whose primary language is other than that of their dominant culture. (1992, pp. 463–464)

These observations are in accord with our own position, the focus of which is on *how test data are interpreted and used* for making important decisions about people's lives. Our objection to exclusive reliance on intelligence tests for data to inform such decisions is primarily that intelligence test data are remarkably subject to misuse, whereas DA data can supply what is missed in the testing of intelligence.

CONCEPTS, ASSUMPTIONS, AND THEORETICAL BASIS OF DYNAMIC ASSESSMENT

Some fundamental concepts and assumptions appear to underlie virtually all approaches to dynamic/interactive assessment. They include the following:

1. Some abilities that are important for learning (in particular) are not assessed by normative, standardized intelligence tests.

2. Observing new learning is more useful than cataloguing (presumed) products of old learning. History is necessary but not sufficient.

3. Teaching within the test provides a useful way of assessing potential as opposed to performance.

4. All people typically function at less than their intellectual capacity.

5. Many conditions that do not reflect intellectual potential can and do interfere with expression of one's intelligence.

The notion that some important abilities are not typically assessed by normative, standardized intelligence tests is not worth much unless one can identify ways to assess those fugitive abilities. One prominent way is to look for conditions that may be limiting a person's access to his or her intelligence, minimize or remove those limiting conditions, and then assess abilities again. This strategy is exactly the one that led Vygotsky to his now-famous concept of the "zone of proximal development":

> Most of the psychological investigations concerned with school learning measured the level of mental development of the child by making him solve certain standardized problems. The problems he was able to solve by himself were supposed to indicate the level of his mental development at the particular time. But in this way, only the completed part of the child's development can be measured, which is far from the whole story. We tried a different approach. Having found that the mental age of two children was, let us say, eight, we gave each of them harder problems than he could manage on his own and provided some slight assistance: the first step in a solution, a leading question, or some other form of help. We discovered that one child could, in cooperation, solve problems designed for twelve-year-olds, while the other could not go beyond problems intended for nine-year-olds. The discrepancy between a child's actual mental age and the level he reaches in solving problems with assistance indicates the zone of his proximal development; in our example, this zone is four for the first child and one for the second. Can we truly say that their mental development is the same? Experience has shown that the child with the larger *zone of proximal development (ZPD)* will do much better in school. This measure gives a more helpful clue than mental age does to the dynamics of intellectual progress. (Vygotsky, 1986/1934, pp. 186–187)

Although there have been some improvements recently in intelligence testing (e.g., Das & Naglieri, 1997; Woodcock, 2002), it remains true that much of standardized intelligence testing relies on assessment of the products of presumed past learning opportunities. Vocabulary tests, for example, are common, and these by their very nature reflect past learning. Comprehension of social situations, humor, and absurdity shows up often in such tests and similarly has to be based on prior learning, as does knowledge of mathematics and skill at calculating. Comparison of any individual's score on such tests with the average score of similar persons in a normative sample requires the logical assumption that all persons of a given age, gender, race, and social circumstance (e.g., urban vs. rural residence) have had the same opportunities to learn – an assumption that is patently untenable. Although old learning is highly correlated with success in new learning (the venerable "principle of postremity" in psychology: the most likely response is the most recent response, or the best predictor of future behavior is past behavior), the correlation is far from perfect and often becomes a self-fulfilling prophecy. An obvious example is the deaf child who comes to school without having had the benefits of training in specialized communication. That child will score poorly on normative tests because he or she will have learned less than have age peers, but the score will not reflect the potential of the child to learn *given appropriate communication methods*. In such a case, attempts within the test to overcome experiential deficits will yield better estimates of the child's ability to learn, given appropriate teaching. Teaching within the test should bear greater resemblance to the criterion situation, in this case classroom learning in a person-appropriate class. If, on the other hand, such a child is given normative tests, scores low, and is placed in learning situations with low expectations and without appropriate communication methods, the prophecy of the normative score will be fulfilled because the assessment and criterion situations are similar.

All proponents of dynamic assessment appear to be more interested in determining potential performance than in assessing typical performance. They recognize that all people typically function at levels far below their capacity, at least in terms of their neural capacity. Assessment of typical performance is invaluable for prediction of future performance. If one wishes, however, to assess what is possible or what would be possible under more optimal conditions – in other words, how to defeat pessimistic predictions derived from assessment of typical performance – then a testing strategy that involves intervention and the seeking of potential is essential.

From the beginning of psychological science, psychologists have been careful to distinguish between "intellective" and "non-intellective" variables. Early psychologists, for example, divided "consciousness" into the three dimensions of *cognition* (knowledge, thinking), *conation* (feeling, emotionality, perhaps motivation), and *volition* (will) (Boring, 1950). Whereas such a division makes for good science in the search for pure effects, uncontaminated by "irrelevant" variables, it does not make for good clinical assessment, especially when assessment of intelligence is based heavily on performance on tests that require prior learning. We know, for example, that intelligence test scores can be affected by motivational variables (Zigler, Abelson, & Seitz, 1973; Zigler & Butterfield, 1968), racial, gender, and linguistic match between examiner and examinee, language competence, previous testing experience, social class, personality of examiner and examinee, and a host of other non-intellective variables (see, e.g., Tzuriel & Samuels, 2000; Tzuriel & Schanck, 1994). Almost all DA advocates, then, try to identify and compensate for the effects of such non-intellective variables and to take them into account when interpreting the data from DA. Some typical sources of poor performance that can be easily overcome include misunderstanding of instructions or expectations (Carlson & Wiedl, 1992a,

1992b), unfamiliarity with materials and content of tests, timidity, and history of failure on tests (Johnson, Haywood, & Hays, 1992).

AN APPROACH TO DYNAMIC ASSESSMENT

Anyone's specific approach to assessment of individual differences in human abilities should derive from and depend on one's systematic view of the nature of human ability itself. We do represent a particular view of that subject, discussed in detail in Chapter 2. We present a synopsis of the applied aspects of that approach here to make it easy to compare it with other approaches within the broad field of DA.

Our approach to dynamic assessment is actually an approach to psychological and psychoeducational assessment in general; that is, we do not separate DA as a complete alternative to more traditional assessment methods. This approach includes the use of DA for the purpose of finding answers to specific questions, as a specific tactic within an assessment strategy that includes more traditional methods, such as standardized testing.

In general, we find that the social–developmental history is the single most important source of diagnostic information, and it often contains clues to fruitful intervention strategies as well. Careful history taking, supplemented by records review, interview, and direct observation in learning and performance situations, is the primary source of the questions to be addressed in the more formal aspects of assessment. The nature of those questions must determine which tactics to employ and in what sequence.

The first major aspect of our approach to DA is our answer to the question, "Why do dynamic assessment?" We distinguish the principal goals of DA from those of static, normative assessment along two axes. The first is to consider what one seeks to find out from administering ability tests, that is, what question(s) one asks of the assessment process. "Intelligence" tests, although initially designed simply to sort out children who might or might not be expected to succeed in "regular" classes at school (Haywood & Paour, 1992), have nevertheless come to be seen as instruments for making inferences about a latent variable – intelligence – that is not observable and not measurable by any direct means. Doing so is important within the context of development and elaboration of theories of human development and functioning. That is not a goal of DA, in which one seeks instead to make inferences about barriers to the expression of intelligence and ways to improve functioning, especially in the sphere of learning, both academic and social. A second goal of standard intelligence tests is classification: placing into categories or ranges of intelligence those persons who score at certain IQ levels. This is done on the assumption that persons who achieve similar scores on the tests have enough characteristics in common to warrant similar educational treatments or settings, such as special segregated classes for "gifted and talented" children or for those with mental retardation or learning disabilities. That assumption and that goal are based on the high correlation between IQ and subsequent school achievement – a group relation, not an individual one, to be sure. The question that remains after a child is classified is what to do with the child. That is, unless the mere movement from one room to another is viewed as a meaningful intervention, we are left with the ultimate question of "so what?" in response to much of what is yielded by traditional procedures. A major goal of dynamic assessment, on the other hand, is not to dispute such classification but actually to discover how to defeat the more pessimistic of the predictions that are made on the basis of standard tests; in other words, one tries to discover how to remove people, to help them escape, from certain classes rather than how to put them into categories. In a very important sense, intelligence testing with standard tests is part of a *nomothetic* enterprise, an effort to find and apply general laws of development and behavior that apply to very many individuals. Dynamic assessment, on the contrary, is part of an *idiographic* enterprise, that is, an effort to find the characteristics, especially the potential for effective learning, of individuals without reference to the performance of others. In the former approach, one compares persons with other persons. In the latter approach, the comparison is within the person: from time to time, without and with teaching, across domains of knowledge and skill. (For a time-honored discussion of nomothetic vs. idiographic psychological science, see Meehl, 1954. Although Meehl argued cogently and convincingly for the superiority of "statistical prediction" models, a principal contribution of his work was to make a sharp distinction between general laws of behavior and the study of characteristics of individuals, thus applying nomothetic and idiographic models to psychology.)

The second major aspect of our approach, in common with most other practitioners of DA, has to do with the role of the examiner in the assessment enterprise, that is, the nature of the intervention that defines DA. This aspect addresses both what the examiner does and how she or he does it. Dynamic assessment methods can be arranged along a continuum of *intensity of intervention* on one axis, and along a different continuum of relative cognitive *depth of intervention* on a second axis. Table 1.2 is a list of some intervention strategies that frequently characterize dynamic assessment, by a suggested (nonempirical) estimate of intensity and cognitive depth, on a scale of 1 (*light intensity, relatively shallow cognitive depth*) to 3 (*intense, deep*). The two axes are not orthogonal, so the same continuum may represent both the variables of intensity and cognitive depth of intervention, varying from attempts to regulate the behavior of the examinee to

Table 1.2. Intervention strategies in dynamic assessment by axis of intervention

Strategy	Intensity	Cognitive depth
Focus attention on relevant aspects of the task	1–3	1
Clarify instructions and expectations	1–3	1
Provide minimal feedback (correct, incorrect) on performance	1	1
Encourage task involvement, intrinsic motivation	1–2	2
Give information, e.g., vocabulary definitions	2	1–2
Provide elaborated feedback (e.g., what aspects were correct or not) on performance	2	2
Pose guiding questions	2–3	2–3
Regulate examinee's behavior (e.g., inhibit impulsivity)	2–3	2
Teach concepts, metacognitive principles, *promotion of self-regulation*	3	3
Suggest or elicit application of concepts, principles, rules	3	3

the actual teaching and application of cognitive concepts, metacognitive habits, and applications of rules.

The third major aspect has to do with the interpretation of the data that one gets from dynamic assessment. Unlike normative assessment, one cannot get a score, refer that score to a normative table, and thereby rank-order the individual's non-intellective performance (by assigning an interpretive percentile rank, for example) with respect to others of similar characteristics. The data must be interpreted in an idiographic way, that is, with the person himself or herself as the referent; for example, performance without and with intervention, performance on different kinds of tasks, identification of apparent barriers to performance, effectiveness of different qualities and intensities of intervention. The ultimate question, of course, is "What can be done about performance deficiencies?"

DATA FROM DYNAMIC ASSESSMENT

Depending on what questions are asked, DA can yield answers to the following questions:

a. *What is the present level of performance, that is, baseline or without help?* Of course, one does not need DA to answer that question. Standardized tests, school grades, teacher reports, and parent interviews all are excellent sources of "present performance" information. Given our conviction that less is more, that is, that the total amount of testing for a given individual should be no more than is essential to answer the pressing questions that we have asked, information that is already available from other sources should not be sought yet again by repeating tests that have already been given. Usually, then, "present performance" is established on the basis of referral information as well as from observation, standardized data, and curriculum-based sources; however, if one wishes to know how intervening teaching and learning will affect postintervention performance on the same tests, either identical or parallel forms, it is necessary to give those tests at the beginning of the assessment rather than to rely on other data to estimate baseline performance. We add here the caution that any norms used to evaluate the pretest data in DA cannot be applied to the posttest data. These can only be viewed as estimates, and examiners should refer to test–retest and standard error of measurement data to aid with interpretation of the gains. What is important is to note the difference but primarily to use the information descriptively to enhance understanding of the planning for the individual.

b. *What are the recognizable barriers or obstacles to better learning and performance?* Answering this question requires a "try it and see" approach, as well as a store of knowledge about child development, learning, and teaching. Often, the path of inference is a circuitous one. The examinee encounters problems, introduces mediation designed to overcome a suspected barrier, and, to the extent that performance then improves, may conclude that the treated domain was, indeed, the problem, or at least one of the problems. In other words, if I provided a treatment designed to overcome a problem and the problem disappeared, then the nature of the problem must have been as I imagined it – provided, of course, that other influencing variables have been controlled. This strategy is reminiscent of the behaviorist tactic of "functional analysis" (Haywood, Filler, Shifman, & Chatelanat, 1975). Careful observation of examinees' behavior also yields data relevant to this question.

c. *How much and what kinds of intervention were required to produce improved performance?* This question can only be answered with any validity if one can assume that the examiner gave only the help that was actually needed, so that "help given" and "help needed" can be assumed to be the same. This has to be a major source of unreliability in DA because different examiners respond to different personal characteristics (their own) in inferring examinees' need for intervention. Much of the validity of the conclusions reached on the basis of DA depends on the training of examiners to limit their intervention to what is actually needed for examinees to incorporate the cognitive and metacognitive principles necessary for them to achieve improved performance. The now familiar caution, "If it ain't broke, don't fix it" applies here. Nevertheless, there should be recognition of the need to take a hard look at intra- and interexaminer reliability with regard to what is or is not broken as well as how to fix it. This is an area in much need of further research because we cannot support an approach to assessment that is completely idiosyncratic and examiner-dependent. The need for flexibility and responsiveness to learner needs balanced with reliable outcomes and interpretations poses a special challenge for DA.

d. *What is the response to intervention?* One can specify what was apparently needed and then give the required help only to find that individuals vary widely in how much that helps. The previous question yields as much information about the examiner as it does about the examinee, but the present one is focused on the examinee and asks, "How much difference did my intervention make?" or "How much improvement was there in the examinee's performance after my intervention?" This is essentially a gain-score question: What is the difference between baseline performance and postintervention performance? It is also important to note that response to intervention can be expected to vary not only from person to person but also according to the type of intervention. For example, if there is minimal response to simple motor focusing (directing an examinee's attention to the relevant aspects of a task, often by simply pointing) but pronounced improvement following verbal focusing of attention, the interpretation of response to intervention must be quite different. We are also aware that level of initial performance plays an important role in interpretation of gains. It surely makes a difference whether the learner begins at a very low or high level of competence in the domains of assessment.

e. *How much investment, of what kinds, may be required to promote long-term gains in performance?* Answering this question requires collating data from the entire dynamic assessment – indeed, from both dynamic and static tests as well as other sources of information rather than from performance on a single task. That is true because (a) one has asked more than a single question, (b) there was probably more than one obstacle to good performance, (c) more than one type of intervention will have been used, (d) response to intervention probably varied according to the nature of the problems' content (quantitative, spatial, verbal, for example) and the type, intensity, and frequency of intervention. The answers to this question, then, must represent an amalgam of data from all aspects of the assessment and further must be different according to the different domains of functioning. Even so, the question is usually answered in a somewhat speculative rather than a purely quantitative manner. Furthermore, no matter how committed we are to DA as a model, we need to acknowledge the limits of any of our efforts to effect change. Therefore, our assessments are best used for relatively short-term, and certainly not lifetime, planning. Assessment is not forever. It should be repeated, the results monitored, and the process repeated as needed. For individuals with special needs, we suggest 1 year as a reasonable period of time for considering the results of the assessment valid. This may well vary with the age of the individual and, of course, is another meaningful target for investigation.

A fourth major aspect of our approach is the observation that DA is properly part of a broader, more comprehensive assessment strategy. The role of DA is to find answers to questions that cannot be answered by other methods of data gathering, such as standardized testing, interviewing, review of social and developmental histories, direct observation of behavior in typical situations, or school records. This observation leads to a related one, that the *combination* of data derived from dynamic assessment and from other, more traditional procedures can produce insights that are not reached on the basis of any single source of information. That is, neither the zone of actual development nor the zone of proximal development suffices. Optimal results are the product of their combination.

Other characteristics of our approach to DA have to do with specific applications. For example, applications to school learning questions have some unique characteristics, such as the melding of DA with curriculum-based assessment, whereas applications in neuropsychological assessment or clinical assessment of persons with psychiatric disorders, responding to different questions, will employ different emphases, such as eliciting maximal performance or distinguishing different responses to language intervention. See Chapters 3–9 for discussion of such specific applications. A final differentiating aspect of our approach is its (perhaps) unique base in particular concepts of the nature and development of human abilities. That discussion is presented in Chapter 2.

MODELS OF DYNAMIC ASSESSMENT

Although there is considerable agreement among adherents and practitioners of DA regarding the most fundamental issues, there is also wide diversity regarding matters of implementation. Haywood (1992b) observed that "'interactive' identifies the major common characteristic of the wide variety of methods, which is a much more active relationship between examiners and subjects than is found in normative, standardized assessment" (p. 233). A further common characteristic is the search for more effective learning and performance capacities than are manifest in static approaches. Here the diversity begins. Haywood (1997) identified three major groups of DA approaches, which he characterized as "restructuring the test situation," "learning within the test," and "metacognitive intervention, teaching generalizable cognitive operations." Sternberg and Grigorenko (2002) further divided the various approaches into the following groups:

> Structural Cognitive Modifiability
> Learning Potential Testing
> Testing via Learning and Transfer
> *Lerntest* Approach
> Testing the Limits
> Information Processing

This finer grouping seems to us to have great overlap but ultimately to be reducible to the "what does the examiner do?" categories. Table 1.3 shows a combination and extension of these two classification schemes.

In the following discussion, we assume some familiarity, at least at a reading level, with the different DA approaches shown in the table. Based on that assumption, and because they have been described in detail elsewhere, usually by their own authors, we do not present them here in any detail; rather, we suggest that interested readers consult these sources: Guthke and Wingenfeld (1992); Hamers et al. (1993); Haywood (1997); Haywood and Tzuriel (1992); Lidz (1987); Lidz and Elliott (2000); Tzuriel (2001).

Unlike Sternberg and Grigorenko, we have not included a "target population" criterion for differentiating these approaches because all of them are applicable to a wide range of learners with varying characteristics and needs. In other words, they are not specialized methods devoted to one group or another, although it is true that all of the various DA authors have been primarily (but not exclusively) concerned with low performance.

DISTINGUISHING DIFFERENT DA APPROACHES

Although the several approaches to DA are not usefully distinguished on the basis of their target population, they do differ in some important respects. One of these is the degree of departure from traditional, established psychometric principles and procedures. On one end of a psychometric continuum are the procedures of Swanson, Das, and Naglieri, which adhere fairly closely to standard psychometric procedures and indeed have been incorporated into standardized tests. Carlson and Wiedl's "testing the limits" procedures can be applied in such ways as not to spoil the normative

Table 1.3. Classification of approaches to dynamic assessment according to two classification schemes

Sternberg and Grigorenko's characterization	Haywood's categories		
	Restructuring the test situation	Learning within the test	Metacognitive mediation
Structural Cognitive Modifiability (Feuerstein et al.)	X	X	X
Learning Potential Testing (Budoff et al.)		X	
Graduated Prompt (Campione & Brown)	X		
Lerntest (Guthke, Hamers, Hessels, Ruijssenaars, et al.)		X	
Testing the Limits (Carlson & Wiedl)	X	X	
Information Processing (Swanson, Das, Naglieri, et al.)	X	X	
Approaches Not Charted by Sternberg and Grigorenko			
Curriculum-based DA (Lidz)	X	X	X
Stimulus Enrichment (Haywood)	X	X	X
DA of Young Children (Tzuriel)	X	X	X

characteristics of the tests; for example, their clarification and elaborated feedback tactics can be applied to test the limits after a normative score has been obtained, in some ways leading to the best of both worlds. The same can be said of Budoff's "learning potential assessment," although in practice one might not wish to subject the participants with mental retardation with whom he has worked frequently to the series of failures that will inevitably occur when tests are given in the usual normative manner. The *Lerntest* approach that is associated with both German and Dutch authors essentially spoils the test for normative purposes but otherwise retains traditional psychometric requirements (relatively standard procedures within their paradigm, insistence on reliable test instruments). Lidz's curriculum-based DA is again the best of both worlds not because her DA procedures conform to psychometric principles but essentially because she employs both standardized and dynamic tests within a comprehensive assessment. Haywood's procedures, characterized here as "stimulus enrichment," establish baseline first, thus allowing for normative interpretation of initial performance, but employ two kinds of intervention: restructuring the test situation (giving enriched information) and metacognitive mediation of basic logic processes (training in comparison, classification, class inclusion), as well as a branching program for the sequencing of tasks. The most radical departures from a traditional psychometric process are Feuerstein's "cognitive modifiability" and Tzuriel's young children approaches, neither of which seeks to classify examinees or to compare them with age norms or with the performance of others.

Response to intervention: DA or not? An approach to educational assessment that bears striking (and perhaps deceptive) resemblance to DA is referred to as "response to instruction" or "response to intervention" (RTI). With conceptual roots in curriculum-based measurement and, to a limited extent, DA, the RTI approach arose in large part as an attempt to redefine the diagnostic category of learning disability (LD) and to reoperationalize that diagnosis. Historically, the principal criterion by which learning disability has been diagnosed has been a significant discrepancy between aptitude and achievement. Specific learning disabilities, for example, in reading, have been associated with discrepancies between aptitude and achievement in a specific curricular domain. Thus, one could have a specific learning disability in reading, in mathematics, or, theoretically, in any domain of academic studies. The discrepancy criterion has not led to agreement among diagnosticians or special educators regarding its validity, but it has led to a very large number, perhaps an unrealistic number, of schoolchildren bearing the LD diagnosis. Kovaleski (2004), citing Lyon et al. (2001), observed that the discrepancy approach "often results in the wrong students being identified for special education, requires that students 'wait to fail' before receiving needed special education services, and does not lead to useful educational prescriptions for the remediation of the student's academic difficulties" (p. 1). Reauthorization of the Education of All Handicapped Children Act, now named IDEA (Individuals with Disabilities Education Act), helped to bring about renewed and critical examination of the definition and operational criteria of the diagnosis of LD. That renewed examination led to abandonment of the IQ–achievement discrepancy criterion in favor of a "response to instruction" one, although the discrepancy criterion has since reappeared in the official (government-recognized) definition. Lyon et al. (2001) recommended "consideration of a student's response to well-designed and well-implemented early intervention as well as remediation programs as part of the identification of LD" (2001, p. 279).

Despite the temporary abandonment of the IQ–achievement discrepancy criterion, the new RTI approach remained a discrepancy and deficit model, requiring both low academic performance (typically two grade levels below grade peers) and poor response to appropriate instruction (Kovaleski, 2004). The latter criterion is frequently determined by use of curriculum-based measurement (CBM; Fuchs & Fuchs, 1986a, 1986b). The use of curriculum-based measurement to define response to instruction helps enormously to rescue RTI from the deficit-model category because the principal goal of CBM is to identify educational procedures that can be successful at improving students' learning effectiveness.

RTI has much to recommend it as an alternative to more traditional procedures for identification of LD, but for several reasons we consider it not to be synonymous with DA. Chief among its assets is its reliance on the concept of continuous monitoring of classroom learning performance, often operationalized by curriculum-based measurement. Fuchs, Mock, Morgan, and Young (2003) distinguished two versions of RTI: problem solving and standard protocol. We see the problem-solving version as a significant advance in assessment, moving from an "everything for everybody" or standard test-battery orientation to one that is more similar to DA, that is, use of assessment procedures that are specifically chosen for and tailored to the answering of individual questions, especially questions about how to promote improved learning. The third asset is RTI's tactic of comparing performances within a person rather than between persons, which is also consistent with DA.

Despite these advantages, we argue that it is not DA, essentially because RTI is still a search for deficits rather than primarily a search for sources of strength. A second weakness of the approach is the undefined nature of the intervention as "appropriate" and "well designed." In the mediational approach to DA, the focus is on mediating tools of logical thinking and systematic learning, whereas in the usual applications of RTI, the focus of the intervention is on the curricular contents of academic learning. The third and perhaps most important difference between RTI and DA is the fact that RTI is a set of procedures designed specifically for classification as a means to classify more accurately pupils with learning disabilities, whereas DA is not properly used to place people into categories; indeed, it is frequently used to remove them from categories. (To be sure, any technique that serves the classification goal may also be used to declassify; it is a question here of the *purposes* of these two procedures.)

Although RTI as presently configured does not constitute DA, it is quite possible and even likely that the two concepts should become more closely related. This can be accomplished, with significant benefit to children, by extending the RTI approach well beyond the mere definition and operationalization of LD and employing the principles of DA in the application of RTI. Clear specification of the intervention in RTI and inclusion of cognitive and metacognitive teaching as an important part of that intervention – that is, viewing the intervention as "extended mediation" of cognitive and metacognitive operations – can enhance the utility of RTI. This is to say that the intervention in RTI could well include teaching, learning, and application of the logical tools of learning. Using RTI to locate the cognitive and metacognitive assets of learners rather than merely to locate their deficiencies is another way to extend its usefulness. Other ways will be found, but at the present stage of evolution of both concepts, it is clear that a period of systematic research is essential. The point is simply that DA can and should be brought into the RTI enterprise, and that enterprise can and should become more like DA.

A RECOMMENDED APPROACH

Our own model of DA, presented throughout the book, is one that we believe will help to make dynamic assessment more accessible to both practitioners and researchers. It emphasizes a particular concept of the nature and development of ability (Chapter 2). It places DA within a broad context of psychological and psychoeducational assessment as a useful extension of assessment specialists' repertoire. It makes use of both abstract and academic content, with emphasis on the asking of appropriate assessment questions and the use of assessment strategies to find answers to those questions. By using this approach to assessment, we attempt to bridge the gap between assessment and classroom practice, in the case of school-age children, and between assessment and treatment in clinical applications. Most of all, we offer specific instructions and guidelines that we hope will encourage professionals to begin their DA journey, as well as provide data and models for further investigation by researchers and procedure developers.

2 A Model of Mental Functioning

The first important step in the search for effective methods for assessing variations in some supposed quality or characteristic is to formulate a systematic conception of the nature of that entity. In the case of dynamic assessment, we are trying to assess variations in ability – specifically, ability to perceive, think, learn, and solve problems in logical ways. In other words, we are asking how to assess mental functioning; therefore, a model of mental functioning is necessary. Without such a model, attempts at assessment would be unsystematic, even chaotic, inconsistent, and ultimately extremely difficult. In this chapter, we present a model that represents our systematic view of the nature and development of human ability.

There are essentially two ways in which one can view the nature of mental functioning. The first is to ask questions such as, "What is ability, what are its components, origins, and correlates?" In other words, one can try to define the nature of the *latent variable*, that special quality of human ability that is unobservable and by any direct means immeasurable, whose existence must be inferred from its presumed effects on and relationships to other, more observable variables. In the assessment of individual differences in intelligence, for example, the latent variable is intelligence, whereas the score on an intelligence test, often transformed into IQ, is the *manifest variable*, the observable and measurable datum on the basis of which we make inferences about the latent variable. All too often, the two are confused, and IQ is seen as the latent variable, or the essential quality of intelligence itself. One sees that error reflected in the incorrect reference to "IQ tests," even by the most sophisticated psychologists. (Of course, there are "intelligence tests," the score of which may be an IQ.) The second is a far more practical question, such as "Ability for what?" According to this second type of question, one is less concerned with defining an unseen quality than with specifying useful means of sorting out assets and liabilities for cognitive and social performance. The model that we present in this chapter is a combination of both perspectives, the conceptual and the applied, because both views are important to our understanding of the ways in which human abilities develop, how individual differences in ability affect such important sociocultural enterprises as academic and social learning, and what can be done to enhance the ability to gain access to and apply one's intelligence to achieve more effective logical thinking, perceiving, learning, and problem solving. To achieve this combination of perspectives on ability, we present two overlapping conceptual schemes, Haywood's *transactional perspective on human ability* (Haywood, 2006; Haywood & Switzky, 1992; Haywood, Tzuriel, & Vaught, 1992; Haywood & Wachs, 1981) and Lidz's *process-focused model of ability* (see Chapter 7, this volume). This integrated model is biological, neuropsychological, ecological, and transactional by its nature and focuses on information processing as the principal mental activity.

TRANSACTIONAL PERSPECTIVE ON HUMAN ABILITY

According to the transactional perspective, the three principal dimensions of human ability (ability to think systematically and effectively) are intelligence, cognition, and motivation. The ever-changing relations of these three dimensions make the model transactional. The general transactional perspective holds to the following tenets:

1. *Ability is multifaceted.* This statement suggests that it is useful to think of different kinds of intelligence, somewhat in the manner of Gardner's multiple intelligences but with a broader scope, so as to include, for example, "emotional intelligence" (Goleman, 1995, 1998) and metacognition. Psychometrists have always been confronted with "sawtoothed" profiles of performance on intelligence tests as well as on school achievement tests: almost always some disparity between verbal and nonverbal estimates of intelligence, but often significant variability even within the verbal and nonverbal domains. It is likely that it takes one kind of intelligence to learn to read, another kind to conceptualize structures in different spatial orientations, another to learn to play the cello, and yet another to be an effective quarterback (i.e., to master and to know when to call different plays or strategies on the football field). The various slants on intelligence are all correlated, some quite strongly, with global estimates of intelligence (g, general intelligence), but that fact does not diminish their unique qualities.

2. *Ability is multi-determined.* Intelligence is viewed as a biological quality that derives from the structure, integrity, and functional efficiency of the brain (see, e.g., the concept of "biological intelligence"; Halstead, 1947; Hebb, 1949; Luria, 1980). The development of its primary mediating

structures is the result of polygenic action, that is, the action of a critical combination of genes. This statement says that there is no single gene for intelligence; rather, individual differences in intelligence arise as a result of a group of genes, each of which may assume different levels, qualities, and interactive characteristics (see, e.g., Bouchard & McGue, 1981; Ehrenmeyer-Kimling & Jarvik, 1963; Jensen, 1991, 1998, 2000; Otto, 2001; Scarr-Salapatek, 1975). Even the most insistent of "nativist" theorists leave some room for experience to affect the development of intelligence, but so far the available evidence suggests that by far the largest source of individual differences in intelligence is one's genetic endowment. (For a detailed examination of the ways in which experience, especially early experience, may affect individual differences in intelligence, see Haywood, 1967; Haywood & Tapp, 1966.) Without getting into the controversy over how much is attributable to heredity and how much to environmental/experiential influences, we acknowledge the very strong role of genetics and also the possibility of a relatively modest contribution of experience. In fact, according to the transactional perspective, it hardly matters how great the role of genetics is, even up to 100%, because intelligence alone is not sufficient to account for individual differences in perception, systematic thinking, learning, and problem solving. It is a necessary but not sufficient condition for effective thinking to occur.

3. *Individual differences in intelligence are not sufficient to account for differences in logical thinking and learning.* We have already noted in Chapter 1 the imperfect correlation between IQ and subsequent school achievement scores. It is also common knowledge that on some tasks, individuals with low IQs may perform at a level that is equal or even superior to that attained by individuals with higher IQs and that individuals with very high IQs sometimes perform quite poorly on learning tasks and do badly in school (Haywood, 2004a, 2006). Thus, the model requires an additional component. One such component appears to be the *development of systematic cognitive and metacognitive processes*. Such processes constitute relatively stable modes of logical thinking as well as habits of using those logic modes in the daily tasks of interpreting information from the senses, perceiving learning opportunities, approaching learning tasks, integrating new knowledge, and solving problems. According to the two sets of theory that have most strongly influenced thinking about cognitive development over the last century, those of Vygotsky and Piaget, there are two principal ways in which these thinking modes may be acquired. From a Vygotskian perspective (Karpov, 2005; Vygotsky, 1929, 1978), the essential cognitive processes consist of symbols, signs, scientific concepts, and similar abstractions.

These are already present in the culture in which children are born and grow up, so their acquisition is primarily a matter of their transmission to children by adults or more cognitively competent peers in the context of interpersonal communication. In the neo-Vygotskian view (Karpov, 2005), acquisition of essential cognitive modes consists of learning or otherwise acquiring culture-based models for gathering and analyzing information. These models are not limited to semiotic means, as Vygotsky held, but include problem-solving strategies and procedures as well. Adults present these models to children and mediate the children's acquisition and mastery of the models in the context of child–adult joint activity. Subsequent effective learning is a matter of applying those models.

The Piagetian perspective is quite different (Piaget, 1952; Piaget & Inhelder, 1969). Each child has the developmental task of constructing his or her unique set of cognitive "structures" (durable, generalizable logical thinking modes). This task is accomplished through successive encounters with the environment that lead to cognitive conflict (i.e., to discrepancies, "disequilibrium") between new information and what is already in the child's store of knowledge. Resolution of the cognitive conflict that arises from these discrepancies (equilibration) is accomplished by way of the twin processes of "assimilation" (incorporating new information into existing structures) and "accommodation" (revising old knowledge so that it accords with the new information).

Although appreciating these two historical views of cognitive processes, we rely even more heavily on a Luria-based perspective in which mental processes are seen as specific mental functions such as attention, perception, memory, language, conception, and metacognition (Luria, 1980).

Whether subscribing to the Vygotskian view or the Piagetian view of acquisition of basic cognitive knowledge, one still runs inevitably into the question of the specific role of adults and other more cognitively competent persons in the cognitive development of children, as well as how best to promote learning. Both Vygotsky and Piaget assigned an important role to adults in this process, a role referred to nowadays as "mediation." Karpov (2003b; see also Karpov & Haywood, 1998) has described Vygotsky's concept of mediation, Haywood (2003a) a neo-Piagetian view of mediation, Deutsch (2003) mediation from the perspective of "mediated learning experience" (the perspective of Feuerstein), and Hansen (2003) mediation from the perspective of Magne Nyborg. This collection of papers on the subject of mediation suggests that it is an important concept across some rather widely differing views of cognitive development and approaches to DA. We do not present a detailed account of mediation here, both because it has been described in some detail by these authors and also because, being a central concept in the special intervention that occurs in DA, we describe it later in the book as part of the "how to" emphasis.

Some process of acquisition and elaboration of fundamental metacognitive processes (systematic thinking modes) appears to be essential for effective learning, regardless of the level of intelligence. That is to say, even the most intelligent children will not be effective learners unless and until they have managed to acquire such processes. The trick in that assertion is simply that the more intelligence one has, the easier it is to acquire the fundamental metacognitive processes, so with very intelligent children the process of acquisition often appears to be spontaneous, unintentional, and effortless. The corollary assumption is that the less one's intelligence, the more difficult it will be to acquire basic metacognitive processes; therefore, the greater will be one's need for help, "mediation," teaching – intervention of one sort or another. Feuerstein (Feuerstein & Rand, 1974) interprets that relation as a differential need for mediated learning experience (MLE). We interpret Feuerstein's position, as well as the implied positions of Vygotsky and Piaget, to mean that although there are large individual differences in the need for mediation, or MLE, nobody is so intelligent that he or she does not require any mediation to achieve adequate cognitive development. Similarly, there is nobody with so little intelligence that his or her cognitive development cannot be accelerated or improved by the mediation of basic modes of logical thinking. Tarzan to the contrary notwithstanding, human beings do not seem to be able to develop cognitively in social isolation! Thus, we see so far that both intelligence and metacognitive processes are essential for learning to take place.

Given that there appears to be a pronounced tendency, even among the most sophisticated psychologists, to use the terms "intellectual" and "cognitive" interchangeably, as if they meant the same thing, it is useful for us to distinguish our use of these terms – and our understanding of the two concepts within the framework of the transactional perspective. Haywood has repeatedly offered a sharp distinction between them (Haywood, 1995, 2003b, 2004a, 2006; Haywood, Tzuriel, & Vaught, 1992). Table 2.1 shows the elements of that distinction.

The most fundamental difference between intelligence and cognition (cognitive and metacognitive processes) is their respective origins. According to the transactional perspective, intelligence is primarily genetic, whereas cognitive processes must be acquired. The corollary assumption is that whereas intelligence is only modestly modifiable, with great effort, systematic cognition, having been acquired in the first place, is eminently

Table 2.1. Distinction between intelligence and cognition according to six criteria: source, modifiability, character, modes of assessment, composition, and developmental requirements

	Comparison of intelligence and cognition	
	Intelligence	Cognition
Source	Genetic (polygenic)	Acquired
Modifiability	Modest	High
Character	Global, *g*	Generalizable
		Specific
Assessment	Achievement	Process
Composition	Intellectual	Mix of native ability, motives, habits, attitudes
Developmental requirements	Genes, nutrition health, safety, fostering environment	Active, directed teaching; mediation of cognitive processes

Note: From Haywood (1995, 2004, 2006); Haywood & Switzky (1992); Haywood, Tzuriel, & Vaught (1992).

modifiable: Whatever is learned can be unlearned, modified, or relearned. Therein lies one of the most useful aspects of the intelligence–cognitive processes distinction. As a medical school faculty member for many years (HCH), one used to hear, and repeat, the advice that if two diagnoses are equally likely, one should render the one that is treatable. In this case, intelligence is not itself eminently treatable. In fact, even when educational intervention leads to significant (but rarely very large) increases in IQ, we are never certain that such increases in the manifest variable actually represent any real increases in intelligence, the latent variable. Such apparent increases might be indications of improved test-taking ability or responsiveness to social desirability factors, that is, increased sophistication in providing the answers that the examiners are seeking. They might also represent improvement in cognitive functioning that is then reflected not only in tests of cognitive functioning but in intelligence test scores as well. The assumption that cognitive processes are fairly readily modifiable leads us naturally to select intervention strategies designed to enhance their development and application. A major aspect of dynamic assessment, following this transactional model, is to identify the cognitive and metacognitive processes that need improvement, the tactics that lead to enhancement of such processes, and the differential responsiveness of individuals to intervention designed to enhance their development and application.

A third distinction refers to the general character of the two concepts. Although intelligence may be subdivided into broad categories, such as verbal and performance, one can make a very strong case for its utility as a global construct, that is, the sum of the various components of intelligence. In fact, it is g, or general intelligence, that has quite high correlations with a wide range of other variables, including learning and a host of performance variables (Jensen, 1998). The term "metacognitive processes," on the other hand, refers to both specific and generalizable modes of logical thinking. Such processes have a dynamic character in that they develop and grow as a function of cumulative experience and, so far as we know at present, are separate rather than additive; in other words, it is not useful to try to take the sum of, let us say, comparison, hypothetical thinking, role taking, quantitative relations, and spatial relations because each is uniquely related to the effectiveness and efficiency of learning and performance. The operative part of the term is "processes" rather than "qualities." They represent ways of doing things that are psychologically important (i.e., of mental functioning).

Most intelligence tests are essentially achievement tests, which is to say that they assess what one has already learned (or not) from past opportunities to learn. There are, of course, exceptions, such as reaction time, speed of the neural impulse, or processing speed, but these are correlates of scores on intelligence tests rather than aspects of intelligence itself. Being tests of knowledge or skill, it is quite appropriate that intelligence tests resemble achievement tests. Cognitive *processes*, on the other hand, do not represent a static state of knowledge; rather, they reflect ongoing tactics, strategies, habits, and modes of thinking; of approaching, defining, and solving problems; and of perceiving the universe. It is thus uniquely appropriate that cognitive processes be assessed by dynamic means.

The composition of intelligence is essentially – well, intelligence. Makers of intelligence tests have been careful to exclude "non-intellective" variables, such as motivation, emotion, and attitudes. Cognitive processes are conceived of as a mix of native ability (overlapping intelligence), motives, habits, and attitudes toward learning and information processing. In that sense, cognitive processes are similar to Feuerstein's (Feuerstein et al., 1979, 1980) notion of "cognitive functions."

By "developmental requirements," we mean to suggest the role of parents and other child-rearing agents such as grandparents, older siblings, and professional teachers. With respect to the development of intelligence, the primary gift of parents is genes that are associated with intelligence. They also provide nutrition, health, safety, and a child-rearing environment that is conducive to realization of intellectual potential. The role of parents and other child-rearing agents in the development of cognitive processes is much more specific and, in fact, vital. They provide active, directed teaching. Depending on which developmental model one adopts, they either "mediate" the preexisting culture to the children or serve as catalysts (also mediating agents) for the individual construction and acquisition of important cognitive processes.

4. *Motivation is an essential component of performance ability.* Just as intelligence alone is not sufficient for effective thinking and learning, requiring the addition of individually developed cognitive processes, the combination of intelligence and cognition is still not sufficient. That combination requires complex transactions in development with task-intrinsic motivation. Although motivation has been regarded historically in psychology as a "non-intellective" variable, not to be confused with intelligence, it is a vital part of the three-way symbiosis within the transactional model of human ability (Haywood, 1992a). The term "task-intrinsic motivation" refers to motivation that is inherent in tasks, what Hunt (1963) referred to as motivation inherent in information processing and action. Hunt meant that the very act of taking in, processing, and acting on information is inherently rewarding, for its own sake, without need of task-extrinsic incentives or rewards. Task-intrinsic motivation is both a situational variable and a personality trait (Haywood, 1971; Haywood & Burke, 1977). As a situational variable, it means that in any given situation an individual may seek and derive satisfaction from variables that are part of the task with which he or she is confronted at that moment (intrinsic motivation) or, alternatively, may look outside the task for incentives and rewards (extrinsic motivation). Although the same person may seek either intrinsic or extrinsic rewards across a variety of situations and circumstances, within each person a relatively stable tendency develops to prefer one or the other (or neither), which then becomes a personality trait. It is the number of different situations in which one seeks and derives satisfaction from task-intrinsic variables that defines the trait, whether one is predominantly intrinsically or extrinsically motivated. It is important to distinguish these terms, "extrinsic" and "intrinsic," from the more familiar concepts of "external" and "internal." The referent for the internal–external distinction is the person, whereas the referent for the intrinsic–extrinsic distinction is the task. Research over the last 40+ years (see summary by Haywood & Switzky, 1986) has led to a rather clear picture of the differing motivational orientations of intrinsically motivated and extrinsically motivated persons, shown in Table 2.2.

An important distinction that one can see in Table 2.2 is the observation that whereas intrinsically motivated persons *seek satisfaction*

Table 2.2. Characteristics of persons who are predominantly intrinsically motivated or predominantly extrinsically motivated

Intrinsically motivated persons	Extrinsically motivated persons
Seek satisfaction by concentrating on:	*Avoid dissatisfaction* by concentrating on:
Task involvement	Avoidance of effort
Challenge	Ease
Creativity	Comfort
Responsibility	Safety
Learning	Security
Psychological excitement	Practicality
Aesthetic considerations	Material gain

Note: From Haywood (2006).

(by concentrating their attention on task-intrinsic variables), extrinsically motivated persons tend not to seek satisfaction at all but rather to *avoid dissatisfaction* (by concentrating on factors that lie outside of tasks). This distinction is reminiscent of the success striving versus failure avoiding tendency. It could possibly account, at least partially, for the superior performance of predominantly intrinsically motivated persons in work, learning, and problem-solving situations. Active seeking is undoubtedly associated with more vigorous engagement in tasks and more enthusiastic pursuit of goals.

The same series of studies has shown that individuals who are intrinsically motivated in a wide variety of situations, in contrast to those who are predominantly extrinsically motivated, have the following characteristics:

a. They work harder; that is, they produce more units of output per time unit.
b. They persist longer in tasks.
c. They learn more effectively; that is, they require fewer trials on average to reach a learning criterion, and they show greater mastery of material to be learned.
d. They retain more of what they have learned over a longer period.
e. They engage in more exploratory behavior.
f. They prefer novelty and complexity over familiarity and simplicity.
g. They prefer to monitor their own activities, rather than to be monitored by others, and to set their own schedules of reinforcement rather than to have them imposed.
h. When they have the opportunity to choose schedules of reinforcement for themselves, they set "leaner" schedules; that is, they require

and apparently prefer modest payoff, relatively infrequently delivered. In fact, task-extrinsic rewards appear to interfere with their intrinsically motivated behavior. (For summaries, see Haywood, 1971, 1988; Haywood & Burke, 1977; Haywood & Switzky, 1986.)

All of these observations suggest that intrinsic motivation is a powerful source of individual differences in the effectiveness and efficiency of learning and performance across a wide variety of tasks. Haywood (1967, 1968), studying the relation of individual differences in intrinsic motivation to scores on a standardized school achievement test in Grades 1, 2, and 3, found that individual differences in intrinsic motivation were associated with school achievement differences as large as or larger than those associated with 20–25 IQ points. Subsequent studies revealed powerful effects on laboratory learning (e.g., Haywood & Wachs, 1966), exploratory behavior (e.g., Tzuriel & Haywood, 1984), work performance and preference for differential incentives (Haywood & Weaver, 1967; Switzky & Haywood, 1974), and child-rearing practices (Tzuriel & Haywood, 1985). In spite of such demonstrations of powerful effects of intrinsic motivation, psychological and educational assessment specialists have typically relegated motivation to "incidental observations" in their testing and test reports. In our model it becomes an integral part of the assessment process.

In the context of child development, children who explore more, who are enthusiastic about new experiences and new tasks, who are able to find satisfaction in engaging in tasks, especially information processing, for their own sake and as their own reward, are more likely than are others to develop a large store of knowledge. Further, they are more likely to be able to apply their intelligence to the understanding of new experiences, to learning, and to problem solving.

We do not believe that either intrinsic motivation or cognitive processes can create intelligence or greatly increase the intelligence that one already has. The primary effect of the development of fundamental cognitive processes and of the personality trait of task-intrinsic motivation is to enhance one's access to and ability to apply the intelligence that one has. "Bad" environments, especially those in which there is inadequate mediation of cognitive processes by adults or poor modeling of intrinsic motivation by adults, do not destroy intelligence. Instead, they serve to mask one's intelligence, to deprive one of the repeated experience of gaining access to one's intelligence and of applying it effectively, especially in learning situations. "Good" environments, especially those that include strong models of intrinsic motivation and a rich history of mediation of cognitive processes by adults, serve to unmask one's intelligence, to make it available and accessible, and especially to help with the development of executive functions. By this latter term we refer to the metacognitive processes of scanning one's store of thinking strategies, selecting appropriate ones to match situations with which one is confronted, and to apply those strategies to perception, learning, and problem solving (see also Borkowski, Chan, & Muthukrishna, 2000; Borkowski, Turner, & Nicholson, 2004).

What makes the relations among the three variables of intelligence, cognitive processes, and intrinsic motivation "transactional" rather than merely interactive is their dynamic, constantly changing nature. Each of them changes both in quantity and in character over time, such that the effect of one on either of the other two depends on the stage of development of each and the history or prior interactions among them (Haywood, 2002; Haywood et al., 1992, esp. pp. 51–52). Thus, we can expect that persons whose intelligence is relatively low might do better than expected on many learning tasks if they have well-developed cognitive processes (the results of frequent, intense, and appropriate mediation) and even better if they can add to their cognitive development a task-intrinsic motivational orientation. Similarly, persons with high intelligence might perform poorly in learning situations if they have either or both inadequate cognitive development and a task-extrinsic motivational orientation. A complicating factor is the observation that high intelligence is associated with relatively easy acquisition of basic cognitive processes, requiring relatively less mediation than would be required by persons of less intelligence; thus, these variables are not independent but are correlated. Further, intrinsic motivation is positively correlated with both chronological age (up to adolescence) and mental age.

Intrinsic motivation is relevant to dynamic assessment in multiple ways. First, and most directly, if we wish to assess potential for higher levels of learning and performance we must recognize, according to this transactional model of ability, that those criterion variables will be affected, often very strongly, by one's level of the personality trait of intrinsic motivation. That being the case, it is useful to assess such individual differences and rather neglectful not to do so. Just as intelligence is assessed by giving intelligence tests and cognitive processes are assessed by performing dynamic assessment of learning potential, intrinsic motivation is assessed psychometrically. Some tests of intrinsic motivation that fit this scheme well are discussed in Chapter 8. The ones to which we actually own the rights are available on the Web at www.cambridge.org/9780521849357 for downloading, printing, and use. Second, to the extent that a goal of dynamic assessment is to promote maximal performance (as an indication of what might be possible under very good conditions), it is necessary to inject into the dynamic assessment situation a quality of interaction designed to promote intrinsic motivation: processing information and working on problem solving for its own sake and as its own reward, the motive to do one's best without expectation of task-extrinsic reward. This kind of interaction is discussed at greater length in Chapter 8. Finally, one can frequently identify task-extrinsic motivation as an obstacle to effective learning and problem solving, and as such it should constitute part of the outcome of the assessment, with recommendations for addressing that problem.

We might ask how the transactional perspective relates to psychological and educational assessment. First, and most obviously, if intelligence itself is not sufficient to produce the known individual differences in learning and achievement, then comprehensive assessment must include what is not assessed by intelligence tests. In this case, that means both development and accessibility of cognitive processes and relative intrinsic or extrinsic motivational orientation. Second, the transactional perspective demands the estimation of learning potential, that is, the ability to learn new material *given appropriate help*. Third, it leads to comparison within the person – for example, from time to time, situation to situation, and across different domains of ability – rather than reliance on cross-person comparison. Fourth, it opens in a major way the possible explanations – and remedial treatments – for ineffective learning and performance. In this last regard, we emphasize that the variables of intelligence, cognitive processes, and intrinsic motivation relate to each other in such a way that intervention in any one of those domains may be expected to result, to some extent, in improved functioning in the others, the magnitude of that effect depending on the prior transactions of the three elements. Thus, assessment strategies can include intervention that is focused on cognitive mediation or on motivation with the goal of identifying those aspects that are most likely to yield to intervention, with the expectation of good effects on the whole system.

Implications of the Model for DA

Because we are drawing a difference between intelligence and cognition and are focusing our assessment on aspects of mental functioning that are modifiable in response to mediation, we advocate a process-focused approach that identifies specific processing targets that characterize any individual being assessed, as well as the demands made by any DA task. These are neurologically based processes that are frequently cited and described in the neuropsychological literature and are generally viewed as important for development and learning. The specific mental processes that we propose as appropriate targets for DA are attention, perception, memory, language, cognition, and metacognition. Each of these reflects capacities with which human beings are typically born; yet each of them develops in response to experience and becomes increasingly guided by the executive metacognitive processes. Metacognition is not restricted to these specific processes, but is also increasingly involved with the so-called non-intellective emotional functions as well, such as motivation.

What we are actually modifying when we offer mediation during the course of the assessment, as well as during the subsequent interventions, are the metacognitive processes as they affect one or more of these more specific processes. That is, if the individual is manifesting difficulty with the specific process of attention, for example, we are not directly affecting the process of attention; rather, we are mediating the ways in which the individual regulates attention.

We view the assessment as a way to discover and explore the nature of the match between the processing demands of the task and the processing resources the individual brings to the task. Both the task and the individual would be analyzed in terms of the same processing elements. The questions for the assessment become the following: What are the processing demands of the task? How does the individual respond to these demands? Which processes are not functioning well? What are the individual's current processing resources? What can be done to improve this match? This includes ideas for modifying both the task and the individual's ability to handle the processing demands of the task in the most generalizable way possible.

Berninger and Abbott (1994) have proposed a model that is similar to ours, based on working brain systems that are related to school functioning, each of which is amenable to assessment and relevant to functioning in learning situations. These systems include the following:

attention (vigilance, sustained, selective, divided, and alternating),
memory (short-term, working, long-term schema, and
    paired-associate),
fine motor (finger function),
oral language (phoneme, rhyme, syllable, lexical, syntax, discourse)
orthographic (coding, imaging),
executive functions (planning, monitoring, organization, regulation,
    metacognition),
social-emotional (affect, social cognition, interactional skills,
    classroom system, family system),
motivation (attribution, goals, proactive strategies, success history),
cognition (abstraction, reasoning and problem solving, constructive
    processes),
reading (accuracy, rate, comprehension), and
writing (handwriting, spelling, composition).

These processes are all documented within brain functioning and are directly relevant to acquisition of new knowledge and skills. Further, assessment procedures are currently available for virtually all of these processes. These authors propose a dynamic assessment model that reflects responsiveness to treatment through development of growth curves (and, in their case, brain imaging).

The specific definitions of the processes and some suggested approaches to their mediation are elaborated in Chapter 7, where we discuss the curriculum-based approach to DA. This approach is also incorporated into the general DA approach we describe in Chapters 1 and 3. Suffice it to say at this point that our DA procedures are not intended as tests of intelligence but as vehicles for exploration of mental processes that are basic to learning. We view assessment as a means for revealing the processing needs of the individual, and, what is unique to DA, we see the sessions as opportunities to develop, in collaboration with the client, a road map for overcoming obstacles to competence.

3 General Procedural Guidelines for Conducting an Assessment That Includes Dynamic Assessment

It is clear from observing how we proceed in our own assessments, as well as from the way we teach others to do assessments, that DA is not all we do, although it can be an important enterprise on its own. Any good assessment is designed to respond to referral questions, as well as to questions and issues that arise during the course of the assessment. We need a full and varied repertoire of procedures and approaches, and we need to be aware of the data available from each of these. We need to begin with establishing the individual's zone of actual development within any of the domains addressed by the assessment, only then moving on to developing zones of proximal development. These zones of proximal development do not need to be established for each and every functional area but are best reserved to target areas determined to be at risk for the specific individual. With this approach, incorporation of DA into the assessment need not add a tremendous amount of time to the process. Indeed, there are many times when only 20 to 30 minutes are needed.

Depending on the referral issues, it is also possible that many of the procedures that assessors automatically administer are not necessary, and the assessor can move fairly rapidly into exploration of the area of concern and spend more time with DA procedures without using unnecessary time on those that fail to provide relevant information. The guiding questions for any assessment should be the following:

- What do I want to know?
- Where will I find that information?

With these questions in mind, we need to remind ourselves of the information that DA can provide and incorporate DA procedures only when this information is relevant:

- The individual's "next" level of development
- The responsiveness of the individual to intervention
- The types of intervention that may or may not be helpful

In other words, although automaticity may be a characteristic that is often desirable in our clients, it should not be a characteristic of the assessment process.

What, then, would be useful general guidelines for the assessment process? These are best outlined in terms of questions and data sources. Assessment is, after all, a data-gathering process to respond to questions that inform decisions.

Question	Data Sources
Is the individual "at risk" in a domain of functioning?	Norm-based procedures; interview; observation
To what extent has the individual mastered the content of a domain or task? What does the individual actually know and not know?	Criterion-referenced and curriculum-based procedures
What can be done to improve the individual's functioning in the areas of risk?	Dynamic assessment and assessor's knowledge base regarding interventions
How well is the individual responding to the intervention?	Curriculum-based procedures, interview, and observation

Thus, it should be clear that we view DA as an important part of the assessment repertoire, but not its entirety. It should be evident that no one approach provides adequate responses to all questions. We use and value all of the approaches for their contributions to the assessment process, when used appropriately. It is too often the case that procedures are used to respond to questions for which they were not designed, or even to questions that were not asked.

We also wish to make it clear that we advocate conducting any assessment within an ecological, or contextual, model. Although we are focusing in this book on assessment of individuals (with some consideration of groups), it should almost go without saying that any hope of understanding the individual requires awareness and knowledge of the environments within which that individual functions. To the fullest extent possible, these environments should be represented within the assessment. This is often done through interview and observation, as well as through consultation with knowledgeable cultural representatives when the referred client comes from a background that is not familiar to the assessor.

With all of these considerations in mind, the assessment typically follows a sequence that should be familiar to most readers:

- Review files
- Interview primary stakeholders
- Observe referred individual in relevant contexts

- Design assessment battery based on issues and questions derived from first three steps
- Administer direct procedures to determine zones of actual development, using normative and criterion-/curriculum-based approaches
- Proceed in hypothesis-generating manner to target and explore areas that appear to present obstacles to the individual's optimal functioning, using DA to create zones of proximal development
- Throughout this process, activate ideas regarding what might account for areas and issues of concern and what could be done to ameliorate these
- Formulate plan for intervention in collaboration with primary stakeholders
- Monitor and follow up outcomes of intervention plan

During the establishment of the zones of actual development, we frequently administer some of the major normative tests that are so often used as the sole bases of assessment by others. We find that the Wechsler tests of achievement and intelligence, for example, are useful for surveying broad areas of functioning; however, even inclusion of these in the battery is done in response to specific questions and not automatically, and other procedures may be found to be more relevant and useful for a particular case.

In general, we proceed in a funnel-like direction, moving from such broad survey types of approaches to increasingly specific and narrow procedures, guided by the information that emerges and the hypotheses that develop from our mental processing of our interactions with the individual. We continually ask ourselves, what do we now know, and what do we need to know? Following completion of each procedure, it is in fact useful to make notes to respond to these questions, particularly the first, because this is what often becomes part of the assessment report. See also the discussion of the continuum of assessment services model, Chapter 8.

Such an outline and procedure in fact describe a comprehensive assessment. It is possible and conceivable that, under circumstances of limited consultation, the assessment could move quickly from files review to interview to observation to dynamic assessment. This would describe what Rosenfield (1987) called Instructional Consultation and would be appropriate when the assessor functions within the school as part of an instructional consultation team. Although Rosenfield relies on curriculum-based procedures for her assessment, we suggest that curriculum-based dynamic assessment would be even more appropriate (see Chapter 5). Under these circumstances, the agenda is not to conduct a full assessment, but merely to generate some "pre-referral" ideas to determine whether the student responds to a low level of intervention. If not, then the more comprehensive approach would ensue.

When proceeding with a comprehensive assessment, we keep the model of mental functioning described in Chapter 2 in mind, particularly the array of cognitive processes. These processes allow us to respond to the questions of what might be the barriers to more optimal functioning of the referred individual, as well as what areas to target for intervention. These functions in fact serve as a means of direct linkage of the assessment with intervention. For example, if attention is the primary obstacle to learning, then attention is the primary focus of intervention, and so on for memory, language, and the other processes.

We think it would be useful at this point to walk and talk through an actual case from the point of referral through the assessment design and administration process. This will provide insight into our thinking as we conduct our assessments and will also reveal how we fit DA into the process.

CASE

This is the case of Karen,[1] who was referred to our summer clinic at Touro College. The summer clinic served as a practicum experience for students in the school psychology program who had completed their coursework and were about to move on to their full school year internship in an educational setting. All cases were done in collaboration between the students and the clinic supervisor, usually with the students working in pairs, but, in the case of Karen, with the student working alone with the clinic supervisor.

Karen was 7 years and 7 months of age and had completed first grade when she was brought to the clinic by her mother. Karen's teacher had recommended assessment by the school's child study team, but her mother preferred doing this independently of the school system. Her teacher noted academic functioning below grade level, and her mother voiced specific concerns about Karen's reading and math skills, as well as her attention span. The questions for the assessment were as follows:

- To what extent does Karen's current academic functioning deviate from expectations for her grade level?
- If significantly low, what are the obstacles to her functioning?
- What can be done to improve her performance?

Because Karen was seen during the summer, it was not possible to observe her within her classroom or to have contact with her teacher. She

---

[1] This name, as all names of cases used in this book, has been changed, with specific personal information omitted. Background information is provided only broadly.

lived with both natural parents and an older brother. Both of her parents were teachers. Although another language was spoken in the home, the dominant language to which she was exposed was English. Early history and development were notable for marital stress between her parents, but otherwise Karen's development progressed normally, and her health was good. Family history revealed that there were others in the family who had mild learning problems. Karen did not begin formal schooling until first grade because of the family's moving from one state to another, and she subsequently repeated this grade. She was recommended for promotion to second grade at the time of the assessment, with concerns, as stated earlier, about her academic skills. The emotional climate at home remained tense.

Karen was an easy child to work with. She was highly motivated, warm, friendly, alert, and appropriately interactive. She persisted when faced with challenge and responded to praise and encouragement with increased effort. She appeared to understand all instructions. Loss of attention and fidgetiness became apparent when she was involved in tasks well beyond her ability level.

We decided to begin with a broad survey of her skills by administering the Woodcock-Johnson Test of Cognitive Ability-Revised [WJ-R] (this was prior to release of the third edition) and the Wechsler Individual Achievement Test [WIAT] (this was prior to release of the second edition). The WJ-R revealed low average to average scores in all areas except Memory for Names and Picture Vocabulary. The WIAT similarly revealed low average to average scores in all areas except listening comprehension (although this area was more solidly average on the WJ-R). This pattern raised the possibility that, despite claims of English language dominance at home, there might be issues related to bilingualism that need to be addressed. The normative procedures did not identify reading and math as significantly deficient, although they were weak relative to her general reasoning ability, reading more so than math.

In response to the referral questions specifically targeting Karen's reading and math skills, we decided to move to curriculum-based assessment. For this we used sample passages from the last two reading books used in Karen's class. Karen was found to be at a frustration level at the beginning of the last reader in the book series and to be at an instructional level at the end of the book just prior to that. Thus, she had not mastered the reading expectations of first grade and was on very shaky ground for her move into second grade. Although she was able to make letter–sound associations, she did not have a stable foundation in phonetic rules, such as knowing that when a word ends in "e," the preceding vowel is usually long. Thus, she made errors such as reading "ride" as "rid" or "made" as "mad." Also, Karen lacked familiarity with many letter–sound combinations such as "th," "ch," "sh," "ou," "aw," "ow, "ph," and "-ing." These gaps reduced her fluency and, inevitably, her comprehension. On the other hand, Karen could at times compensate for these gaps by making use of contextual cues to help her figure out unfamiliar words.

In the math area, samples of Karen's school worksheets and homework were reviewed with her. In this area she was found to lack automaticity for basic money and time facts and lack of knowledge of the rules for carrying and borrowing in addition and subtraction problems. Thus, curriculum-based assessment was much more revealing of Karen's struggle in the domains for which she was referred, and it was possible to highlight specific skills she needed to review and master. In spite of this information, we still did not know much about Karen as a learner or about what approaches might help to optimize her learning. For this, we moved on to dynamic assessment.

The dynamic assessment approach used for Karen reflected the curriculum-based dynamic assessment (CBDA) model described in Chapter 7 of this book. For this, we used a story from the class reader for which she was at the frustration level. Passages from the reader became the pretests and posttests for the dynamic assessment. Her pretest and posttest performance was determined by calculating words and errors per minute, and she moved from a frustration level of 38 words and 9 errors per minute to an instructional level of 44 words and 2 errors per minute. The intervention focused on modeling and eliciting Karen's ability to read for meaning because she was noted to have good reasoning ability and to apply the spontaneous strategy of using contextual cues for word decoding. For this, Karen was taught to think about the basic message of the sentences and paragraphs that she read as she read. Her mother was also encouraged to read on a nightly basis to Karen, emphasizing meaning by sweeping groups of words with her finger as she read. Other interventions that were recommended for use within her home were to employ flash cards to increase her automaticity with words that had the sound combinations she needed to review, and involvement in choral reading of familiar passages to increase her fluency. For math, similar drill-based review of basic facts was recommended, in addition to emphasis on time-telling related to Karen's personal events and schedule. Specifically, it was recommended that she make a schedule in collaboration with her mother, post and review this schedule, and use it to help her learn to tell time. Issues of English mastery and parental marital problems also needed to be addressed and discussed.

The assessor found Karen to be highly motivated to gain proficiency in both reading and math. She was eager to show off her improved ability to read the material used during the assessment.

In this case, the dynamic assessment required only about 45 minutes. More could have been done to address Karen's issues of automaticity in both reading and math, but we can say that important insight was gained into Karen as a learner and some direction provided for intervention in the domain for which she was referred. Other areas related to her functioning were addressed as well, with the dynamic assessment used only to deepen insight into a specific function and to point the way to experience-based intervention.

MEDIATION

Possibly the most intimidating aspect of DA to those who have not yet tried it is the idea of providing intervention, or mediation, during the course of the assessment. Somehow it just does not feel safe when all the lines are not drawn in. First, let us hasten to point out that DA procedures differ with regard to the amount of scripting included. In fact, the procedures we have included in this book vary greatly regarding this feature. We begin our discussion of mediation with the most open-ended, "clinical" approach, associated most directly with the work of Feuerstein (e.g., Feuerstein et al., 1979) as a way to try to reduce the fear factor about this approach. We were certainly not taught to provide such mediation when we were taught to do assessments, and mediation turns DA into the antithesis of all we were taught in our assessment courses. We were told to remain neutral, to provide directions exactly as presented in the manuals, not to "mess" with the test. This is all essential to reliability and validity, matters to be discussed later in the book.

With DA we are not neutral, and we do mess with the test and the learner in order to find routes to move the learner to the next level of development. We have to create a "process" so that we can see how the learner learns and how we can promote increased competence. To do this, we must first create a collaboration between the assessor and the referred individual and place the individual in the position of active participant in the assessment process. To do this, we have to make our thinking as explicit as possible. This begins with what Feuerstein and his colleagues call *intent*. We have to express our intent to the learner: our intent to engage him or her in a teaching–learning process, our need for active participation for both parties, our agenda for what will happen, and our feedback as it happens. Such explicitness allows us to try out hypotheses and to make mistakes. Under these circumstances, we can say, "Well, that sure didn't help," and try something else. The interaction becomes an instructional conversation rather than something that the assessor does to (or extracts from) the individual being assessed.

Form 3.1. Mediation checklist

To Do

❑ Determine whether the learner has the basic knowledge and skill base to proceed with this task. (If not, go back and either teach what is necessary or modify the level of the task to reflect the learner's zone of actual development.)

❑ Decide how you will present the task. How will you give directions, provide supports (e.g., visual aids), modify the task (e.g., simplify, break down)?

❑ Select the interventions that are the most promising for this type of task.

❑ Identify the basic principles and strategies of task mastery or solution.

During the interaction, remember to

❑ Provide feedback that informs the learner about what did and did not work.

❑ Elicit active conversation and input from the learner related to the work.

❑ Collect data and work samples to demonstrate and document changes in competence (show these to the learner).

❑ Be explicit about what you are thinking and decisions you are making during the assessment; model reflective thinking through self-talk related to the task.

❑ Look for opportunities to relate new work to what the learner already knows, and encourage the learner to do this as well.

❑ Gear yourself to match the learner's pace and style and be ready to adjust what you are doing and saying to make it accessible to the learner.

❑ Keep the work within the learner's reach, but also require the learner to reach just beyond what he or she already knows or can do.

❑ End on a positive note of successful accomplishment.

The components of mediation can be rather esoteric, and an operationalization of the characteristics that closely correspond to those proposed by Feuerstein and his associates has been developed into a rating scale by the second author (Lidz, 1991); however, this is more relevant for researchers and trainers than for practitioners. The characteristics of mediation are in fact very accessible and need not rely on such jargon. Mediation is what good teachers and parents do when they promote high levels of mental functioning in their children. The outcome of good mediation for the learner is development of these high levels of mental functioning, including the ability to self-regulate and engage in strategic problem solving and abstract thinking. The specific characteristics of mediation appear in the Mediation Checklist of Form 3.1.

This checklist simply lists the types of behavior that should characterize the assessor's interactions with the learner during the course of the dynamic assessment. They differ from what might be considered the "usual" types of teacher–learner interactions in their emphasis on promoting higher levels of mental functioning (e.g., by focusing on principles and strategies of task solution) and by ensuring the customization and individualization of the experience for the learner. The checklist is meant to serve as a self-evaluation for assessors beginning their dynamic assessment journey, and it can also be used for taking notes so that the assessor can begin the plan for the dynamic assessment.

What we are describing in this section is mediation that characterizes the most clinical approach to dynamic assessment. There are other approaches that are more tightly scripted and that offer interventions that are actually semi- or fully standardized. It is, of course, arguable whether these latter approaches are in fact "dynamic," but we do not wish to engage in that discussion at this point. In this section, we merely wish to introduce readers to the basic concepts that typify this approach to assessment and that characterize what we actually do when we engage in dynamic assessment.

DOING DA

How, then, do we actually proceed to carry out a dynamic assessment? Although there is no simple answer to this question, there are some general guidelines that can be provided. First, it is necessary to target an area of the individual's functioning that warrants further exploration and that raises questions for which DA is an appropriate response. It is critical to establish the individual's zone of actual development in this area. Second is the selection of the specific DA approach to employ, and we hope to provide a repertoire of choices throughout this book to aid with this selection process. We also refer readers to Haywood and Tzuriel (1992) and Lidz and Elliott (2000) for an array of currently available dynamic assessment procedures, each explained by its designer.

It is very important that the content used for pretesting (and posttesting) be just beyond the individual's zone of actual development and, therefore, require intervention or mediation. Dynamic assessment is not dynamic assessment without interactive intervention, and there is no point in providing intervention for content that is either already mastered or so far into the learner's frustration level that it does not build on the current knowledge base and creates problems with motivation and perseverance. It is the interaction between the assessor and the learner that creates the zone of next (proximal) development; this zone does not exist as a separate, external entity.

The attitude that needs to be in place in the mind of both the assessor and the learner is that the zone of next development can be created, that the next step can be reached, and that the primary issue is to determine, through collaboration (assessor leadership, learner feedback, and active participation), how to reach it.

The types of information that can be derived from such an interactive approach include the following:

- What the individual is able to do independently
- What the individual is able to do with support
- Insight into the obstacles to the learner's more optimal performance
- The intensity of effort involved in facilitating the move of the learner from the zone of actual development to the zone of next development
- The nature of the interventions and interactions that seemed to promote this enhanced development

Dynamic assessment, when used in its most clinical, open-ended approach, is primarily descriptive; however, it is also possible to engage in DA using instruments that yield norm-based scores or curriculum-based measures such as the words-and-errors-per-minute scores used in the foregoing case example. When using norm-based information, one must be aware that these are only accurately applied to pretests, and scores cannot be reported for posttests without caveats. Use of norms for posttests can at best only be reported as "estimates," and the assessor should interpret these cautiously and in relation to test–retest and error of measurement information reported in the manuals. The more heavily scripted approaches have been successful in reducing test biases that tend to favor one ethnic group over another, and these have become quite useful for multicultural assessment practices (Lidz, 2001). Assessors should use standardized tests in a dynamic way only reluctantly and with compelling reason to do so, because the DA process by definition destroys the normative value of standardized tests. This is true because the conditions under which the tests were administered are not the same for persons in the normative samples and for participants in DA.

Dynamic assessment is at its best when describing learners in the process of learning, and the subtle changes that take place during the course of the interactions that provide opportunities for assessment viewed as $N = 1$ qualitative and formative research (e.g., Delclos, Vye, Burns, Branford, & Hasselbring, 1992). DA differs from behavioral models in its attention to process, albeit as expressed in observable behavior. Behavioral models can nevertheless be useful in providing means for recording and documenting the pretest and posttest experiences of the learner. Dynamic assessment not only deepens the insights gained from existing traditional approaches, but, even more important, it also adds information that is not available from these approaches.

The case of Karen is an example of DA that was focused heavily on academic content (reading, math); thus, it rather closely resembled curriculum-based methods. In other cases (see Chapter 9), the principal difficulty was found to lie in poorly developed metacognitive operations; therefore, the mediational intervention was focused on the operations that appeared to be deficient, and recommendations were developed based on the outcomes of the DA. Let us assume that Karen had shown difficulty understanding task instructions. An obvious thought would be that she had some receptive language difficulty, given that she lived in a bilingual environment. Had that turned out not to be the case, we would have explored other hypotheses. In that event, we might have discovered that her understanding of task instructions was quite adequate when the instructions were repeated, with slight variation of wording the second time. We might then have concluded that she had difficulty making meaning out of minimal information, that her difficulty was partially overcome within the DA session by the technique of varied repetition. We would regard that as an indication that greater and more durable success in getting her to understand task instructions could be reached in her classroom by advising the teacher to vary her verbal presentation, giving each instruction more than once but in different words. A monitoring check would then be done periodically, because we would expect Karen's ability to understand instructions to improve to the point at which she would no longer need the repetition tactic. We might also have mediated some "careful listening" strategies to Karen during the DA and assessed the degree of improvement from that mediation.

4 Dynamic Assessment in Clinical Settings

The term "clinical settings" in this chapter's title refers to those places and circumstances where people go to get help with psychological, educational, and social problems. We deliberately separate such settings from schools. In the latter case, people go there for learning whether or not they have problems. Thus, clinical settings are by definition problem-solving settings. This emphasis means, for one thing, that assessment activities can have a sharper focus: Although finding the precise nature of problems is often a clinical task, discovering whether problems exist is usually not an essential part of that task. School settings and clinical settings differ in the typical nature of the problems that require assessment and, most important, in the outcomes of assessment. In school settings as well as in clinical settings dealing with school-related problems, the outcomes must have clear implications for classroom management and instruction. In clinical settings the outcomes may be considerably broader, the age span of the clients wider, the services available for follow-up more varied, and the outcomes should have clear implications for treatment. In such settings, DA can be especially useful in getting at elusive information that may be more difficult to obtain than is true in more typical settings, particularly information on abilities and performance potential and on the sources of intelligence masking.

The three major problem groups that we deal with in this chapter are psychopathology, developmental disabilities, and neurological disorders. In keeping with our assessment principle that choice of assessment procedures must depend on the specific questions that one asks, we do not recommend a "standard battery" for assessment within any of these groups of disorders, much less across these categories. It is useful to bear in mind also that dynamic assessment is most usefully part of a more comprehensive assessment. Specifically, it is the part whose emphasis is most sharply on the cognitive and metacognitive processes of logical thinking, learning, and problem solving; therefore, in discussing each of our three categories of disorders, we look for the relation of dysfunction or inadequate development or application of systematic thinking processes to the particular disorder (or both).

The plan of this chapter is, in each of three major sections, to discuss the nature of the disorder category, present some specific aspects of cognitive and metacognitive functioning that one should examine (not excluding others), show and discuss some instruments that have been useful in dynamic assessment, and then present case material.

Many years ago, while working as a clinical psychologist in a psychiatric hospital, I (HCH) observed that psychologists quite often disputed their own test data when writing diagnostic reports. To check out this observation, I examined all of the psychological assessment reports that had been done in that hospital over the most recent 3-year period. The data were even more startling than my informal observation had been. In more than half of the cases in which a standardized intelligence test had been given (which was true of the great majority), the examining psychologist had reported an IQ and then, in the narrative section of the report, had offered the opinion that the IQ was an underestimate of the patient's abilities. Sometimes, but not always, the psychologists offered some conjecture regarding the nature of the obscuring factors: presence of a "thought disorder" such as schizophrenia, inattention and distractibility, motivational deficits associated with chronic hospitalization, difficulty understanding the requirements of the tests. My thought at the time was, "Why bother to give the tests if you are going to argue with the results?" We know now that these psychologists were probably correct and that their opinions, although based on data that they were unable to specify, were probably more valid than were the test scores. Nevertheless, the familiar report-writing dodge "present level of functioning" provided an effective screen and at least protected psychology interns from the wrath of clinical supervisors! Taking psychiatric disorders as an example of the broader realm of clinical psychological practice, we can surmise that psychologists who argue with their test data are (a) dissatisfied with what they get from standardized, normative tests; (b) seeing something in their patients that the tests do not reveal; and (c) in need of some new technology for assessment, particularly of cognitive functioning and intellectual potential. We try to provide that in this chapter.

We noted in Chapter 2 that intelligence is often masked by factors that make it appear that one has less ability, less potential, than is actually the case. Those same factors operate to limit access to one's intellectual resources. Nowhere is that more likely to occur than in those realms most often encountered by psychologists in clinical practice: psychopathology, developmental disabilities, neurological impairment, and learning disorders (this last category not covered in this chapter). There have been suggestions of dynamic approaches to assessment of intellective functioning in psychiatric patients (e.g., Kaniel & Tzuriel, 1992; Sclan, 1986), but they have been timid and tentative, primarily of the "change the test situation" variety. There is a stronger history of dynamic assessment with persons who have developmental disabilities (mental retardation, learning disabilities, autism spectrum disorders; e.g., Budoff, 1967, 1971, 1987; Budoff & Friedman, 1964; Haywood, 1997) and sensory impairment (Keane, Tannenbaum, & Krapf, 1992). What is needed now is a group of specifically dynamic instruments that can be used for just that purpose. In this chapter, we present both some background and some specially designed instruments that can help to gain a picture of the intellectual and cognitive potential of persons who have, or may have, a defined group of disorders. We include in the target populations adults, adolescents, and older children who may have psychiatric disorders, developmental disabilities, neurological impairment, or a combination of these.

DA AND PSYCHOPATHOLOGY

Intellectual Deficit and Psychosis

By their very nature, psychiatric disorders raise barriers to intellectual functioning, leading the classical psychoanalysts such as Sigmund Freud and Otto Fenichel (e.g., 1946) to write of *neurotic stupidity*. The more serious the disorder, the greater the masking of intelligence. Although neurotic stupidity was used to refer to a phenomenon that was quite similar to ego defense mechanisms, allowing one to avoid ego-threatening situations and interpretations (a typical neurotic reaction), the "loss" of intelligence with the onset of some psychoses was thought to be permanent and progressive, the result of brain pathology. In describing *dementia praecox* (the earlier term for schizophrenia), Kraepelin (1919/1971) asserted that its onset is accompanied by just such a loss of intellectual resources, as did Bleuler (1911/1950, 1978). Hunt and Cofer (1944), in a classical review of psychopathology and intellectual functioning, reported an average "loss" of at least 10 to 15 IQ points with the acute onset of schizophrenia, but they also surmised that the loss was not necessarily permanent. That inference was supported by Haywood and Moelis (1963), who retested "improved" and "unimproved" patients with schizophrenia 16 to 142 months after their hospital admission. The improved patients (whose psychotic symptoms were essentially in remission) had regained an average of 7.30 IQ points, whereas the unimproved patients had sustained a further loss of 2.65 points.

In a seminal study of intellectual deficit and schizophrenia, Blaufarb (1962) investigated the notion of masked intelligence, and in the process introduced into the field of psychopathology a form of dynamic assessment. Blaufarb observed that patients with schizophrenia were usually characterized by a deficiency in verbal abstracting ability, that is, the ability to assemble concrete verbal information and construct abstract meaning from it. Interpretation of proverbs had long been used as an informal test in the psychiatric examination of mental patients. In fact, that exercise had even made its way into individual intelligence tests (e.g., Wechsler's item, "What does this saying mean: Strike while the iron is hot?"). Blaufarb suggested that patients with schizophrenia have an information input deficit that makes it difficult for them to derive meaning from minimal information. He gave proverbs tests to these patients and to "normal" adults under two stimulus conditions. In the regular condition, the subjects got 17 single, separate proverbs. In the enriched condition, they got 17 sets, each set composed of 3 proverbs that were concretely different but that all had the same abstract meaning (e.g., "Don't cry over spilt milk," "No use closing the barn door after the horses are out," and "You can't unring the bell"). He had thus changed the test situation, in current dynamic assessment terms. In that study, the patients performed quite poorly on the single proverbs but scored significantly higher on the proverb sets. For the non-patients, there was no difference between the regular and enriched conditions in spite of their not having approached the test ceiling in either condition. These results led Blaufarb to conclude that his patients did indeed experience a deficit in information input channels that was at least partially overcome by changing the stimulus situation, that is, by enriching the input. The non-patients were not helped by the enrichment procedure, ostensibly because they did not have input deficits in the first place. This study was replicated and extended by Hamlin, Haywood, and Folsom (1965), who studied three levels of psychopathology (closed ward, open ward, former patients with schizophrenia) and non-patients. Patients with severe schizophrenia (closed ward) and non-patients were not helped by the enriched procedure, but both patients with a mild form of the disorder (open ward) and former patients showed significant improvement. The authors suggested that the non-patients were not helped because they did not have an information input deficiency, and the patients with severe schizophrenia were not helped because the treatment was not sufficiently powerful to overcome their difficulties, which might have included input deficits and also continuing disorders of thought (delusions) and perception (hallucinations). Improvement with enriched input for the open ward patients and the former patients was interpreted to suggest that these persons did indeed have a deficit in input channels that was easily overcome by stimulus enrichment.

A proverbs test appropriate for dynamic assessment can be found on the Web site. This test is still useful in the examination of persons with psychopathology. The original proverbs test, in the earliest dynamic assessment form, was of the "change the test situation" variety. One can also add mediation of some basic precognitive and metacognitive operations to press further the question, "What level of abstracting ability is potentially possible?" This combination of two intervention approaches is often very useful, especially when done sequentially so as to be able to separate the effects of each. This is most clearly demonstrated with the Test of Verbal Abstracting (TVA; in downloadable tests and forms[1]), which is discussed more fully in our treatment of developmental disabilities. Applying the same principles to the proverbs procedure, the following is an illustrative mediational sequence:

1. Administer form P-1 of the proverbs test (i.e., the 20 single proverbs).
2. After an interval in which one can do some other activity, such as administer another, unrelated test or administer form P-3 (i.e., the 20 three-proverb sets, each set containing the single proverb in P-1 and two additional ones that have different content but the same abstract meaning).
3. If needed (if there still is a low abstracting score, with not many full-credit responses), do verbal mediational training on (a) listening carefully and gathering clear and complete information; (b) different levels of meaning, with illustrations from everyday life; (c) thinking divergently ("What else could it mean?"); (d) expressing meaning in abstract, generalizable terms. In individual cases, other mediation may be needed, such as inhibiting impulsive responding, hypothetical thinking ("What if I said . . .?), self-verification of possible answers, and use of private speech to examine hypotheses.
4. Administer form PV-1 (i.e., parallel form, single statements of proverbs).
5. If there is still little evidence of verbal abstracting (i.e., low total score or few fully abstract responses), administer PV-3 (i.e., parallel form of the three-proverbs sets).
6. To push potential performance even further, one can then engage in a "testing the limits" procedure. In this procedure, the examiner presents all of the proverbs in both forms on which the examinee did not earn full abstract credit in an effort to determine whether an abstract response was available but not selected or expressed. One might say, for example, "Do you remember what you said when I asked you the meaning of the

---

[1] Many of the tests and test forms referred to throughout the book are downloadable from the following Web address: www.cambridge.org/9780521849357.

saying, 'Don't put all your eggs in one basket'? Yes, you said carrying eggs in a basket is not such a good idea because they might bounce around and break. Do you think that saying could have a meaning that has nothing to do with eggs and baskets?" If after a series of such mediational questions the examinee still has not produced an abstract response, the examiner might say, "When asked the meaning of 'Don't put all your eggs in one basket,' some people say that it means 'It is not a good idea to have only one plan,' and others say that it means 'Put things together that go together.' Which of those two do you think is better?" Finally, the examiner might state an abstract meaning and ask, "Do you think it could have that meaning?" If the answer is affirmative, the examiner might then ask, "Would you please think of a common, everyday situation in which that meaning might apply? In other words, when would it be a good idea to follow that advice?"

Thus, using this simple test of interpretation of proverbs, one can assess the effectiveness of (a) changing the test situation by enriching stimulus input, (b) mediating applicable metacognitive operations, and (c) testing the limits. The amount of intervention needed to bring about abstract interpretations can reveal the depth of any deficits in information input channels and the probable investment that will be required to remediate this cognitive aspect of functioning.

This test can be adapted for group administration. See the section on group assessment (Chapter 8) for some detail on how to do this. In the ideal situation, the proverbs test should be part of extended dynamic assessment, that is, assessment that extends over many days. When that is possible, the different forms of the test should be separated by several days to minimize the tendency to remember and give the same answers without any new thinking. When such extended assessment is not feasible, different parts of the test should be separated by interpolated activity of a different nature, such as a nonverbal task.

DA of cognitive functioning and potential is especially useful in psychopathology because of the intelligence-masking nature of neuroses, psychoses, and some personality disorders. It is usually advisable to give DA instruments that reflect several domains of content to verify any deficits in cognitive functioning that might have been discovered with a single test. Some examples of deficits in cognitive functioning (note that this does not say "cognitive development") that are found often in persons who have psychiatric disorders are impulsive rather than reflective responding to problems; tendency to view problems as wholes rather than as analyzable parts or, conversely, a tendency to see only one or two parts (tunnel vision); difficulty managing multiple sources of information; perceptual and conceptual rigidity (e.g., difficulty switching criteria of classification from shape to color to number to size).

SPECIAL APPLICATIONS IN PSYCHOPATHOLOGY

The study of schizophrenia in particular is a natural application of DA, because DA is usually focused on assessment of cognitive and intellective functioning, and schizophrenia is generally regarded as a thought disorder. DA can help one to distinguish clinical subtypes within the diagnosis of schizophrenia as well as to estimate the probable success of cognitive intervention programs, including cognitive approaches in psychotherapy such as cognitive–behavioral therapy (Meichenbaum, 1977, 1982; Beck, 1976, 1991) and cognitive developmental therapy (Haywood, 2000; Haywood & Menal, 1992). DA has also been used successfully to predict readiness of individuals with schizophrenia for rehabilitation (Wiedl, 1999, 2002; Wiedl, Schottke, Garcia, & Calero, 2001) and their ability to deal with medication problems (Wiedl & Schottke, 2002).

In an early demonstration of DA for patients with schizophrenia, Sclan (1986) gave the TVA (Test of Verbal Abstracting; Haywood, 1986) and the Representational Stencil Design Test (RSDT; Feuerstein, Haywood, Rand, Hoffman, & Jensen, 1982/1986; Feuerstein, Rand, & Hoffman, 1979) to hospitalized patients with schizophrenia who had been diagnosed either as "schizophrenia, paranoid type" or as any of the nonparanoid subtypes (catatonic, hebephrenic, chronic undifferentiated). All of the patients were given a pretest in the static mode, then a period of mediation of cognitive concepts and metacognitive strategies related to these tasks, and finally a static posttest. He classified their errors into eight error types. Nonparanoid patients made significantly more errors than did the paranoid patients on six of the eight error types on both tasks. The paranoid patients derived greater benefit from the interpolated mediation than did the nonparanoid patients (greater gains from pretest to posttest), even though their performance was initially higher. Analyzing their performance by error types, Sclan found that the paranoid patients

> made their large differential gains principally with respect to reduction of errors on items that required more sophisticated abstract cognitive processes; i.e., the more cognitively complex and difficult the task, the greater the benefit that the paranoid (but not the nonparanoid) patients derived from cognitive and metacognitive mediation. (Haywood & Tzuriel, 2002, p. 47)

The DA procedure of intervening within the test had allowed Sclan to reveal and document the relatively more responsive nature of the logic processes of patients with paranoid schizophrenia. It is especially interesting that the results of this study were essentially the same on two such different tasks as the TVA and the RSDT, the one a verbal abstracting task and the other a much more cognitively complex task involving perception of problems, visual–spatial relations, systematic comparing, learning and application of rules, managing multiple sources of information, and complex sequencing (see description of RSDT, Appendix A). On the basis of such an assessment, one could not only distinguish clinical subtypes within a psychopathological diagnostic group but also estimate that those who had derived the greater benefits from mediation would be relatively more accessible to a cognitive type of therapeutic intervention. This is not to say (ever!) that those who derived less benefit from mediation would be inaccessible to cognitive intervention; it is merely to observe that they would no doubt require greater effort, and perhaps more frequent and intense mediation, to reach a similar level of improvement.

DA AND LESS SEVERE DISORDERS

DA is, of course, also useful in the psychological assessment of persons with psychological difficulties that are less severe than the psychoses, such as psychoneuroses, attachment disorders, anxiety disorders, disorders of social/interpersonal relations, learning disorders, and even "character" disorders such as sociopathy. We have made quite a big case for DA with persons who suffer the more serious disorders because the masking of cognitive and intellective abilities is more pervasively done than is true in nonpsychotic disorders; nevertheless, there is plenty of masking to go around!

In general, the principles and techniques of DA that are described in Chapter 8 of this volume for adults and seniors can be applied equally to persons with psychoneuroses, interpersonal difficulties, and character disorders. The primary principle in either case is that the selection of tasks and tactics must be done to answer specific questions. The following brief case history is a summary of one reported by Haywood and Delclos (1986, unpublished):

A 25-year-old man was referred by his attorney following the man's arrest for discharging a firearm in a public park. The attorney, who also held a doctorate in sociology, had heard lectures on DA and cognitive approaches to psychotherapy and thought that a cognitive approach might be useful. A graduate student interviewed the young man at the jail and reported that he "obviously" was of good family, had at least average and probably superior intelligence, had no prior police record, spoke with considerable remorse about his misbehavior, and asked for help in understanding his own behavior, especially his motives for his "in-trouble" behavior. Both parents were university professors of high community standing. Both of his older siblings held graduate or professional degrees, were married, and were responsible parents. This young man, though, kept doing things that got him into trouble (but never before in jail). He had a girlfriend whom he was trying to impress when he fired a gun in the park. Standard psychological assessment confirmed the estimate of superior intelligence, and personality assessment revealed a major conflict: On the one hand, he was strongly motivated to satisfy his family's aspirations for him (to graduate from university and perhaps continue to graduate or professional school, to "settle down" in a family role and be a "responsible part of the community"), whereas on the other hand he harbored strong resentment toward his parents and siblings because he was constantly failing to meet their expectations. Amazingly, he did not understand the nature of this conflict and had no idea how to resolve it. To make matters worse, he had never held a job for longer than 3 to 4 months, although he had no difficulty getting jobs, being personable and even charming. The role expectations were made even more distressing because the family was African American, causing him to feel a special responsibility to do well and act responsibly. There were thus intrapersonal, interpersonal, cognitive, and social components to his problems.

DA was centered on Rey's Complex Figure, Feuerstein's RSDT, and the Learning Propensity Assessment Device (LPAD; Feuerstein et al., 1979) Set Variations I and II (see Appendix A for descriptions of these tests). These instruments were chosen because a primary question had to do with planning: To what extent did the young man look ahead, anticipate events that had not yet occurred, engage in metacognitive planning processes, or even possess the level of cognitive development that would make such planning possible? Even more important was the question of response to mediation: How difficult would it be to bring about some change in his planning behavior, even at the micro-level of performance on DA tasks? On all three sets of instruments, his initial performance was quite poor, although on verbal tasks he had been a very high scorer. Mediation mainly addressed planning but necessarily addressed such prerequisites as inhibiting impulsive responding (taking his time, reflecting), hypothetical thinking, anticipation of outcomes, systematic comparison, managing multiple sources of information, and "personal speech," that is, talking to himself about his metacognitive processes. In fact, establishing a general metacognitive focus was the most difficult part to accomplish – just getting him to think about his own thinking. Easy and immediate positive change was produced in most of the metacognitive operations that were mediated. The problem was that he continued to resist applying these same skills to his everyday life.

Treatment then consisted of a combination of cognitive education and a kind of supportive psychotherapy. The most frequent question was, "Did you learn something in the cognitive education sessions that could help you to understand what you are telling me now about your behavior?" The most frequent answer was, "Yes. I need to think about how I am thinking about these matters." Often, his answers would be much more specific, such as, "I do better when I ask myself what else I could do (as an alternative to acting on the first impulse), then compare the alternatives and ask which, if any, of them is most likely to get me where I want to go."

After about 3 months of twice-weekly meetings, half of them devoted to cognitive education and the other half to a more strictly psychotherapeutic approach, he felt that he was in much better control of his impulses and had become a better planner. He had gotten a job, was engaged to be married, and was carefully weighing the possibility of moving to another state.

The role of DA in that case was essentially to develop at a micro-level the behavioral situations in which we could examine the cognitive and metacognitive processes that underlay his planning behavior, or failed to do so. His response to the mediation in DA provided a blueprint for both the client and the therapist in their further work.

It is generally true that a single task can be used to identify a variety of cognitive deficiencies and to estimate the investment that will be required to overcome them; nevertheless, the content of the tasks does make some difference. Dynamic assessors should be equipped with a "cafeteria" of tasks from which to select the ones that, in individual cases, will be most effective in finding answers to the specific questions posed in those cases. Specific tests that are useful in assessment of persons with psychopathology, developmental disabilities, and neurological impairment are discussed in detail at the end of this chapter. From that group of tests, one can select a small number that, depending on the specific questions asked of the assessment, might respond to the following areas that are found frequently to present difficulty for persons with psychiatric disorders (and, of course, to many who do not have such disorders):

1. General intellectual functioning (standardized intelligence tests, being sure to include expressive language use to the extent that the patients are capable of it)
2. Verbal abstracting (Proverbs, TVA)
3. Spatial, temporal, and quantitative relations; field dependence–independence (certain tests from the LPAD of Feuerstein; e.g., Organization of Dots; Haywood's translation and adaptation of Rey's Seriation of Weights and Measures)

4. Reasoning, especially analogical reasoning (also LPAD tests, e.g., LPAD Set Variations I and II, Representational Stencil Design Test; Haywood's translation and adaptation of Rey's Flags Test)
5. Intrinsic motivation (Haywood's Picture Motivation Scale for low-functioning examinees; any of Susan Harter's situational tests of intrinsic motivation; the Choice Motivator Scale; Delclos and Haywood's Mazes Test of Intrinsic Motivation)
6. Memory (any free-recall verbal learning test, including a free-recall memory test following each form of the Proverbs or TVA)
7. Transformation/Stability (Haywood's Transformation Test, Paour's Boîte à Transformation [Transformation Box])
8. Social Perception (Thematic Apperception Test, given in a dynamic way with mediation of metacognitive operations and testing the limits)

DA AND DEVELOPMENTAL DISABILITIES

When I (HCH) moved from research in psychopathology to research in developmental disabilities, I observed that persons with mild and moderate mental retardation appeared to have the same difficulty forming verbal abstractions as patients with schizophrenia had – quite probably for different reasons. I tried to use the proverbs test and found immediately that scores were so low it was clear that persons with mental retardation simply did not understand the requirements of the task. I then changed the task from interpreting proverbs to detecting verbal similarities. In the first of a series of studies, Gordon and Haywood (1969) gave verbal similarities tests under two conditions to two groups of institutionalized mentally retarded persons. The first group had confirmed central nervous system pathology, whereas the second group showed no evidence of brain damage and was diagnosed as having "cultural-familial" retardation. There was a third group of institutionalized but not retarded subjects, equated with the retarded groups on mental age. The verbal similarities were given under "regular" (e.g., "In what way are an orange and a banana alike?") and "enriched" (e.g., "In what way are an orange, a banana, a peach, a plum, and a pear alike?") conditions. The tests were scored in the usual way, with no credit for incorrect answers ("They are the same color"), 1 point for correct but concrete answers ("You can eat them"), and 2 points for correct abstract responses ("They are both/all fruit"). Both groups with retardation made very low scores in the regular condition, with the younger nonretarded subjects scoring higher than did the MA-(mental age) matched retarded subjects. In the enriched condition, the organic retardation group still made very low scores, but the cultural-familial group made significantly higher scores than they had made in the regular condition; in fact, their scores came all the way up to the level of those in the nonretarded MA-matched group. These effects have been essentially replicated by Call (1973), Haywood and Switzky (1974), and Tymchuk (1973). These studies led to development of the TVA (downloadable forms;[2] Haywood, 1986), which was designed for dynamic assessment in the stimulus change, metacognitive mediation, and testing-the-limits modes.

In cases of either developmental disabilities or psychopathology, the search for potential ability often requires greater diligence and more exhaustive instruments than is true of other persons, simply because there may be more barriers to the expression of intelligence. Such barriers include, in the case of developmental disabilities, especially mental retardation, impoverished vocabulary, history of frequent failure, a task-extrinsic motivational orientation and a failure-avoiding tendency, scant knowledge base associated with ineffective learning strategies and/or poor educational experiences, as well as chronic deficient cognitive functioning and consequent (Paour, 1988) inadequate cognitive development. Because of this multiplicity of obstacles, it is especially important to avoid interpreting initial and even subsequent failures on tests as evidence of lack of potential. The familiar expression in the logic of science applies here: Absence of evidence is not evidence of absence. Thus, use of dynamic assessment instruments and strategies such as the proverbs test and the TVA can be especially productive because they allow examiners to do progressive peeling away of possible obstacles. The sequence of administering the TVA illustrates this point:

1. Administer, in a static mode, that is, without help, Form A-2 (Form A, 20 similarities items: "In what way are an orange and a banana alike?").
2. To minimize immediate recall effects, do an interpolated, unrelated task. This is a good opportunity to administer a different test.
3. If the examinee achieves a high score, with many abstract responses, exit the procedure; no need for further examination with this test (see continuum of assessment services model, Chapter 8).
4. If the examinee achieves a low score, with few abstract responses, administer Form A-5 (Form A, 20 five-exemplar similarities sets: "In what way are an apple, a banana, a peach, a plum, and a pear alike?") in a static mode (no help). If A-5 yields a 25% to 50% increase in total score and an increase in the number of abstract responses, exit and conclude that the initial problem was related to difficulty making meaning out of minimal information, which was easily overcome by enriching information input. If the total score is still low, with few abstract responses, proceed to Step 5.

[2] www.cambridge.org/9780521849357.

5. Without delay, mediate systematic comparison, classification, class inclusion, and verbal abstracting, using the training tasks provided with the test or alternative ones provided by the examiner's ingenuity. In addition to the metacognitive training with these materials, use the mediation period to make certain that the examinee understands the requirements of the task. For example, when the examinee has correctly formed groups of toys, traffic signs, and writing/drawing instruments, one might ask, "So if I should ask you in what way a pencil, a crayon, and a pen are alike, what would you say?" Failure to produce the abstraction "writing/drawing instruments" should lead the examiner to continue the mediation.

6. Go immediately to administration of Form B-2 (parallel form of the test, two exemplars of each concept), static mode. Great improvement in total score and number of abstract responses may be interpreted as evidence that the initial difficulty arose at least in part from underdevelopment of the metacognitive prerequisites of verbal abstracting (comparison, classification, and class inclusion) or from failure to grasp the task requirements and that these difficulties were overcome by the mediational training. Lack of or scant improvement could mean that the difficulty might lie at both the information input and cognitive underdevelopment levels (recall that B-2 has only two exemplars of each concept) and was not overcome by either intervention alone. In that case, proceed to Step 7.

7. Following another interpolated task, administer Form B-5 (parallel form of the test, five exemplars of each concept), in static mode. If there is substantial improvement in total score and number of abstract responses, conclude that the examinee was deficient in both information input and metacognitive operations for verbal abstracting and that these deficiencies were substantially reduced (depending on extent of improvement in the score and amount and intensity of mediation required) by the twin strategies of enriching information input and mediating metacognitive operations. If there still is not substantial improvement, it is possible that the examinee experiences a deficit at the expressive level of mental functioning.

8. In that case, go to a "test-the-limits" procedure. Present all items on which the examinee failed to give an abstract response, but this time ask for five ways in which the items are alike. If the abstract response is among the five ways given, it can be assumed that the examinee has the cognitive development necessary to form verbal abstractions but is deficient in response selection (i.e., in differentiating concrete from abstract responses). That information itself can then lead to treatment and educational recommendations.

Here, then, is a task in which it is possible to use at least three of the usual DA intervention modes: changing the test situation, mediating metacognitive operations, and testing the limits. In fact, one can go beyond that. Throughout this verbal task, there is the danger that one might interpret poor vocabulary as evidence of deficient verbal abstracting ability. To avoid such an error, it is necessary to determine that the examinee does indeed know the meanings of the words that form the exemplars. In the item, "In what way are a kettle and a skillet alike?" an examinee might give an incorrect answer because he or she does not know what a kettle or a skillet is. When an examiner suspects that to be true, he or she may ask the examinee, "Do you know what a skillet is?" or "Do you know what a kettle is?" If the examinee does not know, one should define the item(s) in such a way as not to reveal the verbal abstraction (e.g., "A skillet is a frying pan," or "A kettle is a pot usually used for heating water"). In this way, a major obstacle to clear logical thinking, impoverished vocabulary, especially in persons with developmental disabilities, can be removed, clearing the way to examination of cognitive development itself and the application of examinees' intelligence to the solution of this kind of problems.

Almost by definition, persons with developmental disabilities have histories filled with failure, especially at tasks that require application of intelligence to solution of abstract problems. It is not sufficient simply to call attention to that fact; rather, DA should yield some suggestions about how to overcome that obstacle and get more effective performance. One way is to guarantee success over a variety of problems. We do that often by introducing problems that can be solved easily, allowing examinees to demonstrate their competence and to enjoy success. Each successful solution should be met not only with positive feedback ("You are right! You got that one right. Good for you!") but also with "mediation of a feeling of competence" (one of Feuerstein's list of characteristics of mediated learning experience). Thus, the examiner's response to a good solution might be, "Yes, you got that right! Good for you. Do you know why you got it right? It's because you looked carefully at the whole problem, not just at one part, you took your time, and you remembered the rules." Success can be guaranteed also by giving all the help that is needed, that is, by not permitting failure.

It is a good idea in this regard to begin an assessment with relatively easy tasks. Rey's Plateaux test (see description, Appendix A) is one that is often useful for just this purpose, especially with persons with developmental disabilities. It is even useful for introducing the examining situation with persons who have autism spectrum disorders, partly because it does not require any verbal response, involves little social interaction with the examiner, and can be seen as affectively "safe" because of its use of nonpersonal, concrete materials. Examinees with autism who do not communicate with language often do well on this task and even warm up to the examining situation with its use. Following the Plateaux with drawing tasks is a good way to promote continuation of the task investment of persons with autism.

Barriers based on a task-extrinsic motivational orientation (see Chapter 2) are more difficult to overcome. This situation is observed when examinees clearly do not derive satisfaction from engagement with the tasks, do not enjoy working on puzzle-like tasks, and do not expect to enjoy personal achievement. Persons with developmental disabilities are especially likely to be characterized by such an extrinsic motivational orientation and to develop the habit of trying to avoid failure by not investing much of themselves in problem-solving tasks rather than seeking success by trying hard. Examiners should try a variety of tactics. These include the following:

1. *Guaranteeing success.* Give all the help that is needed, in a non-patronizing way.
2. *Avoiding the use of task-extrinsic incentives and rewards.* Even positive verbal feedback (social reinforcement, praise) should be used only in a limited way, combined with discussion of how success was achieved, so as to link the feedback as clearly as possible to the task and the examinee's performance.
3. *Use of task-intrinsic rewards.* The essential idea here is not to avoid rewards but to be sure that the rewards lie within the tasks. Example: "You did a really good job solving that problem. How did you do that? Would you explain it to me?" Example: "You did such a good job on those problems. I think you might be ready for the next level, maybe some harder ones."
4. *Exhibiting intrinsic motivation.* Both children and older individuals with developmental disabilities do a huge percentage of their learning by imitation. One can take advantage of that fact by showing intrinsic motivation. Just a look of excitement and interested engagement with the task, rather than bored indifference, can communicate the idea that the examiner is himself or herself a person who is interested in solving problems and in using one's intellectual resources to do so. To the extent that they can do so without sounding (or being!) phony, examiners can also make such comments as "That was a tough one, but it sure was fun finding the solution."

In addition to working to overcome the performance deficits associated with extrinsic motivational orientation, examiners should consider including a test of motivational orientation in the assessment package (see earlier paragraph on assessing motivational orientation, this chapter, under DA and Psychopathology). In cases of very low developmental age (as in mental retardation), minimal social interaction (as in autism), or low levels of expressive language, one might wish to choose the Picture Motivation Scale,[3] even though it was developed for use with young children. It has the advantage of not requiring any verbal response: Just pointing to one's choice of response suffices; however, receptive language at a minimal level (about 3–4 years) is required. The Mazes Test of Intrinsic Motivation[3] likewise requires no verbal response, but it does require fairly good control of fine motor behavior, including the ability to hold a pencil and to track a line. At high levels of overall functioning, the Choice Motivator Scale, which does require verbal response and the ability to remember choices that one has just made, can be useful. The scores on these tests can suggest the level of difficulty that one expects to encounter in motivating the individuals to engage in and persist in learning and problem-solving activities, and thus can contribute to the "investment required for remediation" estimate that should be an outcome of DA.

Providing Missing Information

We observed earlier that persons with developmental disabilities are especially likely to have scant knowledge bases. It is a cardinal principle of DA that ignorance is not to be interpreted as inability: does not ≠ cannot. It is thus especially important to be wary of gaps in the knowledge base of any examinees, but most particularly those whose overall knowledge base is likely to be depressed. In addition to persons with developmental disabilities, that group includes persons who are new to the culture, such as recent immigrants, persons who have had limited educational opportunity, and to some extent persons with sensory limitations. The most obvious example is impoverished vocabulary, discussed in a previous section. That is easily overcome by providing definitions of operative words. Even in that case, though, the matter is not a one of simply not knowing the meaning of specific words. It is often a case of not having had experience at considering definitions and generalizing meaning, so some practice at defining words and applying them in discourse also helps. In tests in which calculating may be required, it is important to be sure that the examinees have that skill and have had some practice applying it. Example: In one of the clever tests of André Rey, the Signs Test, the examinee must supply a missing algebraic sign ($+$, $-$, $\times$, or $/$) to complete a mathematical statement (equation). In

---

[3] Materials for this and other tests and test forms referred to in the text have been posted at the Cambridge University Press Web site and can be downloaded and printed for professional use: www.cambridge.org/9780521849357.

another, a test of transitive relations, knowledge of equality and inequality signs ($=$, $\neq$, $<$, $>$) is required. Failure on such a test might mean that the examinee lacks the necessary cognitive development to understand transitive relations, but it might also mean that the examinee simply lacks knowledge of these symbols. Explaining the symbols and making certain that they are understood can remove the ambiguous interpretation of low performance.

DA OF ADAPTIVE BEHAVIOR

Although DA has been developed and is used primarily for assessment of learning potential, it is quite possible to extend its application into related domains. One such domain is assessment of "developmental potential" in adaptive behavior. The term "adaptive behavior" is used widely, especially in the field of developmental disabilities, to refer to "activities of daily living" (ADL; another term that has some currency). There are several excellent normative instruments for assessment of adaptive behavior. The ones most frequently used in the United States are the American Association on Mental Retardation Adaptive Behavior Scales (ABS; American Association on Mental Retardation: www.aamr.org), the Scales of Independent Behavior (SIB-R) and its derivative, the Inventory for Client and Agency Planning (ICAP; Austin, TX: Pro-Ed: www.proedinc.com), and the Vineland Adaptive Behavior Scales (Circle Pines, MN: American Guidance Service: www.agsnet.com). They provide a means of assessing the relative competence of individuals who have special needs to perform the personal and social activities that are required in everyday life, ranging from simple motor acts through personal hygiene, dressing, and grooming, to social behavior and management of resources. They usually include subscales of "maladaptive" behavior, that is, behavior that is less associated with competence than with the potential to limit one's independence through behavior that is unacceptable or disruptive to others, such as fighting, running away, fire-setting. These are largely normative scales in which each individual's level of competence or maladaptive behavior is compared with that of others of similar demographic characteristics or degrees of independent living (or both). They are designed principally to identify domains of those activities of daily living that either restrict independence or require further work and sometimes to suggest the most appropriate residential setting, with the least restriction of personal liberty, that is feasible.

Most scales of adaptive behavior are filled out on the basis of either interviews with persons who have good knowledge of the target individuals' daily behavior or interviews and observations of the individuals themselves. Respondents are typically instructed to report only what they have observed rather than merely giving their general impressions.

There is some degree of criterion-referenced assessment implicit in adaptive behavior scales; nevertheless, it is useful to get data on (a) obstacles, especially cognitive obstacles, to acquisition and elaboration of activities of daily living; (b) strategies for promoting more effective ADL; and (c) response to mediation of thinking modes that could help individuals to acquire and exercise more adaptive ADL. Behaviorists have adopted a similar strategy for many years under the rubric of "functional analysis." They attempt to modify some aspect of behavior, analyze what does and does not work in this regard, and modify their strategies accordingly. Dynamic assessment can yield even richer inferences that can be directly related to education and training in ADL. We must point out here that the following descriptions are not the products of systematic research; rather, they have come from clinical experience, our own attempts to use DA for assessing individual differences in the potential for growth in ADL.

As in any other application of DA, the first task is to identify the questions that one wishes to pose through DA. In the case of DA of adaptive behavior, the principal questions are usually such ones as the following: (a) What is impeding this person's development of more adaptive behavior in the domain of _____? (b) To what extent can we promote further development in this domain through cognitive/motivational mediation? (c) How much investment, of what kinds, will be required to promote such change?

We do not need to ask about the individual's current level of adaptive behavior because application of one or another of the standardized adaptive behavior scales will have told us that. Using that standardized scale information as a baseline and as a source of basic data, we follow this sequence:

1. Identify a domain of daily activity that is weak, for example, self-dressing, and use the normative scores of the individual as baseline data in that domain.
2. Choose a specific activity within that weak domain, for example, shoe tying.
3. Mediate metacognitive operations that are required for that activity and that could be generalized to other activities within the same domain.
4. Work to promote intrinsic motivation related to the activity in question.
5. Take note of apparent obstacles to performance (e.g., poor motor coordination, fear of failure, ignorance of spatial orientation information such as right versus left sides, inexperience with knot tying).
6. Reassess after mediation.

7. Test for transfer by requiring performance on another item in the same domain (self-dressing), such as shirt buttoning.

This is a more or less standard formula in DA. In DA of adaptive behavior, working necessarily with persons whose development is delayed or who have significant motor, speech, language, or cognitive impairment, the steps in this sequence will have to be elaborated and individualized according to learners' abilities and responses to mediation.

Achieving transfer of training on one item to others within the domain ("near" transfer) often appears to be unsuccessful at first. Transfer might require specific training on several items within the domain, accompanied by mediation for transfer. Mediation for transfer consists of "bridging" (e.g., "We have learned that we have to go slowly with this job. In what other activities is it best to go slowly, take our time, and do one part at a time?"). In the process of doing that, examiners frequently become aware of the difference between successful and unsuccessful strategies for the particular person. Such observations become important parts of the outcome of DA of adaptive behavior.

Mediation as we have described the process in this book is a highly verbal process. One might well ask whether it is possible and how it can be done with persons whose language communication is markedly impaired, as, for example, in persons with autism spectrum disorders or severe mental retardation. The first answer is that one should never abandon verbal communication with persons who lack expressive language. Most often, such persons have a higher level of receptive language than of expressive language. Even if they do not, good mediators accompany their nonverbal mediation with plenty of language use. Nonverbal mediation makes use of imitation. To get learners to imitate examiners, the examiners frequently must first imitate the learners. Doing so communicates the idea that imitation is what is wanted. Then, while actually speaking the necessary words (e.g., "See what I'm doing? Now you do it."), the mediator may demonstrate an activity and ask the examinee to duplicate it. Slowing down and taking one's time can be demonstrated, as can thinking about how to go about solving the problem, taking on the problem sequentially ("See? First we are tightening the laces, pulling upward on both"), distinguishing right and left sides, crossing the laces, and so on.

Motivation plays an even larger role in the performance of persons with disabilities than it does in persons with typical development. That is because the importance of motivation, especially task-intrinsic motivation (see Chapter 2), increases with increasing difficulty of tasks, and for persons with disabilities, most tasks are difficult; therefore, motivation makes a bigger difference for them than for others. Avoidance of tasks in which there has been a history of failure, or tasks that the person fears because they look difficult, is a major impediment to effective functioning. Mediating the motivation to try, and eventually to succeed, can make a huge difference. That is accomplished in part by breaking tasks into manageable components, moving backward if necessary to very small components until one locates the level at which the person can succeed. It is further accomplished by mediational feedback ("Great. You did a good job there, because you took your time and did it one part at a time!"). Task-intrinsic incentives and rewards may be used to promote performance. These include asking the learner to show others how to do the task, and "progress" comments such as, "You are doing a great job. I think you are ready to take on the next part."

This application of DA provides an excellent example of the chief outcome: Specifying how the individual can be helped to make further progress in development and functioning. Staff members should not be told simply that this person has been shown to be capable of a higher level of performance than he or she has been demonstrating. Doing so without specifying how such a high level can be achieved does more harm than good (see Chapter 9 on reporting results of DA). Clear communication about how to mediate essential metacognitive and motivational modes makes the difference between assessment for its own sake (i.e., worthless) and assessment that actually helps the person being examined.

NEUROPSYCHOLOGICAL DYNAMIC ASSESSMENT

Neuropsychological assessment and dynamic assessment have much in common and make excellent partners (Haywood, 1977). In both enterprises, one is more interested in maximal performance than in typical performance and in prospects for remediation rather than in classification. In both, the examiner intervenes actively to test the examinee's response and to promote greater effort. In both, there is often direct feedback on performance. Thus, application of DA principles and procedures to assessment of the cognitive functioning and potential of persons who might have suffered some type of brain injury or disorder is a relatively easy step, and DA finds receptive employment among neuropsychologists.

The role of neuropsychological assessment has shifted dramatically in the last generation. There was a time when behavioral assessment of functions assumed to be mediated in the central nervous system was undertaken with diagnosis of brain lesions or malfunction as a primary goal (see, e.g., Halstead, 1947; Heimburger & Reitan, 1961; Reitan, 1962; Wheeler & Reitan, 1962). As imaging technology improved and eventually enabled diagnosticians actually to see brain lesions in their precise locations, the need for psychological tests to determine presence or absence, kind, location, and velocity of brain lesions became much less. Since that time, neuropsychological assessment has been more sharply focused on identifying the prospects for remediation of impaired functions (Haywood, 1968; L'Abate, 1968; Reed, 1968).

Development and use of specific instruments for assessment of persons suspected of having central nervous system pathology has generally followed notions of what functions are impaired. Kurt Goldstein observed that German soldiers who had sustained traumatic brain injuries, especially to the frontal lobes, in World War I often exhibited perceptual rigidity. One result was the Weigl-Goldstein-Scheerer Color Form Sorting Test (Appendix A; see, e.g., Weiss, 1964). This test consists of flat geometric shapes in different sizes and colors. Asked initially to sort the figures on a single dimension (e.g., shape), patients then had to shift to a different criterion of categorization. Very frequently they had a difficult time doing that, persisting rather in their initial sorting criterion. This test is still valuable today if used in a dynamic way, with mediation of metacognitive operations that might underlie perceptual flexibility. The question thus shifts from "What can they not do?" to "How much investment will be required to promote perceptual (and conceptual) flexibility?" The test became quite popular and has been used in many applications (e.g., Halpin, 1958; Heald & Marzolf, 1953; Korstvedt, Stacey, & Reynolds, 1954), including clinical examination of persons not suspected of having brain lesions and research on the development of concept formation abilities.

When used in DA, the interpolation of a period of mediation is essential. Following initial sorting, and encountering difficulty changing to a different criterion for categorization, an examiner might first try to promote greater flexibility by simply asking, "Is there a different way you could sort these pieces?" Following is a mediational dialogue that might take place in such an examination:

Examiner	Examinee
	(*no response*)
How did you decide how to sort them?	By color
Yes, that's terrific, color is one way to sort them.	
How do they differ from each other, besides being different colors?	This one's red, and this one's blue
OK. Please look at these. Let's put this one (red circle) here, and this one (red square) over here. They don't go together, even though they are the same color, because now we are looking at them in a different way. How are they different from each other?	Circle and square

Examiner	Examinee
Right! One is a circle and the other is a square. So you could say that they have different . . .	Shapes
Yes, right on. Now please put the ones that belong with the circle here, and the ones that belong with the square here.	(Shows reluctance, not wishing to combine different colors in the same group.)
It's OK to put different colored circles in this group because they are all circles. We are grouping by shape now, so the colors no longer matter.	(Sorts successfully by shape.)
Wonderful. OK, the first time through this one (red circle) belonged to the group of reds. The next time, it belonged to the group of circles. Is it OK for something to belong to more than one group?	Yeah, I guess so.
If we divided up all the people in this hospital into two groups, what might they be?	Men and women.
Is there another way we could divide them?	Boys and girls?
That would be OK, except there are no children here. We need to look at them in a different way, not by gender or sex, but in a different way.	Oh! Staff and patients!
Yes. Good. Then is it OK for somebody to be both a man and a patient?	Sure. That's me!
What did you have to do, to think about, when you shifted from grouping by sex to grouping by activity or role in this place?	I'm not sure what you mean.
What went on in your mind? Was it easy or difficult to change ways of looking at them?	Hard. I guess I told myself that I could look at them in a different way.
Yes, I think you did. Let's imagine that we are at the supermarket and I pick up a can to tomatoes. I might ask you, "Does this can of tomatoes belong in canned goods or frozen foods?"	Canned goods! You already told me it's a *can* of tomatoes.

Examiner	Examinee
Right! You caught me! What if I then asked you, "Does it belong in a group with produce, or in a group with canned goods?"	
	Well, it goes in both, because it is like the fresh tomatoes, but it is also in a can so it's like other things in cans.
Fantastic! What a great job! You thought about *how* the can of tomatoes is like other, fresh, tomatoes, and also *how* it can be like canned peas or asparagus. That's very good. Do you know what else you did that was great? You *shifted* from one way to group things to a completely different way. When did we have to do that?	
	When we sorted out the shapes and colors.
OK. That's great. Let's go back to those objects.	

This is an example of a typical mediation sequence when doing DA with persons who have brain lesions. Given that perceptual and conceptual rigidity are frequently encountered problems in this population, this kind of test, requiring flexibility, is very useful. Other problem domains with this group include verbal abstracting, difficulty using verbal self-mediation, difficulty with spatial organization and spatial relations, difficulty generalizing from concrete to abstract (inductive) and from abstract to concrete (deductive) modes of thinking, difficulty managing multiple sources of information, difficulty relating parts to wholes, and memory difficulty.

When planning DA, it is always useful to think in advance about what comparisons one wishes to make. In cases of brain injury, the essential comparisons include impaired with intact abilities/functions, premorbid with current functioning, different domains of functioning, performance with and without mediation, across different domains.

To compare impaired areas of functioning with intact or less impaired areas, it is necessary to examine a fairly broad spectrum of abilities. At a minimum, one should be able to distinguish between verbal and nonverbal, especially visual–spatial, domains. Comparison of premorbid with current functioning usually requires historical information, often obtained from school records or records of human services agencies or practitioners.

DA of different domains of functioning (not merely comparison of impaired and intact abilities) enables one to assess areas in which great remedial effort will be required and also areas of functioning that can be seen as assets for remedial work. This is not to say that impaired areas should be avoided or "worked around" in favor of working principally with intact functions; in fact, just the opposite is usually true: One tries to establish ways to redevelop functions that are impaired by attacking them directly. So, for example, if there has been significant loss of language functioning, it is a mistake to minimize the use of language in the examination, and certainly a mistake to do so in follow-up redevelopment work. To do so would be rather like saying, "Don't go near the water until you can swim." Although it is very difficult to do, one must attack specifically the domains of impaired functioning. Doing so can be very discouraging for patients (and examiners as well), so one must work carefully to arrange tasks so as to proceed from the easiest and most likely to produce success to more complex and difficult tasks, thus guaranteeing early success and promoting the motivation to continue working.

Of course, in DA the most important comparison is between premediation and postmediation performances. Sometimes it is possible to avoid the discouragement that usually accompanies static (no help) pretests by using preexisting data, such as standardized tests that might already have been given, as a baseline. In such cases, one can proceed directly to the mediation phase, provided the baseline data contain sufficient detail to serve as a guide for the mediational tactics that one will use. In other words, knowing that baseline performance is low does not help much if one does not know what cognitive and metacognitive processes require help. When static pretesting is necessary, one can (should) use the procedure of "distributed mediation" (Haywood & Miller, 2005). In this procedure, mediation is given following each part of a test, as opposed to "massed mediation," in which one gives a whole static test, then mediation of the cognitive and metacognitive operations that may underlie performance on the test, and finally a static posttest.

Haywood and Miller (2005) used Feuerstein's LPAD Set Variations I (variations on Raven's Progressive Matrices) in both ways, distributed and massed mediation, as well as no interposed mediation, with adults who had suffered traumatic brain injuries (TBI) and adults who were diagnosed as having mental retardation or other developmental disabilities (MR/DD). The sequence for massed mediation was

> Static pretest, problems A1–A6, C1–C6, E1–E6 (18 problems)
> Mediation using generic problems A, C, E (3 problems)
> Static posttest, problems A1–A6, C1–C6, E1–E6 (18 problems)

The sequence for distributed mediation was

> Static pretest, problems A1–A6, C1–C6, E1–E6
> Mediation using generic problem A
> Static test, A1–A6

Mediation using generic problem C
Static test, C1–C6
Mediation using generic problem E
Static test, E1–E6

Massed versus distributed mediation made little difference in the per-formance of the MR/DD group, but for the TBI group the distributed mediation procedure was superior to the massed procedure, that is, it was associated with higher scores. As might be expected, in the no-mediation condition there was no improvement from pretest to posttest, but in the two mediated conditions, there was improvement associated with the interposed mediation. This study demonstrated the differential value of spreading out the mediation within DA, especially for adults with TBI.

A further effect of mediation within DA that is often observed is a reduc-tion in the variability of performance scores. This same study yielded data on performance in the TBI and MR/DD groups on the TVA, Rey's Complex Figure, and a free-recall memory score derived from the TVA. There was an overall reduction in variance for the distributed mediation condition on the matrix tasks. On the other tests, there was a consistent and often dramatic difference between the TBI and MR/DD patient groups, with the MR/DD group showing a marked decrease in variability following medi-ation, whereas the TBI group showed a small but consistent increase in variability.

In another part of that same study, the clinical groups were given a test called Which Two Do Not Belong? (downloadable forms[4]). This is a translation and adaptation of another of André Rey's tests, *Élimination de Deux Données sur Cinq*. Each item has a group of five words, and the task is to cross out the two that do not belong with the others. Although both the MR/DD and TBI groups performed poorly, a standard group mediation significantly raised the performance (on a parallel posttest) of the MR/DD group but not that of the TBI group, suggesting that the TBI patients would require more intensive and individualized mediation.

In these studies of MR/DD and TBI patients, DA was very useful in demonstrating some important cognitive functional differences between the two groups of patients, as well as in providing information on produc-tive intervention strategies.

Both Heinrich (1991) and Haywood and Miller (2003) have demon-strated the value of DA in assessing the learning potential and the ability to benefit from mediation of persons who have experienced brain injuries. Heinrich (1991) used the Halstead Category Test (Reitan & Wolfson, 1985)

[4] www.cambridge.org/9780521849357.

with interpolated mediation of essential cognitive and metacognitive operations. He found that the mediation significantly raised the patients' scores on the posttest and on a near-transfer task, but the increase was not significant on a far-transfer task. Heinrich used individual DA. Haywood and Miller (2003) used a group DA procedure to determine first to what extent group DA might be possible with chronic TBI patients (average of 8 years postinjury) and second what kinds of DA tasks might yield the most useful data. Employing the TVA, a free-recall memory task that followed the TVA, Rey's Complex Figure (Osterrieth, 1944; Rey, 1941, 1959), and Feuerstein's Representational Stencil Design Test (Feuerstein et al., 1979; Feuerstein, Haywood, Rand, & Hoffman, 1982/1986), they concluded that (a) group DA is feasible with chronic TBI patients, (b) significant improvement in test performance can be associated with interpolated group mediation, (c) the most dramatic improvement can be seen on the most cognitively complex task (RSDT in this case), and (d) mediation of important cognitive concepts and metacognitive strategies can lead to significant improvement in memory, both verbal and spatial. Both of these studies yielded convincing evidence that persons with TBI have greater potential for redevelopment of impaired cognitive functions than has been suspected.

The foregoing data suggest that one should not expect the same mediational effects in different clinical groups, and also that mediation for persons with brain injuries should be frequent, interspersed with testing, and carefully designed to avoid discouragement and the experience of failure.

ABOUT PRINCIPLES AND INSTRUMENTS

Throughout this chapter, we have discussed principles of DA that, although applicable generally to a wide variety of persons of different ages, ability levels, and problems, are particularly suited to work in clinical settings. We have emphasized psychopathology, developmental disabilities, and neurological impairment. The area of learning disabilities, although officially part of the category of developmental disabilities, has not been included here because the principles and tactics that apply to the LD domain are discussed in the chapter on DA with school-age children. We have referred from time to time to specific tests and tasks (instruments) that are useful in DA in clinical settings, and have presented some in detail while merely mentioning others. Tests that are especially useful in clinical settings are listed here but are described in detail, with sources where available, in Appendix A, together with instruments that are more broadly applicable. Some are presented on the Web site[5] with automatic permission to print

[5] www.cambridge.org/9780521849357.

them and use them. It is necessary to emphasize once more that DA is an approach to assessment, a set of principles and procedures, and not a group of specific tests. This list is illustrative.

Instruments that are especially useful in DA in clinical settings:
Interpretation of Proverbs (verbal abstracting)*
TVA (Test of Verbal Abstracting)*
Rey's Complex Figure**
Certain tests that are part of the Learning Propensity Assessment Device
    of Feuerstein
  Representational Stencil Design Test**
  LPAD Set Variations I and II**
  Organization of Dots**
  Rey's Plateaux **
Tests based on André Rey's tests (translated and adapted for DA by
    Haywood)
  The Flags Test*
  Which Two Do Not Belong?*
  Seriation of Weights and Size Relations*
Haywood's Transformation Test*
Paour's Transformation Box**
Halstead Category Test**
Time Estimation*

*Presented in detail, downloadable tests and forms[6]
**Described, Appendix A

---

[6] www.cambridge.org/9780521849357.

5 Dynamic Assessment in Educational Settings

In this chapter we review the substantial body of work that addresses the need to link information from assessment to intervention in educational settings. The focus, of course, is on dynamic assessment approaches that have been designed and implemented for this purpose. Use of dynamic procedures very much reflects the increased concern in education, and particularly in special education, for assessment to inform instruction rather than lead primarily to generation of diagnostic labels or classifications for program eligibility. The pressure on regular education to meet the needs of all learners continues, and, even in the most restrictive environments, teachers need help implementing their students' individualized education plans. It is no longer sufficient to limit prescriptions to objectives or outcomes. More and more, the call one hears is for realistic ideas for reaching these desired states, and these ideas should reflect data-based evidence; however, one cannot rely solely on research conducted with large groups for the supporting data. Group research can generate useful hypotheses and set directions for program planning but does not accurately target the needs or resources of individual students. Teachers and parents want to know what works specifically for their children, and dynamic assessment provides a basis for generating this information.

In Chapter 7, we describe a procedure for addressing this need: curriculum-based dynamic assessment. This chapter focuses on what others have proposed and designed and the evidence they have produced for dynamic procedures that involve specific curriculum content.

ISSUES OF APPLYING DYNAMIC ASSESSMENT TO SCHOOL ACHIEVEMENT

Nowhere in the field of human endeavors is Vygotsky's concept of "zone of proximal development" (ZPD) more relevant than in education (Karpov, 2003a). This deceptively simple concept also helps to clarify the meaning of the adjective we frequently refer to as "psychoeducational" in suggesting a relationship between instruction and development (Chaiklin, 2003). Instruction is unlikely to result in learning without both leading and remaining within the realm of the learner's developmental capacities, yet these capacities have a range rather than a fixed point, and the range varies with the specific domain. This range is also highly dependent on the individual's acquired domain-related knowledge base. To promote learning, it would be necessary to address the student's emerging, rather than already developed, mental functions and leading these into the next level of development. What makes the concept "psychological" and not purely "educational" is precisely its relationship with mental development (Chaiklin, 2003). The embedded interventions therefore need to go beyond mere knowledge acquisition or training to enhance this development and facilitate the learner's movement into higher levels of mental functioning. As Chaiklin (2003) pointed out, Vygotsky used the term "zone of proximal development," not "zone of proximal learning." This is also what differentiates the ZPD from the concept of "instructional level." It is not merely task-focused instruction that needs to take place within the ZPD, but rather interactions that promote higher mental functioning (Karpov, 2003). Indeed, these interactions can become part of the developmental process itself.

Because Vygotsky proposed that the purpose of assessment should be the identification of maturing functions, from his point of view, the need for dynamic assessment becomes obvious, because these functions can best become evident in the context of support from a more experienced mediator (Brown & Campione, 1986). It is in this interactive context that the emerging functions become evident and their characteristics available for description and intervention.

In contrast to Piaget, who was primarily concerned with describing and explaining development, Vygotsky was interested in deriving implications for educational practice, particularly in relation to individuals with disabilities. From his point of view, intervention was not only critical to revealing cause but also was an important and necessary outcome for promoting development. The outcome of the assessment should reveal both the nature of the individual's functioning and the nature of the interventions that facilitate development. Vygotsky viewed determination of zones of proximal development in specific domains as a relevant basis for instructional grouping, in contrast to IQ, which he viewed as insufficiently descriptive (Chaiklin, 2003). During his short life, Vygotsky only painted in broad strokes the elaboration of specific details on the nature of these collaborative interventions and left for others the tasks of elaborating and investigating them further.

One of the issues of applying any assessment to educational content concerns the difficulty of matching what is assessed to what is taught. The only true match comes from curriculum-based assessment because the content of the curriculum is the content of the assessment (Fuchs & Fuchs, 2002). This is the reason for looking to curriculum-based assessment as one important basis for designing a dynamic assessment procedure (described in Chapter 7). Generalizability of assessment results to the "real" situations of the classroom remains a challenge even with curriculum-based approaches because curriculum is a moving target and traditional psychometric practices are not particularly good at measuring moving targets.

The decision to incorporate actual curriculum content into the assessment is a clear deviation from Feuerstein's approach. Feuerstein and his colleagues have made a point of selecting content that was unrelated to academic achievement. They have argued that the emotional baggage of academic failure would obstruct students' receptivity to their educational program, one that was designed to enhance basic cognitive structures that were presumed to generalize across content domains. In our opinion, this choice risks sacrificing relevance to the academic achievement these researchers have sought to enhance; indeed, it has been difficult to document meaningful positive effects of their approach on academic achievement.

Differences in approaches reflect differences in contexts and purposes. We are convinced that if the results of dynamic assessment are to be directly relevant in educational settings, then the information derived from the assessment must incorporate and be directly applicable to educational content. It needs to go beyond the surface characteristics of this content, but it needs to show a clear relationship. We should be able to provide information that helps children read, solve mathematical problems, carry out written assignments, communicate, think scientifically and globally, and master the pragmatics of a formal learning situation. Furthermore, in the interest of efficiency, the more direct the link, the better. One important lesson from learning research is that generalization can never be taken for granted. Generalization must be addressed consciously and explicitly, or, as Feuerstein suggests, with intent. With this in mind, we offer the following review of what has been accomplished by a wide variety of researchers up to the date of this publication.

Consideration of dynamic assessment applied in educational settings highlights the crucial issue of the relationship between the mediator and the learner. We must pay attention to the characteristics that promote good mediation as well as characteristics that describe good learner reciprocity. Each of these is a huge topic because each concerns the essences of teaching and learning with which theorists and researchers have been engaged for a very long time. Good teaching as mediation seems to have received more attention than good learning, although there has been some recent focus on reciprocity in the dynamic assessment literature (e.g., Greenberg & Williams, 2002; van der Aalsvoort & Lidz, 2002). Not only is each of these activities conceptually huge, but each is messy as well. The messiness requires consideration of qualitative and not just quantitative factors. What constitutes good teaching or reciprocity is less often an issue of how much than of how good. Lidz (2003) has operationalized both mediator and learner variables into rating scales with forms that can be photocopied and applied in the dynamic assessment process. These scales attempt to provide some quantification of the qualitative factors that describe both mediation and reciprocity.

Consideration of the relationship between dynamic assessment and educational settings raises yet another issue: Who should do the assessment? Our response to this question is this: all professionals who are involved in the education and diagnostic intervention of the learner. From our point of view, no one "owns" assessment in general or dynamic assessment in particular. All professionals who deliver a service need to be able to conduct a competent assessment that informs that delivery. We can take this approach because dynamic assessment is not aligned with any particular content domain. Dynamic assessment concerns how the assessment is conducted, not what is assessed. Therefore, it is truly ecumenical. There are applications for psychologists, teachers, reading specialists, learning disability consultants, speech and language professionals, and others who have not yet found their way to these procedures. Education addresses learning processes, and these processes should be matched with a process-based assessment approach for true authenticity and validity. Without this match, the assessment information reflects what Vygotsky referred to as yesterday (the zone of actual development), when, as professionals concerned with learning, we should be concerned about and plan for tomorrow (the zone of proximal development). History is critical for understanding but an incomplete basis for planning.

APPLICATIONS TO READING

Campione and Brown (1987) have been pioneers in their attempts to assess specific academic domains in the framework of DA. Although primarily known for their highly structured approach to DA of mathematics learning, they, and primarily their student Palinscar, also designed a highly clinical appraisal of reading in the context of their reciprocal teaching model (Palinscar & Brown, 1984). Students are observed during reading comprehension groups regarding their abilities to summarize, formulate questions, clarify inconsistencies, and predict what will happen next. The teacher initially models these skills, increasingly releasing the role of group leader to the students. During this process, the teacher continues to model and provides feedback and prompts to enhance the students' development of competence. The possibilities for transfer are maximized because the activities take place in the context to which they are to apply (Campione & Brown, 1985). There is no formal prescription for these interactions and no structure for recording of observations, although it would not be difficult to devise informal ratings or formats for anecdotal records.

Ruijssenaars and Oud (1987, in Hamers, Pennings, & Guthke, 1994), also pioneers in this area, studied a long-term procedure in which they compared the effects of two reading programs with groups of kindergarten children. Intervention was provided by the classroom teacher during fifteen 10-minute sessions. The students were given pretests, as well as posttests that followed each of the lessons, a retention test 2 weeks following the completion of the sessions, and a reading speed test 5 months after completion of the sessions. The researchers found that 49% of the variance in the final criterion measure could be accounted for by the posttests from the final learning sessions.

Some of the earliest work in applying DA to reading was applied informally, on a case study basis, for example, Blachowicz's (1999) work with two seventh-grade students, Brozo's (1990) work with a seventh-grade at-risk student, and Kletzien and Bednar's (1990) work with a fifth-grade student. Bednar and Kletzien (1990; Kletzien & Bednar, 1990) developed a DA procedure using the following format: initial establishment of a reading baseline with a silent informal reading inventory and free association task to determine prior knowledge base, analysis of process and strategy utilization through probes and observation, involvement in a lesson teaching an infrequently used strategy such as visualization through direct instruction and both guided and independent practice. The students' responsiveness to the lesson was rated on the basis of observations of attempts to use the introduced strategy and speed of learning. Finally, the students were given an alternative form of the reading inventory. In an unpublished validity study with 23 participants (Bednar & Kletzien, 1990), the changes in reading levels ranged from 0 to 4. The growth in reading level during the assessment showed a .71 ($p < .01$) correlation with growth in reading 6 months following the assessment, which provided a rare opportunity to see data on the expectation that DA could provide an index of future long-term achievement.

Tissink, Hamers, and Van Luit (1993) applied their learning potential model to specific academic domains, including reading and spelling (their applications to mathematics are discussed in the section on applications to mathematics). Using a pretest–intervention–posttest format, these researchers sought to produce information that would predict later school achievement, profile strengths and weaknesses in children's cognitive functioning, and provide information relevant to classroom instruction. Their domain-specific procedure relevant to both reading and spelling is the Auditory Analysis Test. The components of this procedure include memory for sentences, auditory segmentation of words in a sentence and syllables within a word, "objectivation," to indicate which of two words is the longer and repeating a word leaving out one syllable, isolation of the first phoneme of words, and phonemic analysis segmenting words into their phonemes. Both pretest and posttest consist of 40 items, with 15 transfer items added to the posttest. The intervention offers a series of nonstandardized prompts (repeated presentation, revelation of item structure, provision of solution strategy, and modeling) that are offered as needed in response to learner errors. This procedure is appropriate for children in kindergarten and first grade, or any other children who are in the early stages of reading development. The authors provide data regarding construct, concurrent, and predictive validity; item analysis; and reliability. The domain specific tests were found to be better predictors of school achievement than the domain-general. Also, learning curves of the students differed per domain; that is, there did not seem to be a general trait of learning potential; rather, domain-specific responsiveness to intervention.

Several studies extend the clinical conclusions from such descriptive studies as those of Cioffi and Carney (1983, 1997; Carney & Cioffi, 1992) and Braun, Rennie, and Gordon (1987). For example, Bednar and Kletzien (1990), with 29 students from Grades 9 through 12, adapted selected passages from three informal reading inventories into a four-step individually administered dynamic procedure that involved initial baseline pretest assessment, analysis of reading process and strategy use, involvement in a mediated learning lesson targeting strategy use, and posttest with an alternate form of the reading test. These participants were reevaluated 6 months after this procedure and their teachers were interviewed. For those who showed below-grade-level performance on their pretest, there was a .71 correlation between their posttest scores and their growth in reading. Their teachers reported having used the information provided to them and expressed positive attitudes about the usefulness of the information for their instruction. These researchers also reported substantial agreement regarding the strategies that were targeted for intervention during the assessment. Unfortunately, this study did not include a control group.

Using multiple control groups in addition to the group experiencing DA, Valencia, Campione, Weiner, and Bazzi (1990) studied 196 sixth-grade suburban students. They reported positive, although weak, results for their reading procedure. Merely orienting the students to the use of strategies increased only the scores involving multiple-choice test questions. Groups exposed to moderate and strong scaffolding during the intervention phase increased their scores on both a strategy use and reading comprehension measure immediately following the intervention and maintained the increase in strategy use when retested 5 months later. The strongly scaffolded group showed stronger reading scores 5 months later than did the more weakly scaffolded group, although these differences did not reach significance. The authors noted the possible effects from the lack of match between the interventions provided and the needs of the students because the scaffolding was standardized.

Spector's (1992) study of phonemic awareness with 38 middle-class kindergarten children compared the ability of static and dynamic procedures administered in the fall to predict scores the next spring on standardized tests of reading and phonemic awareness. The dynamic procedure provided corrective feedback and graduated prompts for the students. The dynamic procedure showed the strongest correlations with all spring measures. In multiple regression, the fall-administered dynamic procedure contributed an additional 12% to 14% of the variance to spring measures of phonemic awareness, above and beyond that contributed by the receptive vocabulary test and the standardized test of phonemic segmentation. The dynamic procedure was the only significant predictor of spring scores on the word recognition test used to estimate reading. The dynamic procedure added 21% to the variance in word recognition scores after receptive vocabulary and static segmentation. Related to this, Gettinger (1984) had shown much earlier, in a study with 36 children with reading disabilities, that number of learning trials to reach criterion during a phonics instruction task was able to differentiate among low, average, and high readers.

Kragler's (1989) study with 21 third-grade students receiving supplemental reading instruction demonstrated the utility of DA for group placement decisions. She employed intervention that included modeling, asking leading questions, and engagement in dialogue and found that estimates of the students' reading levels were raised from third (static estimates) to fourth grade.

Meltzer's (1992) work in the area of learning strategies offers evidence of the difference between product and process in learning. Meltzer places her model on the continuum between dynamic and curriculum-based procedures, and adds observation of problem-solving strategies to evaluation of students with learning problems. This information derives from both guided observations of the student's approach to solving basic curriculum tasks and active probes during the course of the assessment. Meltzer authored two measures, the Survey of Problem-Solving Skills and Survey of Educational Skills (Meltzer, 1987). The latter assesses reading, writing, spelling, and mathematics. Meltzer's research (e.g., Meltzer & Reid, 1994) demonstrates that students with learning disabilities show less flexibility in their use of strategies than do successful learners, and cognitive inflexibility interacts with lack of automatization. Despite considerable overlap of this process-based approach with DA, there is no explicit attempt to assess the change in the students' functioning during the course of the assessment. Guterman (2002), who also offered metacognitive intervention during the course of reading, did explicitly frame her work in the context of DA, and applied her procedure successfully with 300 fourth-grade students.

The Abbott, Reed, Abbott, and Berninger (1997) study of 16 second graders with severe reading and writing disabilities offers yet another approach within the broader DA model. These authors framed their study within the concept of "response to intervention" (see Chapter 1) using growth curves as measures, with their tutorial intervention spanning a full program year. The tutorial targeted orthographic and phonological awareness, accuracy and fluency of word recognition and comprehension monitoring, handwriting fluency, spelling, and composing. The sessions began during the summer with 1-hour twice-weekly meetings over the course of 8 weeks; this continued through the school year with 1-hour once-weekly individual meetings over an average of 36.5 weeks. The lessons were standardized and scripted. This study showed gains beyond chance for most of the children on most of the measures but also showed their differential responses to the treatment. The results also generated individualized recommendations for their next school year.

APPLICATIONS TO MATHEMATICS

Campione and Brown (1987) are well known for their research involving a highly structured approach to DA called graduated prompts. Although developed with more generic, process-based tasks, they also applied this in the domain of mathematics, using either human beings or computers as mediators (Campione & Brown, 1987, 1990). The graduated prompt procedure relies on careful task analysis and provision of predetermined hints that progress in their degree of explicitness in response to the failure of the student to solve the problem. The metric for their research is the number of hints required for the student to reach the criterion of two problems solved independently. Campione and Brown chose this approach to generate data that would be amenable to research, admittedly at the sacrifice of learner sensitivity. The findings from this type of assessment are more informative about students' degree of domain mastery than useful for individual instructional planning; nevertheless, the approach does generate information about the intensity of effort required to promote learning, as well as the rate of students' learning in the specific content domain.

As mentioned previously, the domain-specific work described by Tissink, Hamers, and Van Luit (1993) involved mathematics as well as reading and spelling. To assess this domain, they devised the Prerequisites for Arithmetic Test. This procedure consists of arithmetic language (basic concepts), one-to-one correspondence, classification of pictures sharing one characteristic, seriation (placing pictures of objects in order), conservation (comparing two rows of objects following transformation of one of them), and understanding of measurement of length and counting (completion of counting rows using cardinal numbers from various forward and backward starting points). There are 31 items in both pretest and posttest with 5 transfer items added to the posttest. This is described as a "long-term" procedure because each of the phases is administered on consecutive days rather than in a single session. The intervention consists of the nonstandardized prompts previously indicated in relation to reading and spelling that include repetition, disclosure of item structure, revelation of solution strategy, and modeling, as needed by the students. There was reasonably strong evidence of reliability and validity (Hamers et al., 1994), supporting the greater predictive power of the posttest compared with either the pretest or a domain general procedure in predicting future arithmetic achievement.

Also in 1993 (and 1996), Jitendra and Kameenui demonstrated the ability of their DA of math procedure to differentiate between "novices" and "experts" among their third-grade participants. These researchers also showed the usefulness of their procedure as a research tool for comparing the effectiveness of teaching strategies in the content domain of mathematics.

Hamers, Pennings, and Guthke (1994) described another approach to assessment of mathematics using a number series task: the Sequence of Sets Test. This has been applied with students in first grade and is a quick, 15-minute screening of a pre-arithmetic skill. The examiner provides immediate feedback (right/wrong) for each item. Predictive validity was modest.

Gerber (2000) and his colleagues designed a prototype computerized program, called Dynomath, for students with learning disabilities to assess multidigit multiplication. The program focuses on the processes of retrieval and spatial conceptualization of increasingly difficult multiplication operations. After determining the students' initial level of performance (knowledge base) and types of errors, the program provides hints and demonstrations as interventions to improve success rate. Dynomath generates a profile of what the students know, how they solve the problems, and what further work they need. The program makes it possible to differentiate between errors attributable to impulsive responding and lack of knowledge, as well as between problems of retrieval and those related to spatial processing.

Desoete, Roeyers, Buysee, and De Clercq (2002) described a computerized DA procedure that has been used with third-grade students with learning disabilities in the domain of mathematics: the EPA2000, a multilingual, programmable computer version of the Evaluation and Prediction DA. EPA was designed by De Clercq, Desoete, and Roeyers of the University of Ghent, Belgium. This procedure focuses on the metacognitive functions of prediction and evaluation. It can be downloaded from www.dynamicassessment.com, with a complete version obtainable from Anne.Desoete@rug.ac.be. The authors make the point that metacognitive skills are often associated with learning disabilities, including those in the domain of mathematics, and these skills are rarely included in assessments. Tanner and Jones (2002) also included the teaching of metacognitive skills in their mathematics intervention with 11- and 12-year-old children.

Berman's (2001; Berman & Graham, 2002) procedure addresses place-value numeration and is appropriately called STOPV-DA, or the Seven Tasks of Place Value-Dynamic Assessment. This includes tasks involving counting, part-whole representation, notation, and comprehension of the importance of the role of zero in numeration. The students in her study were from Grades 3 and 4 in Australia. During the nonstandardized intervention segment, the assessor offers help and support in response to the students' perceived cognitive, social, and emotional needs. The intervention portion requires no more than about a half hour per student.

Warren (2002, 2003) described the MATHPLAN, A Diagnostic and Prescriptive Task Collection: A Trip to the Toystore, developed by the Balanced Assessment in Mathematics Program at Harvard University (1995) for use with students in elementary school. This is a set of multistep real-life problems with two to six graduated tasks for each of the 11 sections, totaling 44 tasks. The content includes mathematical objects (number/quantity, shape, space, pattern, function, chance, data) and actions (modeling, manipulating/transforming, inferring/drawing conclusions, communicating). Teachers select a task and administer the assessment. Each action is scored with a rubric of no credit, partial credit, full credit, scaffolding applied (no credit), or "did not administer." The teachers receive training for the procedure during which they learn the specifics of scaffolding. Reliability and validity studies are in process.

Jensen (see www.mindladder.com) developed his MindLadder approach that links mental processing with virtually all areas of academic achievement through a sophisticated computer program. Individuals who know the student well complete a Learning Guide rating scale that generates a profile of the student as learner. The examiner administers selected dynamic assessments in processing areas related to the needs identified from a compilation of information from the learning guide. Based on both sources of information (Learning Guide and DA), the examiner can then link the findings with educational strategies relevant to subsequent instruction of the student. This is a good example of an empirical means of selecting areas for targeted DA and further intervention.

APPLICATIONS TO SPEECH AND LANGUAGE

The DA model has been particularly attractive to speech and language professionals (K. G. Butler, 1997; Olswang, Bain, & Johnson, 1992), many of whom are on the front lines of providing services to individuals from linguistically diverse backgrounds. The concept of stimulability is quite familiar to these professionals (Bain, 1994) and is a concept that may relate to their receptivity to the DA approach. Stimulability, after all, involves taking children beyond their current level of functioning to explore their responsiveness to intervention as well as their degree of change in response to this intervention.

Peña and her colleagues (e.g., Gutierrez-Clellen & Peña, 2001; Peña & Gillam, 2000) have been particularly prolific in applying the DA model in the speech and language domain. These researchers have made important contributions that document the ability of their DA procedures to differentiate between children with language differences and disorders. Their procedures include assessment of vocabulary for preschool children, assessment of narratives for school-age children, and assessment of explanatory language for pre-adolescents and adolescents, all using a pretest–mediate–retest model. Because each of these abilities (vocabulary, narrative, and explanatory language) is directly linked to classroom expectations and instruction, the mediated interventions and responsiveness of the children to these interventions allow a direct link between assessment and recommendations for classroom instruction. These procedures also provide the basis for more complete descriptions of language functioning of the students than is typical for traditional speech and language evaluations.

Roseberry and Connell (1991) found that inclusion of intervention in their procedure increased its ability to differentiate children with learning problems related to cultural differences from those with diagnosable learning disorders. Their study included 26 children of Mexican descent. Similarly, Jacobs (2001) found that the addition of a dynamic component to her computerized preschool language screening enhanced the information available for her linguistically diverse preschoolers from low socioeconomic backgrounds (see also Laing & Kamhi, 2003, for discussion of this application).

The use of Lidz's curriculum-based DA by Jitendra, Rohena-Diaz, and Nolet (1998) with linguistically diverse children is discussed in detail in Chapter 7.

DA has also been applied with second-language learners without issues of determining need for special education services (e.g., Barrera, 2003; Kozulin & Garb, 2002; Poehner & Lantolf, 2003; Schneider & Ganschow, 2000. In the Kozulin and Garb (2002) study with young Israeli adults trying to learn English, the authors adapted a standardized test used for college/university English as a Foreign Language placement as a pretest. An alternative form of this standardized test was designed for the posttest. During the mediation phase, teacher-assessors were taught to guide the students through strategies relevant both to the demands of the test and the nature of the students' errors on the pretest. A study of 23 students showed an increase in pretest to posttest scores exceeding one standard deviation (effect size of 1.2), negative correlation between gain and pretest scores, correlation between pretest and posttest of .80, and differential performance profile of a number of the students on pretests compared with posttests. The authors suggest that information from this procedure has implications for intervention, for example, teaching "learning how to learn" strategies to students with average pretest/modest gain scores, offering those with average pretest/high posttest scores more challenging work with opportunities for independent study, and providing students with low pretest/low posttest performance intensive work with reduced challenge.

Barrera (2003) applied his approach with Spanish-speaking Mexican American high school students with diagnosis of learning disability who were trying to learn English. This author focused on handwritten notes, evaluated on criteria of legibility, structure, and information units. In a pilot study seeking to differentiate typically developing second-language learners from those with a learning disability, the 21 students were given curriculum-based pretest measures in reading, writing, and spelling. The intervention involved a "reflection and analysis" journal for vocabulary building before, during, and after classroom lectures. The teachers taught the students principles of note taking over a 2-week period, using the first and last entries as pretests and posttests. The students with learning disabilities showed significant growth following the intervention, with greater gains in reading and writing than in spelling. The author planned further research to investigate the differentiation between the two groups.

Schneider and Ganschow (2000) described an informal DA for students who were struggling to learn a foreign language. This teacher-administered approach focuses on five metalinguistic processing strategies: student response to thought-provoking questions or gestures (or both), provision of rethinking time, focusing student attention on differences within or between target and native language, use of or development of mnemonic devices, and modeling of how to organize language learning in the categories of pronunciation/spelling, grammar patterns, and vocabulary patterns.

OTHERS

Minnaert (2002) is one of the few who have designed a DA for use in higher education in domains other than foreign language. This procedure, called a *Lerntest*, assesses freshman students' study skills in the domain of psychology. The procedure is grounded in an information process-based theory of studying that incorporates the stages of acquisition, transformation, and consolidation of knowledge. The first phase of the procedure involves silent reading of 10 linked and progressively more complex selections of psychology text, each followed by completion of multiple-choice questions. The next section assesses general psychology knowledge base with multiple-choice questions. The third and final section is a closed-book exam tapping the content of the silent reading from the first section. The *Lerntest* is administered to freshmen at the start of the academic year to generate diagnostic information about learner needs. The procedure generates information regarding speed and accuracy of information processing during silent reading, domain-specific prior knowledge, speed and accuracy of information processing during (re)production, and knowledge transformation competence. Minnaert has also applied this model to the domains of economics, law, and medicine. Minnaert admits that this is more of a process- or performance-based than dynamic procedure; although it does simulate the act of studying in a specific domain, it does not include an intervention. Nevertheless, it does provide a framework that could be elaborated into a more dynamic procedure.

Another approach that pushes the boundaries of DA was designed by van der Aalsvoort (van der Aalsvoort & Lidz, 2002) for administration by teachers in their classrooms while working with small groups of young children. In this approach, which has been used with both "standardized" games and curriculum-based tasks, the children complete a pretest and are worked with over several sessions over several days, followed by completion of a posttest. In the research reported, the focus was on helping teachers to improve the quality of their interactions with the children, as well as to determine the relationship between the mediational interactions of the teachers and both the responsiveness of the children and their mastery of the task. With this approach, there are no restrictions regarding the content of the assessment; it can be applied in any curriculum domain. In this case, the intervention focused on the interactions of the teacher rather than any prescriptions regarding presentation of the task. The results documented the effectiveness of the videotaped feedback to the teachers in improving the quality of their interactions, as assessed by Lidz's (2003) Mediated Learning Experience Rating Scale, as well as the relationship between these interactions and both the responsiveness of the children, also measured by Lidz's (2003) Response to Mediation Scale, and their mastery of the task.

Chan, Ashman, and van Kraayenoord (2000) also moved their DA into the classroom where they have employed a model for use with eighth- and ninth-grade students studying biological classification. Their approach strives to provide information about the students' existing knowledge base, their cognitive processing skills, and their responsiveness to instruction. For their study, both pretest and posttest involved sorting cards of members of vertebrate and invertebrate groups into their appropriate classifications and subclassifications. During the intervention phase, in response to an error, a series of quasi-hierarchical prompts was used to provide information or hints that brought the students' attention to the misclassification. Further instruction was provided as needed to promote the students' ability to classify.

Ashman (1992) also described his Process-Based Instruction (PBI), which is teacher-delivered to focus on development of strategic behavior during the course of problem solving. The teacher works with pairs of students who alternate observer and actor roles. The four phases of the process include task orientation and performance (introduction and determination of knowledge/skill base), instruction (identification and reinforcement of student's preferred coding or memory strategy), intervention (identification of obstructions to learning and reinforcement of cooperative learning, demonstration), and generalization (involvement in transfer activities), with each phase including both assessment and instruction. Ashman reviewed the results of two studies carried out by two special education teachers with teenagers with mild intellectual disability during 12 sessions over an 8-week period. The first study demonstrated the positive effects of within-domain strategy training (simultaneous compared with sequential tasks). The second study addressed only sequential processing and demonstrated the superiority of "real life" compared with laboratory types of materials.

Saldaña's (2004) Dynamic Master Mind game also tests metacognitive skills, in this case with individuals with mild mental retardation. His study compared the results of 16 participants with mild mental retardation with those of 13 with average intelligence, with intervention comprising a thinking skills program. He found the dynamic scores, not static scores or IQs, related significantly to metacognitive functioning during participation in the intervention as well as to adaptive behavior. The two groups performed differently on both static and dynamic parameters.

A very early example of the application of DA to vocational assessment is described by Schloss, Smith, Hoover, and Wolford (1987). This informal approach is called Dynamic Criterion-Referenced Vocational Assessment, or DCRV. The authors begin with a detailed task analysis of the job and, observing the worker engage in the task at workstations that simulate the job, they determine the extent of the worker's mastery. The assessor models the task, asks the worker to do it, and offers a series of prompts as needed. Information includes determination of number of trials needed for independent performance of each subskill and the type of prompts that promote successful performance. The authors also noted the necessity of considering the environmental variables that could be manipulated that could affect successful job performance, such as pace, noise level, supervisor, and length of work shift.

Applying DA to yet another domain, Balzac and Gaines (n.d.) described their Dynamic Multiple Assessment (DMA) approach in the content area of electricity. DMA uses computers and multimedia technology and targets the student, the instruction, and the teacher in relation to the individual student's learning preferences and styles. It is similar in some ways to other adaptive computer techniques that involve feedback and probes but goes further in incorporating direct teaching with information provided regarding learning (pretest–intervene–retest) and transfer in addition to domain knowledge, as well as effectiveness of instructional techniques. This approach, as reported, was very much in its formative stages. The authors recorded the positive feedback from four Vanderbilt University students who completed a course in basic electronics. The second author (Daniel M. Gaines) should be reachable through the Computer Science Department at Vanderbilt University.

Finally, Fenwick and Parsons (1999) have applied their DA model to the domain of social studies, specifically to evaluate citizenship participation.

The approaches discussed in this chapter are listed by author in their category domain in Table 5.1.

Table 5.1. Sources for curriculum-based dynamic assessment procedures

Reading	Abbott, Reed, Abbott, & Berninger (1997)
	Bednar & Kletzien (1990; Kletzien & Bednar, 1990)
	Blachowicz (1999)
	Braun, Rennie, & Gordon (1987)
	Brozo (1990)
	Campione & Brown (1985, 1987)
	Cioffi & Carney (1983; Carney & Cioffi, 1992)
	Gettinger (1984)
	Guterman (2002)
	Kragler (1989)
	Meltzer (1992)
	Palinscar & Brown (1984)
	Rijssenaars & Oud (1994)
	Spector (1992)
	Tissink, Hamers, & Van Luit (1993)
	Valencia, Campione, Weiner, & Bazzi (1992)
Mathematics	Berman (2001; Berman & Graham, 2002)
	Campione & Brown (1987, 1990)
	Desoete, Roeyers, Buysee, & DeClercq (2002)
	Gerber et al. (2000)
	Hamers, Pennings, & Guthke (1994)
	Jitendra & Kameenui (1993, 1996)
	Tissink, Hamers, & Van Luit (1993)
	Warren (2002, 2003)
Speech and Language	Bain (1994)
	Barrera (2003)
	Butler (1997)
	Gutierrez-Clellen & Peña (2001)
	Jitendra, Rohena-Diaz, & Nolet (1998)
	Kozulin & Garb (2002)
	Olswang, Bain, & Johnson (1992)
	Peña & Gillam (2000)
	Poehner & Lantolf (2003)
	Roseberry & Connell (1991)
	Schneider & Ganschow (2000)
Others	Process-Based Instruction: Ashman (1992)
	Science lesson: Chan, Ashman, & Van Kraayenoord (2000)
	Social Studies: Fenwick & Parsons (1999)
	Electricity: Balac & Gaines (n.d.)
	Higher education study skills: Minnaert (2002)
	Metacognition: Saldaña (2004)
	Vocational assessment: Schloss, Smith, Hoover, & Wolford (1987)
	Teacher–student interaction: Van der Aalsvoort & Lidz (2002)

CONCLUSION

In his summary chapter that follows the presentation of a large number of DA approaches from an international perspective, Elliott (2000; see also 2003) emphasized the continuing need for progress in linking the work of psychologists and teachers to develop and use procedures that inform instruction and intervention. Although this chapter has documented a number of such attempts, more and wider continuing efforts are obviously needed. Chapter 7 of this book represents our attempt to move this further along; however, these developments should be applied to every domain, and there remains much room for both research regarding what has already been developed and for design of new procedures to match the diversities of both tasks and learners. One of the greatest challenges of this work is to identify treatments that are effective for large numbers of children and to document, through DA, their effectiveness for the individual. One of the most exciting developments in the generation of evidence for the effectiveness of treatments is the use of functional MRI (magnetic resonance imaging; Berninger, 2004; Richards et al., 2004), which promises to create one of the most powerful diagnostic tools for the 21st century.

Historically, psychoeducational assessment has focused on identifying deficits, more recently adding consideration of error patterns; yet there remains a large gap between these identifications and generation of instructional prescriptions. The only way to know that an instructional approach is effective is to use it; nonetheless, children do not have an infinite amount of time to allow their teachers and assessors to experiment with all possible variations and permutations in the process of discovering the best approach for every instructional situation. Therefore, the most efficient strategy would seem to be to employ a combination of evidence from large group studies, plus diagnostic exploration of general and specific areas of strengths and weaknesses of the individual, followed by sampling a selection of the most promising approaches with the individual during assessment trials. In this way, DA builds on other approaches and adds to the logical flow of the assessment process.

The good news is that information about the components and best instructional practices regarding specific academic domains, especially reading and mathematics, has been increasing rapidly. The bad news is that there is still much more to learn and many students who continue to have difficulty learning.

6 Applying Dynamic Assessment with Young Children

This chapter focuses on procedures for applying the dynamic assessment model to children during early childhood, which is usually considered to range from 3 through 8 years; however, our focus here is preschool, or age 3 through 5, and we delegate ages above 5 to the school-age chapter. In this chapter, we present Lidz and Jepsen's Application of Cognitive Functions Scale (ACFS) in its entirety.

OVERVIEW OF DYNAMIC ASSESSMENT PROCEDURES FOR USE WITH YOUNG CHILDREN

Carrying out assessments with young children can be challenging under any conditions, and specialized approaches, techniques, and training are warranted for this population (Lidz, 2003). Carrying out dynamic assessment with young children is not only challenging, but, in the minds of some professionals, even questionable, because the metacognitive functions typically targeted by DA are not yet well developed. Metacognitive or executive functions are nevertheless emerging even at ages as young as 3, and it can be very worthwhile to explore how well these functions can be facilitated within the context of dynamic assessment.

Important contributions to development and application of dynamic assessment procedures with young children have been made by Burns (1980, 1985), Guthke and Loffler (1983), Haeussermann (1958), Hessels (2000), Kahn (2000), Karpov (1982), Peña (2000), Resing (2000), Schlatter and Büchel (2000), Tzuriel, (2001), and Tzuriel and Klein (1985). Most of these approaches, with the exception of Kahn's, are appropriate for use with children in the early primary grades, and the focus tends to be on gaining access to intellective functioning. Kahn's is the only approach to reach down into the infancy and toddler ages. Several of these approaches specifically address issues of cultural and linguistic diversity. The work of

Tzuriel and his associates is particularly extensive and well researched; his many procedures are listed in Appendix B.

Haeussermann (1958) could well be considered the mother of dynamic assessment of young children, as well as a critical influence for applying this approach in educational settings. She appeared to be working with knowledge of Piaget, but without awareness of Vygotsky, and at a time preceding widespread knowledge of the work of Feuerstein. She was motivated by the practical need to assess abilities of individuals whose capacities were hidden by their physical disabilities. She was one of the first to note that

> Use of a standard test . . . does not reveal how the child has arrived at the solution or whether he has had to detour impaired areas of functioning in order to respond appropriately. Neither does a standard test explore the basis for failure when a task is failed. (p. 16)

Through her more than a quarter of a century of experience, she evolved a set of procedures that incorporated probes and modifications of task presentation to explore the nature and causes of children's responses, as well as the routes to increased success and competence that linked the assessment with intervention.

In this chapter, we provide the full technical and administration manuals for the only dynamic approach of which we are aware that applies to children between the ages of 3 and 5 that focuses on objectives that directly reflect curriculum demands of educational settings. Although this procedure, the Application of Cognitive Functions Scale (ACFS), was developed for use in the United States, it has been used successfully with children in England, The Netherlands, Romania, and Australia and is currently in the process of being translated for use with children in Spain. As was the case for Hauessermann, the ACFS evolved over a period of time in response to a perceived gap in dynamic assessment procedures that could be used with very young children and that linked their assessment with the cognitive and academic demands of their programs. Although considerable research has been accomplished, the ACFS was designed by practitioners for use in practice. The goals have always been to inform instruction and to provide descriptions of children in the process of learning.

APPLICATION OF COGNITIVE FUNCTIONS SCALE

Technical Manual

PURPOSE AND RATIONALE

The Application of Cognitive Functions Scale is a curriculum-based dynamic assessment procedure for use with young children. The six subscales represent learning processes that are typically required for success in most U.S. preschool programs. The ACFS yields scores that indicate the degree to which the children have mastered each of the tasks, as well as the children's responsiveness to intervention. Behavior ratings describe non-intellective qualitative aspects of children's interaction with the materials and the assessor. The behavior rating descriptors are the same across the six tasks. The stability of the behavior rating descriptors across tasks allows assessors to compare children's behavior in relation to the type of task, so that assessors have a means of evaluating the effects of the interaction between child and task.

Educators have increasingly advocated assessment that reflects specific curriculum objectives to promote a close relationship between assessment and instruction (e.g., Fuchs & Fuchs, 1996); however, use of actual curriculum content for assessment of degree of content mastery is most appropriately a function of classroom teachers or of educational evaluators. Diagnosticians such as school psychologists (e.g., United States) or educational psychologists (e.g., United Kingdom) need to find ways to remain close to, yet move beyond and below, the content demands of a specific curriculum to address issues that result in referral of children who are not successful learners (Peverly & Kitzen, 1998); however, even among those who have been strong advocates of curriculum-based assessment come warnings that it is possible for assessment to be too close to the curriculum (Fuchs & Deno, 1994).

Diagnosticians need to go beyond what children currently know to understand how they learn as well as to determine obstructions to their successful learning. Lidz (1991) has proposed combining curriculum-based and process-based approaches within a dynamic assessment model as the optimal approach to assessment. Addressing cognitive processes that underlie specific curriculum objectives allows diagnosticians to probe deeply into the nature of children's learning approaches and areas of challenge. Remaining close to the curriculum increases the relevance of the resulting recommendations for the instructional setting. The appropriateness of addressing underlying processes as a means of both understanding children's cognitive functioning and proposing interventions relevant to the curriculum has been supported by a number of studies (e.g., Das, Mishra, & Pool, 1995; Das, Naglieri, & Kirby, 1994; Naglieri & Gottling, 1997; Swanson & Alexander, 1997).

Each subscale of the ACFS is administered in dynamic assessment pretest–intervention–posttest format. The pretest and posttest of each subscale are the same or close variations on the same task, and the instructions for administration of all tasks are standardized. The interventions for each task are semi-scripted and predetermined in an effort to impose a degree of standardization on the procedure for purposes of research, facilitation of interpretation, and ease of administration. Despite this preprogramming, the ACFS induces an instructional conversation between learners and mediators so that the mediators, as assessors, experience what it is like to work with children-as-learners, and the children demonstrate, in a comfortable way, areas of competence and need. Children quickly warm up and show minimal stress, with minimization of the feeling of being "tested."

The interventions reflect current research literature describing effective instructional approaches for the processes involved in the task. The materials used for the interventions are different from those used for the pretests and posttests. The interventions are designed for teaching to the processes, principles, and strategies underlying the tasks that relate to successful performance, without using the actual test items themselves.

The entire procedure requires about 2 hours. A recommended approach when administering the full procedure is to complete three subscales per session. For children who require more breaks, this is possible just so long as the full subscale, from pretest to posttest, has been completed. Taking a break before administration of the posttest will obviously change the nature of the conclusions about the child's ability to generalize. It is possible to administer selected portions of the ACFS; however, to explore the child's functioning across tasks, administration of a minimum of two to three subscales is recommended. Differences between partial and full administration remain to be investigated. To reduce the time needed for administration, the ACFS has been divided into four core and two supplementary subscales.

Many of the tasks of the ACFS have a heavy verbal loading. It is not a procedure for totally nonverbal children, but the procedure can be used with children who have significant language delays. Well-developed language skills are not necessary for any of the subscales, and for children with delays the subscales can provide a vehicle for assessing the children's responsiveness to intervention, as well as used for monitoring their development over time. Subscales with the heaviest verbal demand have been relegated to supplementary status.

As noted earlier, the ACFS is appropriate for use with children functioning within the age range of 3 to 5 years. Preliminary studies and resulting modifications show that the tasks and level of performance required for success are appropriate for typically functioning children of this age. The ACFS can be used with older individuals, particularly those with delays and handicapping conditions, who are functioning within approximately these age ranges, although the nature of the activities or materials may not be appropriate for all older learners.

The nature of information yielded by the ACFS is both quantitative and qualitative, but not normative. The quantitative scores (number of items and percent of items correct) serve as indicators of level of mastery of the task and cannot and should not be interpreted as age equivalents. The ACFS is primarily useful for its descriptive, qualitative information because it provides six opportunities to interact with the child with inherently interesting, age-appropriate, instruction-relevant tasks. Although numbers can be useful for monitoring the child's learning over time, as well as for research, the greater value is its appropriateness for diagnostic exploration, allowing for error analysis, cross-task comparison, and description of how the child approaches the challenges and reacts to the assessor's interventions. Because the interventions are semi-scripted, inferences for instruction, if the scripts are strictly followed, are limited to the types of interventions built into the procedure. If the ACFS is used primarily for diagnostic purposes and the standardized aspects are less important, the assessor is free to deviate from the scripts to explore alternative hypotheses about potentially effective approaches to mediation. It is also possible to follow the script, derive the quantitative information, and then deviate for the purposes of limits-testing and further exploration.

Although experience with the ACFS is limited, to date there have been very few children who have not been able to obtain some scoreable response to at least the posttests of most of the six subscales (there may be some exceptions among children within the pervasive developmental disorder–autism spectrum). Children are not expected to be competent on pretest tasks. These should be challenging to them because the purpose is to create a zone of proximal development where there is need for intervention to move to the next higher level. There appears to be sufficient ceiling for the more capable learners. The ACFS would not be a measure of choice for higher functioning students but would be more relevant for children referred with a wide variety of learning problems or developmental delays. It is an ideal assessment tool for use with so-called pre-referral, intervention or instructional consultation teams, where eligibility for special education is not the issue but recommendations for classroom functioning are of major concern.

THEORETICAL FRAMEWORK

The ACFS is to some extent atheoretical, and in other ways, it is grounded in contemporary models of cognitive development. The content, represented in the choice of processes, tasks, interventions, is largely pragmatic and responds to the following question: What is it that children need to be able to do to succeed with typical academic and social expectations of school? This informs the curriculum-based aspect of the procedure. How this question is answered is more theory-based and grounded in the works of Vygotsky, Feuerstein, and other researchers in the area of cognitive development and, particularly, of metacognitive functioning. This informs the test administration design, scoring, and interpretation of results. The ACFS is not a test of intelligence. How children perform on the procedure is of course influenced by whatever we agree that intelligence is, but conclusions about a child's performance on the measure should not be framed in terms of inferences about the child's intelligence. This particularly applies to the concept of modifiability; that is, there is no necessary one-to-one relationship between intelligence and modifiability. In our opinion, learning ability–modifiability–responsiveness to experience should be part of any definition of ability.

The procedure will provide evidence of the child's development of cognitive functions related to preschool curriculum content, and the child's ability to learn, that is, to profit from the experiences provided by the interventions; however, modifiability or responsivity is not synonymous with intelligence. Experience with dynamic assessment makes it clear that some very high-functioning children are not readily modifiable, whereas some very low-functioning children may indeed show impressive modifiability. It is therefore necessary to consider both level of performance and responsiveness to intervention when interpreting the results of any dynamic assessment. With the ACFS we attempt to assess how children apply cognitive and metacognitive functions that are related to typical preschool curriculum demands.

The ultimate goal of the ACFS is to inform instruction and to provide a means of relating assessment to instruction and intervention. The procedure informs educators about the child's zone of actual development, provides a format for creating a zone of proximal development, and allows inferences about instructional needs and hypotheses regarding potentially helpful interventions. The ACFS is more related to Binet's original ideas than to what became of his ideas when Terman grafted them onto Galton's (Carlson, 1995).

The subscales tap functions that represent universal neuropsychological capacities that undergird learning and that relate to mastery of a wide variety of tasks, most important, literacy, numeracy, and scientific thinking. These are functions or processes that are frequently cited by major cognitive researchers as basic and primary characteristics of cognitive functioning, and include the processes of classification, memory, sequencing, and planning. The idea of perspective taking, which is also included, is central to the basic human capacity for social interaction. It is difficult to conceive of competent social interactions without this skill. Inclusion of the processes of planning and perspective taking in a procedure for young children is unique to the ACFS, whereas memory, classification, and sequencing are tapped by other measures, but not in an interactive, dynamic format. The ACFS does not include all possible processes that provide a foundation for learning, but the subscales that are included represent a sampling of the most important of these. Although there is no specific subscale for language, the ACFS provides multiple and ongoing opportunities to observe language and record language samples. It is particularly useful in setting the stage for the child to demonstrate applications of language within a problem-solving context.

Dynamic assessment rests on core concepts described by both Feuerstein (Feuerstein, Rand, & Hoffman, 1979) and Vygotsky (in Minick, 1987), as well as systematic conceptions of the nature of mental functioning (see Chapter 2). From Vygotsky comes the notion of zone of proximal development and the importance of the social context of learning, represented in the provision of interventions that put assessors in the role of mediators who work to create the conditions that will lead children to the next higher level of competence. Feuerstein's conceptualization of "mediated learning experience" describes the specific types of interactions that help children to develop higher mental functions that facilitate such progress. The transactional perspective on human abilities (Chapter 2) gives a central role to cognitive and metacognitive operations and to motivation, in addition to individual differences in intelligence. The combination of these three perspectives can be seen in ACFS application.

Each ACFS intervention provides information about the basic principles and most appropriate strategies involved in task solution. The interventions provide opportunities to apply these principles and strategies with related, but not identical, activities. The interventions also provide opportunities for the assessor to observe the child's approach to the tasks, as well as for feedback to the child about what seems to be working or not working in the child's problem-solving efforts. Such feedback and verbalization have been found to be very powerful components of mediation (e.g., Carlson & Wiedl, 1980). Adjustments to the script that facilitate the child's success during the course of the interventions are possible when standardization for research purposes is not an issue.

The choice of processes for subscales relies to a significant extent on an information-processing model of cognitive functioning (Cooper & Regan, 1982; Estes, 1982). There is an assumption that each organism has inborn capacities to process and organize information in specific ways and that the content knowledge base is internalized by and mapped onto these inherent capacities. Learning is dependent on the organism's abilities to sense, attend, perceive, encode, store, retrieve, organize, and monitor information. Important issues for education are how to organize and present information in ways that the organism can most efficiently and effectively assimilate and accommodate it, to use Piaget's concepts.

Also critical for the child who experiences difficulty with learning is the ability of diagnosticians to identify the processes underlying basic educational tasks. It is important for assessment to determine the intactness of these processes, as well as the ways in which they function for individuals. Learning outcomes depend on the interactions between these processes and the social contexts that determine the nature of experiences to which individuals are exposed. Thus, the theory or model for the ACFS is interactional and mindful of the importance of social contexts. Indeed, the nature of dynamic assessment is, by definition, interaction grounded in social contexts. During the course of the interactions, manipulations of experiences within a social context, guided by mediational interactions, are provided.

An important aspect of the ACFS is represented in its name: *application of cognitive functions*. Although the subscales focus on identifiable specific functions or processes, these are discrete only in emphasis; any process or function is necessarily complex and interactive with other functions, particularly those that are metacognitive in nature. The focus is less on the function per se than, more important, on what the child does when the function is tapped by an environmental demand. For example, when a task makes a heavy demand on auditory memory, how does the child respond? This distinction has important implications that highlight basic differences among assessment models.

For example, assessment by the ACFS in the domain of memory involves how the child responds to the request to remember, which is a frequent demand of learning situations. The purpose of the assessment is not focused on determining the capacity of memory as some isolated, independent "thing." How a child goes about purposively trying to remember reveals as much (or more) about the child's metacognitive processing and background experiences as it does about the child's inherent memory capacities. The act of intentionally trying to remember is considerably more authentic to a school learning situation than most tasks on typical memory tests. Moreover, the implications for intervention are profound.

When a weakness is found on one of the ACFS memory subscales, the recommendations that follow do not concern memory capacity per se but, alternatively, strategies for memorizing. Again, the focus is on the act of "trying to remember" rather than on "memory." This assumes that the processes can be influenced by experiences and that the way to influence the processes is through optimizing the child's experiences. Processes are merely capacities, not performances, and dynamic assessment is constantly affirming the difference between capacity and performance (see Bortner & Birch, 1969, for historical discussion). This distinction is relevant to the nature of the ACFS procedure, which is designed to assess cognitive functions rather than intelligence. From the observed applications (performances), inferences are made regarding the child's functions (capacities), but only the applications can really be known.

Estes (1982) defined cognitive functions as "such activities as perceiving relationships, comparing and judging similarities and differences, coding information into progressively more abstract forms, classification and categorization, and memory search and retrieval" (p. 216). These activities form the substance of the tasks of the ACFS. Characteristics that are typically called nonintellective, such as motivation and persistence, that also relate strongly to performance but are more difficult to test directly, are integrated into the ACFS through the Behavior Observation Rating Scale. The important aspect of intelligence as it relates to education is what learners actually do with their capacities and what experiences the school can provide to facilitate improvement in the application of cognitive processes. Turning capacity into optimized performance is the function of all education, both formal and informal.

SUBSCALES AND BEHAVIOR RATINGS
The four core subscales of the ACFS tasks are as follows:

1. *Classification*: The child is asked to sort blocks into groups. The intervention uses attribute blocks to help the child focus on what to notice about the materials that serves as a basis for grouping. Scoring includes the ability to abstract distinctive features and evidence of flexible thinking.
2. *Short-Term Auditory Memory*: The child is asked to retell a short story read by the assessor (both immediate and delayed). The intervention teaches the child to build a model of symbols for the story and to use visual imagery to facilitate story recall. Scoring focuses on the ability to recall details, as well as sequential organization of a narrative.
3. *Short-Term Visual Memory*: The child is asked to remember pictures of eight toys placed in front and then removed. The intervention focuses on memory strategies of rehearsal, chunking, verbal elaboration, and visual imagery. Scoring includes evidence of awareness of the need for application of a memory strategy, as well as number of items recalled.
4. *Sequential Pattern Completion*: The child is asked to complete a repetitive sequential pattern initiated by the assessor, using tangrams (plastic geometric shapes). The intervention focuses on helping the child to sense the rhythm of a pattern and to learn to use the cues provided by the sequence the assessor has laid out to determine what comes next. Scoring includes the child's ability to complete the pattern and to justify the basis for each response.

The two supplementary subscales of the ACFS are as follows:

5. *Perspective Taking*: The child is asked to assume the role of teacher and teach the assessor how to draw a picture of a child (provided). The intervention provides a model of how to communicate to influence the performance of the other person, using a drawing of a cat. The posttest uses a drawing of a bear. Scoring emphasizes the child's ability to share thinking with the other person in the assumed role of teacher.
6. *Verbal Planning*: The child is asked to tell the plan for making a sandwich (or another food preparation, if the child is not familiar with this). The intervention focuses on telling the steps of a sequential plan and using planning words of first, then, next, and last. Scoring emphasizes the child's awareness of multiple and sequential steps toward an identified goal.

The decision to assign certain subscales to "core" versus "supplementary" status was based on several factors. First, we wished to reduce the time for administration to reflect the challenges of assessing very young children. Second, we selected subscales for core status that minimized the demands on verbal expression so as to make the procedure as widely applicable as possible. Finally, the processes included in the core tests appear, through the literature, to reflect the most basic foundations of cognitive functioning that are necessary for successful development of higher mental functions.

In addition to derivation of the scores reflecting degree of success on the six subscales or tasks, the ACFS includes completion of a Behavior Observation Rating Scale. The assessor rates seven parameters of the child's behavior during the course of pretests and mediation phases of all six subscales. Six of the parameters are rated in all instances; "responsivity" is rated only during the mediation phases. Assessors are free (and encouraged) to complete the scale during the posttests as well, but this was not built into the ACFS as mandatory, again as an attempt to minimize the testing time and the demands on the assessor.

The ACFS Behavior Rating Scale Components are as follows:

Self-Regulation: Child maintains attention and refrains from impulsive interaction with materials.
Persistence: Child completes task without seeking to terminate prematurely.
Frustration Tolerance: When experiencing frustration, the child is readily calmed and redirected.
Motivation: Child shows enthusiastic reaction to the materials and task.

Flexibility: Child does not repeat unsuccessful task solutions and develops alternative approaches to the task.

Interactivity: Child engages in turn-taking conversational exchanges with some degree of elaboration.

Responsivity: Child is a willing learner and open to input from the assessor.

SCORING

As a curriculum-based procedure, the ACFS relies on raw scores and calculations of percent of items correct. These two types of scores are used for all pretests and posttests of the six tasks. The delineation of items for each task (that is, what to score) resulted from a combination of rational task analysis and observations of children working on the activities. For the task analysis, the authors posed the following question: What do you have to be able to do in order to solve this task? They also asked what types of behaviors would be possible to observe in the children while working on the tasks. Many modifications of scoring resulted from these observations, and we attempted to represent children's actual interactions with the testing materials. Thus, to a significant extent, the scoring was designed on the frame of the client, somewhat similar to the design of custom-tailored clothing.

Typically, accomplishment of each step within a task earns 1 point. One exception is the pattern sequencing subscale in which each level includes two trials; therefore, the child receives 2 points for success with the first trial and 1 point for success with the second. The pretest–intervene–posttest format allows for calculation of a gain, or near transfer, score, in addition to the raw score total. This type of score remains controversial and is generally viewed as unreliable. It is available in the ACFS simply because it is possible to derive, and this makes it a possible target for research. The more important scores are the pretest, posttest, and behavior rating totals. Since the gain score is partially a function of the pretest, its independent meaning is limited.

It is significant that points are awarded not just for successful task completion, but for metacognitive behaviors and higher mental functions as well. For example, in Pattern Sequencing, for each item solved, the child is asked to state the basis for the correct response ("Why was that the best one? Why did you chose that one?"). Visual Memory includes the child's response to the question, "How will you remember these; what will you do to help yourself remember?" The Classification scoring includes the child's ability to change the basis for grouping blocks ("Good. Now show me another way to group the blocks.").

In addition to these "product" scores that indicate the level of mastery of each activity and the child's ability to profit from the embedded interventions, there are also ratings of the child's behavior during the course of all pretests and interventions on the six (during pretests) or seven (during interventions) dimensions described above. Each behavior receives 0 (*no evidence*), 1 (*inconsistent occurrence*), or 2 (*optimal occurrence*). The actual descriptors for raters are more qualitative than appears here and are as behaviorally descriptive as possible to maximize interrater reliability (Download Form 6.7).

Finally, a number of summary scores are available. These include totals for all tasks on pretests and posttests, totals for each behavior rating across all tasks, and total test scores for the behavior rating scale. There is a sheet on which all of the scores, including summary scores, can be recorded so that all the scores can appear in one location (Download Form 6.8).

The ACFS also includes forms for feedback to teachers and parents (Download Form 6.10), as well as one for developing objectives suitable for inclusion in an Individualized Education Plan (IEP; Download Form 6.9). The feedback form briefly describes each task, records the child's level of mastery in percentage of steps accomplished (not percentile ranks), and, most important, provides space for the assessor to describe the child's approach to the task and behaviors during the course of ACFS administration. This information should be recorded with the intent of informing instruction. The steps of task accomplishment can move directly to the IEP as objectives, and the assessor's observations about what works and does not work to help the child learn can be communicated to the appropriate caregivers and teachers. These summary and feedback forms also provide the bases for monitoring the child's functioning over time, and the IEP form in fact provides space for this.

Assessors and researchers from countries other than the United States should make adjustments in vocabulary and concepts, even pictures, to make the procedure appropriate for use within that culture. These changes should preserve the basic intent of each subscale and the ACFS as a whole and should be applied uniformly with all children within that culture.

GENERAL INSTRUCTIONS

The ACFS can be administered either as part of a comprehensive battery or alone, as an exploration of the child's functioning and responsivity to instruction. Depending on the purpose of the assessment, the time available, and the developmental abilities of the child, the assessor needs to decide which of the subscales to administer. It is highly recommended that the assessment include at least two or three to allow comparisons across tasks.

The Behavior Rating Scale should be duplicated so that it can be completed following every pretest and every mediation for every subscale that is administered. The assessor should score the items on the Scale immediately following completion of the relevant sections. Once the assessor becomes familiar with the seven categories, completion requires only several seconds, and the child can be told just to wait a few moments while this takes place; more active children can be given paper and crayons to draw or can play with the blocks while waiting.

Although the ACFS provides multiple opportunities for scoring responses, it is very important for assessors to record descriptive notations of how the child earns these scores, as well as any other observational information elicited by the procedure and the interaction. These descriptions, not the numerical scores, are the core of the procedure. As is the case for any procedure, the ACFS offers an opportunity for a structured interview, and the unique responses of the individual are the most interesting and informative information that is elicited.

ASSESSOR EXPERIENCE

The ACFS is designed for administration by trained professionals. It is most appropriate for use by school psychologists (in other countries, educational psychologists). It may be found useful by speech/language pathologists and educational diagnosticians. These individuals should be trained and certified within their respective professions, with specific training and experience in individual assessment, and highly skilled in test interpretation.

Assessors working with young children need to be proficient behavior managers. They need to be able to keep the child engaged and to keep up a good pace to move the child along. Breaks should be provided as needed, but it is very important to try to administer the posttests immediately following the interventions. If this is not possible, assessors should provide a brief review of the intervention when the child reengages, prior to administration of the posttest.

It should go without saying (but we say it anyway) that good rapport is essential, and assessors should be upbeat and supportive in their interactions. There are few instances of right–wrong responses, so opportunities for failure are rare. Assessors can provide encouragement with remarks such as "good," "you're doing a great job," "you really enjoyed that one," and so on. This should not be overdone, and encouragement combined with feedback can and should be embedded within the intervention portions of each subscale. It is recommended that the assessor not be a complete stranger to the child. Therefore, if the assessor does not have prior experience with the child, it is recommended that the assessor spend some time either within the home or program playing and engaging with the child (and family, if present) to develop some familiarity.

Most children will struggle with the pretests, although many will not necessarily realize they are having significant difficulty. If children express frustration or feelings of failure, they should be reassured that everyone finds the work hard at first and that the assessor will help them learn how to do this kind of work. They will get another chance to do it. Some children respond to challenge with avoidance and acting up; this should be interpreted to them as their response to finding the work hard, and they should be similarly reassured.

What most assessors find difficult about any dynamic assessment procedure is the pacing and "wait time." The agenda of DA is quite different from that of norm- and curriculum-based assessment, in which assessors try to elicit responses quickly and move on or establish a ceiling and stopping place. DA involves learning about the child and providing time for the child to learn. DA begins where other procedures end, moving from the zone of actual development to the zone of proximal development. Assessors should slow themselves down and keep calm, thoughtful control over the assessment situation. There should be a sense of moving along, but not rushing.

Children can be invited into the ACFS with a statement such as, "I brought some fun work for us to do. This will be like playing school. I'll be your teacher, and we'll do this work together and have some fun." (Use your own words; you get the gist.) We avoid telling the child that we will be playing games because the child may be disappointed when it is not like the games he or she plays. We do not avoid the word "work"; it may have four letters, but it is not (yet) a "four-letter word" to the child.

TESTING CONDITIONS

The ACFS should be administered under testing conditions that are appropriate for any other procedure, in a quiet well-lit space, with minimized distractions, and furniture appropriate for the age of the child. The assessor should sit either next to or at a 90-degree angle to the child. It is easier to manage active children when seated right next to them (when necessary, putting an arm around the child with adult's feet wrapped around the chair!). If the child finds it difficult to remain seated and can work better while standing, this should be allowed.

Only the materials required for each subscale should be visible to the child at any one time. The materials for the interventions within each subscale should be kept out of sight until needed, and materials for pretests and posttests should be removed when working on interventions.

SUBSCALE AND BEHAVIOR RATING RATIONALES

The subscales of classification and sequential pattern completion (a type of series completion) tap two of the three cognitive functions that Sternberg (1982) has described as aspects of inductive reasoning (the third being analogical thinking). These are classic functions that have been historically associated with conceptualizations of intelligence and are included in most attempts to assess cognitive functioning. These functions are important to solving problems that require higher order mental processing (Barsalou, 1992; Marzano et al., 1988).

Classification and sequential pattern completion often appear as objectives in early childhood curricula (e.g., Dodge & Colker, 1992; Haywood, Brooks, & Burns, 1992; Hirsch & Holdren, 1996) as foundations for mathematical and scientific thinking. Classification and pattern perception appear as human capacities as early as infancy and seem to represent important inherent neurological-processing capabilities (Goswami, 1998; Jensen, 1998). The tasks as represented in the ACFS require the child to abstract attributes of common objects and to use these abstracted attributes for the basis of either comparative or sequential thinking.

Classification relies on the ability to match on the basis of perceptual cues, an ability that emerges quite early in development (Gelman, 1998; Gelman & Coley, 1990). The ability to ignore some salient cues to allow categorization on an alternative basis is developing rapidly at the ages for which the ACFS is appropriate, and children differ considerably in their levels of success with these types of tasks both within and across age levels (Blewitt, 1994; Campbell, Donaldson, & Young, 1976).

Typically developing children at this age are quite capable of categorizing on the basis of perceptual qualities of objects. At this age, the most salient attributes are color and shape, with size developing somewhat later. Indeed, categorization appears to follow immediately upon sensation and perception, and this basic aspect of neurological-processing organization appears to underlie the ability to compare (Barsalou, 1992). The deeper and wider the knowledge base, the greater the repertory for classification, and the greater the reduction of burden on memory. The capacity for classification is simply brain-efficient (Rosch, 1999).

The approach to intervention for the Classification task (with these objects that have no functional relationship) involves bringing the child's attention to the relevant perceptually distinctive features of the objects. This approach is an attempt to reduce the salience of the desire of most children to manipulate the blocks for building that is elicited by the materials. The intervention also uses language to facilitate the child's conceptual development, providing labels and verbal elaborations as necessary to support and reinforce the perceptual characteristics of the stimuli (Waxman, in Goswami, 1998). Goncu and Rogoff (1998) have shown that the amount of adult support provided for 5-year-old children can positively influence their ability to categorize, and Gelman (1998) reviewed literature demonstrating the importance of verbal labels for accurate categorization.

The Classification task also asks the children to shift the basis for their groupings. The ability to shift rules (change the basis of grouping) is expected to be difficult for children of this age and greatly increases the challenge of this task (Frye, Zelazo, & Palfai, 1995). Some few children have demonstrated this ability following intervention, and it is worthy of note if a child even makes some attempt, even if not completely successful, to change the organization for grouping the blocks in response to this request. Nguyen and Murphy (2003) have shown that children even as young as 3 years are capable of cross-classifying items such as food; however, because of the executive-processing demand on flexible shifting, which is only emerging for children of this age, this request is expected to create a ceiling for this subscale.

In the case of *Pattern Completion*, although children at this age are developing the ability to engage in this type of task, asking them to justify the basis of their selection of pieces adds considerable challenge (Gerard, 1975). Nevertheless, children of this age range clearly have the capacity for causal thinking in their casual conversations (Hickling & Wellman, 2000). Further, pattern completion has been found to be one of the most universally developed abilities and an excellent vehicle for cross-cultural assessment (e.g., Bentley, 1980).

Regardless of the theorists or researchers, when core processes are proposed, memory is inevitably part of the discussion. The ability to retain, encode, and retrieve is central to most conceptualizations of an information-processing model of cognitive functioning (Siegler, 1998; Wood, 1988). Vygotsky considered deliberate memory a higher mental function (Bodrova & Leong, 1996). Although memory is usually discussed in terms of short-term, long-term, and working memory, what is included in the ACFS is best described as both short-term and working memory, including an opportunity for assessment of delayed recall following completion of one intervening subscale. Short term in the sense it occurs in the ACFS is not as short as it occurs in more traditional procedures. The memory tasks are certainly instances of deliberate memory and are modality-specific. There is evidence for storage areas that differ for auditory and visual–spatial information (Brooks, in Barsalou, 1992). Strategic placement into storage and retrieval from these areas are again executive-processing demands that would challenge children of this age and provoke wide variation of levels of response.

The task for auditory memory involves retelling of a story. This requires maintenance of attention to the story for about 30 seconds and encoding and reorganization of the information for retelling, which requires another few seconds. Thus, there are elements of movement of information into the beginnings of long-term memory. Some consolidation of memory is tapped by asking the child to recall the same story after a brief delay. The possibility of revisiting this subscale after a more prolonged delay remains for those who wish to explore long-term recall. It was not built into the procedure mainly for reasons of time. There are practical considerations in the development of procedures intended for the use of school-based professionals that require minimization of time required for procedure administration (related also to the attention maintenance of young children).

Vygotsky considered retelling of a story important for the promotion not only of deliberate memory but of logical thinking and self-regulation as well (Bodrova & Leong, 1996). Story retelling is thought to help the child develop awareness of story grammar that involves awareness of the logical development of sequencing, as well as cause–effect and other relationships among events. Story retelling has also been found not only to have internal structure and logically sequenced components but also to relate to development of written expression (Mason, 1989). The intervention for the auditory memory task is Vygotsky-based (Bodrova & Leong, 1996) in the sense of using external mediators (object symbols), selected by the child (with the help and guidance of the assessor), to represent the elements and sequencing of the story. The objects are offered as symbols; the child builds a model for the story with the symbols, "reads" the symbols as the first step toward independent retelling of the story, and then uses internalized visual imagery as the final phase of independent story recall. If this sounds too advanced and complicated for preschool-aged children, it is not. DeLoache's work (e.g., 1991) has been instrumental in demonstrating the ability of children as young as 2.5 years to use symbols. Largotta's study (2001) clearly demonstrates the ability of 3- and 4-year-olds to use both abstract and figural symbols to enhance their ability to retell the specific story used for the ACFS.

Engagement in the story retelling intervention is also intended to promote visual imagery, which has been documented as a very powerful tool for story comprehension (Barsalou, 1992).

The intervention for the Visual Memory subscale relies primarily on ideas of rehearsal, both simple and complex (Estes, 1982). The benefits of rehearsal for memory tasks have a long history (Wood, 1988). Components of rehearsal include, at the simplest level, repetition, and, at more complex levels, clustering (organization or chunking) and attention to special properties. An important aspect of intervention in this modality, as well as others, is to encourage the child to engage in some proactive, deliberate behavior when instructed to "remember." The awareness that something active needs to be done is a milestone that presents a challenge even for more advanced learners. Because the procedure is intended for use with very young children, elaborate strategic behavior is not an appropriate expectation, although evidence of the emergence of the need to strategize is a reasonable expectation (Wellman, Ritter, & Flavell, 1975), and the ability of young children to profit from use of such strategies has been documented (Siegler, 1998). A large proportion of the children do in fact engage in acts of simple rehearsal even during the pretest phase of the ACFS. Spontaneous employment of strategies for deliberate memory tasks may be a factor that differentiates children with mental deficiencies from children with typical development (Cherkes-Julkowski & Gertner, 1989). The ability to cluster or chunk information should reflect the child's ability to classify or categorize, and this has been found to be an important aid to memory (Basalou, 1992).

We decided to use eight as the number of items to be recalled for at least three reasons. First is that this number extends just beyond the "magic" number of seven, challenging the child's memory capacity and creating a "need" for a strategy (Miller, 1999). Second is that the use of eight items facilitated our ability to use categorization as a teaching strategy, with four items in each group. Three and three was too easy, five and five too difficult. Finally, in working with the children, we found this number to work; however, this is the one subscale for which there can be a ceiling effect for older, high-functioning children. Nevertheless, we do not expect that the ACFS will be the instrument of choice for this type of population.

Perspective taking requires the ability to de-center, which, according to Piaget (Piaget & Inhelder, 1969), does not develop until about age 7. As with many of Piaget's early assignments of abilities to specific age ranges, this ability too can be seen in children at ages considerably younger than 7, with evidence of its occurrence as young as age 3 (Hughes, Bartsch, & Wellman in Cohen, 2002). Furthermore, early occurrence of this ability appears to relate to the child's experiences, with the implication that the ability is susceptible to the influence of training (Wood, 1988). Perspective taking is not only an important social ability (Eisenberg & Harris, 1984) but one that relates to reading comprehension as well (Albrecht, O'Brien, Mason, & Myers, 1995).

The perspective-taking task of the ACFS taps into the child's ability to engage in conversational exchanges that convey information, but, in this case, the nature of the exchange requires particular sensitivity to the presence of "the other" because the directions request that the child both take on a role of another (a teacher) and at the same time, within that role, attempt to influence the behavior of another (the assessor). Pretense within the context of role-play has been found to be a good way to promote this ability (Lillard & Curenton, 1999), which has been referred to as "theory of mind" (Flavell, Miller, & Miller, 1993). This is a complex social skill, yet one that most children with typical development at ages 4 and 5 can negotiate quite successfully. This subscale is virtually unique to the ACFS, and future research investigating relationships to learning and development will be particularly interesting. It is unusual for procedures purporting to assess cognitive functions to include a subscale so explicitly social/interactive. Yet success in the school environment has much to do with social, as well as intellective, abilities, and this function involves complex interactions of both cognitive and affective processes (Copple, Sigel, & Saunders, 1984).

Planning is arguably among the most human of mental processes, and language used as a tool for planning one of the most important functions (Das, Kar, & Parrila, 1996; Luria, 1973). Although the latest of the functions to develop, young children are nevertheless capable of determining goals and of verbalizing, although not necessarily executing, a plan or strategy for reaching that goal (Hudson & Fivush, 1991). This is at a far less complex level than will be developed with time, but the ability to carry out and articulate a plan, capacities that require a social context for full development, are present in young children with typical development; however, there is a very big difference between the planning abilities of children at ages 3 (very low; mostly means–ends), 4, and 5 (Klahr & Robinson, 1981; Siegler, 1998).

The ACFS Verbal Planning subscale provides the goal for the child and asks the child to articulate the plan to reach that goal. The intervention provides a model for the application of verbal tools to articulate a plan applied to a different goal. The content is kept very simple, with referents to experiences the child has had within the home. Preschoolers as young as 3 and 4 have been found to be able to improve their planning abilities in collaboration with adults, so long as the content of the plan is within their knowledge base. The use of the rubric of counting number of steps in the plan as well as evaluating the sequential nature of the plan has a foundation in research of this capacity (Hudson & Fivush, 1991).

BEHAVIOR OBSERVATION RATINGS

A prospective longitudinal study by Teo, Carlson, Mathieu, Egeland, and Sroufe (1996) documented that ratings of preschool behaviors that included many of the variables represented on the ACFS Behavior Observation Rating Scale were good predictors of elementary school achievement. These made an important contribution above and beyond IQ (which some would argue is achievement predicting achievement).

Self-regulation is a metacognitive function that pervades all processes. One of the central characteristics of successful learners is their ability to self-regulate, inhibit impulsive responding, and engage in reflective thought (Bloom & Broder, 1950; Bronson, 2000; Burns, 1980; Schwebel, 1966; Zimmerman, 1990). Self-regulation results from the internalization of external controls so that immediate gratification is delayed in the service of more long-term goals. The ability to self-regulate appears to emerge and begin to consolidate during the second and third years of life, although there is considerable individual variation (Vaughn, Kopp, & Krakow, 1984). The relationship with cognitive development, especially memory, makes this a particularly important developmental accomplishment (Lee, Vaughn, & Kopp, 1983). Externally provided feedback appears to be an important intervention that promotes development of self-regulation (Butler & Winne, 1995).

Persistence, historically considered a variable of temperament, has been found to affect academic achievement and cognitive development (Palisin, 1986). This comes as no surprise because children who persist sufficiently to complete the task would by definition be more likely to obtain higher scores on measures of these variables. Persistence has been related to mastery motivation, which for typically developing children appears to be an innate predisposition related to exploratory behavior (Hupp & Abbeduto, 1991); however, for children with atypical development, this is a variable that may be negatively affected by the nature of the child's disorder, the experiences the child accumulates related to the disorder, or both.

It would be expected that self-regulation would interact with persistence, because the more self-regulating the child, the more likely it is that the he or she will inhibit the impulsive responses that may lead to errors, and the more likely it is that the child will continue on to complete the task with success. Working on tasks that do not extend too far beyond the child's zone of actual development would most likely elicit persistence by promoting expectations of success. Children with high self-esteem, related to previous history with successful task completion, would be more likely to anticipate success and, therefore, persist (McFarlin, 1985). Similarly, persistence would be expected to interact with task intrinsic motivation because the more interesting the child finds the task, the more likely the child will finish without requiring significant intervention (Feather, 1961). Teaching children strategies for task completion shows promise for a positive relationship with persistence (Karnes, Johnson, & Beauchamp, 1989). Keeping the activity below the child's frustration level and use of tasks and materials that attract the child's interest would also be expected to promote persistence.

Frustration tolerance reflects another example of executive control, where the child is able to regulate emotional responses in the service of increased compliance, attention, and persistence. The child who demonstrates frustration tolerance is able to refrain from crying, avoidance, or anger when faced with challenges to competence or when asked to do something the child may not wish to do at that moment. The child may postpone immediate wishes, increase effort, seek help, or change strategy under these circumstances. This ability typically emerges during the third year (Kopp, 1992).

Flexibility as a dimension of thought is closely related to transfer. The more flexible the thinker, the greater the ability to transfer, and, in the view of some researchers, the more intelligent the learner. Campione, Brown, and Ferrara (1982) commented that "the flexibility with which . . . general executive-metacognitive skills are carried out characterizes the intelligent performer" (p. 472). In their research, the ability or inability to transfer is a critical feature that distinguishes between adequate learners and children with mental retardation.

It seems logical that dealing with novelty requires flexible thinking, and, indeed, flexibility has been historically associated with successful problem solving, and the lack of it (called *perseveration*) with impaired brain function (Zelazo, Müller, Frye, & Marcovitch, 2003). Studies yield varied results concerning the degree of flexible problem solving of very young children, and children have been found to differ widely on this dimension; however, there is evidence that children as young as 3, depending on the task, are capable of demonstrating flexibility in their thinking (DeLoache, 1995). Much depends on the complexity of the task. Therefore, ratings of flexibility may vary across ACFS tasks, and this would be a variable of particular interest for further study. The Classification pretest deliberately taps this dimension. In other tasks, it is more likely to be evident during the mediation phase than during either pretests or posttests because these are more highly structured than the mediation segments. Furthermore, some of the tasks provide more opportunity for variations in problem solving, so that the relevant aspect may not be complexity but the nature (e.g., open-endedness) of the task itself.

Motivation is usually thought of as the energizer of behavior, or the "wanting" to do the task (Wigfield, Eccles, & Rodriguez, 1998). This is what promotes and sustains engagement in tasks and would therefore relate to the variable of persistence. Lack of task engagement leads to lack of learning, and this informs the child's self-concept of himself or herself as a learner even during the preschool years. Similarly, experiences of self as an unsuccessful learner lead to low motivation, recycling into task avoidance and lack of learning (Wigfield et al., 1998).

Ideally, motivation is intrinsic, and children learn because they want to. In the case of children with delays, disorders, and histories of failures, motivation relies to a significant degree on external reinforcers. Because not all the goals of learning are set by the child, it is often necessary to induce motivation even in the most typically developing child by external means in the service of socialization and mastery of skills that are useful to society. Nevertheless, it is optimal to use tasks and materials that appeal to the child's inherent interests and desires, to tap into the child's drives for exploration and mastery, and to strive to expand the child's range of activities that are intrinsically motivating. Increasing the child's capacity for intrinsic motivation also increases the child's independence.

The ACFS uses materials that are of interest to children from most cultures and with which most children from the more technologically advanced cultures are familiar. Most of these are manipulable, and the remaining, with the exception of the pre–post Auditory Memory story, are tangible in their two-dimensional forms. Assessors are encouraged to provide external support, encouragement, and feedback, but the intent is that the activities and materials are sufficiently appealing to elicit the child's interest and to promote the desire and motivation to engage in the activities.

It is also important that challenges to the child's ability remain close to the child's zone of actual development, and children will vary considerably with regard to the amount of challenge they can tolerate. Such variation would affect their motivation for the task and is expected to relate to the child's accessibility to teaching and to learning outcomes. Observations of poor motivation should encourage assessors to recommend and try out, when possible, alternative materials or activities that relate to the same educational objective. Ideas for this can derive from discussions with parents as well as from observations of the child during play and during engagement in unstructured work.

Interactivity is one of the most social of the behavioral components. This relates to what Greenspan (e.g., Greenspan, Nover, & Scheuer, 1987) refers to as completion of circles of communication and what speech pathologists (e.g., Craig & Evans, 1993) would call turn-taking. This component offers unique information about the child's pragmatic language abilities. Although the ACFS does not assess language directly, there are ample opportunities to observe and describe the child's language. Most important, the ACFS incorporates language as a tool for learning. The supplemental subscales generally involve a heavier language load than the core subscales, but far greater demand is placed on the assessor than on the child to communicate verbally for any of the activities, particularly for the interventions. Turn-taking appears particularly vulnerable to developmental disorder and has consequences for the social interactions important for learning (Elder & Goodman, 1996). The degree to which this component relates to successful task solution remains to be investigated, but it would be expected to relate to the child's responsivity and ability to use language as a tool for learning.

The *responsivity* of the child, or the openness of the child to influence by another, is central to both Feuerstein's and Vygotsky's conceptualizations of development, learning, and instruction. For Feuerstein, it is modifiability; for Vygotsky, it is readiness to participate in the creation of a zone of proximal development (Wood, 1988). Mediators can mediate from dawn to dusk, but there is little or no learning without reciprocity or responsivity to this mediation on the part of the child. Mediation without reciprocity is teaching without learning. The reciprocity of the interaction between the adult and the child is a definitive concept for dynamic assessment, and descriptions and evaluations of this characteristic of the child can contribute to the assessor's conclusions about appropriate educational environments and interventions.

These behaviors are expected to apply to all tasks and to all learners engaged in an instructional interaction.

Interpretation

SCORES

Although the primary value of the ACFS is to serve as a basis for in-depth description of the child's approaches to problem solving, there is quantitative information available as well; however, assessors must be very careful about interpreting this quantitative information. The ACFS is a curriculum-based, not norm-based, procedure. The studies that have been completed to date provide evidence that the tasks are appropriate for children with typical development between the chronological ages of 3 and 5. The children are not expected to be able to accomplish the tasks with full success during the pretest phase. Some high-functioning older preschool children with typical development may begin the procedure demonstrating full competence, but this, in the authors' experience, is fairly rare. This would not be the instrument of choice for determination of giftedness; therefore, most children to whom it would be administered would be experiencing some degree of developmental delay or learning disorder.

Some children may not be able to demonstrate any competence in some tasks until they have experienced mediation. This is not a problem, although most children would be able to perform some aspect of most of the tasks during the pretest. There is no need to provide mediation for children who have already fully mastered the task, and, in this case, there is no opportunity to observe the child's responsiveness to intervention. The ACFS is designed to promote observation of children in the process of learning; therefore, the child needs to be able to learn something.

The types of scores that are available from the ACFS are as follows:

- Degree of mastery of the task: *percent of items* within the task success-fully accomplished. This is available for the pretest and posttest of each task. This is not a percentile rank, and does not provide information that compares the performance levels of the children. Again, this is curriculum-based, and this number merely indicates the degree of mastery of the child of the specific content of the task. There is difficulty in comparing these percent scores across tasks, and this should only be done in a very gross way to create a profile of educational need. Because each of the tasks has a different number of items, the percent of items accomplished is not totally comparable. For example, 13 out of 15 items accomplished yields a percent mastery of 87, and 8 out of 10 items accomplished yields a percent of 80. In both bases, there are only two items not mastered, but it might appear that the former represents a higher degree of mastery when it in fact does not. Nevertheless, comparing the two does provide a ballpark "feeling" for relative strengths and weaknesses across the tasks.
- The degree of change from pretest to posttest, or the *gain score*, is one indication of the child's ability to profit from instruction. But, again, this score must be interpreted very carefully. The meaning of the gain score very much reflects the pretest score. If the child begins with a high pretest score, there is not much room for growth, and this alone may create a ceiling. A gain of 1 point may be highly meaningful for one child, whereas it may reflect "testing error" for another. Although it is very important to consider the child's ability to succeed with more items following the intervention as one indication of the child's ability to profit from instruction, this should not be the sole indicator. The assessor's observations of how the child reacts and performs the task become important as well. For example, some children show no change from pretest to posttest in the Classification task but do show changes in their approach to building with the blocks, with more confidence and more use of groupings. In one case, a child who offered no indication of grouping during pretest or posttest of the Classification subscale handed the blocks to the assessor for repacking, using perfect attribute grouping! Such observations become critical to interpreting the child's responsiveness to learning.

After completion of the assessment, the assessor should complete the feedback form (Download Form 6.10), recording information directly from the score sheets, along with descriptive and interpretive information that is relevant to teachers and parents. When appropriate, the assessor can also convert the information from the ACFS into objectives for an Individualized Educational Plan (IEP; Download Form 6.9).

SUBSCALE INTERPRETATION

Interpretive information relevant to each of the subscales as well as the behavior rating categories, and ideas for intervention, are included in the earlier section discussing the rationale for each. Ideas for intervention should also include those that are embedded in each subscale.

The ACFS taps basic cognitive processes and learning strategies associated with typical early childhood learning activities. The processes assessed are synonymous with the subscales of the procedure, and these were presented earlier in the chapter. The processes represented by the subscales can be turned into teaching objectives as follows:

(1) Classification:
   (a) Children will group objects on the basis of abstracted features of color, size function, shape.
   (b) Children will change the basis of grouping objects when asked to "do it another way."
   Subskills:
   - ability to detect distinctive features
   - ability to respond to directions
   - ability to make groups based on abstracted distinctive features
   - application of grouping concepts across a variety of materials, such as toys, clothes, foods (real simulations, as well as pictures)

(2) Short-Term Auditory Memory:
   Children will recall and retell a short story immediately after hearing it with correct story elements and event sequencing.
   Subskills:
   - ability to visualize contents and activities of stories read
   - familiarity with knowledge base of story (vocabulary and activity referents)
   - attention span sufficient to sit and listen to entire story sequence
   - ability to communicate stories in narrative form with a beginning, middle, and end

(3) Short-Term Visual Memory:
   (a) Children will tell the names of a series of pictures of objects placed in front of them.

Subskills:
- knowledge base for objects (vocabulary and experience)
- memory span for recall of eight objects

(b) Children will show the need to apply a strategy to facilitate recall.
- strategies for rote recall, such as rehearsal, visualization, grouping
- elaborative self-talk during object play

(4) Sequential Pattern Completion:
   (a) Children will complete a sequential pattern.
   Subskills:
   - awareness of need to proceed in left to right direction
   - awareness of distinctive features of sequenced pattern pieces
   - detection of repetitive features (rhythm) of pattern
   - experience of incompleteness and need for closure based on pattern features
   - comprehension of concept of "next"

   (b) Children will justify the basis for their selection of the piece that completes the pattern.
   - ability to understand cause–effect relationships
   - awareness of oneself as the source or cause
   - ability to articulate a rationale for behavior

(5) Perspective taking:
   (a) Children will communicate with another person in a way that reflects awareness of that person's need for information.
   Subskills:
   - ability to read behavioral cues of others, such as the signaling of emotions
   - ability to comprehend and distinguish among verbal communications of others, such as statements versus questions versus commands
   - ability to provide verbal and behavioral communications to allow another person to engage in reciprocal interchanges

   (b) Children will accurately describe the drawings they perceive.
   Subskills:
   - vocabulary for appropriate labels and spatial locations

(6) Verbal Planning:
   (a) Children will tell the steps in correct sequence of commonly experienced activities.
   Subskills:
   - vocabulary and experience base
   - working memory to allow mental processing of the plan

   (b) Children will determine when they need a plan.

Subskills:

- ability to detect when something is out of order or in need of organization
- ability to anticipate what comes next
- ability to sequence pictures portraying common activities
- comprehension of planning words such as "first," "next," "last"
- use of planning words to communicate a sequence

Important: Interventions embedded in the ACFS that have been found to be successful with the child can be turned into recommended teaching strategies. Interventions that have not been successful should be discussed and alternatives proposed for trial within the instructional setting.

We offer Table 6.1 to facilitate interpretation of information from the ACFS, but it should not be considered comprehensive or final. Assessors need to update their resources and information regarding best practices and should help teachers monitor the effectiveness of their recommendations. Assessors should also provide consultation regarding implementation of the recommendations. Ideas and techniques for monitoring responsiveness to intervention are discussed by Lidz (2003).

TECHNICAL INFORMATION

In this section, we present the studies concerning reliability and validity of the ACFS that have been completed up to the time of this publication. Many of these are from graduate school theses, with participants primarily from the New York metropolitan area. Some of the studies include participants with diagnosed developmental delays, and others include those with typical development. The participants overall are from a wide variety of socioeconomic and ethnic backgrounds.

Because dynamic procedures are most typically administered in a pretest–intervene–posttest format, the expectation is that, for a group, the scores from pretest to posttest should increase. This is the primary source of evidence for the effectiveness of the interceding intervention. To attribute the gain to the intervention would of course require experimental controls, but the first line of investigation with these procedures, even without the availability of such controls, is to demonstrate a pretest to posttest gain. This would be an aspect of construct validity and is explored in a number of the studies elaborated subsequently.

The first cohort of children assessed with the ACFS was a group of 30 high-functioning children attending a private school in New York City. All children from grades pre-kindergarten (PreK) and kindergarten participated in this study, and Lidz was the assessor. The ACFS was revised on

Table 6.1. Samples of interventions that respond to ACFS results

Subscale	Possible interventions
Classification	Work on visual matching to a model object by attribute; place objects with the same color in the designated box. Teach child to sort by at least two attributes; then ask child just to "sort." Once sorted, ask the child to do it another way.
Auditory memory	Read a short story to the child. Help the child build a visual model for the story with shapes or pictures. Ask the child to tell the story while looking at the model. Remove the model and ask the child to tell the story again.
Visual memory	Provide the child with a number of objects just beyond easy memory span. Tell the child that it is important to learn some special strategies to help with remembering. Ask the child to name each and to tell something about each one. Help the child make groups based upon a common attribute. Ask the child to recall the names of the objects without seeing them.
Pattern completion	Create clapping and drawing patterns for the child and encourage the child to think of what comes next. Emphasize the rhythm of the pattern and indicate by pause and gesture that you expect the child to provide the next response. Model verbalization of the pattern, and encourage the child to follow the model of verbalization. Encourage the child to create patterns that you then verbalize and complete. Look for patterns in the environment, such as on clothes or furniture.
Perspective taking	Encourage children who know how to play a game to explain it to the group or to an individual. Pair children as partners and have each take a turn teaching the partner how to draw a picture or build a construct from a simple model. Model how to do this and show the need to be explicit and clear and which points to discuss.
Verbal planning	During circle time, at the beginning of the day, discuss and visually show the plan for the day. Refer to this plan as you proceed throughout the day. When about to begin an activity, briefly discuss the plan for that activity in terms of sequence and tools needed. At the end of the day or activity, ask the children to recall the plan, to evaluate how well it worked, and to say what could be done better next time.
Self-regulation	Model and encourage task-related self-talk. Provide opportunities for role-playing teacher or parent. Change use of time-out from use for punishment into use as a self-selected tool for self-control, that is, from time-out to time to cool out. Use self-calming routines such as placing hands in lap, zipper lip, or making eye contact with teacher/parent.

Subscale	Possible interventions
Persistence	Encourage task completion. Adjust task so that it is completeable. Alternate active and passive activities.
Frustration tolerance	Model verbal expression of frustration and encourage child to use verbal expression rather than acting up or out. Adjust task to reduce frustration.
Flexibility	Encourage child to think of another way to solve a problem. Use the group to problem solve alternative solutions Coach the child through use of an alternative approach. Practice more than one way to solve a problem and ask the child to choose which one to use and then to try the alternative.
Motivation	Offer praise and encouragement. Try to attach program objectives to child's spontaneous interests. Show enthusiasm during interactions. Assure multiple experiences of success for the child
Interactivity	Provide opportunities for one-to-one interactions with adults and peers. Pair child with another who has good prosocial skills and provide coaching as needed. Involve child in activities requiring reciprocal interaction. Ensure positive responsiveness to any of the child's initiations.
Responsivity	Work on development of a strong positive affective relationship with the child. Provide ample opportunity for practice and review, and ensure child's mastery before moving on to new work. Embed new work within what the child already knows. Provide lots of positive encouragement and feedback about what works to promote success. Go as low as needed to ensure success. Make learning as gamelike and fun as possible. Develop predictable routines.

the basis of experience with these children, so there are some differences in the details of the procedure; for example, the first ACFS version had five instead of six subscales. The children were first assessed in the fall, with follow-up in the spring for the Pre-K group only. These results appear in Table 6.2.

Table 6.2 shows significant pretest to posttest gains for Classification, Auditory Memory, and Visual Memory, with the memory tests showing by far the greatest improvement following the intervention phase. These results were similar for children from both grade levels, and there were no significant differences between the performances of children from the two grade levels. During this first phase, the Verbal Planning and Sequential Pattern Completion tasks required substantial revision, and

Table 6.2. Group means and ranges ($n = 14/15$ for each grade level)

Subscale	Pre-K pre	Pre-K post	Pre-K spring post	K pre	K post
Classification	3.33 (0–5)	4.73 (3–6)	5.42 (3–6)	3.86 (2–6)	4.93 (4–6)
Planning	5.07 (2–10)	4.28 (3–8)	6.07 (0–9)	5.71 (2–9)	6.00 (4–10)
Auditory memory	7.00 (1–14)	10.43 (3–15)	12.00 (5–20)	7.2 (1–14)	11.07 (4–16)
Visual memory	7.40 (4–13)	10.27 (5–13)	9.36 (4–13)	7.64 (1–13)	10.85 (5–13)
Pattern completion	5.07 (2–7)	6.20 (3–8)	5.07 (1–7)	5.86 (2–7)	—

Table 6.3. Pretest to posttest gains on the Application of Cognitive Functions Scale (ACFS; $N = 25/26$)

Subscale	Pre mean (SD; SEM)	Post mean (SD; SEM)	t
Classification	3.15 (1.26; .25)	3.69 (1.09; .21)	3.38***
Perspective taking	3.56 (2.40; .48)	4.64 (2.36; .47)	2.65**
Auditory memory	4.38 (2.86; .56)	5.19 (3.30; .65)	1.41
Visual memory	5.81 (2.26; .44)	6.88 (2.86; .56)	1.92
Verbal planning	4.88 (3.05; .60)	6.15 (3.16; .62)	2.42 *
Pattern completion	6.88 (4.01; .79)	9.69 (6.12; 1.20)	3.86***
Total ACFS	28.96 (7.71; 1.54)	36.80 (9.97; 1.99)	6.51***

*$p = .05$; **$p = .01$; ***$p = .001$.

the Classification task showed need for increased ceiling (for these high-functioning students). The revisions are included in subsequent research.

The next study was part of a master's thesis carried out in the United Kingdom by Brooks (1997). This study used only the Classification subscale of the ACFS with a population of 22 preschool children with developmental disabilities (11 in the experimental group and 11 in the control group). The focus of this study was on potential practice effects; the control group of children did not receive the intervention portion but were administered only the pretest and posttest. This study showed that virtually none of the children in the nonintervention (control) group moved from "builder" to "grouper" status, whereas two thirds of the children who received the intervention made this transition. All of the children were described as "builders" during their pretests, meaning that their response to the instruction to "make groups" was merely to build. Because of a scoring error, the *t* test results of group mean differences cannot be used.

SHURIN STUDY

Shurin's (1998) master's thesis, completed in New York City, involved 26 four-year-old children, all but 5 with diagnosed developmental disabilities. This study looked at a number of issues. The first concerned pretest to posttest gains. These results appear in Table 6.3.

Table 6.3 shows that significant gains were found for Classification, Perspective Taking, Verbal Planning, and Sequential Pattern Completion. The only subscales that did not show significant gains were the two memory subscales. This is interesting because of the dramatic contrast with the results of Lidz's earlier study with high-functioning children. This difference could have diagnostic implications for differentiating children with

Table 6.4. Pearson product–moment correlations between behavior observation ratings during mediation and the Application of Cognitive Functions Scale (ACFS) posttest task scores (N = 26)

Subscale	Task score	Mean behavior rating	r
Classification	3.69	1.49	.28
Perspective taking	4.64	1.56	.27
Auditory memory	5.04	1.38	.17
Visual memory	6.88	1.52	.43*
Verbal planning	6.15	1.46	.64***
Pattern completion	9.69	1.38	.39*

*$p < .05$;   ***$p < .001$.

and without developmental disabilities, which of course would require further study. Table 6.3 also shows the standard errors of measurement, which contribute to information regarding the reliability of the ACFS subscales. These are difficult to interpret because the subscales all have different score ranges, but in all cases except the posttest of Pattern Completion, the errors of measurement are well below 1 point.

The Shurin study included the Behavior Observation Rating Scale that is embedded in each of the subscales. The first question explored the relationship between the Behavior Rating total scores and total task scores: Does the child's behavior during the procedure relate to task competence? The correlation of .65 ($p < .001$) between both total scores suggests a qualified "yes."

Table 6.4 shows the degree of relationship of the total Behavior Rating score during mediation to each of the subscales. The results in Table 6.4 show that there is a significant relationship between the total Behavior Observation Rating scores and three of the six subscales: Visual Memory, Verbal Planning, and Pattern Completion.

The next question was the following: Which of the behaviors on the rating scale relates to task competence, and to what degree? These were calculated for total scores, and the results appear in Table 6.5. The table documents significant correlations for Persistence, Frustration Tolerance, and Flexibility.

To look at the Behavior Observation Rating Scale as a scale, the next issue concerned determining intratest consistency, relating each component with the total scale. These results appear in Table 6.6. Table 6.6 shows that all components except Interactivity showed a moderate to strong relationship with the total score, and Interactivity was borderline ($p < 0.06$).

Table 6.5. Pearson product–moment correlations between total behavior observation ratings during mediation and total Application of Cognitive Functions Scale (ACFS) posttest scores

Behavior category	r
Self-regulation	.11
Persistence	.56**
Frustration tolerance	.52"*"
Flexibility	.63 ***
Motivation	.23
Interactivity	.01
Responsivity	.27

*p = .056;   ** p < .01;   *** p < .001.

Thus, the Behavior Observation Rating Scale does show acceptable intratest reliability. What it seems to be measuring most strongly is self-regulation, persistence, frustration tolerance, and flexibility.

During the preparation of Shurin for her thesis by the author, a case was selected for an interscorer reliability check of the Behavior Observation Rating Scale, comparing the scores assigned by Shurin and Lidz. The percentage of exact agreement for ratings during the pretest was 74%; for ratings during mediation, it was 82%. When the ratings for pretest and mediation were combined and the instances of agreements and disagreements for each behavior component across all tasks were compared, the percentage of agreement was 96%. A similar comparison was done in relation to another thesis (Levy, 1999). In this latter case, the exact agreement

Table 6.6. Intratest consistency of composite behavioral rating scale scores (N = 26) Pearson correlations of each behavior component with composite behavior score

Behavior category	r
Self-regulation	.59***
Persistence	.75***
Frustration tolerance	.78***
Flexibility	.85***
Motivation	.57**
Interactivity	.37 (p = .06)
Responsivity	.57*

* p < .05;   ** p < .01;   *** p < .001.

Table 6.7a. Pretest to posttest mean score gains for special needs children
($N = 11$)

Subscale	Pre mean (SD)	Post mean (SD)	t
Classification	2.54 (.69)	2.73 (1.79)	−.31
Perspective taking	1.91 (1.70)	2.54 (2.62)	−1.29
Auditory memory	0.91 (1.37)	2.09 (3.14)	−1.48
Visual memory	4.73 (3.16)	3.81 (3.40)	.97
Verbal planning	3.00 (3.22)	4.45 (3.67)	−1.74
Pattern completion	5.63 (6.20)	7.45 (5.35)	−1.10
Combined total	16.91 (6.20)	4.09 (9.68)	−1.92

of ratings for the pretests was 77%; for the mediations, it was 70%. The percentage of total agreements across all tasks was 67%.

A third attempt to evaluate interscorer reliability involved two independent raters (certified school psychologists) who attended a workshop offered by the first author of the ACFS. The attendees of the workshop were introduced to dynamic assessment and heard an overview of the ACFS that included the Behavior Observation Rating Scale. During a live demonstration of the ACFS, two participants volunteered to rate the child along with the author. Thus, these raters had very minimal exposure to the scale. Nevertheless, the average agreement among all three raters was 74%. The subscales that elicited the highest levels of agreement were Classification (72%), Perspective Taking (83%), and Auditory Memory (81%), and the behavior components that elicited the highest levels of agreement were Persistence (100%), Frustration Tolerance (94%), and Motivation (78%).

Table 6.7b. Pretest to posttest mean score gains for typically developing children
($N = 11$)

Subscale	Pre mean (SD)	Post mean (SD)	t
Classification	2.63 (0.67)	3.00 (1.41)	−1.17
Perspective taking	4.00 (3.79)	7.00 (4.02)	−.92**
Auditory memory	3.91 (3.62)	5.18 (3.89)	−2.71*
Visual memory	6.54 (3.04)	6.73 (2.76)	−.34
Verbal planning	5.18 (4.43)	7.27 (3.35)	−3.20**
Pattern completion	13.36 (6.09)	13.73 (6.36)	−1.17
Total score	35.64 (11.98)	42.91 (15.24)	−4.64**

$^*p < .05;$ $^{**}p < .01.$

Table 6.8. Mean differences on Application of Cognitive Functions Scale pretests between community and special education groups ($N = 21$)

Subscales	Community mean (SD)	Special Ed mean (SD)	t
Classification	2.64 (.67)	2.54 (.69)	0.31
Perspective taking	4.00 (3.80)	1.91 (1.70)	1.67
Auditory memory	3.91 (3.62)	.91 (1.38)	2.57*
Visual memory	6.54 (3.04)	4.73 (3.16)	1.37
Verbal planning	5.18 (3.43)	3.00 (3.22)	1.53
Pattern completion	13.36 (6.09)	5.64 (2.91)	3.80**
Total pre	35.64 (11.98)	16.91 (6.20)	0.60***

$* p < .05;$ $** p < .01;$ $*** p < .001.$

LEVY STUDY

Levy's (1999) study of the discriminant validity of the ACFS compared the results for 22 children between the ages of 4 years 0 months and 4 years 11 months. Half of the children had diagnoses of "eligibility" for preschool services; that is, they manifested a variety of mild to moderate developmental delays (primarily in areas of language, cognition, or both), although half were from the neighborhood and inferred to be of normal development. All children were from mixed ethnic, racial, and socioeconomic backgrounds. The results of pretest to posttest mean scores for special needs and typically developing groups appear in Tables 6.7a and 6.7b.

The results in Table 6.7a show that the children with special needs made positive gains on all subscales except Visual Memory, but none of these reached statistical significance. In contrast, the results in Table 6.7b show that the typically developing children made positive gains on all subscales, reaching statistical significance on Perspective Taking, Auditory Memory, Verbal Planning, and Total Score. This again supports the observation that performance on the memory scales may be particularly important as diagnostic discriminators between children with special needs and those with typical development.

Levy's study also looked at the differences in mean performance on the pretests and posttests of the ACFS subscales and total scores between the special needs and typically developing groups. These results appear in Tables 6.8 and 6.9. Tables 6.8 and 6.9 show that there were significant differences between pretest means for only the Auditory Memory, Pattern Completion, and Total scores, whereas the posttest differences showed significant differences for four of the six subscales (Perspective Taking, Auditory Memory, Visual Memory, Pattern Completion) and the total score. That is,

Table 6.9. Mean differences on Application of Cognitive Functions Scale posttests between community and special education groups ($N = 21$)

Subscale	Community mean (SD)	Special Ed mean (SD)	t
Classification	3.00 (1.41)	2.23 (1.79)	.40
Perspective taking	7.00 (4.02)	2.55 (2.62)	3.08**
Auditory memory	5.18 (3.89)	2.09 (3.14)	2.05*
Visual memory	6.73 (2.76)	3.82 (3.40)	2.20*
Verbal planning	7.27 (3.35)	4.55 (3.67)	1.82
Pattern completion	13.73 (6.36)	7.45 (5.35)	2.50*
Total	42.91 (15.24)	24.09 (9.68)	3.46**

*$p < .05$;   **$p < .01$.

the posttest scores showed stronger discrimination between the groups. When the groups were separated, the Visual Memory subscale did show a significant difference, suggesting that there may be a ceiling effect for children with typical development. This makes the Visual Memory subscale a possibly strong source of discrimination between groups of children with and without developmental delays, supporting the findings from the Shurin versus first cohort studies described earlier.

Levy also looked at differences between the groups in their Behavior Observation Rating scores. These ratings are available for only four of the variables during the pretest phase, and appear in Table 6.10. The ratings for five of the variables during the mediation phase appear in Table 6.11 (mediation allows rating of the receptivity variable, which is not possible during the pretest). Behavioral categories not rated were those not in evidence during the assessment and were dropped from the analyses.

Table 6.10. Comparison of mean Application of Cognitive Functions Scale pretest behavior rating scores between community and special education groups ($N = 21$)

Behavior	Community mean (SD)	Special Ed mean (SD)	t
Self-regulation	1.81 (.27)	1.38 (.39)	3.03**
Persistence	1.85 (.28)	1.47 (.37)	2.69**
Motivation	1.79 (.45)	1.50 (.37)	1.64
Interactivity	1.77 (.33)	1.45 (.52)	1.71

**$p < .01$.

Table 6.11. Comparison of mean Application of Cognitive Functions Scale mediation behavior rating scores between community and special education groups ($N = 21$)

Behavior	Community mean (SD)	Special Ed mean (SD)	t
Self-regulation	1.71 (.32)	1.20 (.53)	2.78**
Persistence	1.80 (.28)	1.50 (.35)	2.28**
Motivation	1.83 (.36)	1.50 (.40)	2.06*
Interactivity	1.82 (.38)	1.53 (.48)	1.56
Responsivity	1.94 (.46)	1.21 (.46)	3.70**

*$p < .05$;   **$p < .01$.

The results in Table 6.10 show mean differences favoring the children with typical development on two of four components (self-regulation and persistence). Ratings for motivation and interactivity did not differ between the groups. Tables 6.10 and 6.11 show that the group differences were more in evidence during the mediation phase, with mean ratings for four of the five components reaching significance (self-regulation, persistence, motivation, and receptivity). Only ratings of Interactivity during mediation did not reach significance. Overall, Levy's findings are supportive of the discriminant validity of the ACFS, with performance during the posttests and behavior ratings during mediation showing the most significant differences between groups.

Levy also investigated the intratest reliability of the scale. These results, comparing pretests and posttests, appear in Tables 6.12. The results in Tables 6.12 document the relatively stronger intratest reliability for the posttests, compared with the pretests. In the case of the pretests, Verbal

Table 6.12. Correlations between total group Application of Cognitive Functions Scale pretests and posttests ($N = 22$)

	Pretests	Posttests
Classification	.25	42*
Auditory memory	.74***	.71***
Visual memory	46*	.68***
Pattern completion	.86***	.78***
Perspective taking	.50*	.67***
Verbal planning	.39	.71***

*$p < .05$;   **$p < .01$;   ***$p < .001$.

Table 6.13. Correlations between total group Application of Cognitive Functions Scale pretests and posttests (N = 22)

	Post:	CI	PT	AM	VM	VP	PC	Total
Pre:	CI	.31	.07	.26	.22	.24	.28	.35
	PT	.23	.70***	.07	.15	.26	.48*	.49*
	AM	.41	.49*	.83***	.51*	.51*	.46*	.78***
	VM	.01	−.08	.30	.70***	.30	.26	.38
	VP	.21	.43*	.61**	.28	.75***	.11	.52**
	PC	.16	.51*	.36	.50*	.25	.81***	.72***
	Total	.30	.67**	.49*	.55**	.51*	.66***	.81***

Note: AM = Auditory Memory; CI = Classification; PC = Pattern Completion; PT = Perspective Taking; FM = Verbal Memory; VP = Verbal Planning.
* $p < .05$;   ** $p < .01$.   *** $p < .001$.

Planning and Classification do not make significant contributions to the total score, whereas in the case of the posttests, all of the subscale scores are significantly related to the total score. This information is supportive of the validity of the diagnostic aspect of the ACFS as well, because the posttests appear to produce a more reliable instrument.

Levy's results portrayed in Table 6.13 show the relationships between the pretest and posttest scores for her total group. As is typical for dynamic assessment data, Table 6.13 shows that there are highly significant correlations for most of the subscale total scores, but not for all, and there are far from perfect relationships even for those with the strongest relationships. This suggests that mediation is associated with differential responses in the children and that the pretests (static) are imperfect predictors of the posttest (dynamic) results. As would be expected, the highest correlations occur between the pretest and posttest of the same subscale.

Finally, Levy calculated the Cronbach alpha scores for both the pretest and mediation Behavior Observation Rating scores for the combined group, resulting in .89 for the pretest and .91 for the mediation phase.

BENSOUSSAN AND MALOWITSKY STUDIES

In addition to the Brooks (1997) study investigating practice effects related to the Classification subscale, studies by Bensoussan (2002) and Malowitsky (2001) explored this issue with the remaining subscales, in both cases with American children with typical development (Brooks's study involved children with disabilities residing in the United Kingdom).

Bensoussan's (2002) study involved 20 children between the ages of 3 and 4 years. The children were administered the Auditory Memory, Verbal Planning, and Perspective Taking subscales with children randomly

Table 6.14. *t* tests for paired groups comparing mean posttest scores (*N* = 10)

	Experimental	Control	t	p
	Mean (SD)	Mean (SD)		
Auditory memory	9.50 (3.5)	4.40 (1.58)	4.17	.002
Perspective taking	11.60 (1.51)	9.10 (1.80)	5.51	.004
Verbal planning	9.80 (1.69)	3.30 (2.45)	5.98	.0002

assigned to experimental (with mediation) and control (repetition of tasks without mediation) groups. There was a slight but significant difference between the pretest scores (*p* = .03) only on the Perspective Taking task favoring the control (no mediation) group. Following treatment, there were highly significant differences between groups on all tasks, favoring the experimental (mediated) group. These results appear in Table 6.14. Table 6.14 shows that the experimental group in all conditions obtained posttest scores significantly higher than those of the control group. That is, children exposed to the mediation obtained significantly higher scores than those who were not exposed to mediation.

To look more closely at the issue of practice effect, the gains made by each group on each task were calculated, and these results appear in Table 6.15. Table 6.15 shows that all groups receiving mediation made significant gains. None of the groups of children in the unmediated conditions made significant gains; in fact, children in the Verbal Planning group showed significantly lower postintervention scores.

Malowitsky's study included 30 children from 3 through 5 years of age. These children were administered the Visual Memory and Pattern Completion subscales, with children assigned randomly to experimental

Table 6.15. *t* tests for paired comparison of mean pretest to posttest gains by experimental and control groups

	M pre (SD)	M post (SD)	t	p
Experimental				
Auditory memory	3.40 (2.50)	9.50 (3.50)	9.28	<.0001
Perspective taking	6.80 (3.42)	11.60 (1.50)	6.74	<.0001
Verbal planning	5.10 (3.64)	9.80 (1.69)	5.57	.0003
Control				
Auditory memory	4.40 (.97)	4.40 (1.58)	0.00	NS
Perspective taking	9.20 (1.48)	9.10 (1.79)	0.22	NS
Verbal planning	5.30 (2.54)	3.30 (2.45)	2.58	.03

Table 6.16. *t* tests for paired comparisons between pretests and posttests for mediated (E) and nonmediated (C) groups

	Pre M (SD)	Post M (SD)	*t*	*p*
Pattern completion				
Experimental	6.29 (5.28)	7.93 (5.26)	2.27	.04
Control	5.71 (3.47)	6.50 (3.65)	1.99	*ns*
Visual memory				
Experimental	4.36 (2.56)	5.50 (2.28)	1.49	*ns*
Control	4.79 (2.55)	5.21 (2.08)	.70	*ns*

(mediated) and control (no mediation) groups. There were no pretest score differences between these groups. Table 6.16 shows the results for pretest to posttest gains for the groups. Table 6.16 shows that there was a significant difference in favor of the mediation group on the Pattern Completion but not the Visual Memory subscale. These results document the lack of "practice effects" for these participants in that there were virtually no significant gains from pretest to posttest for the groups not experiencing mediation, and the only group demonstrating a significant gain was the mediated group on the Pattern Completion subscale. The failure of the gain for the Visual Memory subscale may be attributable to a ceiling effect for these high-functioning children with typical development.

Correlations between pretest and posttest scores for the same subscales provides information related to both reliability and validity. Without intervention, this informs test–retest reliability, and comparisons of correlations with and without intervention inform validity. Combined rank-order correlations for the Malowitsky and Bensoussan studies appear in Table 6.17. (These data were not reported in the theses but were calculated by the first author of the ACFS following completion of the theses.) Classification is omitted because of the inclusion of that subscale in the Brooks study, where there was a scoring error.

The results in Table 6.17 suggest moderate to high rank-order stability of four of the subscales, with Visual Memory and Verbal Planning showing the least and Pattern Completion the most. The subscales show a tendency toward higher stability under experimental (mediated) conditions, with the exceptions of Visual Memory and Verbal Planning, which show the greatest differences. In these studies, the test–retest interval for the control condition was set to approximate the average amount of time required for the experimental condition, that is, about 15 minutes. This is very short term for a test–retest calculation, and the modest results may

Table 6.17. Spearman rank correlations for pretest and posttest Application of Cognitive Functions Scale subscales

	Rho corrected for ties	p
Experimental (Mediation)		
Auditory memory	.85	.01
Visual memory	.12	ns
Pattern completion	.83	.002
Perspective taking	.90	.007
Verbal planning	.73	.03
Control (No Mediation)		
Auditory memory	.65	.05
Visual memory	.61	.03
Pattern completion	.92	.001
Perspective taking	.68	.04
Verbal planning	.37	ns

reflect a somewhat negative reaction of the children to the mere repetition of the test instructions without something "interesting" happening in between. These were all children with typical development. During the interval, the control participants were exposed to the same materials as the children in the experimental groups, but there was no mediation provided. They were merely told they could play with the materials for a few minutes.

ARANOV STUDY

Aranov's (1999) study focused on the embedded Behavior Observation Rating Scale. This study included 25 children from four preschool classes (age range from 2 through 5 years) from a school for children with special needs. All of the children had developmental delays. Aranov compared her ratings on the scale with those of the classroom teachers and speech therapists, also comparing the ratings of the teachers and the speech therapists. These results appear in Table 6.18. (Each teacher and therapist had more than one of the children who were observed by the researcher for the study.)

Table 6.18 shows generally strong interrater agreement for all pairs. The behaviors of self-regulation, interactivity, motivation, and responsivity, as well as total score, showed the strongest levels of agreement, whereas persistence and flexibility were more wide ranging. Frustration is less likely to occur during administration of the ACFS than during the course of the prolonged instruction of the classroom or speech therapy. Cronbach alpha

Table 6.18. Pearson correlations between ratings of researcher and teacher (R/T; $n = 4$) and between researcher and speech therapist (R/Sp; $n = 7$), and teacher and speech therapist (T/Sp; $n = 4/7$)

	R/T	R/Sp	T/Sp
Self-regulation	.81***	1.00***	.90***
Persistence	.74**	.88***	.62**
Frustration tolerance	ns	ns	.88
Flexibility	.58**	.88***	.62**
Motivation	.83***	.78***	.82***
Interactivity	1.00***	1.00***	.92***
Responsivity	.76***	.83***	.83***
Total	.95***	.97***	.94***

$** p < .01; \quad *** p < .001.$

for the seven components as rated by the teachers were .79, and as rated by the speech therapists, .81.

LARGOTTA STUDY

Largotta's (2001) study differed from those already described in that it did not specifically address psychometric issues of the ACFS. This study concerned the credibility of using symbols as mediators during the intervention portion of the Auditory Memory subscale. Because the ACFS is designed for use with very young children, there may be an issue regarding the developmental appropriateness of using symbolic mediators for this age group. The study included 30 four-year-old boys and girls from a wide variety of backgrounds, all with typical development.

Briefly, this subscale involves retelling of a short story. The intervention or mediation segment presents the same story and teaches the children to build a semi-abstract model with geometric shapes to represent the elements of the story as a way to promote memory and sequencing of the narrative. The Largotta study included three randomly assigned groups: children who used the symbols as offered in the ACFS, a second group that worked with pictures of the story elements, and a third group that manipulated small toy representations of these elements. For the posttest, the children were asked to retell the story without the aid of any of the supports.

The children in all three groups made highly significant gains from pretest to posttest, with no group showing superiority. Although these results fail to support the advantage of any specific materials for intervention, the study also documents the appropriateness of all of these props

Table 6.19. Spearman rank correlations for Application of Cognitive Functions Scale auditory memory pretests and posttests administered under three conditions

	Rho corrected for ties	*p*
Toys	.66	.05
Pictures	−.24	ns
Symbols	.22	ns

for this age group, including the use of the semi-abstract symbols. As an addendum to this study (not reported in the thesis but calculated by the first ACFS author following completion of the project), the pretest to posttest correlations provide some provocative findings. These appear in Table 6.19.

The results in Table 6.19 document the least degree of change in rank order of the children's scores under the "toys" condition, with the greatest amount of change in rank order for the "pictures" condition. In fact, there is a negative, although not significant, relationship between the rank ordering of the children's scores in the pretest–posttest pictures condition. These results, therefore, suggest that there may well be different effects of these interventions that are not reflected in the group means and that the "toys" condition appears to be inducing the least amount of change.

TATIK STUDY

Tatik's (2000) study addressed the issue of concurrent validity. Tatik administered both the ACFS pretests and the Leiter – Revised International Performance Test to 15 preschool children with special needs. The hypothesis was that subscales with similar names would correlate significantly and positively, and those with dissimilar names would not. This hypothesis was not supported, and the researcher concluded that the subscales measured different variables, despite the apparent similarity of the labels.

ADMINISTERING THE ACFS TO DEAF STUDENTS

Lidz (2004) administered the ACFS to 13 deaf children of mixed socioeconomic backgrounds between the ages of 4 and 8. The primary purposes of the study were to explore the ability of these children to respond to the demands of the test, to investigate the types of accommodations that would be necessary so that the ACFS could be used with deaf children, and to research the properties of the procedure when used with this population. The mean differences between pretest and posttest scores appear in Table 6.20.

Table 6.20. t test results ($N = 13$)

Subscale	Pre M (SD)	Post M (SD)	t	p
Classification	2.46 (.97)	4.08 (1.66)	−3.88	.002
Auditory memory	2.92 (3.07)	6.85 (4.02)	−4.93	.0003
Visual memory	5.08 (2.22)	7.00 (2.04)	−3.24	.007
Pattern completion	9.69 (4.82)	11.15 (3.69)	−1.96	.07
Perspective taking	8.38 (6.25)	10.92 (5.74)	−1.59	.138
Verbal planning	3.15 (3.31)	5.23 (3.86)	−2.82	.02
ACFS total	31.67 (14.56)	45.23 (16.13)	−6.61	< .0001

Note: ACFS = Application of Cognitive Functions Scale.

Table 6.20 documents highly significant gains from pretest to posttest for four of the six subscales, as well as for the total test score. Gains for Pattern Completion were strong but did not quite reach statistical significance. Perspective Taking was the only subscale not to approximate significance, although the children did make a clearly positive improvement.

These children, as did others in the previously described studies, showed behaviors that were rated significantly higher during the mediation, compared to the pretest, phase of the assessment. The mean rating during pretest was 37.77 and during mediation, 43.54 ($p = .02$). Also, as shown in Table 6.21, the behavior ratings during mediation generally related more strongly to the subscale posttest scores than did the behavior ratings during the pretest. This supports the validity of dynamic assessment because inclusion of intervention is unique to this model.

Table 6.21. Behavior rating scale Pearson correlations with subscales

Subscale	Pretest ratings	Mediation ratings
Classification post	−.28	.22
Auditory memory post	.51	.70
Visual memory post	.05	.12
Pattern completion post	.22	.54
Perspective taking post	.43	.58
Verbal planning post	.40	.60
ACFS total post	.40	.68

Note: ACFS = Application of Cognitive Functions Scale.

Table 6.22. Pearson correlations ($N = 13$) with pretest total score

Classification pre	.22
Auditory memory pre	.85
Visual memory pre	.56
Pattern completion pre	.67
Perspective taking pre	.76
Verbal planning pre	.75
Classification post	.26
Auditory memory post	.82
Visual memory post	.62
Pattern completion post	.91
Perspective taking post	.79
Verbal planning post	.84

Table 6.22 shows the internal reliability through Pearson correlations of pretest subscale scores with pretest total and posttest subscale scores with posttest total.

The results in Table 6.22 show that all of the subscales make moderate to strong contributions to the total scores, with the exception of Classification. There is a tendency for the posttest scores to show a stronger relationship with the total score than the pretests.

The degree to which pretests predict posttest scores within subscales is of interest for dynamic assessment, and these results appear in Table 6.23. The data in the table show strong relationships between the pretests and posttests for all subscales except Classification; however, the variance accounted for by the pretest never exceeds 50% of the posttest, which can be interpreted as a relationship between the "static" and "dynamic" (post intervention) score. That is, the pretest is again an imperfect predictor of the responsiveness of the child to teaching.

Table 6.23. Pearson correlations between Application of Cognitive Functions Scale pretests and posttests

Classification	−.10
Auditory memory	.70
Visual memory	.70
Pattern completion	.66
Perspective taking	.64
Verbal planning	.65

Finally, this study documented a higher correlation between ACFS posttest (.44) than pretest (.11) and chronological age, and a higher correlation between pretest (.40) than posttest (.16) and IQ. This suggests that the posttest is a better reflection than the pretest of developmental status of the students and that the pretest is more closely related to traditional IQ than is the posttest.

Such data add to evidence of validity for the ACFS.

USEFULNESS OF THE ACFS WITH DUTCH CHILDREN

Lidz and Van der Aalsvoort (2005) completed a study involving administration of the four core ACFS subscales to 29 Dutch children in early primary regular education classes.

The study used an alternative, but related, behavior rating scale that was completed during pretests and posttests. This study documented significant pretest to posttest gains for three of the four subscales (Classification, Auditory Memory, and Pattern Completion); Visual Memory showed gains that did not quite reach statistical significance ($p = .07$).

Despite the slightly older age of the children (up to ages 6 and 7 years), there was no ceiling effect for any of the subscales, with means and standard deviations well below maximum scores for pretests and posttests.

The study included correlations between the subscales and standardized measures of language and arithmetic. The Classification pretest (.55), Auditory Memory posttest (.39), and Pattern Completion posttest (.43) showed significant correlations with arithmetic. The Classification pretest and posttest (.57; .37), Auditory Memory posttest (.35), and Pattern Completion posttest (.44) showed statistically significant correlations with language. Behavior Ratings during Pattern Completion Pretest (.65), Pattern Completion posttest (.68), and Arithmetic (.56) were significant. Correlations between pretests and posttests for all subscales were significant but weak (Classification, .39; Auditory Memory, .48; Visual Memory, .38), with the exception of the strong correlation for Pattern Completion (.86).

Finally, significant correlations were found between SES and Behavior Ratings for three of the four subscales (Classification, .53; Auditory Memory, .51; Visual Memory, .38), as well as for both Language (.63) and Arithmetic (.55). The authors concluded that the ACFS could be appropriately used with Dutch children similar to the population of this study and added to accumulating information regarding the construct and criterion validity of the procedure. However, in a later similar study with a larger number of Dutch children, Van Der Aalsvoort and Lidz (in press) were not able to replicate the strength of these findings with this population. In this later study, there were issues of possible ceiling effects and the unknown effects of multiple assessors.

USE OF THE ACFS WITH AUSTRALIAN CHILDREN

Macdonald's (2006) study applied the ACFS with 50 preschool children, comparing the results of two groups, one with children with developmental delays and the other a control group with children with typical development.

Analysis of the results documented the following:

- Significant pretest–posttest total and subtest differences (gains) for students in both groups
- Consistent discrimination between the two groups, with the children with delays obtaining lower scores on all pretests and posttests
- Posttest scores of the children with delays consistently surpassing pretest scores of the children with typical development on all subtests
- Significant but moderate (.56) correlation between the ACFS full-scale posttest scores and the Wechsler Preschool and Primary Scale of Intelligence, third edition (WPPSI – III) for the children with developmental delays, but no relationship between these tests for the pretest scores of the delayed children or for any of the scores of the children with typical development
- Cronbach alpha of .63 for ACFS pretest scores
- Significant discrimination between the two groups on the Behavior Observation Rating Scale, with the children with delays obtaining lower ratings
- Cronbach alphas for the embedded Behavior Observation Rating Scale of .96 and .95 for pretest and mediation, respectively

These data suggest that the ACFS can be applied successfully with this population of Australian children.

SUMMARY

These studies as a group present a beginning foundation for the investigation of the psychometric properties and utility of the ACFS. Most of these studies have involved small numbers and, at the same time, were highly labor-intensive. The participants in the early studies have mostly come from the urban northeastern United States, but participants in later studies have been from other countries. Socioeconomic backgrounds have been mixed, and the studies vary regarding inclusion of children with typical or delayed development. To date, information is available regarding only one group of children with a low-incidence disability (deaf). Gindis has successfully applied the procedure with children adopted from Russia who manifest a variety of developmental disorders (Lidz & Gindis, 2003), though information about this remains anecdotal. Further research with this procedure is needed and encouraged.

SAMPLE CASES AND REPORTS

We present two cases in their entirely, despite their length, to allow readers to view the use of the ACFS information in the context of assessments that use a wide variety of data sources. These reports also reflect differences in writing styles that were left intact, as readers will also differ widely in their report writing styles. Case 6.1 demonstrates the use of the ACFS with a 4-year-old child with essentially typical development but with multicultural issues and concerns about language development. Case 6.2 illustrates the use of the ACFS with a child who is chronologically older than preschool but has significant developmental delays. These cases were contributed by both authors of the ACFS. Examples of how the procedure has been used with children who have been internationally adopted appear in Lidz and Gindis (2003). Obviously, names and any personally identifying information regarding these cases have been changed or deleted.

CASE 6.1

Name: Jason (male)
Age: 4 years 2 months

Reason for Referral

Jason was referred with concerns of both his teacher and mother regarding his development. His mother described him as "spacey" and easily frustrated. He did not express his feelings well at home and had difficulty transitioning from one situation to another. In school, Jason had shown some delays in concept development, although he had made significant progress since the beginning of the term. The assessment focused on a general "checkup" of his development to determine whether there were any areas of concerns in need of further attention, particularly with regard to language development.

Procedures: (test scores at end of report)
- Home Language Identification Survey (NY State Education Department)
- Child Development Inventory (completed by mother and assessor)
- Bracken Basic Concept Scale
- Kaufman Assessment Battery for Children
- Beery-Buktenica Developmental Test of Visual–Motor Integration
- Oral and Written Language Scales
- NEPSY: A Developmental Neuropsychological Assessment
- Application of Cognitive Functions Scale (dynamic assessment)

Background Information

Jason is the younger of two children who live with their natural mother. His older brother attends the same private school. His mother's native language is Spanish, but she is fluent in a number of languages, including English. His father is German-speaking and travels a great deal and sees his son on a limited, irregular basis. Jason has a very complex language history. He was born in Los Angeles but moved to Germany at about 1 year, continuing to reside there until about age 2 years and 6 months; his language base up to that age was German. Jason and his mother moved to the United States when Jason was age 2 years and 6 months, and from that time on, Jason's dominant language became English. Although his mother is fluent in English, she is not a native English speaker, and she feels she does not provide the best language model for him. His caregiver's native language is Spanish, and he hears his mother speak other languages (Italian, French) to her friends and acquaintances, and his father speaks German to his friends (English to Jason). Jason has never spoken any language other than English but most likely understands at least some Spanish and German. Thus, Jason is an English-dominant speaker, built on a foundation of German, but with frequent exposure to Spanish, as well as, less so, to other languages.

Jason's mother reported a normal pregnancy and delivery with normal developmental milestones except somewhat delayed language. As an infant, he cried a lot and was sensitive to touch. He is easily frustrated, and does not express his feelings clearly. It is also difficult for him to make changes, for example, from one place or one activity to another. He is well behaved and presents no significant discipline problems. He enjoys playing with Lego blocks and watching TV. His pediatrician has checked his hearing and reported it to be normal.

Jason had been tested previously (with the WPPSI) for admission to his school. The scores were calculated on the basis of an incorrect birth date (by 4 months) and therefore underestimated his levels of performance. Within the verbal area, his strength was in vocabulary, with weakness in comprehension. Overall, there was a tendency for him to be higher in the verbal than in the nonverbal area; however, with rescoring, none of these levels would be considered at a risk level other than Comprehension (which involves a great deal of verbal expression). The examiner noted some difficulty with word retrieval and with loose pencil grasp. His attention to perceptual–motor tasks was very good.

Assessment Results

Jason was a handsome boy with dark brown hair and big brown eyes. The assessor first observed him within his classroom, before he was aware that she was there for him. His caregiver bid him farewell in English, and Jason then stood at the computer, patiently awaiting his turn. When his turn was granted, he appeared very confident about what to do and operated the mouse with right-hand dominance and good control. He was very intensely interested in the program and interacted pleasantly with the boy sitting next to him, with whom he was sharing turns. As he moved the mouse, he showed some associated movements in his left hand but was soon able to relax it. After spending some time on his preferred part of the program, he asked his neighbor, "You like the trees one?" He soon relinquished his turn without stress and was invited to watch by his partner. He moved around somewhat more than the other child but maintained prolonged interest in the task and pleasant social interaction with the other child. Jason spontaneously repeated the words he heard from the computer. He was reluctant to leave the computer for the next activity and needed some help and encouragement from the aide to exit from the program.

Jason was somewhat late to join circle time [when the entire group sits in a circle for early morning discussion and singing] because of his difficulty leaving the previous task and had a hard time deciding where to sit in the already formed group. He settled against his teacher's legs. He was an active participant in the group discussions but had some difficulty switching topics. His contribution to the conversation about the relationship between getting wet and getting sick was, "If you stay in the water a long time, and you have a cold, you could die." He said "'scuse me" when he wanted to interject his thoughts.

The children selected their next activities, and Jason, by default, selected the sand box. He soon left that area and did not seem sure of where to go next. He then wandered over to his teacher's table. This activity involved size and category comparisons with pumpkins. Jason responded to the question of how the pumpkins were alike with, "If we treat them nice, they won't roll," thus, he was a willing respondent, but not quite on topic. He continued to be eager to share what he knew about pumpkins and said, searching for the correct words, "If the skin comes off, the fruit will come out" and, later, "If you break this, you can put pumpkin seeds." He seemed to use the "if . . . then . . ." context as an outline for framing his thoughts; although he was using "if . . . then" correctly, the content of his sentences at times lacked relevance to the question or issue of discussion, and his teacher needed to stretch to try to make a connection between what he said and the topic at hand.

It became evident while watching Jason during these activities that he did not always follow directions given distally to the group but that at times he needed to have the directions followed up by the classroom aide, who provided individual guidance to help him close down one activity and proceed to the next.

The next classroom activity involved using the pumpkins as a model for a painting. Jason engaged in the act of painting with enthusiasm but focused on painting a series of faces, ignoring the directions to refer to the model. While doing this, he verbalized, "This is his face. He looks like a [indistinct utterance] face." He held the brush with an overhand, fisted grasp.

The children then moved to find toys to use for playing on the carpet. Jason looked at one of the groups of children who were already playing but did not join in; instead, he rolled a car on his own area of carpet and maintained his focus on the nearby group. He remained in an observer role for this activity.

The children left for music, where they were not observed, and then returned for their snack. Jason was upset that the donut he hoped to eat was no longer available by the time he got to his plate because he was the last to arrive. He allowed himself to be distracted onto an alternative donut and was the last to finish. He was the only child to volunteer to help with clean up: "I'll go clean up my place!" He got the sponge and helped with the rest of the places as well.

Thus, Jason appeared to function successfully within the classroom routine, with some holding back for group activities, some difficulty switching activities, and some mild struggle with verbal expression, in the context of strong interest in communicating and willingness to participate and comply. Jason cooperated with the individual assessment for about 45 minutes at a time. He was reluctant to leave his class and puzzled by being taken out, despite attempts to explain this to him. He would comply with a few requests, and then he was clearly finished. Despite his preference for being in his class, he interacted warmly with the assessor and sought close proximity, preferring to work leaning up against her. He tended to avoid challenge and was not a risk taker but could be stimulated to move beyond his preference for safety with enthusiastic and encouraging presentation and promise of imminent relief.

Jason's English dominance was established by interview with his mother and completion of the Home Language Identification Survey, developed by the New York State Education Department. As noted earlier, despite his English dominance, he continued to have exposure to a complex language environment, and his early foundation for language was established in German. Jason was an eager communicator and readily expressed his thoughts, despite occasional struggles with finding the right word. Every once in a while, there was a very slight hint of an accent, and he would more frequently show some syntactical confusion. More often than not, he would get his point across and did not seem inhibited by his mild struggle. His articulation was clear, with a slight lisp evident.

Jason's mother completed a developmental inventory that described his functioning at home. Because of some of her confusion in interpreting the items, the asseseor reviewed and rescored the inventory. The inventory yielded age equivalents and showed that, for most areas, Jason was rated as near or within expectations for his age. He showed strength in the area of language comprehension and relative weakness in the areas of social and fine motor development and expressive language. He was well within expectations for his age in the areas of self-help, gross motor development, and academic knowledge.

Further assessment of Jason's fine motor skill, where he was asked to copy geometric figures, confirmed a weakness in this area. His functioning on this task was at a borderline deficient level. Most of his difficulty appeared related to his grasp, which resulted in poor hand control when he tried to draw. When he was taught to modify his grasp, much better control and more competent drawings resulted. He tended to hold the pencil with an overhand fisted grasp. He also tended to perseverate in his copying and did not observe the boundaries for his figures. His style was to start to draw his figure very close to the model and then allow himself to be weaned gradually into making a more independent drawing. It was difficult for him to switch the orientation of a straight line from vertical to horizontal. Talking him through and demonstrating what to do helped to improve his competence in this area. He needed increased pencil control and more strongly reinforced boundaries to do better with this activity.

Further assessment focused on Jason's general cognitive functioning and specific language abilities. The trend in all these measures was for him to function at or above average. There were virtually no areas of deficiency on any of these standardized measures. On the Kaufman Assessment Battery for Children (K-ABC), Jason showed near superior level ability on the sequential processing subscales, which emphasized rote memory of material presented both visually and auditorally. He was solidly average or above on the simultaneous processing subscales, which look at his ability to integrate information.

A measure of neuropsychological processes tapped his functioning in language and memory and showed levels of development toward the higher end of the average range in both. A subscale of particular interest for him was comprehension of instructions, and this was one of his higher level scores. Although he was not administered the visual–spatial portion of this measure, he showed spontaneous interest in the block construction task and so was allowed to complete this. This was the one area where he showed really well below average level of success. He resisted following the model and wanted to follow his own agenda of building with the blocks. As he built, he tended to switch hands. Once he saw that the task presented some unanticipated challenges, he wished to terminate. It was very difficult for him to move from viewing the drawing in the book to building his own block construction, but when provided with some help, he showed significant improvement and evidence of potential success at an above-average level.

Another specific measure of language functioning confirmed Jason's solidly average level of functioning in both listening comprehension and oral expression. Thus, any possible language difficulty was not documented by these standardized measures. Any indication for concern in the language area could only be gleaned from subtle qualitative observation of Jason's occasional struggle with word finding and his occasional syntactical confusion. In view of the amount of progress he is making in his language development, this is not viewed as an area of concern, but those working with him need to be aware that full mastery of English continues to present some small challenges for him; nevertheless, he is well on his way.

The final procedure used with Jason was a dynamic assessment that involved providing intervention for each of six tasks to see how he responded to these interventions. This was another way of looking at his levels of functioning, in addition to his responsiveness to instruction, with the intent of developing ideas for how to promote his competence. The first task of classification involved making groups with blocks that had a number of attributes, including color, shape, and size. Children function on this task as either "builders" or "groupers." Children are builders if they proceed to use the blocks for building despite the instructions to "show me how you can make groups with these blocks." Children are groupers if they proceed to sort the blocks according to some abstracted characteristic such as color, shape, or size. If they do not spontaneously group, the intervention works to teach them how to group. On this task Jason was a builder and remained a builder. He enjoyed the materials and showed an impressive degree of complexity and flexibility in producing his designs. Although he responded well to the intervention as it occurred, he did not transfer the grouping ideas into the posttest. To indicate how proud he was of what he made, he suggested that we "take a camera of this," meaning, of course, "photograph," but this illustrated the type of expressive language errors he at times would make. The assessor needed to work to hold his attention to the task, at least to the task as defined by the assessor. Relinquishing his own ideas to attend to the agenda of another was a mild challenge for Jason.

The next task asked the child to take on the role of teacher and teach the assessor how to draw a simple picture. The focus here was on the child's ability to communicate ideas to another and to communicate in a way that showed awareness of what the other person needed to know. The intervention provided a model for this type of communication. Jason did so well in his first attempt at this task that his failure to improve following the intervention only confirmed the stability of his high level of communication ability and sensitivity to another person. He would have shown postintervention gains if the picture had been different from the pretest picture; in his case, additional communications seemed repetitive to him and this led him to lapse into his own fantasies and agendas; nevertheless, he maintained his high level of functioning. (This task has since been modified to provide a different posttest picture.)

Jason showed dramatic gains in his responsiveness to the interventions for both of the rote memory tasks. In the case of the auditory memory activity, where he was asked to retell a short story, he came into the session with tornadoes on his mind, and the story quite coincidentally and unfortunately had a tornado in its content. (This task has since been modified.) This resulted in his getting stuck on this concept, although this only affected his performance negatively on the pretest. Once he was exposed to the intervention, he greatly improved his recall of the posttest; however, "tornado" was still the first word on his lips even for the posttest (although he did get beyond this). Getting Jason to improve on these tasks required significant input from the assessor because he very much wished to discuss his own ideas. The assessor needed to tell him "no, tell *my* story." For the visual memory task, he had entered the session with the themes from his classroom play on his mind, and this involved thoughts of danger, which significantly interfered with his ability to attend to the task. During the review of materials for the visual memory task, he showed some language confusion regarding the labels of the clothing items, mixing the words for shirt, skirt, and shorts.

The visual memory activity presented the most initial challenge, and finally had to be interrupted following the intervention. When this activity was resumed at the beginning of the next session, Jason was much more focused and did moderately well. He not only recalled most of the items presented but showed good use of strategies in his attempts to help himself remember them (he named each item to himself and interacted with the materials; these were two of the strategies demonstrated during the intervention). Jason also showed considerable improvement on the Verbal Planning task, where he needed to tell the plan for baking cookies. This proceeded so quickly and smoothly that he hardly noticed he was in a testing situation because he was generally comfortable about being involved in a conversation with some material support (pictures, in this case). His plan changed from "cook 'em and then eat them" for the pretest to "you get a cookie machine and when it's all ready you eat them and you get a little dessert" for the posttest. Thus, he showed improvement in his sequencing and elaboration and required no special management to keep him focused.

The final task of this procedure, Pattern Completion, presented considerable challenge for Jason, and this was the only instance when his level of functioning actually decreased following the intervention. It was very difficult to communicate the sequential nature of the patterns to him. The pattern pieces had a building or construction salience for him, and, when he would agree to sequence, he merely matched the last piece rather than focus on the pattern created over the sequence of pieces (for example, tall/short/tall/short/tall . . .). The visual and motor salience of the materials seemed to interfere with his ability to abstract and conceptualize; he wanted to dive in and construct. This was particularly evident following the intervention, when he became more able to say the correct sequence but would still not do it.

Working with Jason on these tasks revealed how much he brought to each task, and how necessary it was for the adult in the teacher role to try to map instructional goals onto his spontaneous ideas. He seemed to accommodate himself more to the agendas of others within his classroom, suggesting that the group pressure and his motivation to be a good classroom member worked well. Even within the classroom situation, the instructors need to be aware that he is often absorbed in his own thinking and may not be totally tuned into what the teachers want him to learn, so that some additional work may be necessary to switch, capture, and maintain his attention to the teacher's agenda.

There are times when the presence of manipulable materials may interfere with his ability to think, and his involvement with the manipulables may need to be restrained to help him focus on the more abstract concepts. Such interference was evident for both the classification and sequencing tasks, where it was very difficult for him to inhibit his desire to construct and build in the service of the abstract concepts of grouping and pattern completion. Perhaps if these were done with non-manipulable materials such as pictures, he would have had more success. These are not serious deficits and not so different from other young children his age but only indicative of relative areas of weakness and potential targets for instructional focus.

Recommendations

Jason is functioning very well and has made significant progress since entering his current program, particularly in his language and social skills. There are some areas that warrant further attention.

Given his early history of some possible tactile defensiveness and ongoing evidence of relative fine motor weakness, Jason would profit from at least an evaluation by an occupational therapist.

Attention to trying to put Jason with as many good native English speaker models as possible is recommended. This could be in the form of such things as play dates with children from his class or inclusion in summer programs and other recreational activities.

In the long run, his multilingual exposure should become an advantage, and it might even be a good idea for his father to become a German speaker with Jason to promote real bilingualism in him.

The combination of good memory ability and a learning style of "sit back and watch for a while" should also work in Jason's favor. These are ingredients for good learning, and those working with him just need to refrain from trying to push him into a new activity too forcefully at the beginning; it would be better to let him watch for a while and then find his time for more comfortable entry. He can even be asked if he's ready to try it.

Jason likes to use a familiar adult as a point of reference and for reaching out to new situations. He tends to seek proximity to his teacher and leans against even a relatively new "teacher" in approaching a new situation. Adults just need to be aware of this need or preference.

Transitions are a particular challenge for Jason. One approach to help him with this is to give him a routine of warnings whenever possible. Some agreed-on strategy, such as "three warning signals," is recommended when he needs to switch activities. For changes in location, he will similarly need to be prepared and talked through the change with advance notice and enthusiasm. Then, when it is time for the change, the adult needs to do this swiftly and authoritatively, without hesitation. "Now. It's time. Let's go" (hand held out and some pushing away from the old to point him toward the new).

Jason also seems to profit from the readiness of the classroom aide to follow up with him on directions given to the larger group; he needs the proximity of the adult to guide him to completion of an activity and to help him enter the new activity.

Jason would profit from specific attention to concepts of classification and pattern completion. A trial attempt with two- rather than three-dimensional materials is recommended to see whether these promote higher level thinking. There are relevant activities in the "Let's Think About It" program developed by this assessor and Jason's classroom teacher (provided).

There was some discussion about the possibility of considering grade retention for Jason. The agreement was to wait to see how he developed over the rest of the year. At this time, there is a mixed case for this decision.

On one hand, the research literature on retention is not generally support-ive of the effectiveness of this option; however, this does not mean that retention would not be a recommended decision for a specific individ-ual child. On the other hand, Jason is showing some neurodevelopmental immaturities that could profit from more time and attention. Children do develop in spurts, and it is too early to make a firm decision. The possi-bility was raised, and Jason's placement for the next school year will be discussed again further into the spring term.

Test Scores
Child Development Inventory Profile (age estimates):
Social: 2.1
Self-Help: 4.0
Gross Motor: 3.9
Fine Motor: 3.0
Expressive Language: 3.3
Language Comprehension: 4.5
Letters: 4.0
Numbers: 4–3
General Development: 3–6

Bracken Basic Concept Scale (partial) (Mean = 10; SD = 3)
School Readiness Composite:
Standard Score: 12; Percentile: 75
Direction/Position Concepts:
Standard Score: 10; Percentile: 50
   Kaufman Assessment Battery for Children
   Mental Processing Subscales/Scaled Scores (Mean = 10; SD = 3)
   Magic Window: 11
   Face Recognition: 11
   Hand Movements: 10
   Gestalt Closure: 13
   Number Recall: 14
   Triangles: 9
   Word Order: 15
   For the following scores, Mean = 100; SD = 15
   Sequential Processing, Standard Score: 119 (110–128); Percentile: 90
   Simultaneous Processing, Standard Score: 106 (96–116); Percentile: 66
   Nonverbal, Standard Score: 100 (89–111); Percentile Rank: 50

Beery-Buktenica Developmental Test of Visual-Motor Integration
(Mean = 100; SD = 15)
Standard Score: 78; Percentile Rank: 7

Oral and Written Language Scales (OWLS) (Mean = 100; SD = 15)
Listening Comprehension:
Standard Score: 103 (93–113); Percentile: 58
Oral Expression:
Standard Score: 106 (97–115); Percentile Rank: 66

NEPSY: A Developmental Neuropsychological Assessment
(M = 10; SD = 3)
Subscale Scaled Scores:
Body Part Naming: 11
Phonological Processing: 12
Visual Attention: 9
Comprehension/Instructions: 12
Narrative Memory: 10
Block Construction: 5
Sentence Repetition: 13
   For following scores, Mean = 100; SD = 15)
   Language: Domain Score/108 (99–115); Percentile Rank: 70
   Memory: Domain Score/109 (100–116); Percentile Rank: 73

CASE 6.2 [Contributed by Ruthanne H. Jepsen]

Name: Sonia (female)
Age: 9 years 5 months

Reason for Referral
Sonia was referred for an evaluation of her current level of intellectual
functioning and adaptive behavior to assist in developing a comprehensive educational treatment plan. Parents requested this evaluation to assist
in program placement determination for the following school year and
to provide recommendations for approaches that would facilitate Sonia's
learning and assist her in reaching her potential.

Background Information
Information was obtained through a clinical interview with Sonia's mother
and review of records. Sonia lives with her mother, father, and younger
sister. Her mother describes Sonia as a very active child who can be difficult
to manage because of her strong will and stubbornness. She expressed
concern that Sonia has not made sufficient progress in school.

   Pregnancy and delivery were without complication, and early development was within normal range. Until age 4 Sonia was an alert, inquisitive
child who enjoyed reading, playing with her sister, and riding her bike.

At age 4, Sonia sustained a traumatic brain injury from a motor vehicle accident. She experienced an immediate loss of consciousness and was comatose for approximately 2 to 3 weeks. Medical records indicated soft tissue swelling in the right frontal area, hematoma posterior to the area, possible brain stem sheering, and increased intracranial pressure; shunt placement was inserted and intracranial pressure monitored.

One month later, Sonia was transferred to a rehabilitation hospital for comprehensive inpatient rehabilitation. On admission, she needed assistance for dressing, grooming, bathing, toileting, eating, ambulating, transfers, and bed mobility. She demonstrated improvement in all areas throughout rehabilitation. Her status was characterized as Rancho Level 5 at discharge. For the next year, Sonia participated in a pediatric day treatment rehabilitation program 5 days a week.

On discharge Sonia participated in outpatient treatment rehabilitation programming in conjunction with her enrollment in preschool. Therapies included physical, occupational, and speech/language therapy three times per week. Although improvements were noted, Sonia showed persistent difficulty focusing and sustaining attention and a high level of activity. Recommendations were made to assess possible pharmacological intervention for treatment of attention-deficit/hyperactivity disorder. A 3-month trial on methylphenidate (Ritalin) had negative side effects (described by Sonia's mother as "zoning out") and was discontinued. At age 7, Sonia began taking an antihypertensive medication to address attention difficulties and hyperactivity.

At this time Sonia continues to receive the following therapies: occupational, physical, and speech/language therapy. According to her mother, Sonia is increasingly resistant during sessions, often refusing to participate in therapeutic activities. Therapist notes indicate that the intensity and frequency of noncompliant behaviors has increased as well as persisting difficulties with attention and hyperactivity. Sonia is not currently taking medication for these problems.

A neurolopsychological evaluation completed 2.5 months postinjury showed that Sonia demonstrated memory retrieval difficulties and variability in her acquisition of basic cognitive concepts, language, play, and psychomotor skills.

At 1 year and 6 months postinjury, Sonia enrolled in preschool 2 days per week in conjunction with attending the pediatric day treatment program 3 days a week. At this time, she had difficulties with attention and perseveration and poor safety awareness. She was described as physically active with difficulties focusing on task and following directions.

Sonia was evaluated to establish a life care plan. The neuropsychological evaluation revealed continued cognitive difficulties following injury.

The Wechsler Preschool and Primary Scale of Intelligence – Revised (WPPSI-R) was administered. Sonia obtained a Full Scale score of 63, Performance score of 60 and a Verbal score of 73. Her performance on verbal organization and verbal expression tasks appeared more intact than her performance on visual–spatial, visual motor, and visual organization tasks. Her best performance was on tasks requiring her to point to something missing from a picture. Acquisition of basic concepts measured by the Bracken Basic Concept Scale showed an understanding of size, quantity, direction/position, texture/material, and time/sequence concepts. Sonia was able to recall the names of two out of four objects after three trials. Hand dominance was not clearly established at this point. She was able to draw a circle with her right hand and ate at home using a utensil with her left hand.

It was noted that at this time she spoke in a loud voice but that her speech was generally intelligible. She was easily entertained with toys. Assistive devices consisted of bilateral ankle-foot orthoses and a protective helmet, which Sonia used when she played outside. She was described as a competitive child who could be stubborn and prone to temper outbursts when frustrated. She tended to perseverate and was typically hyperactive even in familiar surroundings. A structured, behavioral program was recommended for home and school to optimize Sonia's ability to learn.

At age 7, a neuropsychological examination included the administration of the WPPSI-R. Sonia obtained a Full Scale score of 51, Performance score of 50, and a Verbal score of 61. The report noted that her overall score profile was consistent with her previous performance on the WPPSI-R. Her verbal organization and verbal expression appeared more intact than her performance on visual–spatial, visual motor and visual organization tasks. She accurately identified one of four pictures on the Quick Test (QT), indicating a relative strength in receptive language ability and understanding of verbal information. Expressive speech was characterized by poor articulation and sound substitutions. Poor attention and distractibility during testing were noted as affecting her performance as well as difficulty on memory tasks. Adaptive behavior, measured by the Vineland Adaptive Behavior Scales, showed a relative strength in socialization compared to daily living skill and communication domains. At this time Sonia was taking antihypertensive medication to treat difficulties with hyperactivity in home and school.

Sonia currently is enrolled in the second grade. Academically she is working on counting skills and accurate coin identification. She has more than 50 sight words and is beginning to work on identifying the beginning and ending sounds in written and spoken words. School records indicate continued problems in her behavior in school; Sonia is described as generally compliant to regular tasks and responds to strict rules and clearly defined behavioral boundaries. Areas of concern continued to be "perseverating, interrupting, and difficulty remaining on task and 'disruptive behaviors.'"

Classroom Observation

Sonia attends a self-contained classroom where assistance is provided to help her learn academic concepts. She is also integrated into regular classroom activities where she receives the assistance of a one-to-one aide. She was observed in her second-grade classroom placement. She was aware of her environment and spent a great deal of time watching her classmates and walking over to pay attention to the classroom pet gerbil. She did not engage in activities unless encouragement and prompts were provided. When prompted, she was cooperative and acted appropriately. The teacher reported that Sonia generally required multiple directions to follow classroom rules and completed assignments. During a small group activity, listening to poems read from a large picture book, she was eager to get up and point to characters described in the poem. Her classmates raised their hands to volunteer and Sonia picked up cues from her peers and began to raise her hand but often got up before being called upon. With multiple verbal redirections, she was able to wait until called on by her teacher. When asked to describe the picture, Sonia's responses were concrete with little elaboration.

During academic instruction, Sonia had difficulty following directions, which required her to find items related to the month of September, write the word, and then color the corresponding item in the picture. The multistepped direction seemed to lead to confusion. Sonia was distracted by activity in the room and had difficulty with the sequence of writing the word before coloring the item. Classmates were at various stages in the assignment, and when she noticed that they were coloring, she would pick up a crayon and begin to color. She would state that she was finished and seek adult approval. When other students began to bring their papers to the teacher, Sonia was frequently directed to return to task and provided assistance and reassurance; she would skip steps in an effort to turn in her work. Sonia's focus was no longer on completing the task but how to turn in her paper and talk to her friends.

A paradox was noted in both classroom settings. Sonia relied on her environment for cues while at the same time activities and things in the environment distracted her focus.

Clinical Observations

As the focus of this evaluation was to assist teachers and parents by providing insight on how Sonia processed information and her response to learning, the assessment component of the evaluation was completed in two sessions. This provided time to accommodate for fatigue through scheduling ample opportunities for breaks to reduce fatigue. It also presented the opportunity to observe Sonia's responses to standardized test questions and in a dynamic assessment or mediated learning environment. Both sessions ran approximately 90 minutes. In comparing her performance on two occasions, there were differences in Sonia's ability to sustain attention and work through challenging tasks. Sonia required frequent breaks when working in standardized test format. In the dynamic assessment format, she often stated that she did not want to take a break.

Sonia was accompanied to the evaluation by her parents. She easily separated from them and seemed to enjoy the one-to-one attention the testing atmosphere provided. She was a talkative, charming child, eager to please, and responsive to encouragement and praise. Her speech was at times difficult to understand. She tended to glide the medial consonant, reduce syllables, and substitute consonants (e.g., K/t, g/d, and s/f).

Once she saw the test materials, Sonia tried to change the topic, referring to items of personal interest. We set up a schedule of breaks or talk time, which seemed to help maintain effort and reduce her comments. Generally breaks were taken following each subscale. She was quite social and enjoyed social interaction. This gave the assessor an opportunity to get to know her interests. Sonia continues to enjoy her doll and playing with her sister but no longer rides her bike, although "this was something I really liked before the accident."

Sonia's approach to standardized test material was to answer a question immediately. She did not ask for clarification and relied on trial-and-error guesses rather than establishing a consistent approach. She did not take time to scan items before task initiation, nor did she check her work. Her rather unsystematic ("let me get this done as quickly as possible") approach did not vary between timed and untimed subscales. When test items became increasingly demanding, her concentration decreased, and her motivation and efforts shifted to attempts to avoid the task, behaviors also observed in the classroom. Sonia often asked when the test would be over, stating, "Too hard, finished, I'm tired." She was easily distracted, engaged in off-task behaviors such as leaving her seat. With supportive redirection and reassurance Sonia was able to continue working and refocus on materials. Redirection required verbal directions coupled with a gesture indicating one more.

In our second session, Sonia was initially apprehensive. This was the dynamic assessment using the ACFS, and she enjoyed the learning activities. As the session progressed, she became an increasingly cheerful, happy learner. She did not attempt to avoid tasks and worked diligently and did not request breaks, nor did she need to be redirected to task. She was motivated and responded to encouragement and praise. Sonia enjoyed feeling successful, and her sense of accomplishment maintained her motivation. She was thoroughly pleased when she answered a question correctly and showed gains in learning and trying new strategies. Her approach changed to more careful observation, precise description of task requirements, and the basics of sequential planning and problem solving. She often requested "one more," demonstrating that when engaged in materials she was able to focus and that she retained and applied past experiences to present situations.

Tests Administered
- Cognitive Assessment System (CAS)
- AAMR Adaptive Behavior Scale (ABS-S 2)
- Applications of Cognitive Functions Scale (ACFS) Dynamic Assessment Procedure
- Draw a Person

Cognitive Assessment System
The CAS was administered to obtain a measure of Sonia's current cognitive function. The CAS provides an assessment that requires minimal acquired knowledge so that the child will not fail the test for lack of information. The test is designed to assess cognitive processes and provide an overall measure of intelligence called the Full-Scale Score (FS). The FS is a standard score based on an equally weighted composite of Planning, Attention, Simultaneous, and Successive subscales. The scale has a normative mean of 100 and a standard deviation of 15. Subscales correlate with the structure of cognitive materials used in the classroom and provide a cognitive profile for educational planning and instruction. Sonia's FS of 43 was in the deficit range of cognitive functioning.

CAS – Full scale and subscale areas	Standard score
Full Scale	43
Planning	51
Simultaneous processing	62
Attention	49
Successive processing	65

Planning: This measures the ability to make a plan of action, apply the plan, check accuracy or effectiveness of the plan, and modify or change the plan as needed. The three subscales included paper-and-pencil tasks. (1) Number matching task composed of six numbers per row in which Sonia was asked to find the matching numbers. (2) Coding task required Sonia to fill corresponding codes in empty boxes on an answer grid. (3) Planned connections, number, and number–letter sequencing tasks similar to the Trail Making Test of the Halstead-Reitan test battery.

In matching numbers, she initially scanned the entire row of numbers but focused on the first three numbers as the digits increased in length. On coding tasks, she coded neatly and slowly, by referring to the model at the top of the page before entering a code. On planned connections, she seldom scanned the page for the next number or letter or looked back to the last number or letter.

Sonia obtained scores reflecting that her ability to apply planning strategies effectively was limited at that time. She was able to follow directions and develop a plan but had difficulty self-regulating and modifying her responses. Thus, once she established a plan, Sonia had difficulty altering her strategy. This indicates that she had not yet acquired the cognitive strategies to assess and alter her approach to solving problems.

Simultaneous Processing: This measures the ability to integrate separate stimuli into a meaningful Gestalt. The activities have spatial, logical-grammatical, and memory components. The spatial aspect involves perception of visual images, pictures, geometric shapes, and matrixes. Sonia recognized relationship patterns within a matrix but often failed to discern subtle differences between responses necessary to select the correct form to complete the spatial matrix. Her performance worsened when the spatial aspect involved perception of patterns across horizontal and vertical dimensions involving geometric shapes of varying color and shape. Her score on logical grammatical dimensions was similar. Figure memory was a difficult task for Sonia. She remembered the original figure imbedded in a geometric design. She verbally identified the original figure but proceeded to trace the entire design. It appeared that the salience of the material in front of her overrode her ability to retain the instruction and the single shape.

Attention: This measures the ability to focus, inhibit a response, shift attention, and recognize irrelevant or competing stimuli. The subscales include verbalizing size when an interfering visual stimulus is presented, a number detection paper-and-pencil task was used involving identification of numbers and differentiation of numerical script and a receptive attention task identifying letters that look the same and letters that sound the same. Sonia showed vulnerability to interference effects on these measures.

Her accuracy deteriorated and errors of commission increased as she progressed through the tasks. She worked diligently, and her persistence indicated that although she can sustain attention, she has difficulty shifting and dividing her attention.

Successive Processing: This measures the ability to sequence verbal information, retain information in short-term memory, and comprehend a serial sequence presented verbally. The subscales include repeating a sequence of unrelated words, repeating sentences, and answering questions that demand comprehension of a sentence based on the serial placement of words. Sonia showed vulnerability to interference effects on these measures. She was able to repeat four words in the correct sequence and short sentences composed of color words. Her accuracy deteriorated with the increase in the number of items and length of sentence. Errors of commission increased as she progressed through the problems. Comprehension of sentences was more difficult. Sonia answered these questions concretely. For example, she accurately repeated the sentence, "the white is blue," but when asked, "What is blue?" she responded "the sky."

Sonia's current cognitive profile indicates relative strengths in successive and simultaneous processing. At this time, she has difficulty applying and understanding basic principles of problem solving. It is not that she is unable to make a plan, but it is her ability to alter or modify a plan once a task is initiated that creates difficulty. In the area of attention, Sonia is able to focus but has difficulty sustaining and dividing her attention. For example, when given a problem that requires shifting attention between elements of a task or from one task to another, she tends to rush ahead. This leads to failure to inhibit this first response so that she can accurately initiate a second. Her difficulty sustaining and alternating attention and developing a successful planning strategy contributes to her impatience and difficulty staying on topic.

ACFS Dynamic Assessment
Using a dynamic assessment, pretest–mediation–posttest format provided an opportunity to work with Sonia in a learning situation. Information derived from the previous tests indicated that Sonia's strengths were in skills that require verbal and visual spatial abilities. She had relative difficulties on tasks that required divided attention, memory, visual search, and attending to detail. Through the dynamic assessment procedure, we hoped to ascertain whether application of her strengths could improve her performance.

The ACFS includes subscales that tap interacting cognitive processing areas: classification, pattern completion, visual and auditory memory, planning, and perspective taking. The dynamic format provides information regarding responsiveness to learning opportunities. Sonia was very responsive to the functional format of the ACFS; the materials sustained her attention and focus throughout this portion of the assessment.

On pretests Sonia's initial approach to tasks reflected the same impulsive approach seen in the classroom and on her performance on the CAS, which indicated a limited awareness of the need to seek various methods of problem solving, gathering information, and sequencing steps.

Classification: This provides an opportunity to group blocks of varying sizes, shapes, and colors. On the pretest, Sonia grouped all blocks by color. During the mediation, we first focused on how the blocks were the same and different. We then discussed noticing that groups can change. As we worked together, she demonstrated an understanding of the concepts of color, size, and number. Following mediation she was able to regroup by size and shape, often stating the number of items in a group.

Visual Memory: Assesses the ability to apply memory strategies to recall objects. Given the pretest direction that we were going to try to remember eight toys placed on the table, Sonia briefly scanned the items and then indicated that she knew them. The items were removed, and she could recall none. During mediation, we worked with concepts of repetition, categorization, and creating mental images by telling stories about the items. Sonia's response was enthusiastic. It appeared that using memory strategies was a novel and enjoyable experience. On the posttest, when items were removed, she was able to recall all eight. At the end of the session, she volunteered that she could still remember the toys and recalled six items. Her response indicated that visual memory skills could be improved using the stated strategies.

Auditory Memory: This assesses the ability to recall characters and sequences in a short story. On the pretest, Sonia was given the direction that we were going to try to remember a story about "A Little Toy Train." She listened carefully but recalled only two characters. During mediation, we worked with the strategy of using geometric shapes to represent characters symbolically. Sonia used the concept of creating a symbol; however, once she created a representation it reminded her of other things (e.g., computer game characters). We discussed when it was important to stay on topic: in school, when following directions, and when learning to play a new game. Sonia was able to refocus. On the posttest, she commented that she had to "stay with the story," and her recall of the story improved slightly. Sonia recalled six of the main characters in the story in the correct sequence.

Pattern Completion: On the pattern completion subscale, Sonia was eager to begin the task; she talked about what she was going to do and completed patterns that required matching colors and simple geometric forms. Mediation involved encouraging Sonia to discuss the elements of each model and verbalize relationships before attempting a solution. She was encouraged to use systematic exploratory strategies to define the problem by noticing relationships. By using verbal description, she was able to grasp quickly the principle underlying a problem. On the posttest Sonia's performance showed marked improvement. She completed all the pattern problems. More important was her consistency in carrying over the strategies of scanning and verbalizing each problem. Her precision and restraint of impulsivity were noted in the accuracy of her responses. She completed patterns that involved recognition of color, shape, and size sequences and was confident in her ability to recognize patterns between geometric shapes. During the mediation, we first focused on how the blocks were the same and different.

Planning: This requires the development of a sequence of steps to complete a task. On the pretest, the task involved purchasing candy from a vending machine using picture card cues (old version). Sonia placed the first and last card correctly and used few sequence or planning words. Her focus was on the type of candy bar she preferred. During mediation, we worked on the example of planning and sequencing making cookies. We first discussed making cookies with her mother and familiar items in the kitchen. On the posttest she applied this same process, placing the cards correctly when describing how to purchase candy from a vending machine.

Perspective Taking: This involves giving instructions to draw a picture from a model requiring the awareness of others when providing directions. On the pretest, Sonia copied the model, drawing without regard to the presence of the examiner. Mediation involved understanding the role of the teacher. Following mediation, she provided instructions and checked my work to see that I was accurately doing as directed.

The ACFS provided further insight to Sonia's learning strengths and deficits. Her performance on the auditory and verbal memory pretest tasks revealed that despite poor memory performance, Sonia's scores improved following mediation. There is a wide zone of proximal development, or difference between what Sonia was able to do independently and what she was able to accomplish with the assistance of cognitive strategies. These strategies involved relating tasks to activities in her environment, home, and school and providing visual and verbal strategies to help her make meaning of the task. Language was a strength that helped Sonia to execute activities accurately and confidently. She demonstrated good imitative skills. Awareness of her environment helped her notice the inherent properties of the materials. Discussing task demands and materials helped her to understand and orient her attention to the task, as did the sequence of directions and suggestions provided during mediation.

To provide structure, we discussed the underlying rules and strategies of how to begin and complete the task. With enhanced understanding, she was able to remain focused on the task and own the problem as well as gain confidence in her responses. Effort and frustration decreased when she could relate the order of steps and time to discuss how to organize her approach so that she found the correct solution. Her responsiveness revealed that she was capable of learning more quickly when encouraged to think about thinking.

Generally Sonia was able to focus her attention on multiple units of information and apply rule-based problem solving. Her engagement in the interactive mediation activities as shown by taking turns and listening to instructions, and her use of strategies on the posttest measures showed that with supports, she is an active learner. Her overall performance indicates that she is able to learn and apply new knowledge.

Draw a Person

The Draw a Person is a projective tool that provides some insight into how an individual views himself, others, and his or her relation to the world. It involves three pencil drawings with the student providing a brief description of each. Sonia's drawings were primitive and rapidly done. All of the figures were large and drawn filling the entire page. Her figures had large heads, eyes, mouths, arms, torsos, and legs. The age of the first person drawn was a 16-year-old girl; the second was a drawing of a man, her father, was 50 years old; and the third was a picture of herself at 16. None of the figures showed action or mobility. In contrast to her drawing of a girl and man, Sonia's self-drawing depicted a larger head. While completing the drawing, she became absorbed with making small lines radiating along the side of the "head." When questioned as to what these might represent, Sonia stated that she had "changed, just found out that she was still smart and decided to draw her thoughts, too." When asked what the people were doing, she stated that they were "happy about being able to drive a car and go lots of places." Her descriptions of her drawings suggest that she is looking forward. The ages indicate this view toward the future. The lack of detail and mobility indicate that Sonia's view, although concrete, includes having the hope that someday she will go places. The drawings were done immediately following the ACFS mediation and may reflect the success she had previously experienced.

AAMR Adaptive Behavior Scale

The ABS was administered with Sonia's mother as informant to obtain insight into her ability to cope with the demands of her environment and apply knowledge in daily situations. The ABS is a rating scale to assess independent functioning and social and personal adaptive behavior. The survey yields a standard score with a mean of 10 based on comparisons with same-aged peers without disabilities.

Domain	Standard score	Rating
Independent Functioning	6	Below average
Physical Development	11	Average
Economic Activity	7	Below average
Language Development	6	Below average
Numbers and Time	7	Below average
Prevocational Activity	7	Below average
Self-Direction	9	Average
Responsibility	8	Average
Socialization	6	Below average

Part I of the ABS indicated that Sonia was functioning in the average to below average range of adaptive behavior. Her scores reflected efficacy in practically applying knowledge gained in the classroom, language, and number and time concepts and lower scores in areas of self-help and responsibility. She was able to comply with daily demands of self-help or independent functions, although at this time she requires supervision to monitor and complete tasks. Item analysis showed that her skills in use of household appliances such as care of clothing were less developed. Her motor and sensory skills did not impede her ability to participate in routine activities. She understood and communicated her opinions, made requests, and was generally understood by others. Her understanding of numbers and time indicated that she was able to follow a daily schedule or routine. She was responsible and aware of her environment. She was able to occupy herself by reading simple stories and playing computer games. She participated in a narrowed range of social activities but had difficulty taking turns and sharing with others. She knew the rules of games but became upset if she did not get her way. She was motivated to be independent but had limited opportunities to acquire skills because most self-help tasks were performed for her. Sonia has a good vocabulary and expressed her opinions and ideas.

Part II of the ABS measures maladaptive behavior. This scale indicated that Sonia demonstrated no maladaptive behavior that was atypical of children her age, although items across domains that resulted in lower scores were related to noncompliance, refusal to follow directions or complete tasks, and hyperactive behavior. All have an effect on skill acquisition. Item analysis of the scores indicated that in addition to noncompliance, she had a few inappropriate interpersonal manners such as hyperactivity that could affect her success in school or unstructured situations.

Factor analysis of responses indicated that in the area of Personal Self-Sufficiency, Sonia demonstrated the ability to take care of herself on a daily basis with the support given a typical 9-year-old. The area of Personal-Social Responsibility is a relative strength. Sonia demonstrated the social and interpersonal skills needed to establish and maintain friendships and participate in group activities. Behaviors related to Community Self-Sufficiency or the ability to interact with others and use community resources were a relative weakness. These skills would be necessary for her to move beyond her immediate home environment. Such behaviors that involve community awareness and safety can be taught through the home and school. Proficiency in skills assessed by this factor is indicative of full or at least partial normalization into society.

General Impression
Sonia was a 9-year, 5-month-old girl who was functioning within the mildly retarded range of intelligence and demonstrated below average to average skills in adaptive behavior. Her performance on standardized measures showed scores in the deficit range with weaknesses in attention and planning. Her response to mediation indicated that she had potential to improve her planning and memory skills. During mediation, Sonia demonstrated that she was able to learn and enjoyed learning and working with an adult. Her strengths in successive processing and social awareness permitted her to gain knowledge about her environment and motivate her participation and perseverance. She could apply cognitive strategies in learning new information and focus attention and effort. She was able to inhibit her tendency to use a trial-and-error tactic and analyze components of a problem systematically. Her ability to reason and solve problems improved when tasks had meaning and functional cues were present. When provided structured supports, Sonia was motivated to work to accomplish tasks. Her response to applying memory strategies and verbal self-cueing reinforced her sense of self-direction and encouraged her to take responsibility for solving problems.

Recommendations
- Sonia would benefit from inclusion in a regular school program. Participation in individualized instruction should be part of this program. This coordination of instruction and intervention strategies would provide the consistency she requires to learn and integrate new material.
- To enhance focus, encourage Sonia to describe elements of a problem before working on the task. This approach builds on strengths to build up areas that are currently weak, and it is important to capitalize on her strengths in successive processing and verbal skills.
- Encourage Sonia to make associations with other tasks and activities in home and school. This will help her to develop her vocabulary, word associations, cognitive flexibility, and attention.
- Sonia is able to label items accurately, recognize color, shape, size, and pattern, and count. Provide opportunities before initiating tasks for

her to demonstrate these skills. Emphasis on accurate labeling and identification of objects and concepts will increase her understanding or task meaning.

- When introducing new materials, skills, or applications of current skills, instruction should involve sequencing steps and framing directions that make connections to familiar skills to encourage self-direction in working through problems. Frame directions and provide a concrete sequence of steps.
- When presenting tasks, review and discuss the meaning and demands of the task and how Sonia will approach the task to do her best work. Review task demands at the beginning of each lesson.
- Instruction should provide functional applications of academic work introduced in the classroom as well as introduce visual and verbal strategies to initiate and complete tasks. Functional examples and manipulative materials should be used wherever possible, and materials should be presented through a multisensory approach that integrates tactile, motor, visual, and auditory input and skills.
- When presenting worksheets, ask Sonia to look at the page, notice important features, and discuss her observations. Encourage accurate visual scanning by discussing items from left to right and top to bottom of the page.
- Minimize the number of items on a page and review when the items are completed.
- Sonia responds to a structured approach in which compliance is anticipated. She has developed mild manipulative behaviors to avoid challenges. Parents and teachers should set realistic expectations for task completion such as allowing her to take one more turn or make one more attempt before asking Sonia to evaluate her work to determine whether she has followed directions or completed the task before allowing her to escape from demands.
- Sonia is keenly aware of her environment and attends to environmental cues. She relies upon these cues to help give her direction and structure. To facilitate attention, minimize distractions in her environment and schedule activities to minimize fatigue, work in a designated area with minimal distractions to help Sonia sustain concentration and inhibit attention to competing stimuli.
- Sonia will do best in a supportive environment that minimizes conflicting visual and auditory distractions (e.g., noise, distracting material in her work space, proximity of peers when working). When possible, introduce new tasks in settings that lend logical support to the activity.
- If possible, schedule academic instruction and introduction of new educational material in the morning when Sonia is more alert and eager to learn. When fatigue is a factor, provide short breaks and return to the

task. It may be necessary to intersperse high-interest activities to maintain momentum and motivation.

- Provide organizational supports through color-coding work and keeping work samples in color-coded binders.
- An orientation to the daily schedule will help Sonia organize her day and prepare for transitions. A schedule of the day's activities can facilitate organization and provide awareness of sequences. Review the schedule on arrival to school and refer back to the schedule before transitions. (Example: Use a picture schedule that includes the time and a math problem for math, a book for reading, and so on.)
- A posted schedule of the daily routine at home will help Sonia to sequence and refer to steps so that she can check these herself. She should be encouraged to groom independently, take care of her toys, and assist in chores. Sonia is motivated to be independent. Functional learning through telling time, cooking, sequenced cleaning tasks, and other activities of daily living will increase her sense of accomplishment as well as provide direct application of concepts introduced in school.
- Sonia's ability to retain new information and general memory can be enhanced through practice of memory strategies that include
  - Repetition – repeating the name of an item three times
  - Categorization – placing items to be remembered in categorical groups
  - Visualization – begin with concrete visual models then move to more abstract representations as Sonia becomes increasingly successful
  - Keep in mind that it may take Sonia longer than others to respond. Wait for her to initiate a response before providing assistance or verbal prompts.

APPLICATION OF COGNITIVE FUNCTIONS SCALE (ACFS) ADMINISTRATION MANUAL

Authors: Carol S. Lidz and Ruthanne H. Jepsen

GENERAL INTRODUCTION

Say to the child:

"We are going to work together on four (modify number if supplemental tasks are included) different activities. Some of these activities might be a little hard, but I think you'll have fun with them. Each time we start something new, I'll ask you to do it first all by yourself. Then I get to be the teacher, and we'll work on it together. Then I'll ask you to do it again all by yourself. Let's try the first one so you can see how it goes."[1]

---

[1] A list of materials and their sources is on the last page of this chapter.

I. Function: CLASSIFICATION

MATERIALS:

Pretest and Posttest: 26 wooden blocks.

> The blocks should vary in color (red, green, blue, and yellow), shape (circle, square, triangle, and rectangle), and size (tall or big and short or little). Each characteristic should appear across other characteristics.

Intervention:

> One set of Attribute Blocks varying on the characteristics of color, size, and shape.

PRETEST:

Place blocks in front of the child and say:

> "Do you know what these are?" (Wait for a response)

> "Right! These are blocks. We can do many things with blocks. We can build with them, and we can count with them. We're going to use these blocks for making groups. Show me how you can make groups with these blocks."

Score the child's response [Download Form 6.1].

> ⇒ If the child does not group the blocks or builds with the blocks, score the child's production and go directly to the intervention.

> ⇒ Note gradation in scoring (building items 1–3) and grouping (items 4–6)

If the child did group the blocks, say:

> "Fine. Now, let's mix them all up. Show me a different way that you can make groups with these blocks."

Score the child's response.

> ⇒ If the child made the same classification groups, score and go directly to the intervention.

If the child grouped by different criteria, say,

> "Great! That was good. Can you think of a different way to make groups with these blocks?"

> ⇒ If the child grouped by different criteria, the ceiling has been reached. Go on to the next subscale and do not do the intervention.

> ⇒ If the child made the same classification groups, go on to the intervention.

INTERVENTION

For all children: Put the blocks away (out of sight). Take out Attribute Blocks. Spill them out in mixed order in front of the child.

Say:

> "That was very good. Now I get to be the teacher, and we'll talk about making groups. A group is when things belong together. We might have a group of people or a group of bananas or a group of crayons. Something about the things in our group is the same. Let's think about all the different ways we can make groups with these pieces. I notice that these have different colors, different shapes, and different sizes. This means we can make color groups, shape groups, and size groups. Let's make a group with the same color."

> ⇒ If the child can proceed on his or her own to make the color group, let the child do it.
> ⇒ If the child has difficulty, the assessor should start the group and let the child add to it.
> ⇒ If the child has already made a group during the Pretest using one attribute, acknowledge what the child did and carry out the intervention on the other attributes.

After completing a group, say:

> "Now let's change what we notice and make some shape groups."

> ⇒ The examiner may start each group and then ask the child to continue.
> ⇒ Continue the procedure for size.

> "See how you learned to change what you noticed about the pieces so you can make different groups? One time we noticed the color and made color groups. Next time we noticed the shape and made shape groups. Then we noticed the size and made 'big and little' groups. Now it's time for you to make groups all by yourself."

POSTTEST:

Give child the posttest set of blocks.

Say:

> "Here are the blocks again. Show me how you can make groups with these."

Score the child's response.

> ⇒ If the child builds, move on to the next function.
> ⇒ If the child makes groups based on one of the attributes, mix up the blocks.

Say:

> "Great! What did you notice about these? Fine. Now show me another way you can make groups with these."

Score the child's response.

> ⇒ If the child succeeds in changing the basis for grouping, ask one more time and score the response.

II. Function: AUDITORY MEMORY/STORY RETELLING

MATERIALS:

> Box of Magneforms and magnet board from Magneform storage box
>
> The Story: from "The Little Toy Train" (John Speirs, *Margaret Wise Brown Treasury, 14 Classic Stories and Poems*. Racine, WI: Western Publishing. (A Gold Key Book).

> **The Toy Train**
>
> In the little green house lived a cat and a mouse,
> A girl and a boy, and a man with a little toy train.
> One day the train ran away.
> It was a very little train.
> So it ran down a mouse hole.
> And the cat and the mouse and the girl and the boy
> And the man who were all very little too
> Ran down the mouse hole after the little toy train.

PRETEST:

Say:

> "I'm going to read you a story. Does anyone read you stories at home or school?"
>
> ⇒ Take time to explore the child's experience with listening to stories.
>
> "Well, this is a story called "The Little Toy Train." Listen very carefully, and when I'm all done, I want you to tell me the story."

Read the story to the child with expression, but just as it is written with no elaboration or questioning.

Say:

> "Now you tell the story to me. Just tell me what you remember. You'll get a chance to hear it again, so don't worry if you can't tell it all."

Record number of correct items recalled (number each item recalled so that the order of recall is recorded). [Download Form 6.2]

INTERVENTION:

Use the Magneform board and magnetic pieces. The child represents main elements of the story with these pieces (the house, girl, boy, man, cat, mouse, toy train and circular piece for the mouse hole, placed over each character as they "disappear down the mouse hole").

Say:

> "See this? This is a magnet board and some magnetic pieces that we will place on the board." (Demonstrate.)

> "We are going to use these pieces to help you remember the story I just read to you. I'll read the story again. This time, each time I tell a part of the story, I'll help you find one or two of these pieces to put on the board; that will be a symbol, or a reminder to help you remember the story. We're not going to make the whole picture. We're only going to use one or two pieces to remind you about what happens in the story."

Proceed to read the story, pausing after each element to find two pieces. Encourage the child to select the pieces as symbols, but provide help as needed. Make sure the pieces have some resemblance to the story element, but remind the child that we are not making the whole picture. Put away the unused pieces.

Say:

> "OK. We have all our reminder symbols. Now I'll read the story one more time, and you touch the symbol for each part of the story that I read."

Proceed, helping the child to find the appropriate symbol.

Say:

> "Great, now you tell me the story, and use the symbols to help you remember." Provide help as needed to move the child through the correct sequence of the story.

Remove the pieces.

> "Now I'll put these symbols away and leave the magnet board here."

POSTTEST:

Say:

> "Fine. Now we can't see the symbols. They are all inside your brain. Tell me the story just one more time." If the child struggles, provide a cue by pointing to the location on the board where the story begins.

Score the child's response.

IMPORTANT:

Carry out DELAYED RECALL following the Visual Memory subscale.

III. Function: SHORT-TERM VISUAL MEMORY

Materials: Two sets of eight laminated pictures to include two groupings each [Download Figure 6.3]:

Set 1:   Animals (Rabbit, Horse, Duck, Pig)
   Transportation (Car, Train, Airplane, Boat)

Set 2:   Foods (Grapes, Banana, Strawberry, Orange)
   Clothing (Slacks, Shirt, Dress, Shoes)

PRETEST:

Place Set 1 in front of the child in randomized (mixed or nongrouped) order.

Say:

"Here are some pictures. First, tell me the name of each picture."

⇒ Wait to see if the child knows the name

⇒ If not, provide it and encourage the child to repeat it.

Say:

"We're going to play a hide and remember game. I'm going to hide these pictures, and then you need to remember and tell me the names of the pictures that were here. OK? Now, before I hide them, show me how you can help yourself remember all of these pictures."

⇒ Wait to see what the child does.

⇒ If the child hesitates, say: "Now, remember. I'm going to take these away, and you need to remember them. How can you help yourself remember them?"

⇒ Hide the pictures. Place them in your lap or behind a screen.

Say:

"Now tell me the names of the pictures."

Score the child's response [Download Form 6.3].

INTERVENTION:

Put Set 2 in front of the child in randomized order.

Say:

"Now it's my turn to be teacher again. We're going to talk about how to remember what we see. Here are some new pictures. Tell me the names of these."

Wait for child's response.

"If we want to remember all of these pictures, how can we do that?"

⇒ Wait for response.

Regardless of response, say:

"When I want to remember many things like this, I look at them and say their names over and over again to myself and I can close me eyes when I say them and make a picture in my brain."

⇒ Demonstrate and encourage child to do this.

Say:

"Another thing that helps me to remember is to think of how the pictures go together. Do you remember when we made groups of blocks? We can make groups with these pictures."

⇒ If the child does not spontaneously group the pictures, the assessor starts to form two groups and hands the child a picture to place in the correct group.

⇒ Provide as much help as necessary.

Point to the food group. Say:

"Why did I put these in one group? These are all _____."

⇒ Wait for the child to respond.

⇒ If the child does not give a correct response, provide prompt (things we eat), then identify group, (foods).

Point to the clothes. Say:

"Now, why did I put these together? These are all _____."

⇒ Wait for the child to respond.

⇒ If the child does give the correct response provide prompt (things we wear) then identify group (clothing).

Say:

"Good. It helps when we make groups. Now there are only two groups to remember. Let's talk about the things in our groups. What do you notice about them? We can say something about each of them to help us remember them when we can't see them anymore."

⇒ Review pictures with the child to help the child notice and say something about each one.

Say:

"Now I'll hide these and you tell me which ones you remember."

Record child's response (write in empty space somewhere on score sheet).

POSTTEST:

Say:

"OK. Now let's go back and look at the pictures I showed you before."

With Set 1: Have the child say the name of each picture.

Then say:

"I'll hide these again and you tell me their names. I want you to tell me the names of these pictures again. First, show me how you will help yourself remember these pictures."

⟹ Wait for the child to show a memory strategy.

⟹ If no strategy is shown, proceed.

Score child's response.

IMPORTANT:

Administer delayed memory for AUDITORY MEMORY/Story Retelling Subscale

Say:

"Now, before we do our next work, I want you to try to remember the story I read to you before. The name of the story was "The Little Toy Train." Now tell me what you remember from that story. What happened?" (Be sure to provide sufficient wait time.)

IV. Function: SEQUENTIAL PATTERN COMPLETION

MATERIALS:

⟹ Tangram Set for Pretest and Posttest

⟹ Items (there are 12 patterns, 2 per set); [Download Figure 6.1]

⟹ Intervention: $8\frac{1}{2}$ × 11–inch unlined white paper and box of six primary color crayons

PRETEST:

Place pieces of each item in front of child, with choices placed under the patterned pieces in the order indicated.

⟹ Administer the first item of each set. If the child makes the correct choice, go on to the first item of the next set (Child gets 2 points).

⟹ Administer the second item in a set only when the child does not make a correct choice on the first item in the set (Child gets 1 point if correct, 0 if incorrect).

⟹ After pattern pieces are laid out, cover choice pieces with your hand during directions.

Say:

"Look at these." (Point to each piece.)

Say:

"Try to figure out what comes next. Pick one of these pieces to show what comes next."

If the child makes the correct choice, ask:

"Right. Why did you pick that one? Why was that the best one?"

Score the child's response [Download Form 6.4]. Continue using the same format on consecutive items until a ceiling of failing two consecutive sets has been reached.

After the items are completed, lead the child into the intervention. Say:

"Now we get to talk and learn about this kind of work."

INTERVENTION:

Materials: Paper and box of six primary color crayons

Say:

"This work helps us learn about patterns. A pattern tells us when something happens again and again. Patterns help us figure out what comes next."

"Suppose we have weather that goes:

Sun, rain, sun, rain, sun, _____. What do you think comes next?"
If the child answers correctly, say: "Right!"
If the child answers incorrectly, repeat and then give the correct response. "Sun, rain, sun, rain, sun, rain"

Continue and say:

"Suppose I throw the ball to: girl, boy, girl, boy, girl, _____. Who gets the ball next?"
If the child answers correctly, say: "Right! Good!"
If the child answers incorrectly repeat then give the correct response. "Girl, boy, girl, boy, girl, boy."

Continue and say:

"Suppose I clap my hands like this: Up." (Clap hands in front of your chest.) "Down." (Clap hands on your lap.) "Up, Down, Up, _____. What will I do next?"

If the child answers incorrectly, repeat and provide the correct response.

Say:

"Let's work on some more patterns together."

For the following activities:

⇒ If the child makes an error, the assessor says the pattern, emphasizing with voice the rhythm of the pattern (e.g., STICK, circle, STICK, circle...)

⇒ After completion of each pattern, the assessor should have the child say the pattern aloud, together with the assessor.

⇒ If child is not able to complete the pattern, the assessor should provide as much help as is needed.

Activity 1: Draw circles with alternating colors (yellow, black, yellow, black, yellow, _____.

Say:

"Let's say the pattern together. What comes next?"

Activity 2: Take out another sheet of paper.

Say:

"Now if I draw the pattern: line, circle, line, circle, line, _____, let's say the pattern; tell me what comes next." (Provide help as needed.)

Activity 3: Take out a new sheet of paper. Draw: Big circle, little circle, big circle, little circle, big circle.

Say:

"Now say this pattern and tell me what comes next."

Activity 4: Take out another sheet of paper.

Say:

"Now if I draw the pattern: red, blue, green, red, blue, green, red, blue, _____. Now let's say this pattern and you tell me what comes next."

Activity 5: On another sheet of paper, draw with lines: /, //, /, //, /, // _____.

Say:

"1, 2, 1, 2, 1, 2, 1, 2, _____."

Say:

"Now say this pattern and tell me what comes next."

Activity 6: Using a blank sheet,

Say:

"Great! You've learned a lot about making a pattern. Do you want to make one up for me? You tell me a pattern and see if I can draw it."

If the child does not wish to do this, just go on.

POSTTEST

Re-administer the test patterns. Begin with the last set on which the child obtained a score for selecting the correct piece. The correct reason given is not necessary.

Say:

> "Look at these again, and try to figure out what comes next. Pick one of these pieces and show what comes next."

Score the child's response.

If the child makes the correct choice, ask:

> "Good. Why did you pick that one? Why was that the best choice?"

(Continue administering the items until a ceiling of failure of two consecutive levels is reached.)

SUPPLEMENTAL:

V. Function: PERSPECTIVE TAKING

MATERIALS:

Two primary size crayons and 6 blank sheets of $8\frac{1}{2} \times 11$–inch paper

Simple drawings of a child, a cat, and a bear, each on a separate piece of paper [Download Figure 6.2].

The child can pick whichever crayon is preferred for drawing but use of yellow is discouraged because of the difficulty with seeing the lines.

PRETEST:

Take out the drawing of the child, the crayons, and two sheets of blank paper. Place one sheet of paper in front of the child and one in front of the assessor. Place the picture of the child between the assessor and child and the crayons below the picture.

Say:

> "Now we're going to do something a little different. I want *you* to be my teacher. I want *you* to help *me* to draw this picture. Teach me how to draw a picture of this child. What do I have to do?"

> ⇒ If the child hesitates or starts to draw, prompt once, saying:

> "Don't forget! *You* are the teacher. Show or tell *me* how to draw the picture."

⇒ If the child starts to give instructions and then lapses, provide an additional prompt, saying:

"Don't forget. You need to teach *me* how to draw the picture."

⇒ If the child provides any directions or verbal remarks, the assessor draws exactly what the child says. In other words, the assessor does not wait for the child to tell him or her to draw.

⇒ [Download Form 6.5].

INTERVENTION:

Place the drawing of a cat, a blank piece of paper, and the crayons in front of the child and the assessor.

Say:

"OK. Now it's my turn to be the teacher. I want to teach you how to draw this cat. What crayon would you like to use?" (Avoid yellow.)

Model teaching by verbalizing or demonstrating (or both):

⇒ details of what needs to be done

⇒ where to place lines or parts of the cat's body

⇒ the order in which to draw

⇒ shapes to use in making parts of the cat's body

POSTTEST:

Place the drawing of the bear, two crayons and two blank sheets of paper as indicated in pretest in front of the child.

Say:

"Now it's your turn to be the teacher. Teach me how to draw this picture of a bear. What do I need to do? Don't forget; you need to teach me how to do this."

Score the child's response.

VI. Function: VERBAL PLANNING

MATERIALS:

Set of six sequencing cards selected to reflect content appropriate for the child's background and knowledge base [Download Figure 6.4].

Pretest: Making a sandwich

Intervention example: Pictures of child getting dressed in the morning or culturally relevant alternative

Posttest example: Making a sandwich

PRETEST:

Say:

> "Do you like sandwiches? What kind of sandwich do you like? Have you ever made a sandwich? Have you ever seen anyone make a sandwich?"
>
> "Tell me how to make a [use child's choice] sandwich. Tell me all the things you have to do when you want to make a sandwich." [Use peanut butter and jelly, if you can't elicit something from the child, but make sure the child knows what this is.]
>
> ⇒ If the child is unfamiliar with sandwiches or does not have experience with making sandwiches, use a substitute food (e.g., salad, fruit, or a breakfast food).

Record the child's responses verbatim.

Score the child's response [Download Form 6.6].

INTERVENTION:

Place the sequencing cards showing a boy sleeping and then dressing in order on the table in front of the child.

Say:

> "Now it's my turn to teach, and we're going to use these pictures to help us learn about making a plan. These pictures show the plan for this boy to get ready for school in the morning. [Point to each picture one at a time.] "*First* he hears the alarm clock and wakes up. Then he gets dressed. He puts on his shirt. *Next* he puts on his pants. And the *last* things he puts on are his shoes and socks. Now he's all dressed and ready to go. Now let's look at the pictures one more time. *First*, what does he do? *Then next*, what does he do? Then the *last* thing that he does it what? Great! That's a good plan for getting ready to go to school. What is your plan for getting ready for school? What do you do?"

[Record what the child says.]

POSTTEST:

Say:

> "Now let's think about the sandwich again. Tell me the plan for making a _____ sandwich. Tell me all the things you have to do if you want to make a sandwich."

Score the child's response.

List of ACFS Materials and Sources
Note: All "provided" materials should be downloaded from the publisher's Web site.

Classification:
Pretest: selection from 65-piece blocks set
ASIN: BOOOO96QD1
SKN: 737122
from: www.Imaginarium.com or
www.TOYSRUS.com
Intervention: Attribute Blocks
RA207
from: www.Lakeshorelearning.com

Posttest: same as pretest

Auditory Memory:
Pretest: provided

Intervention: Magnetic Design Board and storage box
LA718; extra magnetic design shapes LA722
from: www.Lakeshorelearning.com

Posttest: same as pretest

Visual Memory:
Pretest: provided

Intervention: provided
Posttest: provided
[All sheets need to be coated with plastic and cut.]

Pattern Completion:
Pretest: Tangrams
RA272
from: www.Lakeshorelearning.com
Intervention: paper and crayons

Posttest: same as pretest

[Assessor must create patterns to match stimulus pictures that are provided; these should be placed in small plastic bags with a cut out picture of each pattern placed in the bag with the pieces for that pattern.]

Perspective Taking:
Pretest: provided
Intervention: provided
Posttest: provided

Verbal Planning:
Pretest: no materials
Intervention: provided
Posttest: no materials

7 Applying Dynamic Assessment with School-Age Children

In this chapter, we go beyond the general model of psychological assessment to discuss how this model can be applied in schools. Assessment in schools or in relation to the school curriculum should be integrated with information from multiple sources, all of which impinge on students' ability to learn and profit from instruction. Increasingly, teachers are asked to address individual needs of children with very diverse backgrounds and needs. If teachers are expected to assume this increased responsibility, then those who provide supportive services to the teachers must address these demands as well.

One of the primary contributions of dynamic assessment in educational settings is the provision of information that optimizes the match between students and the tasks they are asked to perform. In this chapter, we look at dynamic assessment as a source of information that facilitates the ability of instructional settings to meet the needs of individual learners, the ability of assessors to provide information that is usefully and meaningfully applied in educational settings, and the ability of learners to function successfully in educational settings. Dynamic assessment also becomes a tool that addresses the call for information about students' responsiveness to intervention rather than restricting outcomes of assessments to provision of recommendations for placement, referrals, or diagnostic labels. Dynamic assessment is, after all, defined by its interactive nature and its ability to look directly at the responsiveness of learners to interventions that are offered during the course of the assessment.

In this chapter, we describe and provide directions for three specific procedures that are appropriate for use with school-age students from early primary through late secondary years. The first is a generic model that can serve as an overlay for assessment in relation to virtually any curriculum content for students of all ages. This is called Curriculum-Based Dynamic Assessment (CBDA). The second is a procedure that was designed to screen classroom-size groups of students from first through fifth grades (approximately ages 6 through 10). Because this is a modification of the Das and Naglieri (1997) Cognitive Assessment System, the title of the procedure is CAS/GDAP, or Cognitive Assessment System/Group Dynamic Assessment Procedure. The third procedure was designed to identify gifted students from multicultural backgrounds. The dynamic portion of this approach is a modification of the Naglieri Nonverbal Ability Test (NNAT; Naglieri, 1997), called the NNAT/DA.

Attempts to link dynamic assessment with academic curriculum is one of the most active areas of development and research in dynamic assessment (e.g., Barrera, 2003; Campione & Brown, 1987; Machleit, 2000; Nigam, 2001). The work in this area is also one of the most diverse. Mathematics has been a frequently targeted domain (e.g., Berman, 2001; Gerber, Semmel, & Semmel, 1994; Jitendra & Kameenui, 1993; Warren, 2006), with reading (e.g., Abbott et al., 1997; Carney & Cioffi, 1992; Spector, 1992; Swanson, 1992), and language following in close order (e.g., Barrera, 2003; Jitendra, Rohena-Diaz, & Nolet, 1998; Kozulin & Garb, 2002; Olswang, Bain, & Johnson, 1992; Peña, 2001; Peña & Gillam, 2000; Peña, Iglesia, & Lidz, 2001; Peña, Miller, & Gillam, 1999; Peña & Valles, 1995). The need is clear. If dynamic assessment is to be useful in educational settings, it must contribute to the main business of these settings, the curriculum. Teachers and parents must view it as yielding relevant information, and information derived from DA should lead to appropriate programming and positive learning outcomes for students (Delclos et al., 1987). We cannot claim yet to have addressed all of these issues successfully (and neither have designers of normative, standardized approaches), but progress has been made, and work is definitely ongoing.

CURRICULUM-BASED DYNAMIC ASSESSMENT

CBDA is a generic approach that can incorporate virtually any specific content or relate to any domain. Development of this approach represents an attempt to maximize the link between assessment and instruction. Curriculum-based assessment (CBA) has increased in popularity because it links to the curriculum – because it is the curriculum, or, if good, is a representative sampling of the curriculum. CBA by itself offers limited information relevant to learners who struggle in their efforts to respond to the curriculum; it responds to the "what" questions: What does the learner know? What does the learner not know? What is the next instructional step (if this can be defined; not all content is neatly hierarchical)? This is an important first step in school-related diagnosis. Furthermore, CBA offers a means of monitoring the learner's progress during the course of developing academic competence. CBA does not provide information about obstructions to the learner's mastery of the curriculum, nor does it inform educators about how such mastery might best be promoted. The addition of dynamic assessment to CBA provides this missing link.

CBDA begins with selection of relevant curriculum content and construction of an appropriate CBA to serve as both the pretest and posttest. The dynamic component enters after this step, applying the pretest–intervene–retest format with the inclusion of intervention that addresses the *processing demands* of the selected tasks in relation to the *processing capabilities* of the learner. In our model, the delineation of processes of both the task and the learner are virtually identical and are analyzed to determine the extent of the match or mismatch. It is the extent and nature of the mismatch that characterizes the individual's learning problem. The defining characteristic of the diagnostic approach to dynamic assessment is the inclusion of intervention in the assessment process. As described in Chapter 3, the assessor designs the intervention to reflect the steps included in the Mediation Checklist outlined in downloadable Form 3.1.

The overall process of carrying out the CBDA includes the following steps:

1. Determine the content area and how this will be assessed in pretest–retest (e.g., in reading: probes or running record).
2. Conduct a process analysis of the content area: What process demands does this make on the learner?
3. Conduct a process analysis of the learner based on what has been learned to this point from observation, interview, file review, and administration of other procedures.
4. Design intervention that is relevant to the specific content area.
5. Administer the CBDA pretest–intervene–retest format.

The need to carry out a process analysis of the task and the learner is central to the CBDA approach. The process analysis we suggest reflects the model of mental development presented in Chapter 2. The questions posed during this process analysis are, for the task, To what extent does the task make demands on this process? And in the case of the learner, To what extent are the processes demanded by the task developed and intact? The processes that are addressed for both the learner and the task appear in the downloadable Forms 7.1 and 7.2.

Forms 7.1 and 7.2 also serve as worksheets to guide assessors through the process analysis for both the learner and the task. The following information addresses the definitions, issues, and sample interventions regarding each of these processes. Before engaging in this analysis, however, assessors should always determine the learner's knowledge base regarding the content because the gap between what the learner knows and what is expected may by itself account for the collapse of the teaching–learning interaction.

1. Attention

The process of attention includes two aspects, focus and selectivity. Focus concerns the ability of the learner to maintain attention to the target, and selectivity concerns the learner's ability to inhibit reactions to competing stimuli while doing so. The learner's ability to "pay attention" relates to many things, including the learner's neurological predispositions; the learner's sociocultural and familial experiences; the stimulus properties of the target; and the nature, strength, and characteristics of competing stimuli. Closely related to the process of attention is the learner's ability to self-regulate; with regard to this process, it is important to note the learner's ability to maintain attention and awareness of the need to engage in strategies to maintain attention when faced with this demand. Although the learner's state of arousal usually refers to the involuntary state of the organism and can be described as hyper-, hypo-, or optimal, the process of attention is usually viewed as volitional, that is, purposeful and conscious directing of focus. There are generally three types of attention that can be described: selective (ability to focus on the target while ignoring distracters), divided (ability to shift attention between two or more simultaneously occurring stimuli), and sustained (the length of time the learner can maintain focus). It is also possible to describe the learner's attention capacity or the amount of stimuli to which the learner can attend at any one time.

Interventions that relate to attention include promoting self-awareness in the learner of the need to attend and to engage in strategies that will promote the ability to attend. The learner needs to develop awareness of the onset of loss of attention and to develop strategies to reengage. Interventions for attention can also address the perceptual properties of the task in ways that capture the learner's attention, for example, introducing ways of highlighting what is important to notice, use of contrast and novelty, and manipulation of gestures and voice. The learner also needs to develop understanding of the importance of the need to pay attention, to develop strategies that will promote attention across situations, and to make cause-and-effect hypotheses of connections regarding sources of difficulty with paying attention.

Finally, the assessor can manipulate such variables as length of task, number of items, pacing, level of difficulty, use of presentation strategies such as advance organizers, and concept mapping, all in the service of enhancing the learner's ability to attend.

2. Perception

As described by Luria (1973), perception is

> an active process which includes the search for the most important
> elements of information, their comparisons with each other, the creation
> of a hypothesis concerning the meaning of the information as a whole,
> and the verification of the hypothesis by comparing it with the original
> features of the object perceived. (1983, p. 240)

Perception, then, goes well beyond stimulus detection and lays the ground-
work for cognition. Based on a foundation of sensory processing interacting with attention of stimulus detection, types of processing that would
be considered perceptual include stimulus feature discrimination (notation of distinctive features), stimulus recognition (derivation of meaning
relating to previously stored information), stimulus comparisons (notation
and comparison of stimulus features across targets), and implementation
of perceptual strategies (e.g., scanning).

As in the case of attention, the assessor can communicate the need to
notice stimulus features to the learner and help the learner to note relevant distinctive features by increasing the salience of these features. The
assessor can also facilitate the learner's ability to relate percepts to previous experiences and knowledge base and communicate the importance
of precision and detail. Most important, the assessor needs to encourage
the use of relevant strategies to promote the learner's ability to compare,
process, and proceed with the activity.

3. Memory

Flavell (1985) defined memory as "the retention of all the products and
achievements of one's cognitive development to date.... Storage activities [that] put information into memory while retrieval activities recover
information from memory" (p. 208).

Three types of memory are usually differentiated: short term, working,
and long term. Short-term memory concerns what can be recalled within
several seconds of exposure, whereas working memory involves retention
of all that is necessary, combining both short- and long-term, during current
conscious processing of information. Long-term memory is stored in the
brain and accessed as needed. Most assessment issues address either the act
of converting short-term into long-term memory or the ability to retrieve
memory from long-term storage for use as working memory in current
conscious mental activity. There are strategies involved in both storage
and retrieval, as well as in maximizing learning space during the act of

short-term recall that interacts with attention. One of the challenges for assessors is to determine how much of the learner's apparent difficulty with memory is really more an issue of attention than memory (and possibly even of perception related to determining meaning, or knowing to what features to attend).

Interventions for memory again involve communication to the learner that there is a need to remember and to do something to promote memory. The assessor can try to induce some emotional linkage, for example, through attention to prosody in presenting the material or through promoting associations with emotionally laden content or by facilitating awareness of meaningful connections within the materials to be recalled. Intervention can also encourage connections of material to be learned with past and future experiences, as well as promotion of the ability to transfer across modalities. And, as always, the assessor focuses on application of strategies such as rehearsal, chunking, verbal elaboration, and visualization. The assessor also engages in manipulations that maintain the material within the memory span of the learner and breaks down the material to be learned into units small enough to be retained.

4. Language

According to Lahey (1988), the basic dimensions of language are content, form, and function. These refer to what the learner is actually saying, such as the words used and concepts communicated (content), the syntax or order in which this is expressed (syntax), and the use to which this is put (function). She has defined language as the integration of these dimensions to guide actions either with objects or with people. This allows the individual to interpret actions, ideas, and intentions of others; express her or his own ideas and meanings; and initiate and maintain social interaction. All of this is highly culturally embedded and follows a developmental sequence, but typically developing individuals from all cultures share the capacity to use language.

Interventions in the area of language are in the professional domain of speech/language pathologists; however, all those who interact with children either in the informal settings of the home or the more formal settings of the school are in the business of influencing language development. For our purposes, the most important aspects of language have to do with development of academic and social competence. Our questions regarding the learner concern his or her ability to use language to learn, to inquire, to clarify, and to express understanding and develop ideas. Educational settings are also social arenas, and a significant portion of successful learning has to do with mastering the pragmatics and routines (including language routines) of the classroom and playground, and developing the ability to engage in appropriate adult–child and child–child discourse, including generation of personal and academic narratives. Classrooms are highly verbal environments and place heavy demands on language competence.

Good diagnostic assessment is particularly important in the domain of language. It is very important to try to parse out both the nature and sources of difficulty. This is beyond the goals of what we are discussing here. In the context of dynamic assessment of an activity that has a heavy language load, we need to consider if the individual has the vocabulary necessary to engage in the task, and, if not, if direct teaching of the relevant vocabulary is a sufficient intervention. An important intervention can involve simple provision of labels for objects with which the child interacts or for feelings that the child experiences during the course of interaction. Provision of labels can enhance the child's perceptions and widen the child's knowledge base from which to build higher levels of thought. Any of us who have taken art or music courses are well aware of how much more we see and hear once our attention is brought to details we might otherwise overlook, and we become aware of how helpful it is to develop the vocabulary for communicating our experiences.

In this domain we need to consider issues of processing speed and retrieval, as the presentation speed is something that can be adjusted. The speed of speech can be slowed; assessors can also learn to increase wait time before responding and proceeding; repetitions of instructions can be offered with changes in vocabulary as needed. For individuals experiencing difficulties with language, the search for supports from other modalities is also a relevant intervention. The most obvious supports would be visual aids such as pictures or actual materials, as well as use of gesturing by the presenter.

Cueing the student to look at the speaker's lips can be helpful as well, and recommendations may need to include seating the student close to teachers not only for hearing and attention issues but also to promote close observation of the teacher's lips and gestures to enhance language comprehension. Providing the child with appropriate verbal scripts can be helpful to some children who either suffer from retrieval problems or who have simply not learned how to verbalize their messages effectively, for example, suggesting when a child starts to squirm or lose attention that perhaps he or she needs to ask for a break or stating that "the work is getting hard now" when a child starts to react with upset when faced with challenge. The assessor can directly suggest that "You can tell me . . . , when. . . . "

Another important intervention that is easily carried out during a dynamic assessment is to model self-talk during the course of problem solution. Depending on the task, the assessor can provide demonstrations for the child, and should always accompany these with verbalization and "thinking aloud" about the actions involved in task solution. Children should never be discouraged from using self-talk, and those who are shy about doing this can be told that the assessor finds it helpful to talk when working on something that is challenging. Children with significant language issues of course need to be referred for specialized assessment and intervention.

5. Reasoning

Although there is significant overlap between language and reasoning, this category refers primarily to development of higher mental functions, or analytic, representational thinking. These specifically include abilities such as analogical, cause-and-effect, and inferential reasoning. These abilities rely heavily, although not exclusively, on language as a tool, so, in most cases, mastery of language relevant to the higher order task would be considered a necessary part of the individual's knowledge base.

Intervention regarding reasoning relies heavily on a combination of questioning and modeling. The need and expectation to think and reason are induced by the nature of the assessor's questions; the example for how to go about responding to these questions is offered by the assessor's modeling of responses to questions that can be at first rhetorical. For example, the assessor can frame such probes in terms of "I wonder what would happen if. . . . " or "Can you think of a reason for. . . . " and then respond with, "Could it be that. . . . What do you think?"

6. Metacognition (Planning)

According to Luria (1966), a person

> creates intentions, forms plans and programmes of his actions, inspects their performance, and regulates his behavior so that it conforms to these plans and programmes; finally he verifies his conscious activity, comparing the effects of his actions with the original intentions and correcting any mistakes he has made. (p. 80)

Thus, planning is complex and possibly the most human of all mental activities. Planning is the metacognitive, or executive, aspect of mental processing.

Interventions that address planning again need to communicate the need to plan and help the learner determine when engagement in the planning process is appropriate, that is, to recognize the cues for this and facilitate the learner's deployment of planning strategies. The planning or problem-solving process typically involves steps of problem recognition; problem definition; determination of materials, operations, and sequences of steps needed; determination of appropriate strategies; implementation of the plan; evaluation of the plan; and adjustment of the plan in response to this feedback. The ability to engage in this planning process requires development of self-regulation on the part of the learner, and this is facilitated by provision of elaborated feedback and encouragement of the learner's verbalizations (and, most likely, visualizations).

Another important metacognitive function is flexibility. This involves the ability to generate alternative solutions. An important intervention for this ability is to ask the child to think of alternatives, for example, with questions of "what else ... can you think of another way ... ?"

To facilitate the process analysis of the learner, it may be helpful to think in terms of questions such as the following:

1. Attention/Arousal:
    *   What is the child's characteristic state of arousal? How consistent is this?
    *   How does the child manage selective attention?
    *   What factors affect the child's attention?
    *   How does the child apportion resources when divided attention is required?
    *   For how long can the child maintain attention? How does this interact with the content and environment?
2. Perception:
    *   Does the child derive meaning from perceptual experiences?
    *   How efficiently are perceptual experiences processed?
    *   Are there modality differences?
    *   How well does the child note distinctive features?
    *   How well does the child detect patterns?
    *   Does the child show appropriate perceptual strategies?
3. Memory:
    *   What is the extent of the child's working memory?
    *   How well does the child retrieve from long-term memory?
    *   How well does the child move information from short-term into long-term memory?
    *   Does the child show appropriate memory strategies?
    *   Are there modality differences?
4. Language:
    *   How well does the child understand language?
    *   How developed is the child's expressive language?

- How appropriate are the child's pragmatics?
- What are the functions for which the child uses language?
- Are there any issues regarding voice and articulation that require referral?
5. Reasoning:
   - Does the child show evidence of analogical reasoning?
   - How well does the child make cause–effect connections?
   - Can the child engage inferential reasoning?
6. Metacognitive Processing:
   - How well does the child recognize/define the "problem"?
   - How well does the child determine relevant strategies?
   - How well does the child apply relevant strategies?
   - How effective is the child's self-regulation?
   - How well does the child evaluate and adjust performance?
   - How does the child generate alternative solutions?

The *analysis of the task* addresses exactly the same processes as the analysis of the learner. Each task is looked at in terms of its processing demands (attention, etc.), and the focus is to determine the match between the task and the learner.

Scoring rubrics for the pre- and posttests should be appropriate for the specific content. In the case described in Chapter 3, words and errors per minute were used for the reading task that was involved. In the case of the spelling example used in this chapter, either part or whole word scoring can be used. Part scoring would be the more sensitive and could include scoring for beginning, middle, and ends of words, as well as for errors that approximate sounds versus those that do not. The important point here is that CBDA results, even though not normed, can be quantified in the same way as CBA results. Such quantification is useful for determining degree of mastery of curriculum content as well as for monitoring the student's performance over time and for estimating the responsiveness of the student to intervention. Assessors should never forget to take copious notes that describe the student's performance during the course of learning and should not rely solely on scores to characterize the student.

An example of a spelling task is used in this chapter to illustrate how to carry out this process. The goal of the task is to teach the child a predetermined list of spelling words, presumably a sample of those that are involved in the child's curriculum. Prior to the assessment, however, it would be useful to determine whether these spelling words are within the child's reading range. If not, a more appropriate list of words should be selected: those within reading range but that the child has not yet fully mastered for spelling. We can process analyze the spelling task into heavy loading on memory, with special perceptual importance regarding sequential ordering (the order of the letters is important). A specific child may have difficulty with attention or perception, and the child's linguistic background may either interfere with or enhance the child's ability to relate to the perceptual qualities of the task. For example, if the same letter sounds one way in English and another way in the child's language, this may serve to confuse the child's ability to spell the word. If memory is the primary process requiring mediation, the assessor needs to engage the child in these strategies in relation to the spelling task.

The assessor would then determine the special features of the words the child might notice; for example, should the child pay special attention to the fact that all the words have short vowels or vowel combinations? Are all the words nouns? The next step would be to relate the words to experiences with which the child is likely to be familiar. Most important, the assessor needs to determine appropriate strategies for learning the words as well as decide how they will be presented. For example, learning spelling words involves memory, so appropriate strategies for memory need to be reviewed, such as visualization (look at the word; close your eyes and try to see the word; now spell what you see) and multi-modal involvement (have the child look at the word, then look away from it and trace it in the air).

The CBDA approach has the advantages of flexibility and generalizability. On the other hand, it has the disadvantage of reliance on the assessor's time, knowledge, and ingenuity. The information it yields, although quantifiable, is obviously more valuable for descriptive elaboration of the learner. Some may view CBDA as a form of testing the limits, and to some extent this is true; however, CBDA involves far more than the simple offering of additional time or presentation of materials with altered vocabulary or modality of presentation. In addition to the emphasis on embedded interventions, the CBDA model requires the assessor to apply in-depth analysis of both learner and task and to seek what was advocated many years ago by Hunt (1961): the optimal match between the two. Its usefulness in the domain of language has been demonstrated by Jitendra, Rohena-Diaz, and Nolet (1998).

COGNITIVE ASSESSMENT SYSTEM/GROUP DYNAMIC ASSESSMENT PROCEDURE

The Cognitive Assessment System/Group Dynamic Assessment

Procedure (CAS/GDAP) was designed by Lidz and Greenberg (1997) as a program evaluation tool for the Cognitive Enrichment Network (COGNET) Follow Through Project. It was first used at a COGNET site with

75 first-grade regular education students from a school in rural Montana (United States) located on a Native American reservation, with half of the children from the two tribes comprising the population of the reservation. Because COGNET was founded on principles of cognitive education with roots primarily in the work of Feuerstein and his colleagues, the intent was to target basic processes associated with learning that were expected to improve as a result of experience with the program. The Das/Naglieri Cognitive Assessment System (1997), grounded in the theory of Russian neuropsychologist Alexander Luria, was selected as an appropriate core model. Because the CAS was designed for individual administration and was a standardized, normative procedure, it was necessary to make modifications that would permit its administration to classroom-size groups of children, and to add interventions to turn it into a dynamic assessment approach. Since then, it has been used successfully with students in Grades 1 through 5 from both regular and special education. Because of the group administration, we consider this a screening procedure and not an in-depth diagnostic test. As is appropriate for screening purposes, students who are identified as low performers should be referred for more comprehensive diagnostic assessment. The information from this procedure can also be used to group students who have similar remediation needs so that supplemental instruction can be provided. Assessors who wish to administer this procedure need to secure the Das/Naglieri CAS and use the protocols that come with the complete kit.

The CAS taps the four major areas of mental processing described by Luria (Attention, Planning, Successive, and Simultaneous) with four subtests for each process. One subtest per process was selected for the GDAP modification, based primarily on the criterion of ease of modifiability for group administration. The only area that could not be modified was Successive, and this was administered on an individual basis. The subtests selected included Receptive Attention, Simultaneous Verbal, Word Recall (for Successive), and Planned Codes. Because only the Simultaneous Verbal subtest involved right or wrong responses, the same subtests were used for both pretest and posttest phases of the dynamic assessment. An alternate form was created for the Simultaneous Verbal subtest by substituting the words "right" for "left" and "circle" for "square" in the otherwise unchanged instructions. Other changes involved removing the printed instructions for the Simultaneous Verbal subtest and reducing the number of items in the Word Recall subtest.

The specific subtests involve the following tasks:

- *Receptive Attention*: This is a cancellation task typical of many that have been traditionally used to assess attention in individuals of all ages. In this case, there are two sections with a practice sheet for each. Both sections involve pairs of letters (or, for younger students, pairs of faces). The first task is to strike out all pairs that have letters that look the same. The second task is to strike out all pairs that have letters that sound the same.

The student is told to strike out as many as possible in 60 seconds. The score is the number correctly canceled, subtracting errors from this total.

- *Simultaneous Verbal*: The student receives a booklet of 16 pages with six geometric drawings on each page (or figural drawings for younger students). The student crosses out the one drawing in the page that matches the directions that are read by the assessor, for example, "Put an X on the picture of a square inside a triangle to the left of a circle." Each direction is read twice, being sure to proceed clearly and slowly so as to reduce the memory load. The score is the number of items answered correctly.
- *Planned Codes*: This involves two sections with a practice page for each. There is a code for the letters A (e.g., XO), B (e.g., OX), C (e.g., XX), and D (e.g., OO) at the top of the page, and the student must copy the code into the empty spaces with letters in rearranged order throughout the page. The code is rearranged for the second section, and the placement of the empty spaces made more complex. The student is told to copy as many as possible in 60 seconds. The score is the number of codes filled in correctly, subtracting errors from the total.
- *Word Recall (Successive)*: The student repeats unrelated word sequences of increasing length read aloud by the assessor. Scoring is 2 points for exact repetition and 1 point for inclusion of all the correct words but not in exact order.

The general instructions to the students are as follows:

We are going to do some new and special kinds of work with you. This work will help us find out how you learn best and how we can teach you. This is how it will go. Over the next few days, we are going to go through some work that we will do more than one time. In fact, we will do everything two times! And in between those two times, we are going to help you learn how to do the best job possible. Then you will get the work again and have a chance to try out your new ideas. The important thing is for you to try to learn how to do a better job the second time.

Do you understand? The idea here is to try to learn how to do a good job with this work and to do an even better job when you get it again. This will not be very hard work, and you may even know a lot of it the first time you try it. But it's always possible to do just a little bit better, isn't it? We will work together to help you do even better the second time.

What we want to learn and what we hope you will learn is how you learn best and what helps you to learn. That means it is really important for you to do your own work and not to copy from your neighbor or friend. You won't get grades on these tests, and this will not go on your report card. Let's think about how to fix your desk or place at the table so no one else can see your work. [Take time to do this.]

Each session requires about 1 hour. Depending on the circumstances of the classrooms and students, sessions can be scheduled at the rate of one or two per day. These should be done to minimize the intrusiveness into the regular schedule.

SESSIONS 1 and 2: all pretests
SESSION 3: Receptive Attention intervention and Posttest
SESSION 4: Simultaneous Verbal intervention and Posttest
SESSION 5: Word Series intervention and Posttest (requires 5 minutes per student and needs to be administered in a quiet place)
SESSION 6: Planned Codes intervention and Posttest

In all cases, the intervention portion begins with reminding the students of the pretest for the process to be discussed. (These are shown to the group, but not redistributed to the class.) The intervention guidelines are followed in reviewing these sheets. Each mediation session (for each process) follows these guidelines. The assessor reviews the pretest with the students, posing the following questions (the specific vocabulary needs to be tailored to the age level of the children; these questions need not and should not be read or asked verbatim):

1. What did we need to do here? What was the task?
2. What do we need to be able to do or need to know so we can do this? What processes are involved? (Arrive at identifying the relevant process of the test.)
3. Why is this process important? How does it help us with our learning? (Arrive at derivation of a principle expressing the importance of the process in "if . . . then . . . " format.)
4. What strategy did you use? What would be some good strategies for this kind of work?
5. When and how do we use this process in other situations? At home? In school?
6. Let's apply our ideas in another similar situation. (Provide elaborated feedback and encourage learners' verbalization.)

DO THE INTERVENTION ACTIVITY.
7. Let's summarize what we have discussed. What was the important principle? What were some good strategies?

> When is this important in our lives? Can you think of how you will apply this to doing better on the work we just did?
> Try to use what we have talked about to help you do better when you do the work again. (Pass out clean subtest sheets.)

The specific interventions for each process are as follows:

Attention

This activity involves an age-appropriate poem.

The poem is read three times, first to familiarize the students with it, second to ask the students to raise their hands whenever they hear a preselected word (select one that is frequently occurring), and third, to raise their hands every time they hear a preselected sound (such as "s-s-s").

The assessor discusses with them how they are able to control their attention by first listening for one thing and then switching to listen for something else. The assessor then passes out sheets from another cancellation task, unrelated to the CAS pretest, and discusses good strategies for proceeding with this type of activity. These should be elicited from the students as much as possible. Strategies such as proceeding systematically, trying to visualize the target as you proceed, and verbally describing the target and repeating this as you proceed, and not stopping to erase, should be included. Students should be encouraged to try the strategies and find those that work for them. After they complete the worksheet, there should be further brief discussion about what worked and what did not work for them.

Simultaneous Processing

The assessor selects a student from the class to stand in front, and asks the class, "Is she (or he) tall or short?" Discussion ensues regarding the point that there is no answer to this without comparing the student to someone else. The assessor then selects someone else to stand next to the first student and asks the same question, with subsequent discussion. The point is made that some things cannot be known without knowing the whole picture to see how one thing relates to the next.

The assessor then draws shapes on the board and asks the students to label these. These shapes are selected from the Simultaneous pretest, and this is done to ensure that the students have the vocabulary knowledge base for the task.

The assessor then draws shapes in various relationships to the others and asks students to volunteer to describe what the assessor has drawn. The assessor then asks the students to describe shape relationships for the assessor to draw on the board – for example, a circle under a triangle to the left of a square. The activity for the class is then to break up into groups of two and take turns drawing a set of shapes and describing these to the partner (who does not see the drawing) to see whether the partner can do this accurately. The partners then switch to do the same activity. The results are then briefly discussed with the class to talk about how they did, what made this difficult, what helped, and so on.

Successive Processing

This intervention involves clapping the syllables of names of students from the class and then representing these as lines and dashes on the board. The assessor discusses the importance of order and the effect of order on accuracy; changing the order would change the name and the meaning would be lost. The assessor then talks about how this applies to reading, spelling, and math; for example, how it makes a difference to write "cat" or "cta" or "49" versus "94" or "please put the book on the chair" versus "book put the please chair the on."

Because the task also involves memory, the assessor discusses strategies to help memory, such as visualization.

The students are then asked to break up into pairs and to practice remembering strings of words for objects around the room, using visualization. Each partner should begin with a string of three and build up as high as possible with the partner. Each partner should be given more than one trial for difficult sequences; for the repetition, the partner should be encouraged to do it with closed eyes and to try to make a mental picture of the object.

Planning

A page needs to be created for this task for the purpose of "researching" the most effective strategy for each student. The page should have small pictures of animals across the top, with a number code written in for each animal underneath the animal (numbers 1 through 5, for example). Then pictures of these animals with blank spaces are placed below on the paper in a way that suggests an organized plan for proceeding. The students are given two copies of this page, and discussion ensues regarding the best strategies to use to fill in the codes. There should be two basic strategies derived from this discussion. The students are then asked to try the first strategy on the first paper, and the next strategy on the second. They are given 30 seconds for each sheet and then calculate their own results. This ends with discussion about what worked best and the general conclusion that it can be helpful to have a strategy when there is a lot of work to do.

Scoring

Because the CAS/GDAP involves modifications of the CAS, the norms of the CAS cannot be applied. It may nevertheless be helpful to refer to the normative information in the case of the pretest scores of students who perform at a low level in relation to their classmates as a way of gaining perspective regarding their level of risk in relation to the national population. This should be done only with regard to making decisions about follow-up referral rather than for the purpose of reporting their scores.

Instead, the raw score information from this procedure can be used for information about the students' functioning relative to the other students in the class, as well as for profiling the functions of individual students. Observations of students during the course of the interventions by their teachers can be particularly enlightening because teachers are often surprised with the involvement and participation of students who they have perceived as low functioning. In fact, it is helpful to ask teachers to focus and record observations of three to five students about whom they have particular concerns. It is of course also relevant to check to see how these students complete their pre- and posttests.

As a screening procedure, the pretest and posttest information should be used both to identify students in need of further diagnostic assessment and to inform instruction. Students who start low and remain low are those with priority for referral. Students who start low and make significant gains may be responsive to more intensive instruction in the class that focuses on the processes shown to be at risk. A number of authors (Carlson & Das, 1997; Churches, Skuy, & Das, 2002; Kroesbergen, Van Luit, & Naglieri, 2003; Naglieri & Johnson, 2000; Parrila, Kendrick, Papapoulis, & Kirby, 1999) have documented the effectiveness of interventions directed at these processes for improving academic competence in both reading and mathematics. The relationship of these processes to both academic areas using the CAS/GDAP procedure is documented in the studies in the section that follows.

Research

In the Lidz and Greenberg study (1997) with 75 rural first-grade regular education students, three of the four posttest scores correlated significantly with standardized reading achievement test scores (Attention, Simultaneous, and Successive), whereas none of the correlations with pretest scores was significant. Planning posttest (not pretest), Attention pretest and posttest, and Simultaneous pretest and posttest scores correlated significantly with standardized mathematics test scores. The Successive posttest (not pretest) correlated only with reading, and the Planning posttest (not pretest) correlated only with Math; thus, these two subtests were the most discriminating regarding the academic domain. Further analysis showed that the significant gains on all but the Successive subtest were made primarily by students whose pretest scores were in the lower 40% of the group, and correlations between the subtests and reading were generally stronger for students with low pretest scores (Attention posttest, .40; Simultaneous posttest, .48; Successive posttest, .37). The Simultaneous posttest was a good predictor of math for students with low pretest scores (.45).

Lidz, Jepsen, and Miller (1997) investigated the relationship between CAS/GDAP scores and standardized reading and math scores with 66 students with a variety of physical and mental disabilities. The age range for this study was 11 to 21 years (mean of 14.95, SD of 1.92). Three of the four subtests (Attention, Successive, and Planning) showed significant pretest to posttest gains. Pretests and posttests for all subtests correlated highly significantly with both reading and math scores. The Attention posttest was the strongest predictor of both reading and math. Factor analysis showed Simultaneous and Successive processing to be independent, with Attention and Planning related to each other. Only the posttests of Attention and Simultaneous loaded on the "achievement" factor for both reading and math. Stepwise multiple regression showed the posttests of Attention and Simultaneous subtests accounting for 67% of the reading variance, with Attention posttest alone accounting for 56%. For math, Attention posttest, IQ, and Successive pretest accounted for 67% of the variance; Attention alone accounted for 56%, with IQ contributing 9%. For the participants in this study, with Wechsler IQs ranging between 32 and 112 (mean 57.75, SD 17.04), CAS/GDAP posttest scores were better predictors of both reading and math than IQ.

The Jepsen and Lidz (2000) study investigated the reliability and validity of the CAS/GDAP with the same population as in the Lidz, Jepsen, and Miller (1997) study. The performance of 26 adolescents who had participated in the previous study (Lidz and Jepsen, 1997) was compared with the results of 22 who had not previously participated. This allowed the authors to look at the stability of the results for the first group of participants (reliability), as well as providing a control group of new participants, who completed the CAS/GDAP pretests and posttests without intervention (validity).

To assess test–retest reliability, the four CAS/GDAP posttests were re-administered to the previous participants two weeks following initial administration. No significant differences were found between means of the two GDAP administrations for the previous participants for Attention, Planning, and Simultaneous scores. Attention and Planning showed nonsignificant continued improvement. Successive showed a significant decrement.

In the case of treatment and control group comparisons, there were no differences for Attention (both made significant gains), and there were significant differences favoring the treatment group for Successive, Simultaneous, and Planning. In the case of Planning, the pretests for the treatment group were significantly lower than control group, and the gain resulted in equal scores for both groups. For these participants, the Attention results appeared susceptible to possible practice effects.

For the new control group of 22 students, their CAS/GDAP pretest results were compared with IQ in relation to curriculum-based assessment of reading and math. This was carried out by their classroom teachers, and thus reflected their actual classroom performance. IQ showed no relationship to either academic domain. All CAS/GDAP subtests, however, showed significant relationships, with the exception of Successive/math. The correlations for reading are as follows: Attention (.59), Simultaneous (.59), Successive (.53), Planning (.63). The correlations for math are as follows: Attention (.75), Simultaneous (.50), Planning (.61). These in many cases outpredicted or equaled the .59 correlation between reading and math. These results speak to the validity of the CAS itself as representing cognitive processes that are highly related to basic academic domains. Administering the CAS with dynamic assessment modifications seems only to increase these relationships, and, most importantly, both sources provide data about processes that can be targeted for intervention. This avoids the question, Can we improve IQ? We can respond affirmatively to the question of, Can we improve attention, planning, and simultaneous and successive processing? Moreover, directing interventions at these processes shows positive effects on academic functioning.

Finally, the second author carried out an unpublished program evaluation during the spring of 1994 and 1995 for the Department of Special Education of the Detroit Public Schools. At this time, the system had a Center for Mediated Learning, and this Center worked with selected schools to put the COGNET program in place. The program evaluation involved two regular education classes (Grades 1 and 2) and one special education (mixed diagnoses) class from one of these schools. Only the Attention and Planning subtests, modified for group dynamic assessment, were used. Results were compared with those from the standardized achievement tests given to all students throughout the District. For Grade 1 ($n = 22$), only the first Attention scores showed significant gains; for Grade 2 ($n = 29$), both Attention tests showed significant gains; and for special education ($n = 15$), only the second Attention tests showed significant gains.

For Grade 1, relationships between CAS/GDAP and reading were .50 or greater for Attention but not for Planning, whereas the relationships between Attention and math were even stronger, in most cases exceeding .70, but, again, not for Planning.

For Grade 2, the only strong relationships were between Planning and math, and these were notably higher for posttests than for pretests (e.g., .77 compared with .47). The second administration of the Attention posttest yielded a moderately good prediction of math for the special education group (.53).

In this study we also looked at the relationship between CAS/GDAP and the achievement gain scores because we had the reading and math scores on the same achievement measure for both years for Grade 2 students. The strongest predictor of reading gain was Attention posttest (.70), and the strongest predictors of math were Attention pretest (.71), Attention posttest (.60), Planning pretest (.60), and Planning posttest (.55). Correlations for special education students were low and sometimes strongly negative, except for Planning posttest and reading (.45). In this study, the students in the special education class were so heterogeneous that any generalizations regarding results were impossible.

IDENTIFYING GIFTED MINORITY STUDENTS
WITH DYNAMIC ASSESSMENT

At a conference in the late 1990s, the second author was approached by one of the school psychologists and the special education supervisor of a school district located north of Philadelphia about a problem. The problem concerned their district's determination of eligibility of students from minority and immigrant backgrounds for their gifted program. Whereas the district found an average of 5% of its students to be eligible for this program (based primarily on Wechsler IQ), in the school where more than 60% of the students came from minority or immigrant families, typically only one or two, that is, fewer than 1%, of the students qualified. The psychologist and special education supervisor knew that the second author was involved with dynamic assessment and wondered whether it would be possible to apply this approach to address their problem.

The second author worked with the psychologist from this district to design a procedure that would be culture-fair, truly use multiple sources of information, and incorporate dynamic assessment. Because the gifted program accepted students only from first grade and up, kindergarten students were not included in this project. The specific school that was involved included students through fifth grade, totaling 473 (excluding kindergarten). The design involved two sets of procedures, one for initial screening of the entire student population and one for the final determination of eligibility from the pool of students who survived the screening. Although Pennsylvania had specific standards for determination of eligibility for gifted programming that involved IQ, the researchers were able to obtain permission to place students who qualified on the basis of the study in the gifted program.

Both researchers (Lidz & Macrine, 2001), with the help of two graduate students, administered the screening procedures. The researchers selected screening procedures to reflect recommendations of authors of current research and literature. These procedures provided input into the identification process by all relevant parties, including teachers, parents, and peers, and included the following:

- Gifted and Talented Evaluation Scales (GATES; Gilliam, Carpenter, & Christensen, 1996) (completed by teachers)
- Iowa Tests of Basic Skills (ITBS; Drahozal, 1997) (Reading and Math)
- Sociometric Questionnaire (completed by peers)
- Parent Questionnaire (Downloadable Form 7.3)
- Group Dynamic Assessment Procedure of the Attention subtest from the CAS/GDAP (used for observation of classroom participation) (see Downloadable Form 7.4 for Teacher Rankings sheet)

Inclusion of the scores of the group dynamic assessment of the Attention subtest from the CAS/GDAP in the analysis of the results was aborted because of technical difficulties related to the administration by the graduate students.

Following completion of the screening, the authors reviewed the results and selected students who scored in the top decile on at least two screening measures. This resulted in a total of 85 children (18% of the students in grade levels 1 through 5) who were then eligible for individual assessment (by the researchers).

The individual assessment included the following:

- Kaufman Assessment Battery for Children (K-ABC; Kaufman & Kaufman, 1983; Mental Processing Composite [MPC] and nonverbal scores)
- Naglieri Nonverbal Ability Test (Naglieri, 1997), modified for individual and dynamic administration (NNAT/DA; as of this writing, this test is available for individual administration)

- A Student Interview (Downloadable Form 7.5) was constructed and administered, but the results were not scored or included in the project because of time and labor constraints, and in view of the large amount of data available from other sources. Nevertheless, the form is included here for interested readers.

The DA intervention for the NNAT was designed to be as conservative as possible, yet representative of meaningful mediation for the student. The intent was to remain as close to the original as possible. The instructions for modifying the NNAT for dynamic assessment were as follows:

Following completion of the pretest (according to test directions), the assessor provided mediation for the first *five* items that the student *missed*. The student was reassured that s/he had done a fine job, but that no one obtains a perfect score. They were then told that the items that they found difficult would be re-administered. The mediation involved three steps:

1. The students were told what they had selected and that this first response was not correct. They were asked to look at it again to see if they could generate a better response. If the student then gave the correct response with no further prompting, they were granted a (1) or full score. Even in the case of a correct response, they were asked to defend their answer (why was that a good choice; what was wrong with their first choice . . .), and the assessor interacted with them to reinforce the correct basis for their selection.
2. If the students did not give a correct response following Step 1, the assessor brought their attention to the details of the matrix, and said, "Look at how this (pointing) relates to this, and how this (pointing) relates to this." If the students then spontaneously selected the correct response, they were granted a score of .5 for that item.
3. If the students did not give a correct response following Step 2, the assessor talked them through the correct solution of the item, and no further credit was assigned.

These three steps were followed for the first five items that the students did not correctly solve during the pretest. The students were then asked to solve the remaining items that they had missed on their own, with no further intervention. Their posttest score was made up of the pretest score, the scores they accumulated during the brief intervention (maximum of 5), plus any further successes (1 point each) for the re-administered items, minus the test–retest score of 2. Both the pretest and posttest scores were converted into standard scores, using the NNAT norms. In the case of posttest scores, these, of course, are *estimated* and need to be referred to as such. They serve only as a source of comparison and to describe the student's functioning with minimal support.

As mentioned earlier, the scores from the previous year's Reading and Math subtests of the Iowa Tests of Basic Skills (ITBS) were included in both the screening and the final determination of gifted status. For screening, students in the 90th percentile qualified, and for final selection, students in the 97th percentile qualified. That is, the scores of students who scored at or above these levels would count toward determining their eligibility for either individual assessment (90th percentile) or gifted program selection (97th percentile).

In an attempt to proceed as conservatively as possible, identification as gifted was defined as performance at or above the 97th percentile on any two of the three major instruments used, that is, the K-ABC (Mental Processing Composite, or Nonverbal), the NNAT (pre- or posttest), or the Math or Reading sections of the district's achievement test (ITBS). That is, the students had to obtain scores in the top 3% range across two measures, not in one measure. Because the achievement data were not available for students in first and second grades, the criteria for these students relied on their performance on the two measures administered by the assessors (K-ABC and NNAT/DA), and the students had to perform at or above the 97th percentile on both. Also, there were one or two exceptions such as the case of a student who obtained a composite score on the K-ABC of 160, but did not obtain a score above the 97th percentile on other measures. We could not in our minds justify his exclusion from eligibility with such a high score on this standardized test.

The teachers completed the GATES for all of the children in their classes. Using a score of 127 or higher (97th percentile), the teachers correctly identified 20% of the students who later qualified as gifted, therefore failing to identify 80%. The teachers identified five students as gifted who did not qualify. Only the subscales related to academic talent were used because the district's program was not designed for artistic or musical ability.

The total return rate of questionnaires by the parents was 55%. This was fairly even across the grade levels. Sixty percent of the parents of the children who passed the screening returned questionnaires ($n = 48$), which was somewhat higher than the total return rate. That is, it was only somewhat more likely for the parent of a higher functioning child to return the questionnaire. Among these, 15 (60%) of the parents whose children were identified as gifted returned questionnaires. The hit rate for these parents in correctly identifying their children as gifted was 50%. Thirteen children from the total population who were not identified as gifted by this project were identified as gifted by their parents. It was an interesting finding that parents in fact did not identify their children as gifted in large numbers. In fact, many parents of children who were eventually determined to be eligible for the gifted program did not rate their children as gifted.

Logistic regressions were used to determine which of the screening measures were the best predictors of gifted status for the total group. The scores from the GATES Intelligence subtest and the ITBS Math achievement subtest made the only significant predictions of final gifted status. These analyses further documented that neither minority nor immigrant status resulted in differential predictions of gifted status based on the GATES or ITBS scores. It is important to note that the route to determination of final "gifted" status was quite diverse and in fact involved all of the screening measures used. To exclude any one of these would have meant excluding at least one of the students from eventual eligibility. Despite the statistical significance, the poor hit rate of the teachers is important to note.

There were 25 students who met the final criterion of attainment of 97th percentile or higher on two of three parameters (K-ABC Mental Processing Composite or Nonverbal), ITBS Reading or Mathematics, NNAT pre- or posttests (with minor exceptions noted earlier). This represented 5% of the total school population, equal to the proportion of students identified as gifted by the school district. At least two students from each grade qualified.

Furthermore, the categories of ethnic distribution of students who qualified for gifted placement approximated the proportions of the populations of the school. Therefore, the distribution was diverse, with 60% of the students who qualified as gifted coming from either ethnic minority or immigrant backgrounds.

Of the 25 students identified as gifted, 23 met criteria on the basis of their performance on the *posttest* of the NNAT, that is, in response to dynamic assessment. Only five of these students met the gifted criterion on the pretest of the NNAT. Ten of the students met criteria based on their achievement test scores, and, in all of these cases, their high scores were in the area of mathematics. Fourteen students met criteria on the basis of their K-ABC mental processing composite scores, and ten on the basis of their K-ABC Nonverbal scores. Scores on the Nonverbal portion of the K-ABC made no special contribution for these students, as any student who obtained scores in the top 3% on the Nonverbal subtests met this criterion on the other K-ABC subscales as well.

Four of the students met the gifted criteria on all three components, that is, on the ITBS, the K-ABC, and the NNAT. Twelve of the students met the criteria on the combination of K-ABC plus NNAT posttest. The rest of the students met the criteria on the basis of combinations including ITBS plus either the K-ABC or NNAT posttest.

Logistic regressions were used to analyze the relative contribution of the individually administered measures to the determination of gifted status.

None of the measures differentially predicted gifted status across immigrant groups.

K-ABC MPC significantly predicted gifted status, controlling for minority group, NNAT pretest, and NNAT posttest. NNAT posttest significantly predicted gifted status, controlling for minority group, K-ABC MPC, and NNAT pretest. ITBS Reading and Math significantly predicted gifted status, controlling for minority group. None of the measures differentially predicted gifted status across the minority groups.

An intervention segment was added to the NNAT to create a dynamic assessment measure for individual administration to the participants in this study. We performed further analyses to determine the validity of this procedure. Analysis of pretest to posttest gains for the 81 students selected for individual assessment yielded a change in mean scores from 104.48 (SD 20.26) to 118.46 (SD 19.79), with a t of -15.66 and $p < .001$. This documented a highly significant increase in mean scores from pretest to posttest on this measure. This explores a parameter of construct validity.

Evidence for concurrent validity of the NNAT/dynamic assessment was determined by means of correlations between the NNAT pretest and posttest scores and the K-ABC MPC. These correlations were .64 (pretest) and .74 (posttest), both significant at $< .001$. The relationships between the NNAT residual change score and all K-ABC subtests were significant ($p < .01$).

One attempt to correct for possible practice effect on the dynamic assessment (that is, the retest of the NNAT) was to subtract the estimated test–retest score from the posttest raw score before determining the standard score for each student. These corrected scores were used for identification of the students for the gifted program.

To conduct a further check of the validity of the gains made by the students in response to the retest, the scores were checked against the standard error of measurement range information provided for simultaneous processing subtests of the Das-Naglieri/Cognitive Assessment System (1997). These results appear in Table 7.1.

Table 7.1 shows that all but one set of gains (those made by students whose pretest scores were between 81 and 90) were 80% or higher. That is, by far the majority of the gains made by the students following the intervention portion of the dynamic assessment exceeded the gains that might be expected from re-administration of the test without intervention. Furthermore, the distribution of the gains across groups argues against regression to the mean because students obtained a similar percentage of gains in all but the one level of pretest score groups. Calculations were not made for the highest performers because they were at such a high level and maintained this level for the retest without a sufficient ceiling to show gains out of an expected range; however, their scores did not regress. A total of

Table 7.1. Percent of students obtaining Naglieri Nonverbal Ability Test posttest scores beyond expected gains

Score range	N pre	N post	M pre	M post	Exoected range	Percent beyond expected range
70–80	5	0	74	NA	62–93	100
81–90	7	3	86	88	72–102	57
91–100	23	4	96	94	81–111	83
101–110	14	14	107	105	90–120	80
111–120	12	12	114	114	99–129	82
121–130	16	23	125	125	108–138	88
>130	3	22	136	142	Not computed (ceiling scores)	

82% of the students obtained posttest scores beyond expected gains. This information contributes to evidence for construct validity of the dynamic assessment procedure.

Although it was not possible to follow up all of the students who were placed in the gifted program as a result of this project, Lidz and Macrine were able to track down 11 of the original 25 during the term following the completion of a full year in the program. The five fifth-grade students who qualified went on to middle school and were lost to follow-up, and a number of the remaining students most likely transferred to the new charter school that opened for the fall term following the project; some students mentioned this intention during the course of their assessment.

The teachers of the gifted classes for the elementary-level gifted program completed the Scale for Rating Students' Participation in the Local Gifted Education Program (Renzulli & Westberg, 1991) for all of the students in the program. The 11 project students obtained a mean score of 39.00 (SD 10.51; R 24–50), and the 78 non-project students obtained a mean score of 39.87 (SD 7.03; R 12–50). This difference is not statistically significant ($t = -.360$; $p = .7196$). The scores on this scale range from 0 (*not applicable*) through 5 (*very high*). Calculating the proportion of students who obtained scores with totals at the high and very high levels (40+), 64% of the project students and 56% of the non-project students attained this level. Three of the project students were experiencing some difficulty dealing with the challenges of the gifted program, and six of the non-project students obtained scores at similarly low levels. Seven of the eleven project students obtained high to very high scores.

These results suggest that the students who were placed in the program as a result of this project fared as well as those placed through results of traditional assessment. Without the project, few of these students would have qualified as eligible for the gifted program. In fact, during the year of the project, only one student from the project school qualified by the traditional means of identification.

There is one more approach that can be applied with school-age children in instructional settings, and we describe it here despite the fact that it is not strictly a dynamic assessment.

Use of the Mediated Learning Experience Rating Scale for Teacher Consultation

The Mediated Learning Experience Rating Scale was designed by Lidz (1991, 2003) to evaluate the mediational repertoire of primary mediators such as parents and teachers. Although not in and of itself "dynamic assessment," the scale nevertheless reflects what should characterize the examiner's behavior during the course of the intervention portion of the dynamic assessment. The full scale and its explanation are available in the 1991 and 2003 publications. The scale has been used for both research and diagnostic purposes; however, it can also be used for instructional consultation (Rosenfield, 1987) with teachers in regard to their interactions with both groups and individual students. Because of its relevance for classroom instruction and because this information was never previously reported, we present a case example that was carried out particularly well as part of a graduate school seminar assignment by Janet Rubien, who was at that time in the school psychology doctoral program of Temple University. The consultation followed a single-subject design using a baseline–mediation–maintenance model such as that employed by Vye, Burns, Delclos, and Bransford (1987) and Tawney and Gast (1984). Continuous baseline data were collected over a minimum of 3 consecutive days, with the intervention introduced after a zero acceleration trend had been established. The teacher and student participants were from an urban early intervention program. The process of instructional consultation followed the stages suggested by Rosenfield (1987) and included entry and contracting, problem identification and analysis, implementation of interventions, and termination.

The participating teacher volunteered after hearing the description of the project. She selected a student aged 4 years 10 months who was functioning in the moderate range of mental retardation. The teacher selected the target behavior from the child's Individualized Education Plan and that involved pointing to (receptive language) and labeling (expressive language) actions and emotions displayed in pictures. The child was to identify one of two pictures presented by the teacher. The consultant served as observer and rater (on the Mediated Learning Experience Rating Scale).

To reduce observer effects, she and another observer-rater were present in the room for three sessions before the onset of the data collection. Two observers who were independent of the project (for purposes of reliability and objectivity) then determined the pretest baseline, asking the teacher to work with the child on the selected instructional objective for 10 to 15 minutes. Each interaction was rated on the scale (this portion of the project may be too cumbersome for most practitioners). The teacher was then asked to assess the child's pretest performance level. There were then three baseline sessions when the teacher and child worked together without intervention (for the teacher) on the selected objective. These were rated by the consultant-observer for the purpose of future feedback to the teacher and to gather generalizable samples of the teaching interactions. Intervention involved four sessions when the consultant met with the teacher following observation of the teaching interactions (the number of sessions can be adjusted to suit the case). The consultant solicited insight from the teacher regarding her impressions of the session, and provided feedback reflecting the components on the MLE Scale. The consultation sessions combined review of past performance with setting of goals for improvement for the future. The components on the scale were shared freely with the teacher because the scale is designed to be "criterion-referenced" and intended as a teaching instrument. We very much wish to "teach to the test"; however, the scale provides basic principles and concepts and does not suggest a specific script or scenario for the interactions (macro rather than micro). The teacher assessed the child's level of mastery at the end of each session, and the two independent raters observed the teacher's interactions at the end of the project.

In the Rubien project, the teacher showed an increase in her total MLE score. More important, the teacher showed her own individual profile, and some components were more amenable to change (for this teacher) than others. The components showing the most growth were Meaning, Task Regulation, Praise/Encouragement, Challenge, Affective Involvement, and Change. The child was generally positively responsive, and, although not rated in detail, the observers anecdotally noted a marked improvement in his attentiveness. The child's level of mastery of the content also showed positive change. An interesting by-product was the consultant's observation that the child's assessment warranted modification. Labeling and pointing were insufficient indicators of task mastery for him because he demonstrated increased awareness and comprehension by acting out what he saw portrayed in the pictures. The consultant noted the relevance of the setting in which the observations were made (on the one hand, consistency enhances measurability, but, on the other hand, it reduces generalizability). She also noted the fact that some of the components appeared

8 Applying Dynamic Assessment with Adults and Seniors

Even though they are typically not in school and usually may be presumed to be free of psychopathology or developmental disabilities, adults (including, for this chapter, adolescents and senior citizens), encounter many situations in which it is especially useful to be able to identify obstacles to good performance and to specify ways to overcome those obstacles. Integrating dynamic assessment of cognitive functioning and potential into a more comprehensive assessment that includes personality and social variables can enable examiners to go well beyond the standard vocational aptitude assessments that characterize, for example, employment services. Even when psychological barriers, including psychopathology (see Chapter 4), may be impeding the performance of adults, one can identify the cognitive component of those barriers and find ways to overcome at least that aspect. In fact, improving logical thinking can be a key to liberation of the personality and to improved personal, social, and occupational performance (e.g., Beck, 1976, 1991; Haywood, 2000; Haywood & Menal, 1992; Meichenbaum, 1977, 1982). In this chapter we discuss the application of dynamic assessment in work with adults, from adolescence into maturity and old age, using the usual combination of theoretical aspects, assessment techniques, and some specific assessment instruments.

THE TASKS OF CHILDHOOD AND ADULTHOOD

Whereas the primary task of childhood is to gain knowledge of the world and competence in interacting with one's environment, with heavy emphasis on education, the primary tasks of adulthood are work, child rearing, social interaction, and learning in non-school contexts. Those differential tasks define, in a major way, the problems that children and adults encounter and consequently the questions that assessment professionals are called on to answer. The most frequently asked question regarding children is, "Why is he or she not learning more effectively, and what can

205

be done to help him or her learn more effectively?" With adults, one still encounters that question, but the more frequent questions have to do with job adjustment, social interaction, and, in the case of senior citizens, declining performance and abilities.

Another major difference between adults and children that obviously affects assessment approaches and techniques is the difference in development rate. Throughout childhood, development of the nervous system and of the behavioral repertoire proceeds at a very fast rate as the cumulative processes of learning take place. The classical intelligence tests such as the Stanford-Binet Intelligence Test and the Wechsler Intelligence Scale for Children (in its several revisions and updates) have usually suggested a division between adulthood and childhood somewhere between 14 and 16 years of age. Neuroscientists agree that although the brain may continue to develop and elaborate well into adulthood, the rate of such development declines sharply after about 12 years of age. In fact, the rate of brain development is most rapid in the prenatal and early infancy periods and declines steadily thereafter, approaching an asymptote around age 12 years. For assessment purposes, these differences suggest a differentiation between initial acquisition of both information and the metacognitive tools of learning, in the case of children, and the processes of learning on the basis of previously acquired knowledge or of metacognitive learning that is out of the usual developmental sequence in the case of adults. Of course, the progression from childhood to adulthood is a continuous process (although not at a steady rate) rather than a sharp dichotomy, so older children may perform more like adults than like younger children; nevertheless, it is useful to make a broad distinction because such a distinction influences the questions one asks in assessment situations, the assessment strategies one selects, the specific tests and other assessment instruments one uses, and even the interpretation of assessment data.

Frequently, some of the developmental tasks of childhood are incomplete in the adult years. The "critical periods" hypothesis in developmental psychology led many psychologists and others to suspect – and to assert – that developmental milestones that had been missed, for whatever reasons, in childhood could not be made up later. Piaget has been misinterpreted frequently to suggest that cognitive development must occur in an "invariant" sequence. (He meant, of course, not that it *must*, but that cognitive development usually does occur in a sequence that is predictable and "constant" – a better translation of *invariant* – across persons.) As it has turned out, the "soft" statement of the critical periods hypothesis is more correct than was its initial statement: Certain developmental aspects are more easily acquired during "maximally sensitive" periods, which suggests that their out-of-sequence acquisition can be expected to require greater effort and more time.

Here is an example of out-of-sequence metacognitive development, as well as an important role for DA. A second-year law student at a very prestigious university was referred because, in spite of excellent predictor scores and a good first-year performance, her grades in the second year had begun to decline, especially on essay exams but also in courses that required critical discussion of case law in class. Dynamic assessment, using mainly The Organizer (an instrument from Feuerstein's LPAD; see Appendix A) revealed that the ability to manage and interpret multiple sources of information simultaneously had not developed satisfactorily, regardless of the content domain, but the assessment also revealed that she responded very well to specific metacognitive training that was focused sharply on integrating information from multiple and diverse sources. A brief training program was sufficient to overcome her difficulty, and her professors reported a very positive gain in her classroom and exam performance. We have seen many graduate students whose superb academic records in high school and undergraduate school would have predicted little difficulty in graduate school, but who did indeed encounter difficulty when faced with the necessity to call on information that was clearly in their knowledge base, evaluate the relevance of that information, integrate it conceptually, and bring it to bear toward the solution of new problems – a major task with which advanced thinkers are confronted quite regularly.

In general, whereas the chief *cognitive* developmental task of childhood is acquisition and elaboration of fundamental cognitive processes (structures, functions, operations), by adulthood the chief cognitive task has gradually shifted to one of selection, application, and metacognitive control of those cognitive processes and of the base of acquired knowledge. Thus, the assessment task itself is frequently one of identifying presence or absence of habit structures (metacognitive habits, such as identifying presence of problems, defining the nature of problems, scanning one's store of problem-solving strategies, applying and evaluating solutions) and estimating what investment will be required to strengthen such habits.

ASSESSMENT OF APTITUDE

Scholastic Aptitude

Having just observed that going to school is a major task of the developmental period of childhood, let us now observe that it also occupies the time and energy of a very large number of adolescents, adults, and even senior citizens. A large part of that effort is devoted to assessment of aptitude for college and university studies, followed by aptitude for graduate and professional school and by aptitude for specific kinds of vocational training. Although use of DA has not become widespread in these domains of aptitude assessment, there is little doubt that a dynamic approach, as one component of aptitude assessment, can be quite useful. The major predictors of academic success at the postsecondary level are (a) high school grades and (b) predictor test scores, such as the SAT and the ACT.[1] Both are imperfect predictors; that is, both yield less than perfect (sometimes far less than perfect) correlations with postsecondary school achievement. This is not necessarily due to bad tests. There are many variables other than aptitude that influence the subsequent achievement of individual students, including focus on non-school factors, differences in motivation to learn and achieve, poor fit between students' aptitudes and interests and the work they encounter at the university level, interruptions in the educational sequence (e.g., military service, marriage), and financial circumstances. There is also the now-familiar fact that past performance, as reflected both in high school grades and in aptitude test scores, is not a complete predictor of future performance. That is precisely where DA may enter the assessment process and make significant contributions: how to exploit that part of the variance in postsecondary performance that is not predicted by aptitude tests or previous school achievement, and, at least as important, how to defeat the pessimistic predictions made by those factors that will indeed be valid without informed intervention.

In spite of the admirable inclusion of reasoning tasks in the ACT and SAT (i.e., tasks that are based less on prior accumulation of information than on "pure" ability to apply logical thinking to the solving of problems), the tests used for prediction of academic success still leave much to be desired. The most obvious problem is that they do not include learning tasks. That is a problem because, as psychometrists have been observing for many years (Anastasi, 1965), the best test of any performance is a sample of that performance. Thus, as Haywood (2002) has pointed out, if one wishes to predict success at operating a drill press, giving a Rorschach test would not be the best way to do that; one should instead give a test that includes a sample of the tasks involved in operating drill presses. This principle is shared by DA and performance-based assessment. The major task in postsecondary education is learning – but not just learning; it is learning at least in part by way of teaching. Some way of answering the question, "How much, and under what circumstances, does this person derive benefit from teaching?" would be an obviously valuable addition to these tests (see also the section on response to intervention [RTI] in Chapter 1). That is precisely the kind of answer that can be provided, to

---

[1] The ACT and the SAT are standardized tests administered in groups to high school students in the United States to assess their aptitude for postsecondary (college and university) study. They are typically used as part of the decision process for admission to colleges and universities.

a considerable extent, by DA. It would be most interesting to add actual learning-given-teaching tasks to scholastic aptitude tests to see how much their predictive validity would be improved. One must recall, however, that prediction itself is not a primary goal of DA. Even if the predictive validity of the tests were to be improved greatly, one would still be faced with the question, "What, then, is to be done with individuals for whom failure is predicted?" In other words, we are asking once again how to defeat the pessimistic predictions. This is the other major way in which using DA in assessment of scholastic aptitude can make a major contribution.

As usual when faced with DA tasks, the first thing we need to ask is, "What do we need to find out?" To answer that question, we must first try to analyze the cognitive, metacognitive, and motivational requirements of scholastic work. We assume that standardized intelligence tests and standardized scholastic aptitude tests do a good job of assessing individual differences in general learning ability: Persons who make high scores on them are typically good learners, and those who make low scores are typically poor learners. Relying on the standardized tests, however, has two major problems. The first is the qualification "typically," that is, relying on group norms to forecast individual performance, characteristic of the nomothetic approach discussed in Chapter 2. The other problem is the absence of teaching in these tests. Thus, we want DA to fill in both of these lacunae by becoming idiographic investigations and basing forecasts and prescriptions on learning-with-teaching.

To accomplish those two tasks, DA must make use of complex tasks rather than simple ones, as well as tasks that require learning and that have a place for teaching. Two that come to mind immediately are both part of the LPAD (Feuerstein et al., 1979, 1986; see Appendix A): The Organizer and LPAD Set Variations II. Both require the gathering of information from several sources and the simultaneous application of that information to finding problem solutions. It would he useful if both tests actually had somewhat higher ceilings so as to avoid the possibility of extremely high levels of performance, leaving room for mediation of complex combinations of metacognitive operations. It is axiomatic in cognitive–experimental psychology that the more subtle the phenomena one wishes to discover, the more complex must be the task. Let us recall also that it is often necessary to sample a rather broad universe of content in our assessment efforts. Difficulty or ability that might not show up in testing of one domain of content might well appear in another content domain. So the tasks should be complex, varied, and responsive to teaching.

The following is an example of mediation that might occur using one of the generic problems, item B, from LPAD Set Variations II with a college-bound high school senior.

Examiner	Examinee
Have you seen anything like this before?	
	Yes, it's pretty much like the ones we did before [refers to Set Variations I].
Yes, it is. Is it exactly the same?	Well, pretty close.
Try to make a picture in your mind of the problems we worked on before. Is this one the same?	
	Not exactly, but some things are the same.
Good. You are comparing them. What is alike?	
	Well, both have these rows and columns of designs, and one place where something is missing.
Good comparing! What is different?	Well, the others had two rows and two columns, and this one has three rows and three columns. So I'll bet it's going to be harder!
Yes, you are right about the rows and columns. The others were hard at first, but what happened then?	
	When I learned how to do them, they got easy. Maybe that will happen here.
I'll bet you are right! Any other differences that you can see?	
	Yeah, I had to pick the answer out of six choices before, but now we have eight choices.
You are really a sharp observer! That's exactly right. But did you just pick out the answer?	
	No. Actually, I worked it out in my head, made a picture of what the answer should look like, and then found the one at the bottom that matched my mental picture.
Fantastic! You remembered exactly how you did those other problems. Do you think you will solve these in the same way?	
	Yes.
What makes you think so? Are all problems alike?	
	No, but these look alike. I mean, they are designs arranged in rows and columns, and there is one part missing, and that makes me think

Examiner	Examinee
	they are probably the same kind of problems.
Excellent analyzing. You looked at all the information, compared the two sets of problems – one set in your mind and the other in front of you – and found the common elements. But you found some differences as well. What made you think mostly of the similarities?	
	The ways they are alike seem more important than the ways they are different. The differences are mostly just about the number of parts.
Right you are! Good thinking. If the principles are the same, it doesn't matter how many parts you have to deal with, does it?	
	No. It's a question of scale.
Great. Now. Do you remember why I am covering up the possible answers at the bottom of the page?	
	Yes. It's so I won't look at the answers before I have worked it out in my head. You don't want me to be impulsive.
Right again, but it isn't just what I want, is it? When did you do better, when you were impulsive or when you were not?	
	OK, you got me. I did better when I worked slowly, a step at a time, and followed the rules.
Wonderful! I think you are not going to have one bit of trouble with these, because you remember so well the easier ones that we did before. Look here (indicating top row) and tell me what you see.	
	Circles.
How many? And what else is there about the circles?	
	Oh, yeah. Three circles, with lines in some of them.
Do you think you could be more precise than that? Your answer about the number of circles was precise, but what about the rest of the description?	
	OK [sighs]. In one, there are no lines, in the second one it has part lines, and in the next one it is all lines.

Examiner	Examinee
Good. Much more precise but not quite there yet. "Part lines" does not tell me much, and "all lines" suggests that there are no spaces. Imagine that I cannot see the page, then describe it to me so that I could draw an exact picture of it.	That's pretty hard. Besides, you can see it! OK, OK, I'm on the case. The FIRST circle is empty, has no lines. Zero lines, just a plain empty circle. Moving to the second circle in the row, half of the circle has lines in it. Then, moving to the third circle, the whole circle has lines in it.
Great. I'm getting the picture. But I don't know what kind of lines.	Just lines. Straight lines.
OK, straight lines. What is their orientation?	What do you mean?
Are the lines vertical or horizontal, standing up or lying down?	Oh, yeah. They're vertical.
So the lines are straight and vertical.	Yeah.
Are there any other kinds of lines? Horizontal? Diagonal?	Nope. Just vertical.
OK. Now you are being very precise. Please tell me then everything you know about the top row.	[Sighs] OK. There are three circles, all the same size. The first one is empty. Half of the second one has vertical straight lines in it, and all of the third one has vertical straight lines in it. There are no other lines.
Fantastic! I know from the other work we have done that when you describe things that precisely, you usually do very well. Is there any other time, at school or anywhere else, when precise description helps you?	Yeah, when I'm telling my friend about a girl I like. Just telling him she's really cool doesn't help him to get a good picture of her, so I have to tell him about her height, her hair, her

Examiner	Examinee
	eyes – but mostly about her personality!
Good example. OK, then, do you think you can discover the rule about what happens across the top row, or will you need more information?	I can make a rule, but it might not apply to the next row.
Right you are. What do you remember about that?	If it is the right rule, it has to apply to the next row, and I guess to the next one also, since there are three rows here.
Yes, and what if it doesn't work in the second row?	Then it was the wrong rule, or I made a mistake trying to apply it. I have to check it out in the top row again, then be careful applying it. If I didn't make a mistake, the rule was wrong and I have to look for another one to explain what's happening.
Exactly right! You really know a lot about working these problems. What might the rule be in the top row?	As you go from left to right, you have to add more lines.
OK, let's see how that helps out in the second row [NOTE THAT THE EXAMINER DID NOT POINT OUT THE LACK OF PRECISION REGARDING EITHER THE PROPORTION OF THE CIRCLE THAT HAS LINES OR THE VERTICAL NATURE OF THE LINES, LEAVING THAT FOR THE EXAMINEE'S DISCOVERY.]	
	Hmmmm. In this one you have some horizontal lines, then both vertical and horizontal lines, and both again in the third circle.
So what's the rule? What was the rule that you established in the top row?	Well, I added more lines each time across the page, and that's what I did in the second row, but things are looking funny.

Examiner	Examinee
Maybe you were not precise enough about that rule from the top row. Would you tell it to me again, this time being as precise as possible?	
	OK. In the top row, the rule is that the number of vertical lines goes from zero to half to full. Oh, I see. It's kind of a math problem: zero to 50% to 100% filled with vertical lines.
Excellent. You see how precise you can be? It's just a question of remembering to be precise, and practicing doing it, not just when we are learning something new. Did the rule mention horizontal lines?	No, except I could just say that there are not any of them.
OK, so what kind of lines is the rule about?	Vertical lines.
Good. Now look again at the second row and apply your rule.	OK. Ah, I see. Zero vertical lines, 50% vertical lines, 100% vertical lines.
What about the horizontal lines?	Nothing about them. They're not in the rule.
Right. But you can now put them in the rule in case it might help. What did the horizontal lines do in the top row?	Nothing. Oh, I see. Just like in the other problems, while some things changed, other things stayed the same. So here, the number or percentage of vertical lines changed, but the horizontal lines stayed the same: zero, zero, zero in the top row; 50, 50, 50 in the second row. Let's see what happens in the third row.
Great. Go ahead. You're cruisin'.	OK, the vertical lines will change from zero to 50% to 100%. The horizontal lines will stay the same, and since they are already at 100% they will be that way all the way across the row. So here where the figure is missing we should have a circle with 100% vertical lines and 100% horizontal lines!

Examiner	Examinee
Good for you! Now shall I uncover the answer choices?	
	Yes, but I know there will be one that has 100% of both kinds of lines, and that one will be the right choice! Yes! It's number 2.
Right! You knew it would be right even before we looked at the answers! How could you be so sure?	
	I made the picture of it in my head, and I knew it was right because I applied the rule and it worked.
Is there a way you could check it, just to be sure you are right?	
	Well, you told me I was right.
But you don't have to believe me. You can check it for yourself. What if I was trying to play a trick on you?	
	OK, no tricks please. Yeah, I remember that in the easier problems I could work them out by columns as well as by rows, and get the same answer. [Quickly works by columns, arrives at the same answer.] It works out. Same answer, but the rule is about horizontal lines changing and vertical lines staying the same.
OK. Great work. What's wrong with choice number 1?	
	It has 100% horizontal lines but only 50% vertical lines, so it doesn't have enough vertical lines to be right.
Right! Which is the worst answer?	I guess I'd pick number 8.
Why?	
	Because its lines are all diagonal, none vertical and none horizontal. Besides, it only has one kind of lines.
I'll buy that! Number 8 is a bad one. Would it be OK if you just rotated it a bit so the diagonal lines would become vertical?	
	Nope! It would still need to have 100% horizontal lines.
That's great. You did a terrific job. Would you tell me now what you did in your mind, what kinds of thinking,	

Examiner	Examinee
that helped you to do so well at solving that problem?	
	OK. First I looked for a rule. No, that's not right. The first thing was, I looked for all the information that was there, and described it. I also gave a name to everything: the shape had to be a circle, the lines were lines and not bars or stripes. But that would have been OK, they just had to have a name. Then I compared the first and second circles, and then the second and third ones. How they were alike and how they were different helped me to find the rule.
Very good! Did the rule come to you right away?	
	No. I had to think about it, and ask myself what kind of problem it was, I mean, what was changing. The only thing changing was the number of lines, so it had to be about "how many" or "how much."
Very nice. It is really good to see you have so much confidence in your answers. It must be because you feel pretty secure about how you are analyzing, finding rules, and applying them. I think the biggest gain you have made is in being more precise, both in describing what you see and in forming pictures of the solution. Do you agree?	Yeah, I guess.

In the "distributed mediation" procedure, this examinee would then be tested, with no help, on problems B-1 through B-15. Throughout the B series, the same strategies apply, but the complexity increases in a power series.

The following things can be observed about the mediation. First, the examiner began by asking for an answer from the examinee. Doing that communicates confidence that the examinee is capable of supplying the answer, as well as the expectation that the examiner will ask for further answers. Second, that question was only a descriptive one rather than an analytic one, which virtually guaranteed a correct answer or at least one that could be accepted. Third, the examiner asked the examinee to relate present to past experience: "How is this like what you have done before, and how is it different?" Over time and many repetitions, doing so can help to establish a habit of calling on one's store of prior experience for help in understanding and coping with new experience. Fourth, the answers were not only accepted in a very positive manner, but they were also analyzed; that is, the examiner helped the examinee to understand exactly what he did that was good, correct, precise, and contributed to the solution of the problem – always focusing on metacognitive operations: "Yes, you described the parts of the problem very precisely, and that helped you to find the rule." Feuerstein (Feuerstein et al., 1979) referred to this as "mediating a feeling of competence," meaning a great deal more than just helping the person to feel good about himself or herself. Fifth, there was at least a minimal attempt to generalize the metacognitive operation that seemed to be the problem with this examinee (i.e., precision and accuracy). This was done by "bridging" (see Feuerstein et al., 1979, 1980; Haywood, 1988), that is, asking the examinee to relate the principle of being precise to familiar experience in his everyday life. In cognitive teaching, bridging is seen much more frequently. It has a place in DA as well, but there is not usually time – or the need – to do as much of it as in cognitive classroom teaching. It is important to note that the examiner's attitude is always positive, supportive, and encouraging, but that he or she does not sacrifice accuracy for the sake of being positive; incorrect answers, wrong paths, are not accepted, but the examinee is redirected with focused questions. Note also that the examiner does far more asking than telling. The kinds of questions the examiner asks are process questions, relating to the examinee's metacognitive operations and not merely to the possible answers. Haywood (1987/1993) has described these principles of mediational teaching in greater detail in the context of cognitive education. They apply as well to the mediation phases of DA as to cognitive education in the formal sense.

ASSESSMENT OF VOCATIONAL APTITUDE

Vocational aptitude assessment occurs at two critical times in the lives of adults (and adolescents): transition from school to work and transition from job to job within the workforce. The first of these is usually a general assessment, whereas the second is usually problem oriented.

Hays (2001), drawing on discussions of assessment validity by Anastasi (1986), Reschly (1987, 1997), Salvia and Ysseldyke (1991), and Sattler (1988), has cited a number of problems with traditional vocational ability and aptitude assessment. One such criticism has to do with a problem that is shared by virtually all of psychological testing, that of content validity: Test items may not adequately represent the criterion domain of vocational skills. A closely related problem is that of concurrent and predictive validity (Lubinski & Dawis, 1992): "the behavior elicited in the relatively limited and artificial test setting does not reflect that likely to occur in other, more realistic settings" (Hays, 2001, p. 1). In the assessment of aptitudes, the usual large difference between the samples of behavior in tests and the population of possible criterion behavior to which one seeks to predict is even larger: tiny sample of items, giant population of criterion behavior (see Messick, 1995). A third difficulty is poor correspondence between persons being tested and those in the tests' normative samples. This is a particular problem in vocational aptitude assessment of persons with disabilities, who are only rarely represented in the normative samples. Even if the normative samples had included a representative number of persons with disabilities, the estimate of overall aptitude may say little or nothing about a person's ability to meet a specific requirement of a job. It is at best a gross estimate.

The use of criterion-referenced tests is, to be sure, an improvement over exclusive reliance on norm-referenced tests, but there are also problems with it. If one uses industrial performance standards for vocational tests (Owings & Siefker, 1991), there is still a discrepancy between requirements (set by the job itself) and standards (set by employers or supervisors). Overall, vocational aptitude assessment may be too much linked to specific job skills and aptitudes (Elrod & Tesolowski, 1993; Szymula, 1990) rather than to generalizable aptitudes that might cut across a variety of on-the-job applications. Thus, we come to a familiar argument: In dynamic assessment, one tries to identify generalizable abilities, metacognitive operations, and habits that can be applied across a wide variety of occupations and activities.

An alternative to exclusive reliance on norm-referenced, or even criterion-referenced, tests of vocational aptitude is incorporation of dynamic assessment procedures into the total assessment process – as we have advocated throughout the book.

There are at least three general approaches to DA of vocational aptitude. In the first approach, "content free," one administers tests of cognitive and metacognitive abilities, regardless of their content (e.g., categorizing, classifying, estimating time, building stencil designs, connecting dots), to locate generalized metacognitive barriers to effective performance. Reports of such assessments look very much like other DA reports on adults' performance and potential, reflecting baseline performance, amount and kinds of mediation given, response to mediation and its generalization, and interpretation of what will likely be required to get more effective performance. Such assessments are indeed useful but lack the specificity that vocational counselors need to see. The second approach is to give standardized, normative vocational aptitude tests in a dynamic mode, that is, with interpolated mediation of specific metacognitive operations and habits. Of course, doing that violates the standardization of those tests and makes it impossible to compare the examinees' performance with the norms of the tests. One way to avoid that spoiling of normative tests is to administer them first in the standard way, deriving standardized scores from that initial performance. Following the initial administration, one then mediates essential metacognitive operations and habits that were observed to be deficient during the initial performance. Such operations might (and often do) include, for example, spontaneous comparing; inhibiting impulsive responding; considering problems in manageable parts rather than as overwhelming wholes; use of metamemory strategies such as mental imaging, rehearsal, and associative clustering; abstracting and applying explanatory and procedural rules; managing multiple sources of information simultaneously; use of private speech; looking for and requiring logical evidence for one's choices; and metacognitive awareness and control of executive functions.

The third approach is one that we have used often in the DA of children, adolescents, and adults, especially those who are in the care of others. Useful with either the content-free or content-oriented methods, its purpose is as much to demonstrate to other people the examinees' capacity for more effective behavior and cognitive functioning as it is to discover that information. In the demonstration approach, one arranges to examine either a single examinee or a group, with responsible others observing. In one such situation, we were working with a group of intellectually low-functioning adolescent boys who were in the custody of the state department of corrections. Our efforts to convince the staff members at their facility that these boys could be challenged to learn more effectively and that they had far more capacity – including intelligence – than was apparent (and more than the staff members gave them credit for!) had largely fallen on deaf, if not actively hostile, ears. Confident that the boys would perform well, we gave them a group administration of the Representational Stencil Design Test (RSDT) from Feuerstein's Learning Potential Assessment Device (see Appendix A), with several staff members observing from behind a one-way-vision window. A graduate student assistant was in the observation room with the staff members, who were also allowed to take the test. One could have predicted the outcome: The boys solved the problems more readily than did the adult staff members, even though the boys were presumed to be functioning intellectually at a mildly mentally retarded level and were clearly the products of a life spent so far in poverty and social disadvantage. Further, most of the boys (but not 100%) responded very well to mediation of essential metacognitive operations and demonstrated that response by performing significantly better after mediation than they had at pretest. Staff members wanted to pose all sorts of hypotheses about why the boys learned within the test situation (Had they been coached beforehand? Were we slipping them the answers?) but finally were able to see that there was heretofore unsuspected potential in the boys, and that realization alone helped our group to work with them to improve the boys' educability. The second-level result of the demonstration was that the staff members were able to witness the successful mediation of metacognitive operations, which enabled them to begin to acquire some new skills for interacting with their charges.

We typically invite parents and others who are responsible for the care, education, habilitation, and treatment of examinees – with the examinees' permission, of course – to sit in and observe DA. Certain rules have to be established: (a) The observers are not to participate; (b) the observers must not express approval or disapproval of the examinees' performance or be distracting in any way; (c) the observers should not try to clarify the examinees' responses or to prompt the examinees to respond. These rules are not made to preserve the standard qualities of the tests but rather to protect the mediational interaction between examiners and examinees. When the rules are followed, it is often true that the observers gain more insight than they can through written reports or even oral feedback from an assessment that they did not observe. For research reports on effects of observed and reported DA, see Bransford, Delclos, Vye, Burns, and Hasselbring (1986); Delclos, Vye, Johnson, and Bransford (1987); and Delclos, Burns, and Vye (1993).

CONTINUUM OF ASSESSMENT SERVICES

As a general model for broad-ranging assessment, the CAS (continuum of assessment services[2]) model serves well. The central idea is that the least expensive services should be those provided to the largest number, because relatively few in a large group are likely to need highly sophisticated services, whereas the most expensive services – the most sophisticated and time-consuming – are reserved for those few who have the greatest need. Following that idea, group screening takes place using group normative, standardized tests (of intelligence, vocational aptitudes, interests). A very large percentage of those who receive such group-administered assessment may then fall out of the assessment sequence because they have satisfactory scores and present no particular questions or problems. The remaining

[2] The general model came out of the Cognitive Development Research Group at Vanderbilt University and was a product of "group think." The name was undoubtedly suggested by Dr. Susan Burns, who was a member of that group at the time.

Table 8.1. A continuum of assessment services model

Recipients of service	Type of assessment	Outcomes
Large groups	A. Standardized, normative, group-administered tests	High scorers exit; low scorers go to next level
Low scorers from A	B. Group DA	High gainers exit; low scorers and non-gainers go to next level
Low scorers from B	C. Individual DA	High gainers exit; non-gainers go to next level
Non-gainers from C	D. Extended (in situ) DA	Feedback to treatment or education plan

examinees are then given group-administered dynamic assessment that is a continuation of the screening process. The usual result of group dynamic assessment is that some percentage of those who made low, unsatisfactory, or problem-suggesting scores on group standardized testing subsequently show greater potential with group dynamic assessment. Some number in that group may then exit the assessment process, provided they show no indication of problems that need to be addressed – either from their performance in group dynamic assessment or from other information such as school or clinic records or their own statements. A very small group can be expected to continue to yield low, unsatisfactory, or problem-suggesting performances, and that group should be given individual dynamic assessment. Individual DA usually reveals both the nature of those individuals' problems and some indications for remedial procedures. Often, there is a much smaller group whose difficulties were not specifically addressed in individual DA and who continue to get low scores on all or most of the tests. These individuals go into an "extended assessment" group in which DA (or some other version of RTI) or CBM is carried out in the classroom or adult setting. Table 8.1 shows the CAS model.

The presentation of the CAS model in Table 8.1 is somewhat over-simplified for purposes of clarity. People just do not fall so handily into categories. Often they give mixed results across different tests. The model allows for such diversity and inconsistency by generous inclusion at each level: When in doubt, continue the search. It is also true that idiosyncratic problems may be revealed at any stage of the CAS procedure.

The model may appear to depend too heavily on global scores. Because of that possibility, one must be especially sensitive to both individual differences within groups and variability across domains of functioning within individuals. Indications that a person should continue to the next level (smaller group or individual) of CAS include the following:

1. significant variability across domains of functioning
2. at least one domain of very low functioning, in relation to his or her other scores
3. one or more domains of very high functioning in relation to other scores
4. informally observed signs of poor work or learning motivation
5. questions raised prior to group testing that have not been answered so far

Intraindividual variability is important for a variety of reasons. First, in spite of the concept of general intelligence (g), which is a real and well-established phenomenon, intraindividual variability across domains of functioning is also real and well established. Because intelligence subtests tend to be substantially correlated with each other, as well as with the total score, one must be suspicious of some interfering agent or circumstance when the variability among them exceeds normal limits (see, e.g., any of the manuals of the Wechsler scales for discussion of significance of subtest deviations). That caution has to be combined with the observation (see discussion of the transactional perspective on human ability, Chapter 2, this volume) that ability is multifaceted, meaning that some deviation is expected. This combination of observations suggests that intraindividual variability is not diagnostic but is rather suggestive of the need for further investigation, if for no other reason than just to determine whether there might be additional indications of an interfering agent or circumstance, that is, some mask on one's intelligence.

One advantage of working with adults, including senior citizens, is their greater accessibility via group DA. Group assessment procedures may certainly be used with younger children (see Chapter 7) as well as with persons who have psychiatric disorders and developmental disabilities (see Chapter 4) but are more easily employed, perhaps in larger groups and with fewer helpers, in groups of mature adults.

PROCEDURES AND PROBLEMS WITH GROUP DA

Everybody agrees that DA is a time-consuming and often expensive process (although it does not have to be so; see Chapter 3). Many have noted that use of DA would be more practical if it could be done with groups of persons at a time. In fact, that can be done and has been done, usually for research purposes. There is no good reason not to do group-administered DA for non-research purposes, but one must understand that the inferences one can make on the basis of the DA are not necessarily the same as those made from individual DA. The CAS model of assessment, discussed in a previous section of this chapter, has a clear place for group DA. Following are some principles that apply to group DA.

1. The tasks must be ones that are suitable to all of the participants, so relatively homogeneous groups, in terms of age, general ability levels, and adaptive functioning, are usually advisable. Homogeneous grouping helps to minimize variability in work efficiency and the resulting boredom and off-task behavior that can be expected when some individuals finish with a given part of the task well before others do.

2. Instructions must be quite clear in order to avoid the necessity to work at an individual level with one or two persons in the group.

3. The mediation that will be interpolated between static pretest and static posttest should be standard; that is, it should be developed and written out in advance so it can be given to all participants simultaneously but with room for individualized mediation as needed.

4. The examiner must have the capability of responding individually to questions and to difficulty with the tasks. This usually means having one or more "monitors" or co-examiners who can move from participant to participant, answering questions, clarifying task requirements, and amplifying the mediation. Individuals within the test group may also pose their questions to the examiner, who then may respond "publicly," that is, to the whole group. Remember, this is DA, so it is essential that the examiner standardize the "proximal stimulus" (i.e., what is actually understood), especially regarding instructions and task requirements, rather than control of the "distal stimulus" (i.e., what the examiner says). That means, of course, that some individual clarification will be required in almost any group. Obviously, the greater the degree of disability or special need in the group, the greater the need for co-examiners.

5. Use of tasks that do not require extensive written responses is recommended. Minimal response requirements will reduce the likelihood of extreme variability in the participants' response time, make the responses easier to score, and increase the reliability of the tests – all at a price, of course.

6. The examiner should control the pace of the testing so that all participants are working on the same problem at the same time. Failure to do so means that some participants will move ahead quickly and then be confused by any supplemental mediation that is required and bored while waiting for the slower participants to catch up.

With group DA, the questions that one wishes to ask, and consequently the instruments that one chooses to try to answer them, cannot be as specific or as finely matched as is possible with individual DA. The group that is assembled for assessment must have been constituted for some reason, and generally that reason (or those reasons) will suggest the questions to be asked. Here is an example from the experience of one of the authors. In one group DA episode, the assessment was done at a U.S. Army post. Initial enlistments in the army were conducted on a fairly open basis; that is, very many enlistees were admitted, some large percentage of whom might not be expected to make careers in the army. The army's attitude was that those who wished to have military careers should have leadership capability and that implied the ability to derive significant benefit from further education and technical training. The task that the army faced was that of determining who should be encouraged to re-enlist and who should not. The "who should not" part of the question did not fit as comfortably with the principles of DA as did the "who should" question, but answering the latter automatically implies some answer to the former unless 100% of those who wished to re-enlist should be encouraged to do so – clearly not the situation that we faced. "Who can benefit significantly from further education and training?" and its corollary, "Who has leadership potential?" then became the assessment questions. The group was far too large for individual DA to be practicable, and members of the assessment team were convinced in any case that group DA could yield relevant information, if not definitive answers, regarding those questions.

We followed a modified CAS procedure, using standardized test scores and personal interviews that were already in the record to identify those individuals who seemed to be very good candidates for future leadership. Those persons did not participate in the DA, but we had suggested that they be moved into the next stage of the army's independent assessment, which consisted of a review of their service records and another personal interview. We reasoned that, although some error would inevitably occur, the outcome of permitting the re-enlistment of some soldiers who might not then become leaders would be far less serious than would be the outcome of denying further opportunity to some who, given the opportunity, might have a good chance of succeeding. In other words, exclusion was considered in this situation to be relatively more serious than overinclusion would be.

Learning tasks were certainly indicated. We chose to use the LPAD Set Variations I and II in a "distributed mediation" format (see Chapter 4; Haywood & Miller, 2005), a group version of the Test of Verbal Abstracting (TVA), and the Representational Stencil Design Test from the LPAD, to examine 400+ soldiers divided into eight groups of 50 each. For each group there was a "lead" examiner (the one who gave instructions and did the group mediation), with four monitors (roving examiners whose task was to be sure all the participants understood the instructions and were on task and to answer individual questions). All stimulus materials for Set Variations I and II and for RSDT were projected from slides onto a large screen in front of the participants. Individual answer sheets for Set Variations I and II were not merely numbered according to the numbers of the items but contained instead reproductions of the response choices usually given at the bottom of the problem pages, in the manner of a multiple-choice test. On the RSDT, participants had to write down, in proper sequence, the numbers of the stencils required to make up the "problem" designs, by item number. The TVA required the most writing. They were asked to write the way in which the items in each pair (or group of five) of exemplars were alike. In the total group of more than 400 examinees, only two papers were "spoiled," that is, were unusable because of mixed-up item numbers and responses.

Overall, there was a significant increase in scores from static pretest to static posttest on all three instruments. We were more interested in individual gains (or not) than in group means and upon examination found that the data conformed very nicely to Budoff's (1967, 1987) categories of High Scorers, Gainers, and Non-gainers. All participants who failed to gain at least 20% over their static pretest scores were then given individual DA using a single task, but this number was surprisingly small: fewer than 40 out of the original group of 400+. Even many of the initial high scorers made further gains with mediation. The participants who made no significant gains in either group or individual DA were not recommended for re-enlistment, but individual reports were written suggesting areas of their development that needed further work; that is, they were not simply dumped into the failure bin but rather were identified as remedial prospects with suggestions of how to accomplish the remediation. Such suggestions ranged from remedial reading classes to a combination of remedial academic education and cognitive education, in that case the Instrumental Enrichment program of Feuerstein. These soldiers could then be returned to civilian life with better prospects for success. Those who made large gains under mediation were recommended to the attention of their officers as persons who had more potential for growth and learning than might be apparent, with some suggestions about how to achieve progress toward their potential. In this example, the use of group DA was highly successful.

The original script for group mediation has not survived, but it is possible to reconstruct one for RSDT to illustrate group mediation. RSDT (Representational Stencil Design Test) is one of the instruments of the *Learning Propensity Assessment Device* (*LPAD*; Feuerstein et al., 1979, 1986). Based on the *Grace Arthur Stencil Design Test*, it is "representational" in the sense that one does not actually manipulate stencils; rather, the examinee must look at pictures of stencils and determine which ones must be stacked, in what order, to construct designs that are presented as the problems. There is a "poster sheet" consisting of 6 solid-color squares (no designs) and 12 pictures of actual stencils in different colors against a uniform gray background. Each of the stencils has a different design (e.g., a small circle, a large circle, an octagon, an X, a Greek cross, plus some more complex, apparently superimposed, designs), making the stencil look like that design has been cut out. There are three sets of problem designs, that is, designs that must be constructed (mentally) by stacking the stencils that are on the poster sheet; for example, there is a red pointed cross (or plus sign) in the center of a yellow square. On the poster sheet one finds a solid red square to place on the bottom and a yellow square with a cross cut out of its center of the same size and shape as that in the problem design. The solution, of course, is to place the solid red square down first and to put the yellow stencil that has the cross cutout on top of it, thus producing a red cross in the center of a yellow square. The three sets of problem designs may be used as pretest (static administration), learning (with mediation of essential cognitive and metacognitive operations and habits), and posttest (static, but with additional mediation as needed to overcome hurdles – such posttest mediation is always recorded).

The first task is to get the examinees to describe the poster sheet, being certain that they are aware of the dimensions of shape, color, and size and of the obvious difference between solid-color squares and cutout stencils. This can be done by calling on the group to name the colors of the solid ones and the cutout shapes of the stencils. Sometimes the stencils are not perceived as cutouts but as paste-ons; that is, the designs may be seen as having been added rather than as holes. The gray background is useful in mediating this difference. Of course, the idea of holes in the stencils is essential for the stacking process because of the necessary idea that one can see through them to colors and bits of shape that lie underneath them. It is necessary also to be sure that the examinees understand that each stencil (and solid) on the poster sheet has a number; further, it is useful if they discover that there is some order in the numbering, with same-color stencils/solids having adjacent numbers. Thus, the solid blue one is number 5, and the blue stencil that has an X cut out is number 6; the solid white is number 15 and the three white stencils (small circle cut out, square cut out, square rotated 45 degrees cut out) are numbers 16, 17, and 18. That system is not conceptually important but contributes to efficiency in solving the problems. The idea that one can imagine making the problem designs by stacking the stencils in the correct sequence is occasionally difficult; this may occur with one or two persons in any large group being examined. Overtraining of the whole group on this idea is far preferable to the alternative of bypassing the ones who have difficulty with it, because that idea defines the essential task and, as usual in DA, one must not allow examinees' failure to understand the task requirements to be interpreted as inability to solve the problems or as lack of adequate cognitive development to solve the problems.

For group administration, one should provide each participant with a copy of the poster sheet (the source of stencils for stacking), but the problem designs may be presented as slides projected on a large screen. That procedure depends on the nature of the group being examined. With adults who are presumed to be relatively problem-free, it is even possible to use two projectors, displaying the poster sheet on one screen and the problems on the second screen. For quite difficult situations (e.g., group examination of adults with traumatic brain injuries; see Haywood & Miller, 2003, 2005), one will wish to avoid the possibility of perceptual confusion wherever possible, so it may be best to present only one problem at a time rather than a whole page of problems and to have all of the examinees work on the same problem at the same time.

Only when the examiner is sure that all participants in the group understand the materials and the nature of the task can one proceed to give the static pretest. The only help that may be given during the pretest consists of clarifying task requirements and procedures – a good reason for trying hard to be sure these are understood before testing begins. For many groups, this phase will be quite frustrating and discouraging, whereas for others it will be seen as a welcome challenge, a sort of puzzle game. The temptation to help the more frustrated members of a group is frequently very strong, but if the data are to be useful, it should be resisted.

Once the pretest has been done, the participants might be given a brief break – or not, if they seem fresh and eager to continue. The learning phase follows. Following is a hypothetical script of group mediation during the learning phase of RSDT (skipping some problems to cut down on repetition – which should not be done in actual practice):

Examiner	One or more group members
1. What shape has been cut out of this one?	A circle.
Yes, a circle. Would you say it is a big circle or a small one?	Big.
Yes, big because it takes up almost the whole stencil, doesn't it?	
What color is the circle?	Depends on whether you look in the middle of it or around it.

Examiner	One or more group members
OK, what color is the middle?	Yes, you are being very precise, telling me everything about it. Good. But the circle itself is yellow, and that is important. Why is it important to identify that color in the middle?	Yellow, with green around it.

Examiner

OK, what color is the middle?

Yes, you are being very precise, telling me everything about it. Good. But the circle itself is yellow, and that is important. Why is it important to identify that color in the middle?

Do we have to find a yellow circle? Isn't the yellow circle already part of the problem? What do we have to find?

Right! So we know we are going to need some yellow. Let's look on the poster sheet and find out where we can get the yellow, and where we should put it.

Great! Are those the only two possibilities?

So which of those two would be better for us to use in making this design, problem number 1?

Fantastic! Now you are looking at more than one part at a time: the color, and where the color must go. So how can we get the shape we need?

Are you sure? How did you know that?

Great. You are right. Is there any other clue that number 11 is correct?

What a sharp eye! You are right, of course. Which is the better place for us to get the green we need, number 11 or number 12?

One or more group members

Yellow, with green around it.

Because we have to know to look for a yellow circle.

Oh, yeah, we have to find yellow, so yellow will be seen through the cutout circle.

We can get yellow from either number 13 (the solid yellow) or number 14 (yellow stencil with pointed cross cutout).

Yes. No others have yellow.

Number 13, because the other one is not yellow all the way to the center.

Number 11 (green stencil with large circle cut out).

It's the only one with a large circle cut out.

Well, it has green around the outside of the circle, but number 12 is also green.

I think number 11.

Examiner	One or more group members
Why?	Because it has two right things; it is the right color and has the right shape cut out.
Does everybody agree? Anybody disagree?	(All agree.)
OK. We all agree that we need number 13 and number 11. Is that enough? Do we need any more?	Nope, that's it. Two will be enough.
Yes, you are right. How did you know that?	I could just tell by looking that two would be enough.
Well, sometimes just looking is OK, but when we know the reason we can check out our looking.	OK. For one thing, we have two colors, so we have to have two stencils. Two colors, two stencils.
Sounds reasonable to me. Do you think we should make that a rule? The number of colors tells us the number of stencils we will need?	Yes! It's a rule!
Well, let's keep it in mind as a hypothesis, and then we can find out as we go along whether it holds up as a rule.	OK, but it will! [Grumbling, disagreement in the group.]
Not everyone agrees about that rule. Let's just see as we move along. (Examiner is preparing the group for hypothetical thinking and hypothesis testing.)	
If we need two stencils, 11 and 13, where do they go? Which on the bottom and which on top?	Put down number 11, and put number 13 on top.
Why?	Because we need the circle to be yellow.
If we put a solid on top, what will we see?	Yellow.
What happened to the shape, the circle, and where is the green?	Oh. Yeah. They're covered up by the yellow.

Examiner	**One or more group members**
Right! Could we find a rule there?	[Much discussion; finally, the group members discover and enunciate the rule that the solid always goes on the bottom. In the process, they discover another useful fact: If you want to know what color should be on the bottom, look in the center of the problem design.]
Great rule! You are discovering rules all over the place! Good for you. That means you are depending more on your thinking than just on your seeing! Here's a good rule. It's not a rule of life, just a good rule for this stencil making we're doing: Always start at the bottom by telling me what goes down first and will be on the bottom of the stack. Do you agree that it would be a good idea to work that way?	[General agreement]
7. Now let's look at this one. How many stencils will we need?	Two!
You sound pretty sure about that. How do you know we will need two?	We made a rule: The number of colors tells us how many stencils we will need.
Was that a rule or a hypothesis?	OK, but it's true here.
So how do you know that?	Well, we need a blue diamond inside a white square, so, two stencils!
OK, but is that shape actually a diamond?	[Other person] No, it's a square! It just looks like a diamond because it's turned up on one of its corners.
Right you are! [Here one can take time, or not, to teach the difference between a diamond and a square. The decision should be made on the basis of the importance of precision and accuracy; i.e., Does that aspect of metacognitive functioning need to be strengthened in this group?] What stencils from the poster sheet will give us the ones we need, in what order?	5, 17.

Examiner	One or more group members
Great! You are right. You did so many things right that time: You said the bottom one first, you got the shape right, and you got the colors right. So how many things do you have to think about to solve these design problems?	About a hundred!
Well, maybe not quite that many. Be precise!	OK, we have to think about the color that goes in the middle, what shape that is, and what color goes around the outside. That's three things.
Yes, you do have to think about all of those. Anything else?	Oh, yeah, the order you put them down in.
Right. Order makes a whole lot of difference in these designs, doesn't it? Remember what we would see if in this problem we put 17 down first and then put 5 on top?	Yeah, yeah, nothing but blue [showing a bit of impatience, which suggests that the examiner may be overmediating, unnecessarily going over points that the group members already understand clearly. It is better to do that than not if there is a possibility that some slower members of the group may be lagging in their understanding of the basic aspects of the task.]
Great job!	

The examiner then continues through the 20 problems of the learning phase. Essential mediation continues to consist not of giving clues to the correct answers, but of mediating the metacognitive operations and habits: looking carefully, gathering clear and complete information, undertaking the task sequentially (what comes first? what next?), considering multiple sources of information, developing a need for logical evidence and an impatience with inaccuracy and imprecision, enhancing the intrinsic motivation that comes with increasing competence and satisfaction with one's own efforts, inhibiting impulsive responding in favor of careful reflection, questioning the validity of purely perceptual information and seeking verification.

SPECIAL CONCERNS REGARDING DA WITH SENIORS

Just as one has to be concerned with the developmental curve in the assessment of children, developmental concerns with seniors are important, especially to the DA process. In static, normative assessment, age norms are in place, and they help to allow for the progressive loss of cognitive functions that typically accompanies old age. At the same time, age norms conceal the quite large individual differences in the rate of functional loss and in the specific areas of loss. Even more important is the observation that in the DA of senior citizens, one is searching less for deficits than for sparing. The most important questions are those having to do with what people can still do or can do even better than when they were younger. It is well known among psychologists that intellectual growth, although typically declining in overall rate after early adolescence, may continue well into maturity and even quite old age, the eighth or ninth decades, provided those persons remain intellectually active. We know that intellectual functioning in maturity can be affected by many variables; for example, sensory impairment, polypharmacy (use of multiple prescription drugs), slowed motor activity and reaction time, motivation, educational level, and variety and intensity of intellectual interests and activities. We must therefore question to what extent assessments of mental abilities mean the same thing in senior citizens as in younger persons. Loss of effective memory is one of the most obvious areas of decline in old age, but there is plenty of evidence that for the great majority of persons (who do not suffer from age-related memory deficit or Alzheimer's disease), such loss is not necessary. It can be prevented and remedied. The urgent questions we ask of DA are thus questions relating to how selected functions can be maintained and improved.

Many of the DA procedures suggested for use with adolescents and young adults are also useful with seniors, sometimes with modification. DA usually does not make use of timed tests, but avoiding timed tests is even more important when doing assessment with seniors because slowing of motor behavior generally occurs at a more rapid rate than does impairment of cognitive functioning; thus, speed may be less related to overall efficiency of cognitive functioning in old age than in earlier years. This is not to suggest that areas of potential difficulty should be avoided. On the contrary, it is important to assess functioning as well as potential in those domains that are likely to cause special concern among older citizens, the most obvious being memory. Fortunately, the research literature is replete with evidence of the utility of metacognitive strategies for improving one's memory. They include, for example: (a) rehearsal, repetition; (b) associative clustering (i.e., grouping items that are to be remembered according to their essential similarities); (c) making mental images of the items to be remembered; (d) making lists; and (e) relating new information to familiar information, so that they can occupy the same category; (f) relating memory and motives (i.e., being aware of why one is trying to remember something). All such strategies can and should become part of the mediation interposed between pretest and posttest, together with personal strategies that may be suggested by the examinees themselves.

Restricting attention is a good metacognitive strategy for improving learning in older persons. One authority on aging suggested that old musicians should concentrate on fewer pieces of music and practice them more. This suggests that the range of items that may occupy the focus of one's attention becomes more restricted in old age, but it does not suggest that the ability to learn and to acquire new skill levels is impaired. Thus, in mediating on problem solving during DA, the examiner might work especially on getting the examinees to restrict their attention to the most directly relevant aspects of a task, to analyze problems into manageable parts, to attack solutions sequentially ("What should I do first?" is a better question than "What should I do?"). In a five-part problem, after mastering the first two or three parts one might return to the beginning and ask the examinee to relate the solution from the beginning. Just as is true with younger persons, success has a cumulative effect on motivation to engage in the tasks. We like to do what we do well. Thus, providing plenty of opportunity to succeed will help one to reveal the potential of older persons to learn new things, to solve problems, to remember, and to think logically and systematically.

Some aspects of DA with older persons are easier than with younger persons; for example, older persons have had much more experience with rules and can be expected to have a better understanding of the importance of rules. Most of the time, they are also less fearful of having their ignorance or inability discovered. Whatever their abilities or limitations, they probably already know about them, so they can be less defensive.

One should be careful to avoid: (a) the fine print, that is, stimuli that require sharp vision; (b) unclear auditory stimuli; (c) background noise (because of the frequent loss of hearing acuity at high frequencies – in the speech range); (d) problems whose content is intellectually unchallenging – and may be seen as insulting or patronizing.

Some abilities may appear to have been lost when instead they have become "de-automatized." This means that skills that were once performed without conscious thought or deliberate action might now have to be "cognitized" and "re-automatized." Haywood (2004b) has discussed these concepts and procedures in some detail. Luria (1979) related a pertinent episode in Vygotsky's experience. Vygotsky was working with a group of patients who had Parkinson's disease at such advanced stages that the patients could no longer walk. One day he distributed sheets of paper randomly across the floor and asked the patients to go from one side of the room to the other without stepping on the papers. To everyone's amazement (except Vygotsky!), they did it. The point is that an activity that was so familiar and well-practiced had become automatic and was performed without conscious thought about it. When Parkinson's disease interfered with the automaticity of that well-practiced skill, the patients were unable to do it – until Vygotsky "cognitized" the activity by requiring the patients to think about what they were doing. Slowing down, de-automatizing, and then cognitizing (requiring the behavioral sequence to run through the metacognitive processes of conscious and deliberate thought) can sometimes restore skills that seem to have been lost. Haywood (2004), in relating that incident, warned against the "centipede effect," that is, thinking so much about an automatic activity that one cannot do it; nevertheless, de-automatization and cognitizing can work in cases in which previously acquired skills appear to have been lost. Once some level of the skill has been recovered through cognitization, repeated performance of it can restore speed and automaticity. At some level, this procedure is incorporated into dynamic assessment at almost every level of its practice. Mediation itself is designed to promote metacognitive awareness followed by improved executive functioning. The example given here is just an extreme case.

Helping senior citizens to rediscover abilities that they thought were lost, helping neurologists and other health care persons to see potential for recovery of abilities that might have been temporarily lost or masked by disease (stroke, for example), and helping seniors to find new interests and abilities can be among the most rewarding aspects of DA with senior citizens.

9 Writing Reports and Developing IEPs and Service Plans with Dynamic Assessment

In this chapter, we demonstrate how information from dynamic assessment can be integrated into both clinical and psychoeducational reports, with the ultimate objective of developing Individualized Education (IEPs) and Service Plans. These plans should flow directly from the information revealed throughout the course of the assessment, which, in turn, should flow logically from the referral questions and the approaches used for data gathering. Embedding interaction-based interventions in the assessment, which is at the core of dynamic assessment, should generate reports and plans that appropriately address individual needs and improve individuals' responsiveness to instruction and intervention. This chapter includes samples of both psychoeducational and clinical reports.

REPORTING TO EDUCATORS

Reports written by psychologists have generally not served teachers well. Teachers want specific, instruction-relevant, feasible suggestions. They want ideas for action, and they want the actions to work. Through the process of assessment and reporting, psychologists are expected to be able to pose specific, measurable referral questions, tailor assessment procedures to respond to these questions, integrate information to address these questions, and develop ideas for interventions to respond to these questions, reducing the gap between children's current levels of functioning and areas of need and the system's expectations.

Most recommendations regarding report writing emphasize the need for clarity, readability, and relevance. Clarity is achieved by avoidance of jargon and use of a conversational tone. Readability is enhanced by good organization, focusing on interpreting the information in relation to its meaning for the child, use of descriptions of task demands rather than test names, along with anecdotal descriptions of how the client approached the tasks. Reports that wear the readers down are filled with numbers and look like boilerplate documents where the client's name was merely inserted into a blank space. Relevance is facilitated by addressing the referral issues throughout and in providing specific, intervention-related recommendations. Consumers of psychological assessment want to understand the children better and to know what to do to improve their functioning. If this kind of information is not in their reports, the consumers are likely to be dissatisfied and to view the assessments as useless.

Linking Assessment with Intervention

Linking assessment with intervention is one of those things we often say we need to do, but rarely do, and even less often do well. Good intervention flows in a logical way from the assessment process itself. If there is good problem clarification at the start of the assessment, and if the process proceeds in good hypothesis-generating, problem-solving fashion, then a repertory of interventions naturally unfolds. It is also incumbent on assessors to update their own awareness of intervention possibilities continually. There is increasing advocacy for use of evidence-based treatment, so professional psychologists need to build a library of resources as these emerge. Because there cannot be adequate research-based evidence for each and every intervention suggested for each and every individual, it is also necessary to build in evidence collection for each client to document his or her response to the recommendations.

In the case of education, placement of a child in a program is not in and of itself an intervention. The movement of a child from one location to another provides no information regarding what to do with or for the child following relocation. Something has to be done within the setting, and we need to inform ourselves about the possibilities of what these might be. There is no homogeneity regarding children's needs or approaches to learning. If teachers are to individualize their programs, they need some guidance to inform them of the needs of the individuals within their domains.

As we indicated at the beginning of this text, dynamic assessment should provide information about at least three major issues:

- the responsiveness of the examinees to intervention,
- results of attempts at intervention that worked or did not work, and
- in-depth understanding of processing strengths and weaknesses.

Different assessors have different styles of report writing. Some include information from their dynamic assessment as a separate section of their report. We prefer embedding the information in the discussion of the function to which the DA approach was applied. This reflects our view of DA as an addition to and extension of traditional approaches to assessment. There is no throwing out of babies with bathwater here; however, there is more revolution in the use of these approaches than may be apparent from such a point of view. It is difficult to revert to old ways once one has crossed over the DA line. There is only great frustration and dissatisfaction with the information that is generated by traditional approaches. Once one has crossed over, there are feelings of "aha" akin to those of the chimpanzee that realizes the stick's potential for reaching the bananas.

Dynamic assessment is process-oriented. The implication for report writing is that reports are most relevantly organized according to basic mental processes or functions in accordance with the model of mental functioning discussed in Chapter 2. This approach is also typical of a neuropsychological approach to assessment, and we tend to extend our assessments, which are clearly strongly influenced by neuropsychology, by dynamic assessment related to brain processes. Therefore, we typically organize reporting of assessment results into the functional categories of sensorimotor, attention, perception, memory, language, cognition, and executive processing. In the case of psychoeducational reports, the knowledge base is discussed in a leading separate section on academic achievement.

In what follows, we present reports of five cases to illustrate how we embed dynamic assessment in a comprehensive psychological assessment to extend the information that is offered by traditional approaches. Careful reading of these reports should make it evident to what extent they differ from traditional approaches. We follow each case with a brief discussion that highlights the role and function of the dynamic portion of the assessment for that specific case. All personally identifying information about these cases has been removed; other background information has been abbreviated and, in some cases, changed.

CASE 9.1

Name: Tiffany
Age: 9 years 3 months
Grade: 3

Reason for Referral
Tiffany is currently in a regular education program. She has been referred with concerns about language comprehension, impulsivity, and attention. She has difficulty understanding language, which affects all areas of achievement, particularly reading, and shows difficulty regulating her behavior both at home and in school.

The questions addressed by this assessment include the following:

- Does Tiffany need additional educational support to supplement her current program?
- If so, what is the nature of her needs?
- How would these best be met?

Background Information

Tiffany was adopted at birth. Her birth weight was 4.5 pounds, the result of a full-term pregnancy. She was kept in the intensive care unit for 7 days following delivery because of her low birth weight. Her adoptive mother thinks her Apgar scores were around 7 or 8. Once home, she was healthy, developed well, and had no physical issues. She learned to crawl and walk early but had delayed speech. She occasionally runs a fever up to 103, but this does not last more than 24 hours. She has no history of ear infections, and her mother reports normal vision and hearing, as a result of screening by her physician. She also passed the school screenings. Tiffany remains small and slender, but it was noted that her birth mother was a small woman. Tiffany is currently taking a stimulant medication for an attention deficit.

Reports from Tiffany's kindergarten teacher indicated difficulty with following directions and with remembering math facts. She also struggled with spelling and phonics. Her first-grade teacher noted her difficulty with understanding both oral and printed communication, her short attention span, and her frustration when she failed to understand.

Tiffany's mother notes that she can read well but struggles with phonics, relying on visual memorization. Her comprehension is described as "terrible." When Tiffany can see something, she will understand, but when people try to use just verbal explanation, she has significant difficulty. At home, her mother uses visual support and acting out to help her learn. This comprehension difficulty has negative consequences for both reading and math. Her mother also notes that, despite Tiffany's preference for minimal structure, she functions best with strong structure; however, she does not do well in an environment with a large number of people, whether structured or not.

Tiffany is currently involved in speech/language therapy both at home and in school, as well as tutoring once a week at home. The tutor focuses on organization, and the speech/language therapists focus on auditory processing. It is also the routine at home to work on a phonics game on Sundays. Tiffany has also completed a sequence of Fast ForWord sessions during the previous summer. The school's speech/language therapist noted that the main concerns are her poor comprehension, focus, and impulsivity.

These difficulties negatively affect her pragmatic skills, particularly turn-taking. She tends to become upset if not called on and has difficulty listening to others. The therapist is trying to teach her to formulate a question before raising her hand, because she tends to raise her hand immediately in class before she has even heard the question.

Tiffany's teacher notes her serious language concerns, with difficulty processing both written and oral language, as well as problem solving in math. Behaviorally, she is extremely impulsive and moves around the classroom a great deal. It is difficult for her to wait for the teacher to complete directions before raising her hand. Tiffany appears anxious and perfectionistic and seeks frequent feedback about her performance. Despite her struggles, Tiffany does not wish to have her work modified because she is aware of what the other students are doing and does not wish to be different. In the area of reading comprehension, Tiffany needs to review and retell her work. She has difficulty summarizing, as well as with organizing her thoughts and answering inferential questions. She at times does not comprehend the question being asked. Her teacher feels she needs the support of a resource room, which would offer the advantage of work in small groups. Tiffany is highly motivated to achieve and responds well to (and needs) extra attention.

Everyone who works with Tiffany notes her strong social skills and her diligent work effort. She is comfortable with seeking help from her classmates and often asks them for guidance and clarification. At home, she loves to shop and is good at organizing social events.

According to her mother, Tiffany is experiencing a good deal of frustration with learning. She seems to feel that she should know everything and is uncomfortable with and unwilling to ask for help from adults. Feeling in control is important for her; when she fails to comprehend, she feels out of control.

Assessment Results

Academic Skills
Tiffany's reading levels in both word reading and comprehension are in the low average range, when compared with a national sample of children her age; however, Tiffany attends a high-performing school, and in this context, her reading levels would be low. Nevertheless, she was able to read some difficult words (e.g., known, column, courage, phonograph, cleanse). Despite her history of difficulty with phonological awareness, Tiffany actually showed strength in phonological processing for this assessment. This may reflect the intensity of work she has had in this area. She would occasionally recite a rule that she learned from her Sunday practice

sessions, and she was able to sound out some words, showing phonological awareness even in her errors.

Tiffany is a fluent reader who shows word comprehension as she reads, which is sufficient to allow her to proceed with appropriate voice inflections and observations of punctuation. She tends to read for the purpose of getting through the text rather than for the goal of comprehension, and, once the words are removed, she has not retained or integrated the meaning of the information she has read. This occurs even when she is specifically told that she will be asked questions following the reading, as well as when she has been provided with the questions prior to her reading. For her, reading appears to be more of a perceptual than conceptual task, and she does not treat it as a source of communication of meaning. When asked a question about the text, Tiffany needed to reread the passage, and then would read the answer straight from the text. It was extremely difficult for her to restate the meaning of the written material or to make inferences beyond what was provided. One obstruction to her comprehension may be her reactions to the length of the text. Tiffany appears quick to notice the amount of work demand that she faces, to evaluate it as "a lot of work," and to set herself the agenda of getting it done (reducing the load).

The most significant obstruction for Tiffany, however, relates to language comprehension. She will often overlook or fail to process critical words in the text that serve as cues for responding to questions. It is not that she fails to comprehend the word in isolation (she certainly knows what "because" means), but she fails to use the word in context as a clue for comprehension.

Tiffany was provided an opportunity to take a timed reading test under a variety of conditions that included extension of time, large print, and reading aloud. Although there was no clear advantage to any of the conditions in terms of effects on her success with multiple-choice test items, she was only able to complete the reading of the stimulus paragraph with extended time, and she also appeared more relaxed under the extended time condition. Her success with the multiple-choice test items under all conditions was below average in relation to the national norms. This suggests that the interventions of time extension, enlarged print, or allowance to read aloud are not sufficient to improve her reading comprehension. This also suggests that she needs extended time to read through the material as a bottom line before she can respond to questions about it.

The time extension allowed her to begin to review her reading as a strategy for aiding her comprehension, but much more guided intervention is necessary to promote her comprehension. In this procedure, Tiffany did not have the reading material available while she answered the questions, and the ability to look back at the text to seek the answers to the questions was an important resource for her. In this context, it was necessary for her to place the information into memory as she read, and she did not do well with this demand.

Tiffany's teacher provided a sample of the work she has already completed in class as well as a lesson from the curriculum that she had not yet attempted. In the work she had already completed, it was evident that Tiffany was having difficulty responding to the meaning of the sentences, particularly when they required some inferential thinking. It was also evident that she would at times overlook critical cue words, resulting in errors in her responses. The content of her reading does not appear to be retained to allow for further processing, and she also makes errors in her initial registering of the information, which promotes inaccuracy even for the bits that are retained. Her teacher also notes that she is not specific in her language (e.g., overuse of the word "it"), a factor that was also evident throughout this assessment when Tiffany was asked to provide elaborations or descriptions. As indicated earlier, when she can refer to the text to answer questions requiring specific factual information, she does well.

When working with Tiffany on the reading lesson prepared by her teacher, she showed considerable anxiety and resistance. She had a great deal of difficulty maintaining her focus and moved around the room and seat frequently. Tiffany does not seem to be integrating the material into a coherent message as she reads, and she does not appear to be visualizing the meaning of the message as she reads. When she retells a story, she shows some theme retention but offers gross generalities with little detail or precision. Some details can be elicited receptively, so she has registered them, but when asked to retell the story, she is not retrieving them. We tried many conditions to see what would help to improve her ability to maintain attention, without success. These included having Tiffany read to herself, reading the material to her, reading the questions first before reading, and reading first before answering questions. I tried to get Tiffany to provide insight into what she thought helped her, and she showed great resistance to this. When I used a magnet board to support her ability to visualize the elements of the story, she became overinvolved with the materials and did not use them constructively to relate back to the story. What seemed to be going on throughout this episode was Tiffany's resistance to admitting that she had a problem in the context of working in the very area that was most problematic for her. Her high anxiety, her distractibility, and her difficulty placing information she reads into memory all coincided to make this a very threatening experience for her. Despite the lack of success of the various approaches to intervention, it would not be accurate to conclude that none of them held any promise for helping her. During the assessment, she was not in a frame of mind to allow any of them to be of help, and further exploration would be necessary before concluding that they were of no use.

Tiffany was most obviously stressed during the written expression testing. It was during this time that she began to make somatic complaints. Her low average score on the standardized test is an overestimate of the quality of work she was able to produce. Written expression places demands on fine motor control as well as language. Further, the particular task of the test requires changing some of the information that is presented (individual sentences need to be combined into one sentence). The need to go beyond what was presented and to make changes in the sentences were very difficult demands for Tiffany. She is able to print legibly and is helped by the presence of lines for writing. She leaves clear (almost too wide) spaces between words. The paragraph she wrote in response to the prompt: "On a rainy day, I like . . . " was to list several activities that she enjoys. She only elaborated one sentence and did not present an integrated message. Also, she did not really write a coherent sentence because she followed the prompt with "to do is: . . . ." and then made her list.

Tiffany's level of functioning in the area of spelling is similar to her other achievement levels – in the low average range, compared with a national sample of other students her age. Her errors usually made auditory sense (e.g., rough/ruff; owe/oh). She did not usually succeed with words that had multiple spellings and depended on context, such as two/too, knew/new, owe/oh. It is interesting in this area that her errors were more reflective of visual memory rather than auditory/phonological processing. Tiffany usually self-corrects to improve her performance; however, in the case of spelling, her two self-corrections changed correct spellings into errors.

Tiffany's level of functioning in mathematics is estimated in the low average to average level in relation to a national sample of students her age. Again, this would be lower in comparison to the students in her high-performing school district. There is a significant difference between her relatively higher reasoning skills compared with her considerably lower numerical operations skills. Tiffany appears to know her basic addition and subtraction number facts. She made an addition error when she had to carry, and she made an error of adding when she should have subtracted for one of the more difficult subtraction problems (may be an issue of attention to details with a lapse in attention). She did not attempt problems with decimals and solved multiplication problems by use of multiple addition (she does not know any multiplication tables or understand the concept of multiplication). Her next instructional levels in math would include the operations of multi-digit subtraction and addition with regrouping, subtraction with regrouping using decimals, and basic facts of multiplication.

Although Tiffany was able to solve the math reasoning tasks at a higher level than math operations, she often required repetition and clarification of the problems before she proceeded. She was able to do problems using measurement, time, patterns, graphs, some fractions, and money. She did not have the knowledge base to solve problems involving fractions above 1/4 or 1/2 or involving multiplication. She may have had more success with these items because they are more applied and related to real-life issues.

There was insufficient time to work on the curriculum sample provided by Tiffany's teacher, but review of the content of this sample shows that the work is very problem- and application-oriented, which may present specific difficulty for Tiffany because of the demands on reading comprehension and inference. This is an area where she receives support in school and that she describes as stressful.

Sensory/Perceptual

Tiffany shows adequate vision and hearing from parental report and observation during the assessment. Her near vision was screened for this assessment with a chart of numbers, and she had no difficulty reading numbers on the 20/20 line. She occasionally held the reading page somewhat close to her eyes, so this just warrants monitoring and does not appear to be a significant issue at this time.

Both her auditory and visual perception appear adequate as well. She performs at a high level on visual matching tasks and shows good auditory discrimination through her high level of competence with phonemic awareness. Her ability to derive meaning from what she sees and hears also appears adequate (when memory and integration are not involved; that is, when items are presented in isolated units).

Motor

Tiffany's execution and integration of fine motor movements showed mixed results related to the strength of her medication. There were two opportunities to evaluate her ability to copy designs, and she showed more control and accuracy when on a higher dose of medication. When on her usual level of medication, her writing tended to be more scribble-like. She shows right hand dominance and writes with an intermediate (thumb over) grasp.

Of most significance in the motor area is her difficulty with self-regulation. She moved around a great deal, leaving her seat frequently and changing her position on her seat. She tended to mark her papers above and beyond what was necessary for the task. When working on written expression and copying tasks, her poor self-regulation results in frequent erasures. She does have good checking-back-to-the-model strategies and is able to improve her productions following her erasures. Having an eraser to use was an important support, and she was considerably more anxious when it was necessary to do a paper-and-pencil task using a pencil without an eraser.

Her gross motor movements were not specifically assessed. From informal observation alone, she appears adequate in this area.

Attention

Attention, like most processes, is a very complex area of functioning. Because of this, it is rarely possible to say that anyone has an attention problem per se, as if "attention" were all one thing. With this in mind, Tiffany showed differences in her functioning among different types of attention. She showed excellent vigilance; that is, her orientation to and reaction to the occurrence of auditory or visual stimulation was at a high level. In fact, it is possible to say that she is hyper-vigilant; that is, she tends to pay attention to too much. One consequence of her difficulty with maintaining attention is that she fails to note details. Her attention is pulled from one stimulus to another, but she does not register precisely the details she surveys.

Tiffany struggles not only with inhibiting and regulating her attention to things that go on around her, but also with regard to her own thoughts. She is easily distracted from her work, and she will frequently engage in elaborations of her thinking that serve to distract her from the task.

Tiffany also has difficulty with sustaining her attention or focusing over the period of time necessary to absorb directions, as well as in her ability to persist from the beginning to the end of a task. This difficulty with sustained attention interferes with her ability to take in information that she needs to store in her memory. She will often respond that she "knows what to do" after hearing just a small portion of directions or after taking a brief glance at the materials placed in front of her. She is often wrong in her conclusions about what she will need to do because she has not heard the full message. Thus, she is acting on incomplete and at times inaccurate information.

It is also possible and likely that Tiffany's high level of anxiety about dealing with her weaker areas of functioning increases her inattentiveness. It became increasingly clear to her that I was working with her to probe into her areas of need. Her very strong desire to avoid, deny, and escape recognition of any needs that may make her different from others manifested as anxiety and resistance throughout the sessions that followed her initial highly controlled efforts.

Memory

Difficulties with working memory are particularly characteristic of children with attention problems, and Tiffany shows considerable difficulty in this area. Her ability to take in information and store it for processing is significantly obstructed by her limited sustained attention. Her short attention span results in her missing important key or cue words in both auditory and visual messages. Her ability to hold a large amount of complex information in her memory is compromised, and this in turn reduces her ability to integrate and process what she experiences. Thus, she often doesn't "get it." When she misses important cue words, she in fact is responding to partial, and therefore incorrect, information. Although Tiffany profits from visual support for auditory information, she does not show strength in the visual domain per se unless there is a pairing of visual and auditory input. This pairing does help her. Tiffany showed that she needed time to consolidate her memory, and she at times (not consistently) did better after a brief passage of time than immediately following the presentation of the material to be remembered.

Cognition

Tiffany's current levels of cognitive functioning are estimated to be in the low average range for most tasks, when compared with a national sample of students of her age, although there is considerable variation in her levels of functioning related to the nature of the task. There is a tendency for her to be more successful with verbal, compared with nonverbal, tasks, yet she obtains some of her highest levels on specific nonverbal tasks that tap her very good ability for signal detection and response speed. Attention to details and integration of information for visually presented materials presented problems for her. Again, this supports the observation that, although visual stimuli may provide helpful support for her memory, she does not do well relying on visual presentation alone. With timed tasks, which many of the nonverbal subtests were, she became overly concerned with speed, sacrificing precision. No reassurance that precision was more important than speed would modify her attempts to beat the clock. She preferred to be finished rather than correct.

In the verbal area, Tiffany experienced difficulty elaborating beyond her initial responses, and she tended to provide very minimal responses, lacking in precision and detail. She needed to embed her responses in meaningful contexts and did best when questioning prompted her to think in meaningful contexts.

The most difficult task for Tiffany involved picture sequencing. For this, she had to reorder pictures to create a story. This meant that she had to change the order that was presented to her to match the story in her mind, and this elicited what was frequently observed as her tendency to be "stimulus bound." That is, she can respond well when all of the information she needs is in front of her; however, when she needs to think about it and reorganize it, she experiences a great deal of difficulty.

When she needs to move away from what she can perceive, she struggles. In this way, her difficulty with attention affects her memory, and her difficulty with memory affects her ability to infer and predict, and this all interacts to create a problem with comprehension because she struggles to hold information she needs for integrated understanding in her memory.

Tiffany uses self-talk while working on challenging tasks, and this serves as a useful strategy for her. She also needed to begin challenging work from an easy base where she could gain confidence before tackling challenge.

When I engaged Tiffany in a mini lesson that involved noting the difference between a diamond and a square, she became very resistant and inflexible. It was very difficult for her to modify her thinking to consider a challenge to her initial idea. At this time, she became very defensive.

Language

This is an area for which she is receiving specialized support. This assessment documents the highly significant difference between her expressive (higher) and receptive (lower) language. Tiffany showed particular strength regarding word fluency, when she needed to generate lists of words relating to a single theme. She struggles with retrieval regarding production of precise language when more elaborate language is required, that is, beyond single-word labeling. This appears to reflect her problem with maintenance of focused attention.

Tiffany needed a good deal of clarification and some repetition and restatement when provided with directions. Once provided with these, she was usually able to proceed with the task. She did at times miss the meaning of what she heard, which appeared related to her failure either to take into consideration or to miss the meaning of small key words in the communication.

Executive

Executive processes have to do with self-regulation, monitoring, planning, and organizing, as well as flexibility and ability to retrieve memories. Tiffany's struggles with self-regulation and memory retrieval and her limited flexibility have already been discussed. She does show good ability to plan what she needs to do over the short term, but poor organization of long-term and complex projects, at least with regard to work related to school. Her difficulty with retaining and integrating complex information seems to interfere with her ability to organize, and, as her mother notes, her tendency to get distracted by the details pulls her off-task and results in disorganization.

The ratings by her mother support the diagnosis of attention-deficit/hyperactivity disorder, combined type, in that her attention, impulse control, and activity level are all affected. Her ratings on this scale show elevations (concerns) primarily in the areas of Tiffany's ability to inhibit, shift, and organize, as well as poor emotional control and limited working memory.

Social and Emotional

The area of social skills is clearly where Tiffany excels. She is able to make and keep friends. She is well liked and personable and generally strives to please. She is comfortable communicating with adults.

In the testing situation, her interactions with me were quite ambivalent. She fluctuated between being cooperative, friendly, and chatty, and being angry and resistant. The testing situation presented her with the ultimate challenge of making her face and deal with her areas of weakness. She sought to deny, avoid, and escape ("I would rather die than do more!").

Tiffany was quickly overwhelmed by what she perceived as a lot of work ("That's too much work for a third grader!"), but with encouragement and reassurance, she would do it and show some interest in some of the content. She continually checked her watch and sought time parameters. When the time came that she thought she should return to class, she got up, gave me a hug, said, "thank you," and proceeded to start to march out the door.

Tiffany refused to complete the rating scale that accessed her feelings. She explained this by saying that she did not see why this was any of my business. I explained that, as a psychologist, this was my business and that the information she communicates can affect how she learns. I also explained that it gave her a chance to speak for herself because her parents were also completing a rating scale. She would not comply, saying these are things that she talks about only with her mother. She specifically referred to the issue of stomachaches (as being one of the issues that were none of my business). When I asked her if she got stomachaches, she would not elaborate. The few items that Tiffany marked on her rating scale before deciding not to continue concerned worry about what others think of her, feelings of loneliness and sadness, and, on the positive side, feeling that what she wants does matter. Thus, she let down her guard very briefly but quickly resurrected her defenses to avoid sharing her feelings. Interestingly, in Tiffany's drawing of a person, she portrays a girl much older than herself (age 21) who "likes shopping and she has to be Miss Perfect...."

Tiffany seems to feel that she needs to know what to do and what the correct actions are with only the smallest amount of cueing. Her ego seems to be on the line with the correctness or incorrectness of every item. She briefly looks at materials or listens to part of oral directions, and says, "I know what to do." She views attempts to teach her something new as a personal affront unless the lesson is clearly directed at all of her peers – that is, when she is not treated any differently from the others. When going through material where she provides answers to questions, she either knows or does not know the answer, and is unwilling to guess or take a risk. Her response to not knowing is usually that she does not remember (rather than "don't know," which to her means that she is dumb). Her response to being told the correct answer is "I know."

Tiffany provides her own statement to describe her concerns with receiving support services: "Then I'll be a baby and everyone will look at me." She interprets any modification of her work as treating her like a baby. For example, when I placed the magnet board in front of her as an intervention for reading comprehension, her immediate reaction was, "I'm not a baby!" When I reassured her that I would never give these materials to a baby, she readily engaged in the task. I tried to work with her on this attitude, suggesting that she instead could feel proud of herself, proud that she recognizes her need for help and has the courage to do something about it. She responded positively to this idea, but it would take more than this brief comment to get her to absorb it.

On the behavioral rating scale, Tiffany's mother rated her in the normal/average range on all parameters except attention problems. At home, Tiffany is difficult to work with regarding schoolwork, but her social-emotional functioning otherwise appears to be adequate. Specific concerns in the attention domain include listening to directions, giving up easily when learning something new, distractibility, listening attentively, and completing work on time or without breaks. She shows some difficulty with emotional control, at times showing a low threshold for reactivity and some emotional lability (mood changes).

When I observed Tiffany in her class during two lessons, one with the speech therapist and the second, with her regular classroom teacher, her tendency to raise her hand frequently before directions were provided was in evidence. During this observation, she did not show as much body movement as she did throughout the individual session, although her teacher reports frequent movement around the room. The lesson focused on key words as an aid to story recall. Tiffany was generally on task and was able to add one key word to those generated by her classmates. She required more time than the others to begin the independent part of the work and sought clarification before she began. She also asked the teacher an off-task question before beginning. She showed a good word-checking strategy once she began her work and asked a useful and relevant clarifying question (if they could use a word more than one time). She needed more time than her peers to complete her work, related to her tendency to become distracted by her environment.

Conclusions and Recommendations

In response to the questions posed for this referral:

a. Does Tiffany need additional educational support to supplement her current program?

Yes. This assessment clearly documents Tiffany's need for supplemental services.

b. If so, what is the nature of her needs?

Tiffany's areas of need include regulation of attention and motor functions, reading/language comprehension, math operations and problem solving, and her emotional reactions to having a need for additional support.

c. How would these best be met?

Regulation of attention

- Tiffany currently takes what she calls "focus medicine." Although a higher dose did improve her ability to attend, control her movements, and engage in learning, the increase in undesirable side effects suggests that an ongoing increase is not an option. Some other possible additions to continuation of her current medical treatment would include working with her at home and in the classroom to create an environment that would optimize her ability to pay attention and *reduce potential distractions*. For this, it would be important to consider where she is sitting, the possible distractions that would occur, and what she needs to do to help herself focus.
- A recently developing intervention that may be helpful to her is *neurofeedback*, where she would be trained by looking at "games" on a computer screen to help her to learn to regulate her own attention. Evidence regarding this technique is still developing, but it does seem to be helpful to some students, and requires a limited number of sessions, plus occasional "booster" sessions spread out over a number of years. This might be something to consider as a summer activity. It is important to use a professional with adequate training in this approach.

Regulation of motor functions

- It may also be helpful to involve Tiffany in *recreational activities* that address regulation of body movements, such as dancing, one of the Asian martial arts, swimming, or therapeutic horseback riding. The selection of any of these should reflect her interest and choice. These would provide some fun opportunities that would not be seen by her as making her any different from her peers yet would meet her needs for further support.
- Tiffany's struggle with control of her body movements may respond to intervention provided by an *occupational therapist* (OT), and referral for this evaluation through the school district is recommended. If ongoing treatment is recommended, how this is provided would be an issue, related to Tiffany's extreme sensitivity to being taken out of class and being treated differently from her peers. Possibly, the OT could work with the family on a consultative basis to recommend and demonstrate exercises to do at home, while scheduling ongoing evaluative monitoring to check her progress (and make her accountable for doing these).

General recommendations

- Tiffany's difficulty with academic work that involves language comprehension is her most serious need. She is already involved in speech/language therapy both in school and at home. Referral to a *resource room* for supplemental and more individualized help is strongly recommended. This will require her to be taken out of her class, and she will need help to deal with this.
- Tiffany would profit from *cognitive strategy coaching*, which would address both her academic and emotional needs. Tiffany needs to develop increased insight into her approaches to learning, to be involved as a collaborator in developing ways to cope with her challenges, and to modify her emotional reaction to being in need of further support. This requires a combination of academic and psychological intervention.

Specific suggestions for intervention in the school (and home) setting are as follows:

- Help Tiffany deal with large and complex work by dividing it into smaller units, assign estimates of time needed to accomplish each unit (these can be revised as needed), and have her use a *checklist* to mark accomplishment of each subtask. For relatively shorter assignments (those to be accomplished in one lesson or homework session), she should build in breaks (assigned time limitations) and think about what she will do during her breaks. She may find use of a timer helpful, although it needs to be determined whether this would be more of a distraction than help. A clock may do as well.

- Tiffany does profit from *additional time* for her assignments and for testing; however, there needs to be a balance between provision of sufficient time for her to get through the whole assignment and feeling some pressure to complete the work as efficiently as possible. That is, she does not profit from a total lack of time limits. For high-stakes testing, it may be best to have her join other students who require additional time in a separate environment, such as the resource room. Some trials with how much time is needed should be made. As a start, I would recommend at least a 50% increase, moving up to 75% and 100%. The point is that she needs sufficient time to get through the material, and this may vary with the content, such as reading versus math.

Reading comprehension

Addressing Tiffany's *reading comprehension* needs is a complex issue and requires further work with a reading specialist. Some ideas resulting from this assessment include the following:

- Use of small amounts of text, with multiple opportunities for review and repetition, appears to be important for Tiffany. It is important to reduce her feelings of being overwhelmed by the amount of work and to try to get her focused on the aspects of the work that are important. She needs to continue to review with guidance as often as is necessary for mastery, moving beyond her agenda of just getting it done and out of the way.
- Despite her claims to the contrary, Tiffany does not seem to be using adequate visualization. One approach to this would be to give her text to read without pictures. Have her read a portion (as well as at times, have the teacher read portions) and stop to ask her to describe what that "looks like" in her head. Keep reminding her to "run the movie in your head" as she reads and as she listens to others talk or read.
- Tiffany makes some errors because of her impulsive approach that results in her rushing ahead to be done. In the course of this, she misses important cue words. The regular classroom curriculum already addresses the issue of key words, and this needs to be reinforced and reviewed on a more individualized basis with Tiffany.
- When asking Tiffany to make predictions, it may be helpful first to ask her to try to find the information in the text, and then, when she

has difficulty, to ask her if she needs a cue. If she does not respond accurately to the first cue, provide others, increasingly explicit, until the question is answered adequately. Part of the intent of this is to train Tiffany to feel comfortable asking for cues and to get her to understand more clearly what a cue is and how it can be helpful. Getting her to provide cues about something she wants to communicate can be helpful as well.

- It was not clear whether it was more helpful to have Tiffany read through the text first before answering questions, review the questions first before reading the text, or listen to the assessor-teacher read the text first. Because of her defensiveness, she resisted providing insight into strategies that can help her. It is recommended that these strategies be reviewed to explore what works best for her and to encourage her to think about what feels like it is working for her.
- It may be helpful to Tiffany to have her read to children much younger than herself. When doing this, she should be encouraged first to read directly from a book but then to try to retell the story without reading it. She would need to be told that she should read the story with the idea of retelling it without reading it. Using the pictures from the book would provide structure for her to guide her thinking. Also she would not be embarrassed by using what she would perceive as a "baby" book; yet with the simpler materials, she could practice comprehension and summarization much more comfortably.
- Tiffany seems to be helped by acting out stories, and acting is an activity that she reportedly enjoys. Participating in recreational acting may be an enjoyable way to help improve her comprehension.

Mathematics
Help Tiffany recognize the key words in math problems and provide her with structure (e.g., a series of questions) to help her determine what she needs to do to solve the problem.

Emotional reactivity
- Although Tiffany would profit from therapy to address her reactions to needing help with her schoolwork, the best approach would be to embed this in the cognitive strategy training recommended earlier. Combining these treatments would also be more efficient and would help Tiffany to feel less "different" and needy.
- Tiffany needs to be helped to develop the vocabulary for how she will tell her friends and herself about her need for additional support. Getting her to role-play what she will say to others may be helpful.

Test Scores
Wechsler Intelligence Scale for Children – Third Edition
(100 = average; SD = 15)

	Standard score	Percentile rank
Verbal IQ	89 (83–96)	23
Performance IQ	73 (67–83)	04
Verbal Comprehension	88 (82–95)	21
Perceptual Organization	65 (60–77)	01
Freedom from Distract.	90 (82–101)	25
Processing Speed	111 (100–119)	77

Subtest Standard Score (average = 10; SD = 3)

Information	09
Similarities	08
Arithmetic	09
Vocabulary	06
Comprehension	08
Digit Span	07 [6 forward; 4 backward]
Picture Completion	05
Coding	12
Picture Arrangement	04
Block Design	05
Object Assembly	02
Symbol Search	12
Mazes	07

NEPSY: A Developmental Neuropsychological Assessment
(100 = average; SD = 15)
Attention/Executive: 92 (83–104); 30th percentile rank
Language: 99 (90–108); 47th percentile rank
Visuospatial: 88 (80–100); 21st percentile rank
Memory: 83 (76–95); 13th percentile rank
[Sensorimotor omitted]

Subtest	Standard score (10 = average; SD = 3)
Tower	10
Auditory Attention/Response Set	10
Visual Attention	07
Phonological Processing	13
Speeded Naming	06
Comprehenson/Instructions	11
Design Copying	07
Arrows	09
Memory for Faces	07
Memory for Names	10

Wechsler Individual Achievement Test, Second Edition
(average = 100; SD = 15)

	Standard score	Percentile rank
Word Reading	96 (92–100)	39
Reading Comprehension	93 (87–99)	32
Pseudoword Decoding	109 (104–114)	73
Numerical Operations	85 (75–95)	16
Math Reasoning	105 (97–113)	63
Spelling	96 (89–103)	39
Written Expression	90 (79–101)	25
Listening Comprehension	79 (66–92)	08
Oral Expression	109 (99–119)	73

Developmental Test of Visual-Motor Integration
Scaled score: 11 (mean = 10; SD = 3)
Percentile rank: 67
Age Equivalent: 9 years 4 months

Das/Naglieri Cognitive Assessment System

Scaled scores (average = 10; SD = 3)

Planned Connections	12
Nonverbal Matrices	11
Figure Memory	11
Expressive Attention	10
Receptive Attention	09

Children's Memory Scale (average = 10; SD = 3)

	Scaled scores	Percentile rank
Stories:		
Immediate	04	02
Delayed	01	<01
Delayed Recognition	02	<01
Word Pairs		
Learning	08	25
Long Delay	11	63
Delayed Recognition	12	75

Dynamic Assessment of Test Accommodations

	Mean scores	Norm group mean/SD
No Accommodation	3.00	4.69 (4.51)
Large Print	1.33	4.00 (4.04)
Extended Time	2.67	7.58 (5.91)
Read Aloud	−2.67	5.20 (4.19)

Behavior Assessment System for Children (Parent Rating Scales)
(50 = average; SD = 10)

	T scores	Percentile rank
Hyperactivity	48 (39–57)	47
Aggression	50 (43–57)	55
Conduct Problems	51 (41–61)	61
EXTERNALIZING PROBLEMS COMPOSITE	50 (45–55)	55
Anxiety	48 (41–55)	45
Depression	47 (41–530)	46
Somatization	41 (33–49)	19
INTERNALIZING PROBLEMS COMPOSITE	44 (38–50)	30
Atypicality	50 (39–61)	60
Withdrawal	40 (31–49)	15
Attention Problems	68 (60–76)	95
BEHAVIORAL SYMPTOMS INDEX	53 (48–58)	65
Adaptability	49 (41–57)	49
Social Skills	59 (54–64)	79
Leadership	44 (37–51)	30
ADAPTIVE SKILLS COMPOSITE	51 (46–56)	52

Behavior Rating Inventory of Executive Function (Parent Form) (50 =
average; SD = 10) [higher scores indicate more concern]

	T scores	Percentile rank
Inhibit	60	84
Shift	65	93
Emotional Control	58	82
Initiate	52	68
Working Memory	68	94
Plan/Organize	71	96
Organization of Materials	40	20
Monitor	55	73

BEHAVIORAL REGULATION INDEX: T = 55 Percentile Rank = 88
METACOGNITIVE INDEX: T = 60 Percentile Rank = 82

Case Discussion
In Tiffany's case, dynamic assessment was first used to explore the effects
of three different conditions on her reading comprehension. Despite the
fact that the scores yielded did not support the superiority of any of
the conditions, observations of Tiffany's behavior during the course of
engaging in the three trials showed that extended time was helpful but

not sufficient to affect her reading problem. The dynamic assessment approach used in this case was a highly structured one designed by Fuchs, Fuchs, Eaton, and Hamlett (2003) that specifically addresses reading accommodations. It provided the opportunity to observe Tiffany's performance and yielded results that were more helpful descriptively rather than quantitatively.

The next interjection of dynamic assessment occurred when reading curriculum taken directly from Tiffany's classroom was used. Although there again was no clear advantage to any of the approaches attempted, this episode again provided a valuable opportunity to observe the degree of defensiveness and anxiety that Tiffany brought to working in her area of difficulty. Both episodes were helpful in revealing the process-based barriers to Tiffany's language comprehension problem.

There was an unplanned opportunity to compare Tiffany's functioning with and without medication. In her case, her improved level of motor functioning with medication was evident. There were also embedded opportunities to derive small ideas for intervention, such as the need for her to have a pencil with an eraser for security purposes.

Another, very brief, use of dynamic assessment occurred following administration of one of the tasks of the intelligence test. This involved trying to teach her the difference between a diamond and a square, in response to a labeling error she made during the course of the testing. Again, her defensiveness and lack of willingness to modify her responses became quite evident.

In Tiffany's case, the referral questions did not concern her level of intelligence or academic achievement. These were not really issues for either her mother or teacher. Her mother and teacher also brought a rather high level of understanding of the nature of Tiffany's struggles, at least on a descriptive level, but they did not know the underlying bases for these struggles and were most eager to gain information about how to proceed with helping to improve Tiffany's competence. Without the insights provided by the dynamic assessment (along with heavy reliance on process and error analysis), the assessor would have been reduced to repeating back to them what they already knew. In Tiffany's case, it was clear that she needed more than just more teaching of reading, writing, and arithmetic. Her executive processing problem with self-regulation and its consequences for attention, memory, and, ultimately, language comprehension needed to be addressed. Her defensiveness made it difficult to determine strategies that would be of potential use for her, but the opportunity to observe her in learning situations both in school and in the assessment provided the basis for generation of ideas leading to an array of recommendations.

CASE 9.2

Name: Sarah
Age: 11 years 10 months
Grade: 6

Reason for Referral

Sarah was referred in relation to a potential Due Process hearing. Sarah has been included in regular education with special education accommodations throughout elementary school. She is a child with autism who is about to transition into middle school, and her parents are concerned about her ability to function in this setting without more intensive intervention than has been suggested by her school district. The questions for this assessment are as follows:

- What are Sarah's current educational needs?
- How can these best be addressed?
- What is the most appropriate school setting for her?

Procedures administered (Test scores are found at the end of the case study)

- File review
- Parent interview and completion of Behavioral Assessment System for Children (BASC) S)) Structured Developmental History
- Woodcock-Johnson Tests of Achievement – Third Edition
- Woodcock-Johnson Psychoeducational Test Battery – Third Edition
- Adaptive Behavior Assessment System
- Stanford Binet Intelligence Scales, Fifth Edition: Abbreviated Battery
- NEPSY: A developmental neuropsychological assessment
- Das/Naglieri Cognitive Assessment Scale: selected subtests
- Curriculum-Based Dynamic Assessment of selected content objectives
- Behavior Assessment Scales for Children (Parent Version)
- Behavior Rating Inventory of Executive Function
- Autism Treatment Evaluation Checklist [Autism Research Institute, www.autism.com/ari]
- Integrated Visual and Auditory Continuous Performance Test
- Miscellaneous sensorimotor screening
- Human Figure and Affect Drawings

Background Information

Sarah lives with her natural parents and younger sister. Sarah was born prematurely at 28 weeks gestation with a birth weight of 2 pounds 9 ounces. Labor was induced and lasted for 12 hours, complicated by lack of water. The pregnancy was further complicated by bleeding during the first trimester. She required intensive care for 3 months following birth and was treated for a couple of days with oxygen for apnea and followed with a monitor at home. She was jaundiced following delivery and was treated with bilirubin lights for 1 week.

Sarah's developmental milestones were somewhat delayed; for example, she began walking at about 17 months. She was followed at a developmental clinic up to age 18 months. At age 2 years she stopped speaking the few words she had, and her parents brought her to a specialized hospital for pediatric services. At this hospital she was found to have a questionable/abnormal electroencephalogram. She began receiving wraparound therapeutic services with a focus on socialization, safety, and frustration tolerance. She has been taught to use stress reduction techniques to manage her anxiety.

Sarah was underweight for a period of time following birth but has since caught up and is now average. She has no problems regarding eating or sleeping but has some gross motor limitations, for example, with skipping, riding a bike, and throwing and catching a ball. These motor limitations relate to her history of low upper body tone. Her only illness was chicken pox at about age 9 years, and her only surgery, removal of tonsils and adenoids at about age 8 or 9 years.

At age 5 years, she received a psychiatric diagnosis of PDD, NOS (pervasive developmental disorder not otherwise specified). In addition to her autistic-like symptoms, she was also noted to have high anxiety and language/auditory processing problems. Currently, her diagnosis, in addition to the above, includes ADHD (attention-deficit/hyperactivity disorder). She has been receiving speech and language services to improve her articulation and sentence structure. Sarah takes no medications.

Socially, she belongs to the Girl Scouts and functions in a follower role. She prefers to play by herself. She enjoys music, computer games, trampoline, swimming, and sewing. She has attended day camp but continues to have difficulty with socialization in her various social settings.

At home, Sarah's behavior is described as generally happy and compliant. She does not present significant management difficulty and responds to verbal controls and explanations. Sarah lacks social skills as well as any interest in social participation. She does not initiate play but, instead, will follow along when asked. Homework is a major source of stress, and she is not able to do homework with her mother. She is receiving some help in this area from the wraparound therapist, but it remains a significant irritant for her. Sarah's parents' goals for her include increasing her independence and developing her ability to work in a job that she enjoys.

Sarah began her schooling at age 3.5 years. Six months later she transferred to a local elementary school, where she continued through fifth grade. She has been included in regular education since kindergarten. She has been assigned a full-time aide since first grade. During fourth grade, she became involved in a Learning Support class for mathematics. Word reading and memory (and, therefore, spelling) have been her strengths, with reading comprehension and mathematics her weaknesses. Handwriting and written expression are apparently also issues because she is receiving services for these. In general, she is a strong visual learner with weakness in auditory processing and need for support with planning and organization. Social skills are a strong area of need as well.

In addition to receiving help for mathematics, which is taught to her by the Learning Support teacher, she is involved in the following additional services: occupational therapy (OT) 30 minutes/week, speech/language therapy (individual and group) 30 minutes twice/week, and physical therapy (PT) 30 minutes/week. She also has a one-to-one "personal care assistant" for both academic and behavioral support. This individual provides verbal and physical prompts to facilitate Sarah's task involvement and work completion. The assistant also helps Sarah to organize her materials at the beginning and end of each day.

According to her most recent evaluation report, Sarah has demonstrated the following needs, along with positive response to the following interventions:

- Attention to task: visual cues
- Anxious, self-stimulatory behavior in testing situations, unexpected schedule changes, and homework: taking 10 deep breaths, sensory breaks (jumping jacks, stress ball, Play-Doh manipulation), use of humor, squeezing or picking up a koosh ball, and a visual social story

Her need for and positive response to a schedule, forewarning regarding changes in routine, breaking down of complex tasks into small units, use of a checklist (for following schedules and task directions), and visual cue cards to signal her to continue working and listening are also noted. For written assignments, she responds well to graphic organizers.

Speech and language objectives for Sarah include articulation, pragmatics, and social skills. Intervention has included verbal and visual prompting, as well as repetition and rehearsal to promote generalization. Occupational therapy includes work on attention, speed of task completion, pencil grasp, and hand muscle strength. She continues to need work in these and the general areas of visual motor integration, visual perception, and fine motor skill. Physical therapy has addressed improvement of upper body strength. She profits from use of visual cues, organizational guides, and breaking down of tasks into small steps. For written assignments, she needs to follow an outline to help her organization. In her classroom, she profits from opportunities to move around and have brief breaks to engage in deep pressure or resistance activities that help to calm her.

Her most current evaluation report notes the challenges of Sarah's struggles with attention maintenance, impulse control, and frustration tolerance. Her educational levels were assessed with the Brigance Diagnostic Comprehensive Inventory of Basic Skills. According to these results, her word recognition was at fifth-grade level, but her reading comprehension was much lower, below a third-grade level. Her math was at a second-grade level. The results of testing with the Kaufman Test of Achievement were above those of the Brigance, and estimate her math computation at a low fourth-grade level, math applications at low third grade, reading decoding at low eighth grade, reading comprehension at low sixth grade, and spelling at low eighth grade. This is likely to be an overestimate of at least her reading comprehension because anecdotal descriptions in the report note her difficulty with making inferences.

Sarah's results from the Gates-MacGinitie Reading Test, which was administered to her class in the fifth grade, estimated her reading vocabulary at the mid-fifth-grade level and reading comprehension at the high seventh-grade level, compared with national norms. Again, this high level of reading comprehension differs from comments from her teachers, who find this an area of relative difficulty for her when the issue involves inferences rather than showing literal understanding. Her evaluation report from last year noted her continuing need for direct, small group instruction in mathematics and writing, as well as a modified, individualized general curriculum, specifically with regard to quantity and rate of information she is expected to cover.

Sarah's most recent psychological assessment notes concerns regarding continuing self-stimulatory behavior that appear to increase with onset of fatigue. Her socialization skills remain poor and her anxiety quite high in relation to homework and other academic expectations. She also has poor safety awareness. There was no testing attempted at that time. The assessor expressed concerns about Sarah's ability to deal with the transition to middle school and recommended a doctoral-level behavior specialist to work with Sarah and her teachers and aides for 4 hours per week. The assignment of therapeutic support staff was also recommended for up to 5 hours per week, along with services of a case manager for 4 hours per month.

All of the recommendations from the psychological were incorporated into the request for wraparound services. Wraparound services have addressed goals to improve her attention, impulse control, social reciprocity, stress management, and safety awareness. Specific objectives include increasing her ability to listen, follow directions, and complete a two-step task, invite other children to join her play, employ stress reduction techniques, make appropriate eye contact, and safely negotiate playgrounds and parking lots using "stop and look" skills. Triggers that elicit stress behaviors from Sarah include mentions of a test, challenging schoolwork, transitions, and highly stimulating conditions such as noise and crowds. She responds positively to praise, is a willing helper, and enjoys her learning successes.

Sarah's parents are specifically requesting that she be assigned to a small, language-based class that incorporates speech and occupational therapy within the curriculum. They also wish for her to continue her speech and OT on an individual basis. They wish for Sarah's teacher to be well trained to deal with students with her types of needs and would like this teacher to be knowledgeable about and utilize applied behavior analysis, as well as able to address Sarah's needs in the areas of auditory processing, socialization, and community-relevant functional skills.

Assessment Results

Behavior

Sarah is a pretty, slender girl of average height with a full head of curly brown hair. Her back is mildly curved with slight stomach protrusion, related to her low muscle tone. She is quiet and cooperative throughout the assessment, speaking when spoken to and initiating no comments. She usually looks away, at times to the side, but occasionally offers direct eye contact, especially when being read to. Her emotional expression and vocal prosody are generally flat, but she will occasionally provide some intensity of emphasis (e.g., responding with emphatic "no" to a silly test statement, conveying her understanding of the item), and she provides a subtle feeling of enjoyment of her competencies.

Sarah responded well to praise and encouragement and needed occasional verbal prompting to continue work that required independence (e.g., fluency items). She needed to be taught to indicate when she had "finished." When she returned for testing on the second day, she made the turn into the wrong office (turning right instead of left). When she left the office on the last day, she turned in the wrong direction when exiting into the hall. When her seat needed to be brought closer to the desk, she at first waited passively, but then followed through with adjusting it herself. She appropriately indicated, "I don't really know" to difficult questions. She tolerated mild frustration in the form of challenging work, although I generally managed the level of challenge by cutting short some of the establishment of ceilings when it was clear that she had reached her limit. During moments of brief waiting, she would engage in mild self-stimulation, mostly with head movements, but this was infrequent. She showed anxiety only during the last session when we worked on a board copying simulation; for this task, she experienced momentary confusion regarding expectations and began to tense and vocalize stress. As soon as instructions were clarified, she calmed down and set to work. Most important, she was able to move from her physical response into telling me that she did not know what to do.

She would occasionally smile to herself but could not communicate what her related thoughts were. She worked well under the optimal conditions of morning scheduling and a quiet, peaceful environment. We took a brief break during an incident of hiccups. Her mother asked her if she needed to use the bathroom, and she declined but then quickly went into the bathroom to use it without seeking privacy.

Academic Achievement

Reading
As has been previously documented, Sarah is a competent word reader, and she succeeds at or near grade level with this. She is able to use her good phonological skills to read words well above her level of comprehension. In contrast to previous testing results, on this assessment Sarah shows very limited and low-level reading comprehension, which, for her, parallels her listening/language comprehension. Her reading comprehension was estimated at a second-grade level, quite in contrast to her word identification at a mid-fourth-grade level. Thus, the written words do convey meaning to her, but she can only process them at a simple level. Nevertheless, she is able to determine whether simple statements make sense or not. The low level of her comprehension will present a severe impediment to her ability to use reading as a tool for learning and to deal with reading content in subject areas such as social studies and science in a regular education curriculum. Her reading comprehension was helped somewhat by asking her to read aloud.

Sarah's ability to learn specific facts is an area of strength. She has a well-developed knowledge base and is able to label at a low average level compared with a national sample of other students her age (i.e., estimated at a mid-third- to mid-fourth-grade level). She knew information such as naming who wrote *Hamlet* and *Macbeth*, the meaning of a cappella (she sings in a choir), and defined a neighbor as "someone who lives quite near you." She recognized the picture of Abraham Lincoln, named pictures of a canoe and a tambourine, and knew which part of the body exchanged carbon dioxide for oxygen. What she struggled with was going beyond the facts into the realm of inference, prediction, and determination of cause and effect. The more abstract the work, the more difficulty she had.

Sarah has had ongoing difficulty with mathematics, related to its abstract nature. Her level of calculation is estimated at a mid-third-grade level, with her ability to solve applied problems much lower, at a mid-first-grade level. When there were many problems or items on a page, it helped to use a paper to cover the items not being worked on. This was more of an issue for math than for reading. Having a lot of writing on a page did not seem to bother Sarah for either reading or writing. Sarah was able to carry out calculations for simple addition and subtraction, as well as for single-digit multiplication. She was able to carry when adding three groups of large numerals. She is not able to divide or work with fractions and could not solve the more complex multiplication problems. In applied math, Sarah was able to solve problems involving addition but had difficulty with subtraction, finding it difficult not to include items she could see in front of her. Although she could name coins, she could not determine their value or compute change. She was able to tell time to the hour (which was all that was tested).

A specific IEP goal addressed with curriculum-based dynamic assessment included Sarah's ability to determine the value of money and add up change to calculate the total amount. A key was made for her with photocopied pictures of coins and a dollar bill, with written cues to indicate the worth of each in terms of number of cents. I first had her name and match real coins with the pictures and state the value of each (using the picture cues). She showed confusion between nickels and quarters that continued throughout the assessment. I then placed three coins in front of her and worked with her to determine the total amount of change of these coins, varying the combinations. She successfully learned to transfer this onto paper as an addition problem. We briefly tried to work with subtraction in the context of getting change back from a purchase, but this is much more complex and will require more attention at a later time. She is ready to continue her mastery of determining the total amount of change, using her cue sheet. She will need to reinforce her ability to discriminate between a nickel and a quarter. Getting her to use the size and pictures of the coins as visual cues seems to help.

Spelling and writing are areas of strength for Sarah. Her spelling is particularly strong, related to her good phonological ability, similar to her strength in word reading. In writing, she is able to construct good simple sentences when provided with printed words in mixed-up order as cues; that is, she is able to rearrange the words and add needed words to create a meaningful sentence. She did not use punctuation and only added one period when cued for this. She does use capital letters to start the sentences.

We did not work on essays. It is likely that she will need a great deal of help with this and will certainly need to follow an outline. Organizing her thoughts will present the main challenge, and she may profit from provision of partially started sentences to complete. Her written expression is limited by her language ability. She is able to write what she is able to understand, and the use of writing is a good vehicle of expression for her.

Sensorimotor Functions
Sarah easily read the visual screening number chart at the 20/20 level and was able to locate the direction of finger rubbing screening of her hearing. Her vision and hearing are reported in her records as normal. She had no difficulty with visual field testing. She did have difficulty with eye tracking and was not able to keep her eyes focused on the target; I had to hold her chin to keep her from moving her head along with her eyes (she tolerated this without a problem).

Sarah's fine motor movements are rather stiff and awkward, and her grip for handwriting is usually a fist; however, when she copied an increasingly difficult series of geometric drawings, she began with a fist-like grip, graduated to a mature grasp during the more challenging items, and reverted to the fist when they became very difficult. For writing and drawing, she shows left-hand dominance. She writes with manuscript, which is readable, although fluctuating in size and spacing. Her letters and numbers are large in size, which is an issue for school because it would be necessary to provide sufficient space for her to record her work (e.g., in math when lining up of numbers is important). Her mother reports that using a paper with lines and wide spacing is helpful for her writing.

Sarah was not touch avoidant, but she had some difficulty processing touch as evident in her very poor performance with finger localization. She was able to determine which fingers were touched when her eyes were open, and she could refer to a numbered chart that matched her hand (I drew this by tracing her hands and numbering each finger; this was necessary because the nature of the task seemed too complex for her). She was not able to communicate which finger was touched when she could not see her hands. I did not specifically test her strength because this has already been determined to be an area of need from OT and PT evaluations, and she has been receiving services to address her hypotonia and upper body strength.

The specific learning goal addressed with curriculum-based dynamic assessment in this area was Sarah's ability to copy homework assignments from the board legibly. I simulated this by writing a multi-sentence message to her on a sheet attached to the wall. I asked her to copy the message. This is when she momentarily stiffened and began some anxiety-related self-stimulatory behaviors; however, she stopped these herself and told me that she did not know what to do. I was then able to change my directions to a simple, single statement, and she readily copied the first line. She then went on to re-copy this first line. I responded with erasing the line she completed and told her to put the next words on her paper, erasing each line as she completed it. I had first expected that her difficulty in this area would be related to the fine motor and possibly spatial demands of the task, but this was not at all the case. The issue for her concerned her understanding of the directions. Her copying was fine. I was prepared with paper with lines of various widths, but did not need to use these. She made a very readable copy on unlined paper, although the sentences would have been straighter with the aid of lines. After completion of two unrelated tasks, I returned to this and wrote a new message. This time, I just told her to copy it. She did this successfully, with no need for further or modified directions.

Attention

Sarah's attention was assessed primarily through a computerized continuous performance test that tapped both auditory and visual attention. Sarah did quite well using the computer and was able to click the mouse appropriately as indicated by the directions, showing adequate finger control. As she took the test, which lasted about 15 minutes, I noticed that she was much more responsive to visual stimuli, often ignoring the auditory. Even with visual, her attention would occasionally drift, and she would briefly look away. She did this during the examiner-administered testing as well and needed encouragement to resume her work (which she did quite readily). The scores on the attention test are not entirely valid because of her difficulty with holding the directions in mind. She was to click only when she heard or saw the number 1. Despite this, she clicked almost as often in response to the number 2 as 1. This is reflected in her scores as questionable comprehension. Her tendency was to click in response to any stimulus, with minimal discrimination regarding when to proceed or withhold her response. The test scores show that she had good stamina, which reflects the fact that she persisted and was responsive through the entire procedure. Her level of vigilance appears much stronger in relation to visual compared with auditory stimuli. Her impulse control (termed "prudence" on the test) was at a low level for both modalities. The test results suggest a relatively similar level of poor focus for both auditory and visual stimuli, with a slight advantage for auditory, but I question this equality because of the observed randomness of her responses and tendency to respond to all stimuli (again, the prudence score). Her reaction time for responding to the stimuli was observed to be generally good. These results support the ADHD aspect of her diagnosis. High activity level is not an observable aspect of her behavior; in fact, she is rather passive and phlegmatic. Her bursts of activity at home appear related to tension release related to her buildup of anxiety. Nevertheless, this test picked up her inattention and difficulty with response inhibition; the latter is a characteristic that is subsumed under hyperactivity.

Perception

Sarah appears to have adequate auditory and visual perception. Her visual matching is good, despite slow speed. Her phonological skills are an area of strength. Processing of touch, however, is an area of difficulty for her.

Memory

Sarah shows one of her greatest needs in the area of memory, particularly with working memory, which describes what she is able to hold in her memory at any one period of time for conscious thinking or thought processing. Sarah's very limited working memory significantly contributes to her difficulty with language comprehension, resulting in her ability to process only relatively short bits of information. This also accounts for the significant difference between her ability to process auditory, compared with visual information, as the visual support serves as an external memory sketchpad.

Interestingly, what at times appears to be impulsivity really is Sarah's attempt to manage her working memory. For example, when she was asked to repeat a number of sentences of increasing length, as the sentences became longer, she began to respond before I finished. At first I thought this was her inability to inhibit her response, but I realized that the point at which she began to respond seemed to correspond with the amount of information she was able to hold in her memory. She had not shown this tendency when the sentences were short and well within her span.

A learning objective in this domain that was addressed by curriculum-based dynamic assessment was Sarah's ability to remember and retell a short story. She is very limited in her ability to retell a narrative just from hearing it. For this assessment, I addressed her need for visual supports and added a visual component to the stories. For our first story, we built a model of each story element with small felt symbols. We proceeded through the steps of first finding the symbols for each part of the story. Sarah then was asked to locate each symbol as she reread the story. She was then asked to tell the story herself by "reading" the symbols, and, finally, she was asked to retell the story without the support of the symbols. She moved from telling an incorrect story that contained no more than three story elements, to communicating the correct story with almost all of the elements in a coherent narrative. We also tried some stories with Sarah making quick drawings of the story elements and then using these as supports to retell her story (again, ending with removal of the visual props). This worked very well also. She was able to make quick appropriate drawings and in fact seemed to enjoy this approach very much. This provides strong support for the effectiveness of using visual scaffolds for Sarah's learning of auditory-language related material.

Language
Sarah's spontaneous expressive communication is quite limited. She often even waits to be asked about her basic needs such as eating and toileting. She answers direct questions appropriately, with minimal answers, but is quite capable of using appropriate complete sentences to answer test items. Her speech is intelligible, despite mild sound substitutions for which she receives speech and language services. She has good prosody when reading, despite reduced prosody in her conversational speech. Her prosody during reading appears detached from the meaning of the words because she exhibits an equal amount of intonation with nonmeaningful as with meaningful sentences.

Sarah has significant limitations in her language comprehension and occasional word retrieval difficulty in her verbal expression, although she has an impressive vocabulary and general knowledge base. Her verbal expression is to some extent reduced by her passivity and general reticence to initiate engagement. Her mild struggle with word retrieval may exacerbate this reticence, and it is worth thinking about a trial use of sign language to enhance both her expressive and receptive language. This would not need to be at a complex level but mainly involve signs for critical words to facilitate her communication of her needs and her comprehension of directions. It would be another form of visual cueing. There were a number of instances when she first responded with an incorrect or nearly correct word to a question, only later to pop up with its correction.

Sarah has relatively good comprehension of language at the single word level. She is able to define words and think of alternative words. She even comes up with interesting and relevant errors in defining words she does not know. For example, her definition of "repose" was "to take a second picture." Because her difficulty with receptive language occurs when she has to retain and process groupings of words, as well as directions, my interpretation is that her difficulty lies more in the area of working memory than language per se. This nevertheless has a negative impact on her ability to process language. The shorter the language load, the better is her ability to comprehend. Furthermore, and very importantly, she relies on language as a tool for learning. Within her ability to attend and retain, language is an area of strength for her.

Cognition
Estimation of Sarah's levels of cognitive functioning is complex because of the large discrepancies in her functioning. No single score can come close to estimating or describing her abilities. The Stanford Binet Abbreviated Battery offers an estimate of her cognitive functioning based on one verbal and one nonverbal subtest. These combined scores yield an estimate in the low average range. There is a highly significant discrepancy between the scores of these two subtests, with nonverbal lying well below average and verbal (vocabulary) lying well within the average range.

Selected subtests from the Woodcock-Johnson were also used to assess Sarah's cognitive functioning. These results further document the discrepancy between her higher verbal, compared with lower nonverbal, problem solving. Her verbal comprehension in terms of single-word vocabulary and generation of synonyms, antonyms, and analogies was in the average range, compared with a national sample of other students her age. She obtained the greatest level of success with simple naming and generation of opposites, compared with her comparatively lower level ability with synonyms and analogies; however, she did succeed with some of these as well. Although Sarah attends best to visually presented material, her speed of processing visual information is slow. Nevertheless, she was able to solve problems that involved visual–spatial processing at a low-average level when speed was not a factor; in fact, she attended quite well to one of these tasks and appeared to derive some enjoyment from it. Thus, she is able to deal with visual–spatial problem solving when this remains uncomplicated by demands on logical reasoning.

Sarah's strength is her ability to learn language and to use verbal labels and information in direct, literal form. Her best mode of learning is through the combination of her relatively good attention to visual stimuli along with verbal stimulation. She is not able, in most cases, to go beyond this direct learning to the point of inference. What she sees and hears is what she understands and expresses. The extent to which she interprets verbal messages literally at times leads to poor judgment and social ineptness. She will respond to exactly what was said and not take it any further. She is, nevertheless, capable of conceptualizing words in terms of same and opposite at a low level; she cannot, however, extend the concepts of same or similar into a simile or metaphor. Teachers need to be mindful of directions given to Sarah and modify these as necessary to ensure her understanding. She is improving her ability to indicate appropriately when she does not comprehend.

Metacognition

Metacognition concerns the ability to self-regulate, as well as to plan and to organize; it involves the ability to function flexibly and to retrieve relevant information from long-term memory into working memory. These are all areas of significant struggle for Sarah. Her behavior was well regulated during the course of the assessment. She was even able to monitor her written work and self-correct as needed. By report, it seems that her low sensory thresholds and ease of becoming overstimulated account for incidents of loss of regulation at home and at times in school. Mostly, she will show this through anxious self-stimulation (e.g., head and hand movements and vocal noises), although at home, she lets more out and becomes highly active (helped by doing activities such as jumping on her trampoline). Of greater concern are Sarah's difficulties with planning/organization and flexibility (e.g., dealing with transitions). These struggles are typical of individuals with autism and usually require external supports of schedules, advance preparation, use of overlearned routines, and visual guidelines. She did show some flexibility when she wrote, in that she was able to manipulate the order of the stimulus words to create a meaningful sentence, even adding needed missing words. She was more stimulus-bound in math, where she found it difficult to subtract items she saw in front of her.

Social–Emotional Functioning

In the autism spectrum, Sarah's level of functioning is rated at about a middle level of severity, according to her parents. In relation to a range from mild to severe, she is most consistently at or below (that is, more toward mild than severe) the 50th percentile. Her relative strength is in the development of speech/language, with her social skills and sensory/cognitive awareness at a somewhat more impaired level. She has significant interpersonal strengths in that she is generally cooperative and agreeable, as well as responsive to praise and encouragement. Anxiety elicits her most autistic-like symptoms of self-stimulation and agitation. When not anxious, she will show some direct eye contact and awareness of and responsiveness to others, but she tends to be passive, requiring external stimulation, yet having a low threshold for becoming overstimulated. She walks a fine line between requiring and overreacting to stimulation.

Sarah was able to show clear differentiation of basic affective states in her drawings, although she did not associate these with any particular content. Her drawings are generally well done and show stable figures with good attention to detail and spacing. The stunting of social skill is apparent. She shows more social–emotional awareness than may be apparent in her expressive behavior.

Sarah's behavior, as rated by her parents, documents areas of concern regarding attention and hyperactivity, as well as her atypical and withdrawn behavior. Her adaptive skills are rated as generally low, particularly in the area of socialization. Her occasional incidents of toileting accidents and attempts at self-injury (banging her head when frustrated) were noted as well.

Adaptive behavior addresses how Sarah functions at home in relation to her self-care and ability to carry out tasks relevant to community access. According to the ratings of her parents, she needs further improvement in the following [I am only listing selected items that have the most relevance for her practical functioning and that should be able to be addressed in an educational setting]:

- Communication: telling others about activities, answering the telephone appropriately, listening to others when they speak, taking turns during conversations, starting conversations on topics of interest to others, and giving verbal directions
- Community Use: packing up supplies, using the school library, finding restrooms in public places, carrying out shopping transactions
- Functional Academics: keeping score in games, using measurement tools, using money for purchases, writing messages, making lists, finding telephone numbers in the phone book, using reference books such as a dictionary
- Home Living: simple chores of cleaning, using electrical appliances, returning items to proper places, basic cooking
- Health and Safety: following safety rules for fire alarms, obeying traffic signals
- Leisure: inviting others to participate in games, planning for leisure activities during school breaks
- Self-care: fastening and straightening clothing before leaving restroom, keeping her hair neat during the day, using the restroom independently, cutting food into bite-sized pieces
- Social: saying thank you when given something, describing how she feels, moves out of the way of others when appropriate, describing feelings of others

These are all practical, applied behaviors that are being worked on and need to continue to be targeted for intervention.

Conclusions and Recommendations

What are Sarah's current educational needs?
Sarah's needs are primarily in the areas of working memory, language, metacognition, and social skills. She has strengths in some aspects of

long-term memory, language, and definitely in the visual modality. She reads and spells well, although she has reached a plateau because of the literalness of her understanding. Math is an area of ongoing need. Specific details of her needs in all areas are indicated earlier in the case report.

How can these best be addressed?
Sarah should be involved in the more challenging academic learning tasks during the morning, when she can concentrate best. She needs to be in a small classroom with direct access to a teacher who has the appropriate training and experience for working with students with autism and who can adjust and adapt the lessons to Sarah's needs. If the purpose of the lesson is to teach specific academic content, there is little need for opportunity for socialization other than reciprocal interaction with the teacher. Sarah does need opportunities to develop her social skills, and this is appropriately done through involvement with and exposure to students with typical development, but these opportunities need to be specifically structured for her, with the other students coached on how to interact with her. Appropriate opportunities for social interaction need to be worked out collaboratively between the school personnel and her parents so that these activities can occur both in the community and at school. There are times when assignment of a peer buddy would be appropriate. There may be other times when Sarah could interact with children much younger than herself, for example, perhaps to read stories to children in kindergarten.

Because the regular education academic work is becoming increasingly abstract and complex and Sarah has specific difficulty dealing with these types of demands, the content of her curriculum needs to be reconsidered to develop priorities for what she needs to learn for practical functioning. Her ability to use reading as a tool for learning is limited. It would not be appropriate for her to be expected to carry out complex projects. Certainly, the regular education mathematics curriculum would be well beyond her reach. She needs to be able to read the information available in her environment, for example, to follow directions for cooking and operating simple appliances. She needs to learn routines for safety and basic money utilization and management. She needs to learn how to shop and take care of her personal needs and how to communicate her needs more effectively.

Continued use of a written schedule, advance planning of changes and activities, written directions, and automatized routines will be necessary. With Sarah's relative strength in writing, it should be possible to work toward teaching her to write out some of her own visual props. For writing that involves planning and organization, she would need an outline and guided practice to teach her to follow this outline. It would be necessary to include time to go to the bathroom in Sarah's schedule at times that would anticipate these needs. She does not always communicate her need to go to the bathroom, and development of her signaling for this needs continued attention.

Sarah's mind can drift during the course of her work. She needs cues to resume and continue, but the teacher needs to discriminate between those times when she is looking off in the distance to think (related to issues of word retrieval and problem solving) and those times when she has disengaged from the task. An effort should be made to teach her to communicate the difference. For example, she could be asked if she needs time to think or if she has lost attention, and then have her state (following the model) which was the case, even if she is not entirely accurate at first. This could be graduated to saying something such as, "You are looking away from your work. Tell me what happened. [Are you thinking or did you lose attention?]"

Sarah would profit from more intensive attention to her fine and gross motor functioning. Some of this would be available from OT (see independent OT report for specific recommendations) and PT, but it is also recommended that objectives from these therapies be reinforced in an adaptive physical education program and that she be excused from participation in regular physical education. Her program should address her need for periodic energy release, development of motor regulation, and increasing her general body strength.

The issue of homework warrants specific consideration and further discussion. Despite the fact that her current homework assignments are modified, this remains a significant area of stress, and it is logical to ask if and to what extent homework is really necessary for her. At the very least, her assignments need to be remodified to the minimal, most necessary components. The more that assignments can be related to practical, home-life activities, the better. Homework needs to be rethought and custom designed for her, asking the question of what she is supposed to get out of it and at the same time evaluating what she is getting out of it.

It is recommended that her speech/language therapist consider offering a trial of sign language, using signs for basic needs and directions. If she responds well, these would need to be taught to her teachers and parents.

I would recommend that Sarah have the benefit of a comprehensive functional behavioral assessment in her new school environment. This should include having the analyst follow her throughout a full typical day to observe and assess her ability to function in the various settings and to chart her needs as she moves through her day. The current assessment has not had the benefit of being able to observe Sarah in her school setting, and this would be important to more comprehensive determination of her needs.

What is the most appropriate school setting for her?
Sarah has significant needs in almost all areas of her functioning and requires a great deal of adaptation and individualization of her curriculum. Under the current conditions of inclusion, many of her IEP goals do not seem to have been addressed. The teachers have large classes and are under a lot of pressure to move through the curriculum. It is difficult to imagine how Sarah's needs can be met in a regular education setting, particularly in relation to the changing demands of the middle school. Even opportunities for socialization need to be carefully structured and programmed. It is not sufficient merely to place her in proximity to other students her age. She needs to interact in a structured context (e.g., games), and the other students need to be coached how best to interact with her in a facilitative way. For these reasons, I support Sarah's parents' pursuit of a more restrictive (i.e., treatment-intensive) environment for her.

Test Scores
NEPSY – A Developmental Neuropsychological Assessment
[mean = 100; SD = 15; subtest mean = 1 SD = 3]

Subtests	Standard scores	Percentile ranks
Tower	03	
Auditory Attention/Response Set	02	
Visual Attention	08	
ATTENTION/EXECUTIVE	78 (73–96)	07
Phonological Processing	04	
Speeded Naming	11	
Comprehension of Instructions	08	
LANGUAGE	86 (79–96)	18
Fingertip Tapping	11	
Imitating Hand Positions	04	
Visuomotor Precision	08	
SENSORIMOTOR	109	73
Design Copying	06	
Arrows	01	
VISUOSPATIAL	56 (52–70)	0.2
Memory for Faces	06	
Memory for Names	05	
Narrative Memory	01	
MEMORY	74 (68–84)	04

Woodcock-Johnson III Tests of Achievement: (Mean = 100; SD = 15)

CLUSTER/Test	Percentile rank	Standard score	Grade equivalent
ORAL LANGUAGE (Ext)	01	65 (61–69)	1.7
ORAL EXPRESSION	08	79 (74–84)	2.4
LISTENING COMPREHENSION	01	67 (62–71)	1.3
TOTAL ACHIEVEMENT	06	76 (74–78)	3.5
BROAD READING	14	84 (82–85)	3.6
BROAD MATH	01	66 (64–69)	2.3
BROAD WRITTEN LANGUAGE	35	94 (91–97)	5.3
MATH CALCULATION SKILLS	03	71 (67–75)	3.0
WRITTEN EXPRESSION	21	88 (84–92)	4.5
ACADEMIC SKILLS	31	92 (90–94)	4.7
ACADEMIC FLUENCY	12	82 (80–84)	3.9
ACADEMIC APPS	01	66 (63–69)	2.0
ACADEMIC KNOWLEDGE	24	89 (85–93)	4.6

Subtests

Letter–Word Identification	32	93 (91–95)	4.6
Reading Fluency	21	88 (86–90)	4.2
Story Recall	01	62 (54–71)	K.2
Understanding Directions	05	75 (70–80)	1.4
Calculation	09	80 (75–85)	3.5
Math Fluency	00.2	57 (54–60)	1.7
Spelling	56	102 (98–107)	6.6
Writing Fluency	19	87 (82–92)	4.6
Passage Comprehension	02	70 (66–74)	2.0
Applied Problems	01	62 (59–66)	1.4
Writing Samples	30	92 (85–100)	4.3
Story Recall–Delayed	–	–	–
Picture Vocabulary	22	88 (84–93)	3.6
Oral Comprehension	02	68 (63–73)	1.2
Academic Knowledge	24	89 (85–93)	4.6

Woodcock-Johnson III Tests of Cognitive Abilities
[mean = 100; SD = 15]

CLUSTER	Percentile rank	Standard score
VERBAL ABILITY (Ext)	21	88 (84–92)
COG EFFICIENCY	<0.1	51 (47–54)
COMP-KNOWLEDGE (Gc)	21	88 (84–92)

CLUSTER	Percentile rank	Standard score
Subtests		
Verbal Comprehension	46	99 (94–103)
Spatial Relations	15	84 (80–88)
Visual Matching	<0.1	35 (32–39)
Numbers Reversed	4	74 (68–79)
General Information	8	78 (73–84)

Das/Naglieri Cognitive Assessment Systems
[subtest mean = 10; SD = 3]

Selected subtests	Standard scores
Planned Connections	Attempted, but unable to complete
Verbal–Spatial Relations	1
Figure Memory	7
Expressive Attention	6
Sentence Repetition	10

Stanford-Binet Intelligence Scales: Fifth Edition, Abbreviated Battery
[mean = 100; SD = 15; subtest mean = 10; SD = 3]

Subtest	Standard score
Nonverbal Domain	
Fluid Reasoning,	
Object Series/Matrices	4
Verbal Domain	
Knowledge: Vocabulary	10
Estimated IQ: 82 (76–92), Percentile Rank = 12	

Behavior Rating Inventory for Executive Functions
[T scores: mean = 50; SD = 10]

Subscales	T scores	Percentile ranks
Inhibit	57 (42–62)	81
Shift	70 (64–76)	94
Emotional Control	68 (62–74)	94
BEHAVIOR REGULATION INDEX	67 (63–71)	92
Initiate	69 (62–76)	95
Working Memory	79 (74–84)	98
Plan/Organize	78 (73–83)	98
Monitor	76 (69–85)	99
METACOGNITIVE INDEX	76 (69–83)	94

Behavior Assessment System for Children, Parent
[T scores: mean= 50; SD = 10]

Subscales	T scores	Percentile ranks
Hyperactivity	60 (52–68)	84
Aggression	32 (25–39)	02
Conduct Problems	37 (28–46)	04
EXTERNALIZING PROBLEMS COMPOSITE	42 (37–47)	20
Anxiety	46 (39–53)	39
Depression	51 (44–58)	59
Somatization	39 (31–47)	09
INTERNALIZING PROBLEMS COMPOSITE	44 (38–50)	30
Atypicality	67 (56–78)	94
Withdrawal	60 (51–69)	85
Attention Problems	68 (61–75)	95
BEHAVIORAL SYMPTOMS INDEX	56 (51–61)	75
Adaptability	47 (39–55)	37
Social Skills	24 (19–29)	01
Leadership	30 (23–37)	02
ADAPTIVE SKILLS COMPOSITE	31 (26–36)	03

Adaptive Behavior Assessment System [Mean = 100; SD = 15; subtest mean = 1; SD = 3]

Adaptive skill areas	Scaled score	Percentile
Communication	1	
Community Use	3	
Functional Academics	5	
Home Living	1	
Health and Safety	2	
Leisure	4	
Self-Care	3	
Self-Direction	3	
Social	1	
General Adaptive Composite	54 (52–57)	0.1

IVA Continuous Performance Test: [mean = 100; SD = 15]

Response control	Full scale quotient
Auditory	60
Visual	65

Response control	Full scale quotient
Response Control subscales	
Auditory	
Prudence	46
Consistency	77
Stamina	102
Visual	
Prudence	45
Consistency	77
Stamina	102
Attention Full Scale Quotient	
Auditory	46
Visual	78
Attention subscales	
Auditory	
Vigilance	40
Focus	82
Speed	67
Visual	
Vigilance	88
Focus	77
Speed	86

Autism Research Institute's Autism Treatment Evaluation Checklist

	Ratings	(Range possible)	Centile (range from mild to severe; 0–100)
Speech/Language/Communication	8	(0–28)	30–39
Sociability	13	(0–40)	40–49
Sensory/Cognitive Awareness	15	(0–36)	40–49
Health/Physical/Behavior	16	(0–75)	30–39
Summary Score	52	(0–180)	30–39

Case Discussion

The first attempts to inject DA into Sarah's assessment probably qualify more as testing the limits than a full-fledged dynamic assessment. This first occurred during testing of reading comprehension, when she was asked to read aloud, and the assessor informally determined that her level of functioning improved under these conditions. This was also the case during assessment of mathematics, when the assessor established that Sarah's ability to calculate was improved when items she was not working on were covered.

The first instance of full-fledged curriculum-based dynamic assessment (addressing an objective taken directly from her IEP) occurred in relation to teaching Sarah how to calculate change. With the advance knowledge that visual cues seemed to help her, the assessor developed a visual cue card to support Sarah's ability to determine the value of coins and then to use the card as support for addition problems with the coins. The degree of her confusion between nickels and quarters was revealed, and her ability to profit from this approach even over the short term for the operation of addition was documented. Based on this actual learning experience, it was possible to set specific educational objectives within her zone of proximal development along with evidence of a potentially helpful instructional approach.

Farther along in the assessment, there was another brief opportunity to test Sarah's limits. This involved the finger localization task, when it was necessary to provide visual support to overcome her failure to understand the directions.

This pattern of difficulty understanding directions and ability to profit from visual support was clearly documented in the next curriculum-based assessment. This addressed the issue of Sarah's difficulty copying her homework from the board. In this case, a simulation of this demand was created. Without this simulation, the assessor would have inferred that Sarah's difficulty most probably involved the combination of motor and spatial demands of the task. Instead, the opportunity for direct observation of Sarah in this situation provided evidence that, again, the issue was her comprehension of directions, and the most effective intervention, simplification of the verbal directions. This simulation also provided a very valuable opportunity to observe Sarah's ability to cope with her stress under these challenging conditions. She first began to show subtle signs of onset of regressive behavior but was then able to muster a very appropriate verbal communication of her lack of understanding which served as feedback to the assessor, so adjustments could be made in the demand. This loop of effective communication provides a very reinforcing basis for learning for her.

The next opportunity for dynamic assessment addressed Sarah's difficulty with working memory. It was becoming increasingly evident that memory played a significant role in her struggle with language comprehension. Process and error analysis revealed that her comprehension was better when the memory load was low. In this case the dynamic assessment again used the idea of visual support, this time as an aid to memory. The intervention went further to address the issue of increasing Sarah's independence in applying a strategy within this domain by moving from symbols created by the assessor to those created by Sarah. In both cases, the effects on her memory were strongly positive.

CASE 9.3

Name: Scott
Age: 11 years 8 months
Grade: 6

Reason for Referral

This assessment was done at the request of Scott's parents, who wish for information about his educational needs and recommendations for accommodations. He has been classified as Other Health Impaired (with ADHD) and is currently receiving learning support services, but his mother wishes for more specifics than have been provided, as well as input from an independent evaluator. For the first time, Scott has developed behavioral problems, and his parents feel this may relate to lack of appropriate accommodations. The questions for this assessment are as follows:

- What are Scott's educational needs?
- What accommodations are recommended for him?
- What characteristics of an educational program are recommended for him?

Procedures [**Test scores are at the end of the case report**]
- File review
- Parent (mother) interview
- Classroom observation
- NEPSY: A developmental neuropsychological assessment
- Das/Naglieri Cognitive Assessment System
- Selected subtests from the Wechsler Intelligence Test for Children, 4th edition
- Woodcock-Johnson Individual Achievement Test, 3rd edition
- selected subtests from the Wechsler Individual Achievement Test, 3rd edition
- Dynamic Assessment of Test Accommodations
- Behavior Assessment Scale for Children (Parent and self reports)
- Behavior Rating Inventory for Executive Functions
- Dean Woodcock Sensory Motor Battery
- Integrated Visual and Auditory Continuous Performance Test
- Sentence Completion
- Drawings

Background Information

Scott lives with his mother and older brother. His parents are divorced. His father has remarried and has a preschool-age daughter from this marriage.

Scott was the product of a full-term pregnancy, with birth weight of 5 lbs 7 ounces. He was jaundiced at birth and treated with bilirubin lights. Labor was induced, and delivery was by C-section. He was able to leave the hospital with his mother. At 4 months, he was diagnosed as failure to thrive and was underweight because of difficulties with feeding. Scott's low birth weight (despite full-term pregnancy), his subsequent feeding problem and failure to thrive, and a later occurrence of unexplained, brief loss of consciousness and migraine headaches and attention problems may all relate to his disorder, which was initially diagnosed as Russell-Silver syndrome. The nature and cause of his growth disorder is currently considered "unknown." Scott's developmental milestones for sitting (11+ months), walking (15–16 months), and speech were delayed. He had tubes for fluid in his ears when young, but these had to be removed because of calcification, leaving a scar on his left eardrum, which has limited elasticity.

Scott is currently taking a stimulant medication for attention deficit, as well as medications for depression and for appetite stimulation. His focus remains poor. He has had both PT and OT in the past related to mixed tone. He has a history of absence of righting reflexes from infancy through toddler years, which affected his accomplishment of developmental milestones. His only childhood illness has been chicken pox at the age of 8 months. Last year he had several instances of "repeated movements" (e.g., making figure eights with his hands, saying he couldn't stop); he was taken to the emergency room and was told the cause was psychological, and he was given medication for stress. He experiences dizziness related to positional hypotension. His mother describes Scott's mood swings and notes that he has expressed self-destructive thoughts. He is currently involved in therapy with a psychologist who is focusing on stress reduction.

Scott's mother questions his current hearing status because he sometimes jumps when someone walks into the room. This needs to be checked further.

Scott was previously evaluated as an infant and was found eligible for early intervention. At this time, he also qualified for speech and occupational and physical therapies. He was terminated from OT and PT services; however, it was noted that he needed to have a chair of appropriate size. Speech therapy continued, related to moderately delayed auditory comprehension and expressive language. He had been determined to have a hearing loss and received monthly itinerant hearing services. Accommodations for his hearing were made to include seating close to the teacher, away from noise and directly facing the teacher; in addition, the teacher was to gain his attention prior to speaking to him, and comments by other students were to be repeated for him. During this time, it was noted that he needed to have frequent, high-carbohydrate snacks. Issues of focus, impulsivity, and work completion were mentioned as early as first grade. He was seeing a psychologist for behavior management concerns.

In an evaluation by a school psychologist when he was about 7 years, attention and hyperactivity emerged as issues on both behavior ratings by his parents as well as in direct observation by the evaluator. He appeared to be an enthusiastic, motivated student who was easily distracted and had difficulty sustaining his attention to the task. His tested intelligence was in the average range, with some significant variability between deficient and high average. His lowest scores were on visual–motor speed, visual attention to details, and auditory rote memory subtests, and his highest scores were on subtests tapping verbal expression and perceptual analysis. On a specific test of memory, he had difficulty recalling visual abstract designs and auditory stories. His teacher reported that he was reading at a pre-primer level. He was an outgoing, willing student, who needed extra time to learn new things and was easily distracted. He had shown improvement in response to a behavior management chart. He got along well with his classmates, more so in structured settings; less structure tended to elicit his impulsivity. He was provided with extra time to complete his work. His academic achievement was estimated to be in the average range in all areas.

Scott was recently reevaluated by his school's current psychologist. Although continuing to document his level of cognitive functioning essentially in the average range, there were several significant decreases in subtest scores, compared with his previous assessment; these occurred in both verbal and nonverbal areas. His academic achievement showed significant scatter, from superior (word reading and spelling) to below average (reading comprehension and mathematics reasoning). Numerical operations and written expression were both in the average range. There was also wider scatter than in his previous assessment, although the tests used were different. On a parent rating scale of his behavior, he was high in the areas of somatization and attention problems. His scores on a depression scale were not significant. The evaluator concluded that he continued to present as a child with an ADHD and continued to be eligible for special education services under the category of Other Health Impaired. Discontinuation of OT services was recommended. Specific recommendations included specially designed instruction in language arts, counseling, preferential seating, multisensory instruction, private signal cues, extended-time/repetition/practice, breakdown of multistep tasks, and assistance with note taking.

According to Scott's December 2003 IEP, he was included in regular education for math, science, social studies, and all special subjects. For reading and written expression, he attends a Learning Support class. He was receiving weekly Occupational Therapy but was recommended for termination. He was involved in individual counseling twice monthly. Although he was said to be able to take notes appropriately, it was also commented that he profited from provision of outlines to be filled in. He was said to have benefited from short breaks, books on tape, and extended time. He is to have several snacks throughout the day and was to have a streamlined binder and two copies of books, with one set in each class and one set in his home.

In math, he is in the lowest of three groups in his class. In reading, his instructional level has been estimated at fourth grade. In writing, his level is described as "basic (second lowest out of four levels)." He has difficulty organizing his thoughts and getting them onto paper. It was noted that he needed to have the assignments broken down into small parts. He was approved for Learning Support and participation in standardized testing with accommodations of small group administration, directions read aloud, breaks as needed, and 30 minutes extended time for reading, math, and writing.

On the state standardized achievement test administered in Grade 5, Scott's level in math was described as "proficient" and his level in reading as "basic."

Scott was involved in early intervention at age 11 months. He attended a regular education preschool and then transferred to a program for children with developmental delays; however, he was asked to leave because of some incidents of aggression. During kindergarten, he received speech services, as well as some physical adaptations related to his growth disorder. He proceeded normally in regular education through the elementary grades, although he struggled with reading comprehension and short attention span and never liked to read. His grades have recently declined, and he is currently involved in Learning Support twice daily for help with reading. There has been a change in his behavior for the worse since he entered middle school. His mother attributes this decline to his frustration related to insufficient accommodations for his special needs. He spends about 2 hours on homework that should take only 1 hour.

Scott's mother notes his difficulty with independent work and says that he hates to read. She finds that she needs to ask for specific accommodations for him and is disappointed that these have not been forthcoming from the school. For example, she has requested that tests be read aloud, and she has found that he responds well to books on tape. Scott has a tutor for reading once a week. He has particular difficulty with sustained reading. It is relevant that Scott has had experience with the use of reading as punishment from his father, who would tell him to go to his room to read when he misbehaved.

Scott's teachers consistently note his difficulty with maintaining focus and his need for frequent cueing and reminders. They also consistently comment on his good motivation, desire to please, and his good ideas. Nevertheless, they find his work inconsistent and note his difficulty getting his ideas onto paper and working independently. He works well with others and has good social skills, although he tends to be overly interested in activities of those around him.

Assessment Results

Behavior
Scott related very comfortably during the assessment. Despite his reported lack of enthusiasm for engaging in the assessment, he never showed this during the actual process and was always fully cooperative and pleasant. He communicated freely and well and showed good awareness of himself. He even showed some reluctance at the end to leave. He conveys a feeling of an intelligent person when engaged in conversation. To accommodate his small size, we needed to make some adjustments to his seating so that he would be more comfortable; I added pillows to his chair and an overturned wastebasket to support his feet. Despite offers for breaks and snacks, he mostly chose to persist, preferring to move toward the finish line. He worked solidly in sessions spanning between 2 and 4 hours with good attention and motivation.

Academic Achievement
There is a large discrepancy between Scott's very strong ability to read individual words (grade equivalent 12.7) and his ability to comprehend what he reads (grade equivalent 4.0). To a significant extent, his relatively lower comprehension appears related to his limited knowledge of vocabulary (grade equivalent 4.5) and general knowledge base (grade equivalent 3.9; information subtest of the Wechsler Intelligence Scale for Children below average as well). When he is allowed to read aloud without time restrictions, his level of reading comprehension improves to the low average level (grade equivalent 5.6). This in turn may reflect his relatively strong oral/listening comprehension; that is, when Scott is able to hear information and not rely just on reading, he comprehends well, even if he is listening to himself. Reading aloud also serves the purpose of slowing him down, thus imposing some self-regulation. He is able to derive meaning from the narratives he hears from contextual clues when he does not know

the meaning of specific words. Scott says he also profits from the technique of previewing, where the content of the material to be read is reviewed, and specific questions are posed in advance to guide the reading. He reports getting helped with graphic organizers.

Scott's retention of information gleaned from exposure to new information is limited (grade equivalent 3.9) and well below expectations for his learning ability (well within average range). Even when he hears information presented orally, despite his good understanding of what was said at the time, he has difficulty placing this information into long-term memory.

Scott's need for accommodations on tests involving reading comprehension was estimated with administration of the Dynamic Assessment of Test Accommodations. Only two of the three accommodations were tried because of time limitations. Scott did show a positive response to the extended time accommodation. Without the extended time, he did not complete his reading of some of the work; with the extended time, he was able to complete the readings as well as improve his accuracy with the comprehension questions. The read-aloud condition did not result in significant improvement and, in this case, increased the time he required to complete his reading. This confounded the positive results that could have resulted from this accommodation because it was administered (according to instructions) under the reduced time conditions. It was noticed on other occasions that when given the choice to read silently or aloud, Scott would choose to read aloud, and this was accompanied by an improved level of performance in his reading comprehension. Therefore, despite the lack of support from the Dynamic Assessment Test Accommodations (DATA) procedure, it is recommended that the option of reading aloud be offered as an accommodation when testing involves reading comprehension (in addition to extended time).

Scott's skills in math are an area of relative strength, particularly his basic calculation ability. Although his numerical concepts and reasoning are somewhat below grade level (fifth-grade equivalent), these are considered to be in the average range when compared with others his age, but he is lower in his ability to work out word problems.

Written expression has been an area of ongoing need for Scott. His essay writing has been evaluated at the "basic" level according to district and state assessments. There are issues of organization and complexity of expression. He will need to learn such strategies as using outlines and mapping. His handwriting, although generally legible with effort, is poor, which relates to his struggle with motor control. His spacing, ability to stay on the line, and formation of letters all suffer.

When observed in his morning classes, Scott was consistently an eager and active participant. He frequently raised his hand and was often correct in his responses. The only instance when he did not actively participate was during the reading comprehension lesson of his language arts class, which was the only class observed where Scott was not mainstreamed (i.e., this was the Learning Support class). During his Learning Support time, all the students in the class were offered the same lesson. During this time, he maintained a low profile, with no initiation of participation. When debriefed at a later time, Scott acknowledged that this was the type of work that was difficult for him.

This is a transitional year for Scott and his classmates. That is, this is his first year in middle school, which presents new demands on performance and adjustment. Scott seems to be handling the building navigation and movement from class to class adequately but is stressed by the increased academic demands. He says he just feels lost and overwhelmed by the work.

Sensorimotor and Perceptual Functions

Scott's sensory and motor functions are for the most part intact and show no serious concerns. He passed both the visual and auditory screenings easily. He does have a history of hearing deficit and has received services for this in the past. Both he and his mother have remarked on the fact that he has some difficulty hearing her approach in their home, and he has been startled by her appearance. Therefore, further investigation of his hearing status is warranted. He already has preferential, front-row seating in his classes, and his teachers tend to teach from the front of the room. He says he has no difficulty hearing them, and he showed no difficulties with hearing during the testing sessions.

In the motor area, Scott scored mildly low on the grip strength task when compared with others his age. He is considerably smaller than his peers, and his relatively weaker grip can be attributed to this; it is not considered a problem. He showed some very mild difficulty processing touch, missing some items on the object identification task (one in his right hand and two in his left). His responses for two of these three items were in the correct "ballpark." The third (scissors), he could not figure out.

Of most consequence was his drawing of a clock, which showed poor organization and planning. He was accurate regarding the details included, but his spatial placement was poor and not preplanned. Also, he did not express dissatisfaction or recognition of the problem once he completed his picture. This is primarily an issue of executive functioning, which is discussed in a separate section of this report.

When observed in his classroom, Scott appeared uncomfortable in his chair, which was much too large for him. His feet did not touch the floor, and his back did not touch the chair; he tended to work either with his legs folded under him or sitting on his knees. When asked about this, Scott recalled that the OT from his previous school had used a step and pillows to improve his seating. When we placed an overturned wastebasket under his feet and pillows behind his back during the assessment, he was much more comfortable.

Related to this, Scott carries a very large loose-leaf notebook around all day. The size is appropriate for his peers but is very large and heavy for him. His mother is currently consulting with a chiropractor to try to figure out a way to reduce the burden for Scott. This is also an issue for an OT.

Attention

Scott shows good attention when this function is directly assessed. Yet his teachers consistently describe him as having difficulty with maintaining his attention in the context of the classroom. The issue, then, for Scott is that he is having difficulty with controlling or managing his attention. He is paying attention, but he is paying attention to too many things and not regulating his attentional resources to select what is important and ignore what is not. This is more of an executive than an attention function. Of course, under the conditions of the testing situation in which he was in a quiet room in a one-to-one situation, his ability to attend was optimized.

Scott's ability to attend would also be negatively affected by his emotional stress, as well as what might be a hearing problem that reduces his hearing in the context of background noise. This needs to be explored further. In any case, the issue of self-regulation and impulse control remains, and this has been a concern since he began school.

Memory

Memory is an issue for Scott. Although his short-term rote memory is adequate, he struggles both with placing information into long-term storage and with working memory. His ability to retrieve information that is well learned appears adequate. He will need the aid of both external supports such as worksheets for writing out information for problem solving and for organizing and internalizing information he needs to learn. Most of all, he needs adequate practice and review. He should not be moving on to new information without consolidating the information he needs to deal with the new input.

Scott shows some ability to remember what he sees better than what he hears (see NEPSY results), which is interesting in the context of his better comprehension of what he hears than what he sees. The most sensible implication of this is that he really needs multilevel support for optimal learning. He would have to hear the information, see some visual expression for this information, and verbalize the information. What is not likely to help is hands-on, visual–motor input because of his motor impulsivity and tendency to get caught up in motor manipulations not necessarily related to the task to be learned. Opportunities for manipulative experiences such as building or drawing may be useful for time-out, relaxation between moments when he needs to concentrate.

I tried a visualization strategy to help Scott retain information from a story read to him. Although he denied using visualization, his retention after being cued to visualize ("make a movie in your head") dramatically improved. Thus, either he was using visualization despite his denial or the review itself with periodic pausing helped his retention, at least for the short term.

Language
Language is an area of strength for Scott. His listening comprehension and oral expression both appear strong. The use of language – for example, in terms of reading aloud and talking himself through visual presentation of information – is a good strategy for him. He is very verbally expressive and enjoys using the vocabulary he has learned, although his vocabulary repertory remains an area in need of improvement.

Cognition
Because Scott had a recent psychological assessment by his school district's psychologist, I did not re-administer a basic standardized test of intelligence. The information provided from this assessment, in addition to previous assessments, clearly establishes that Scott's levels of intellective functioning vary in and around average range; however, some subtest results have changed between assessments. I did decide to re-administer subtests that were low or had shown change to explore the nature of his errors and to document again his levels in these areas. I also administered subtests that had not previously been given to him.

Scott's functioning on the Information and Picture Arrangement subtests of the WISC was the same as previously obtained. This documents his limited long-term memory of basic academic facts, even those related to work he is currently covering in his classes. In a number of cases, Scott remembered having been exposed to the information but said he had forgotten it. In the case of Picture Arrangement, where he had to reorder a series of pictures to create a story, his impulsivity accounted for many errors, leading him to overlook important details that served as cues to the story. When given the opportunity to redo some of the stories he failed, he did improve his success somewhat but still remained below average.

Asking him to tell the story for the picture did help him improve his focus on the details. This again documents the importance of verbalization (see information related to reading aloud earlier in the report) in optimizing his functioning.

Despite Scott's relative strength in math, his success with the Arithmetic subtest was lower in this re-administration than it had been previously. This subtest is not so much a test of math as it is of working memory. Also, when given the opportunity to retry some of the items with the support of a worksheet, it could be seen that he was having difficulty translating the word problems into mathematical operations. Thus, if he is given a problem where he is told he has to subtract, for example, he does fine; however, if he is given a problem where he has to infer subtraction as the appropriate operation and also determine how to set it up in terms of what gets subtracted from what, he has more difficulty. It definitely does strain his working memory, as well as challenge his knowledge base.

In the case of the Block Design subtest, which he had performed adequately when it was first administered in first grade with subsequent difficulty in his most recent assessment, Scott performed at a very adequate level, well within the average range. The reason for his relatively poorer performance in his previous assessment is not clear. In this re-administration, he proceeded systematically. Although he was not quick to process the perceptual relationships, he did find his way to the solutions for all but one of the items. Thus, it would be concluded that he does not have difficulty with these types of perceptual analysis tasks, as long as speed of processing is not an issue.

Social–Emotional Functions

On a behavioral rating scale, completed by Scott's mother and two teachers (one from regular education and his learning support teacher), the levels of risk and concern are generally rated at a higher level in school than at home. In school, there is more concern about his externalizing, or acting out, behaviors of hyperactivity and aggression. All agree that he has difficulty in the area of attention. Scott rates himself as having significant feelings of inadequacy. He is quite aware of his difficulties with self-control, of his thoughts as well as of his behavior. His tendency toward mood swings and self-destructive thoughts is noted by both Scott and his mother. All, except Scott, generally agree on his low degree of adaptability.

Scott was very responsive to the use of drawings to elicit emotional content. He drew without hesitation and was able to develop elaborate descriptions and stories about his productions. In one instance, when asked as part of another test to draw a child, he spontaneously turned this into a very developed story about his main character who sprouted swords and daggers. His content suggests a huge amount of anger that is controlled with some difficulty; he may be small, but his anger quite outsizes him. In his words, buried in his anger is a desire and search for peace, but he feels that the chance for realization of this peace is not very optimistic. He tends to divide the world sharply into good and bad, destructive and peaceful, and has difficulty resolving the idea of possible coexistence.

Scott's human figure drawing of a boy shows a freakish teenage rapper, with hair piled high on his head and a hat on top of the hair, combining to increase his height considerably, and weapons held in both hands (about to be used). His female figure, spontaneously drawn first, is full of controlled emotion and nurturance; he assigned this figure a very young age (7 years), although she looks more like a woman than a girl. Both figures are drawn on a large scale, and there are some minor spatial planning issues with regard to sufficiency of space for the legs and feet. They are, however, of generally stable appearance; however, the boy is rather fearsome and threatening.

Scott feels quite burdened by the things on his mind, to the point where he has wanted to hurt himself, although he says this is not true at this time. Other than his problems with his brother, he describes positive feelings about his family and himself. He is able to see a positive future for himself, when he will drive, have a girlfriend, and have his own children.

Scott's mother describes him as bossy and stubborn when interacting with peers, although she feels that peers do seem to like him, even though they don't call him at home. He seems less mature and has no close friends. Scott refers to friends he has in school, and he describes his peers as seeing him as funny and cute. According to his teachers, his peer interactions in school have improved and are not of concern at this time.

Executive Functions

Executive functions have to do with such things as the abilities to self-regulate, plan, organize, show flexibility, and retrieve information from memory. This is the primary area of challenge for Scott, and this is what makes a diagnosis of ADHD appropriate. Controlling his attention and regulating his movements are significant challenges for him. On the positive side, this is what contributes to his being an outgoing, responsive, gregarious, curious, and involved person. On the negative side, this is what leads to errors and his difficulty with slowing down and taking the time needed for dealing with work when it becomes more challenging and complex. He tends to deal with complex work at about the same pace as easier work. Adding visual input to auditory tends to slow down his reactivity and reduce his errors; thus, having something to look at while he listens could be a way to improve his focus and maintenance of attention, and having something to do while he looks and listens would be the most optimal for sustaining his focus.

Scott is a fast processor and responder, and he is often accurate in his responses. He does not adequately regulate the speed of his response when the work becomes more challenging, requiring more focused processing and problem solving. His responses tend to be impulsive, and this impulsivity can result in his overlooking important details, leading to errors. One example of this occurred during administration of the picture-sequencing task from the Wechsler test, in which his sequencing errors typically resulted from his failure to notice an important detail of the picture that served as a clue to correct solution.

Ratings of Scott by his mother on a scale tapping executive functions highlight all but one area at the level of risk and concern. Her ratings suggest difficulties with inhibiting his responses, shifting his thinking, controlling his emotions, initiating activities, working memory, planning and organization, and monitoring his behavior. The area that she rates within the normal range is his ability to organize his materials. All of these would work against Scott's ability to function independently. He continues to rely a great deal on external structure and guidance.

Scott's difficulty with self-regulation also characterizes his motor responses. He is not hyperactive in the sense of having a great amount of body movement, but when he is asked to engage in controlled fine motor movements such as tracing a trail down a narrow path, he has difficulty staying within the boundaries and does not slow his pace when faced with increasing difficulty.

Conclusions and Recommendations

What are Scott's educational needs?
Scott is currently very stressed by the transition into middle school, particularly with regard to the level of academic expectations. The transition into seventh grade would be even more of a blow to him at his current level of functioning, as the level of work reportedly escalates at an even more rapid rate. The level of support currently provided for Scott does not appear adequate to meet his needs, and a more intensive, individualized level of academic support is warranted. The combination of stresses from both home and school has resulted in behavior problems that were not characteristic of Scott's past history, and his need for both academic and emotional support are clear. He is involved in therapy to address his emotional needs, but more specific interventions are needed to address his academic issues.

Scott needs to improve his vocabulary as one route to increasing his reading comprehension. It is suggested that important vocabulary words for each subject be selected and written onto index cards that are periodically reviewed with him.

Scott needs to have work that involves reading appropriate to his current reading levels. For independent reading, this means fourth grade, and, for supported instruction, fifth grade. This also applies to mathematics that involves reading of word problems.

Scott's strongest need is to improve his awareness and application of memory strategies. His most basic need in this area is for sufficient exposure and practice, that is, adequate time for repetition and revisiting of what he needs to learn. He also needs visual support for orally presented information, both because of his difficulty with maintaining attention and his history of hearing deficit.

In view of his history of hearing loss and continued concerns regarding his hearing status (and its possible interaction with attention/focus issues), Scott should have a thorough audiological evaluation. He has received hearing services and accommodations in the past, and these accommodations may need to be reinstated at this time. It was noticed that he sat in the front of his current classes, but no special actions seemed to be made to stay face-to-face when speaking with him or to gain his attention prior to asking him a question or restating to him what other students have said. He would continue to require preferential seating, and his teachers need to be told that he needs to see their face during moments of oral instruction.

Sustained reading is a particular challenge for him. He will need to break down any extended reading assignments into smaller units, setting goals before he proceeds regarding how much he thinks he can accomplish in one sitting. After he completes a reading segment, he should try to summarize what he has read, and then take a short break, reading his summary before he resumes. He should also be encouraged to read his work aloud to himself. When he has difficulty comprehending, he can review what is difficult by having someone read the passage aloud to him. Another supplementation would be for him to read what he needs to learn onto a tape and then to play it back for himself.

Scott easily relates to art as a medium for his emotional expression. He draws vividly and well and is able to combine his drawing with verbal communication of content that clearly represents his thoughts and concerns. Despite the somewhat metaphorical nature of this, he communicates awareness that he is really speaking about himself, but he does so very comfortably using this medium. Incorporation of art into his therapy is therefore recommended, and Scott was also encouraged to use art at home as a means of self-expression and emotional release. Access to art opportunities for recreational purposes may also be beneficial for him.

What accommodations are recommended for him?
Scott learns best when he is involved in a small group. He works well with peer partners and when he can have ready access to teacher attention for both responsiveness to his needs for clarification and monitoring of his comprehension. Reciprocal teaching that involves small groups may be a promising approach to try for him. He profits from the accommodations of extended time, reading aloud, and previewing.

Seating during class time may contribute to Scott's difficulties with paying attention. Although by this time he has accustomed himself to dealing with oversized chairs, it is nevertheless recommended that some adjustments to enhance his comfort be considered. For example, he might try placing his feet on the side of a wastebasket placed in front of his chair, and some pillows could be placed behind his back. Of course, a smaller chair would also be appropriate. Such accommodations will need to be worked out with him, however, because he may not be comfortable with having all these adjustments in place.

Also, the size of the notebook he carries, although similar to those of his peers, is very large for him. It has already been recommended that he have a smaller notebook; this needs to be reviewed and put in place. He could also use a small piece of luggage with wheels to carry it from class to class. This issue warrants consultation with an OT.

His need for extended time, outlines of classroom presentations, multisensory instruction, and books on tape have all been recommended and approved, but it is not clear the extent to which they are being implemented. The opportunity to read aloud when he is taking a test that involves reading comprehension needs to be added to his accommodations. These need to be put in place and monitored by a case manager who is familiar with Scott's needs and can serve as a central point of communication for Scott and those working with him. If not already in place, a case manager should be designated to ensure that all needed accommodations are put in place and maintained. It would also be important for this case manager to help Scott with his organizational needs. He also needs time to meet with this manager-advocate to complete his classroom work so that he does not have to bring it home as additional homework.

According to his teachers, written assignments need to be broken down into small parts. He needs to learn specific strategies relevant to written expression such as outlining, mapping, and dictation. He should also have access to a computer to supplement instruction in reading comprehension and written expression. In math, he should try graph paper to help him improve his alignment of numbers.

What characteristics of an educational program are recommended for him?

Scott needs a program in which the work is truly individualized. His current program provides some accommodations, but the level of work expected does not seem to vary in relation to the level of knowledge and skills of the student, at least not in his case. He needs to have ongoing access to an individual who serves in a case management role to provide direct support as well as advocacy and communication among Scott, his teachers, and his family.

Discussion between Scott's mother and his current therapist is recommended regarding the advisability of psychiatric evaluation regarding Scott's mood swings and, at times, self-destructive thinking. It is certainly likely that if Scott felt more able to cope, he would feel more adequate and less self-destructive. For this to happen, he would need more support and less stress and pressure at both home and school. This is why he is in therapy.

Test Scores

Wechsler Intelligence Scale for Children – Third Edition [subtest mean = 10; SD = 3] [Selected subtests only]

Subtests	Standard scores
Information	8
Arithmetic	1
Digit Span	10
Picture Arrangement	3 (5)
Block Design	11
Mazes	10

NEPSY – A developmental neuropsychological assessment [mean = 100; SD = 15; subtest mean = 10; SD = 3]

Subtests	Standard scores	Percentile ranks
Tower	05	
Auditory Attention/ Response Set	13 14	

Subtests	Standard scores	Percentile ranks
Visual Attention	14	
ATTENTION/EXECUTIVE DOMAIN	104 (93–113)	61
Phonological Processing	11	
Speeded Naming	11	
Comprehension of Instructions	11	
[Verbal Fluency	12]	
LANGUAGE DOMAIN	105 (95–114)	63
Fingertip Tapping	14	
Imitating Hand Positions	N/A	
Visuomotor Precision	08	
[Finger Discrimination	acceptable]	
SENSORIMOTOR DOMAIN	not determined (see Dean Woodcock)	
Design Copying	13	
Arrows	10	
VISUOSPATIAL DOMAIN	110 (98–118)	75
Memory for Faces	19	
Memory for Names	05	
Narrative Memory	10	
[Sentence Repetition	08]	
MEMORY DOMAIN	109 (99–118)	73

[] indicates this is an extended subtest and not calculated into domain score

Das/Naglieri Cognitive Assessment System [mean = 100; SD = 15; subtest mean = 10; SD = 3]

Subtests	Standard scores	Percentile ranks
Matching Numbers	09	
Planned Codes	11	
Planned Connections	10	
PLANNING SCALE	100 (91–109)	50
Nonverbal Matrices	11	
Verbal–Spatial Relations	09	
Figure Memory	12	
SIMULTANEOUS SCALE	104 (96–112)	61
Expressive Attention	09	
Number Detection	08	
Receptive Attention	11	
ATTENTION SCALE	96 (87–106)	39
SUCCESSIVE SCALE	Not administered	

Woodcock-Johnson III Tests of Achievement Form A (mean = 100; SD = 15]

CLUSTER/Test	%Percentile rank	Standard score	Grade equivalent
ORAL EXPRESSION	29	92 (83–101)	4.4
BROAD READING	65	106 (102–110)	7.4
BROAD MATH	46	98 (94–103)	5.8
READING COMPREHENSION	26	90 (85–96)	4.2
MATH CALC SKILLS	56	102 (94–110)	6.5
MATH REASONING	37	95 (90–100)	5.1
ACADEMIC KNOWLEDGE	17	86 (77–94)	3.9

Woodcock-Johnson, III Achievement Test (M = 50; SD = 10)
Form A of the following achievement tests was administered:

Subtest	Percentile rank	Standard score	Grade equivalent
Letter-Word Identification	96	125 (117–134)	12.7
Reading Fluency	55	102 (98–106)	6.7
Story Recall	19	87 (74–100)	2.9
Calculation	61	104 (93–115)	6.7
Math Fluency	46	98 (93–104)	6.1
Passage Comprehension	28	91 (84–99)	4.0
Applied Problems	37	95 (89–101)	5.1
Story Recall–Delayed	–	–	–
Picture Vocabulary	37	95 (85–105)	4.9
Oral Comprehension	55	102 (92–111)	7.1
Editing	59	103 (95–111)	8.3
Reading Vocabulary	30	92 (86–98)	4.5
Quantitative Concepts	38	95 (87–104)	5.1
Academic Knowledge	17	86 (77–94)	3.9
Punctuation and Capitals	81	113 (100–126)	8.8

Wechsler Individual Achievement Test – Second Edition [mean = 100; SD = 15]

Subtests	Standard scores	Percentile ranks	Grade equivalent
Reading Comprehension	97 (90–104)	42	5.6
Listening Comprehension	108 (94–122)	70	8.2

Behavior Rating Inventory for Executive Functions, Parent Form
[T score: mean = 50; SD = 10]

Subscales	T scores	Percentile ranks
Inhibit	73 (68–78)*	98
Shift	77 (69–85)*	99
Emotional Control	69 (63–75)*	96
BEHAVIOR REGULATION INDEX	77 (72–82)*	98
Initiate	79 (72–86)*	99
Working Memory	71 (66–76)*	95
Plan/Organize	70 (65–75)*	94
Monitor	57 (51–63)	78
METACOGNITION INDEX	72 (69–75)*	95

* Indicates elevation of score into area of concern.

Behavior Assessment System for Children-Parent/Teacher Forms [T scores: mean = 50; SD = 10]

Subscales	T Scores		
	Parent	SE teacher	RE teacher
Hyperactivity	63*	65*	79*
Aggression	60*	67*	69*
Conduct Problems	53	59	87*
EXTERNALIZING PROBLEMS COMPOSITE	66*	65*	81*
Anxiety	53	48	52
Depression	55	42	54
Somatization	62*	44	51
INTERNALIZING PROBLEMS COMPOSITE	59	44	53
Attention Problems	71*	69*	80*
Atypicality	63*	43	47
Withdrawal	50	47	48
Learning Problems	–	57	61*
SCHOOL PROBLEMS COMPOSITE	–	64*	71*
BEHAVIORAL SYMPTOMS INDEX	66*	57	67*
Adaptability	36*	–	54
Social Skills	44	40	36*
Leadership	39*	36	37*
Study Skills	–	34	31*
ADAPTIVE SKILLS COMPOSITE	38*	36*	38*

Note: RE = regular education; SE = special education.

Behavior Rating Scale for Children, Self Report [T scores: mean = 50; SD = 10]

Subscales	T score	Percentile rank
Attitude to School	53	65
Attitude to Teachers	53	70
SCHOOL MALADJUSTMENT COMPOSITE	53	68
Atypicality	63*	87
Locus of Control	48	47
Social Stress	48	47
Anxiety	44	34
CLINICAL MALADJUSTMENT COMPOSITE	51	56
Depression	48	56
Sense of Inadequacy	63*	87
Relations with Parents	45	21
Interpersonal Relations	53	46
Self Esteem	57	73
Self Reliance	54	58
PERSONAL ADJUSTMENT COMPOSITE	53	50
EMOTIONAL SYMPTOMS INDEX	49	53

Integrated Visual–Auditory Continuous Performance Test [mean = 100; SD = 15]

Response control	Auditory	Visual
Prudence	97	84
Consistency	91	97
Stamina	78	77

Fine Motor Regulation Quotient: 104

Attention	Auditory	Visual
Vigilance	91	109
Focus	98	112
Speed	90	97

Reaction time slower to visual than to auditory stimuli.
Random responses higher for auditory than for visual stimuli.

Dean-Woodcock Sensory Motor Battery
Lateral Preference: right
Sensory Assessment:

Near Point Visual Acuity	WNL*
Visual Confrontation	WNL
Naming Pictures of Objects	WNL

Auditory Acuity	WNL
Palm Writing	WNL
Object Identification	Mild to WNL right; mild impairment left
Finger Identification	WNL
Simultaneous Localization	WNL

* Within Normal Limits

Motor Tests:

Gait and Station	WNL
Romberg	WNL
Construction copying	WNL
Clock drawing	mild impairment
Coordination	WNL
Mime Movements	WNL
Left-Right Movements	WNL
Finger Tapping	WNL
Expressing Speech	WNL
Grip Strength	WNL on left; mild impairment on right (see narrative)

Case Discussion

Scott's case includes three examples of the use of dynamic assessment. The first showed that his reading comprehension improved by a year and a half when allowed to read aloud. When more formally assessed with the DATA, this advantage for reading aloud did not emerge because of the limitations of this particular procedure. The success of the read-aloud intervention became apparent only through direct observation and informal assessment.

The second use of dynamic assessment occurred in relation to Scott's difficulty with working memory. In this case, there was a discrepancy between his subjective experience and the objective findings. Scott denied using the visualization strategy suggested as an intervention; nevertheless, following this opportunity, his memory of the story read to him improved dramatically. To understand what happened here would involve further exploration, but the potential for the success of this intervention to facilitate his auditory memory was supported by the evidence.

The third instance demonstrates the use of dynamic assessment as a means of exploring and extending the findings of standardized testing, in this case, of Wechsler subtests. In some cases, the previous results were supported. In other cases, there were some very interesting and important differences, as well as opportunities to interject some interventions. These were of course done following standardized administration of the tasks. Asking him to tell the stories for Picture Arrangement led to some improvement along with some insight into the nature of his difficulty with this task. Providing a paper and pencil for Arithmetic led to important insight into the nature of his difficulty with this type of work. In the case of Block Design, simply re-administering the subtest allowed the assessor to rule this out as a problem area because of his very competent performance that required no intervention.

Use of Dynamic Assessment in Clinical Settings

Most of the principles associated with use of DA in educational settings are valid and generalizable to clinical settings, with some important differences. First, examiners in clinical settings encounter a preponderance of older children, adolescents, and adults (see Chapter 4) (with the obvious exception of clinics that specialize in or include family services and young children). Second, the persons who will receive the reports of clinical assessments are not likely to be limited to school personnel but may instead be primarily concerned with questions of psychological treatment, social integration, or vocational performance. Thus, the data from DA are expected to be generalized to a rather different universe of inference. Third, although issues of intrapsychic and interpersonal functioning do indeed arise in educational assessments, they are ubiquitous in assessments conducted in clinical settings; that is, one responds to a much broader range of questions, rarely restricted to learning effectiveness (which obviously may be affected by such psychological variables). Adolescents and adults have a more extensive history, by definition, and that history constitutes a rich source of diagnostic information.

In clinical reports, one usually wants to see at least the following information:

Anamnestic data: Identification of the examinee, with such information as name, gender, age, and occupation if relevant.

Referral information: Source of referral, principal reason(s) for referral, referral question(s).

History: Relevant aspects of the social, developmental, occupational, and assessment/treatment history. The focus is on the qualifier "relevant aspects." It is not necessarily true that the more information one has (and reports), the better. Leaving out irrelevant information (e.g., what the examinee was wearing, family history that might have nothing to do with the examinee's problems) will make it possible to focus on the most relevant aspects, without distraction. An important part of the history has to do with previous assessments: procedures, by whom, when, where, why, with what results, and interpretations. That information can often constitute baseline ("performance" or "zone of actual development") data and save both examiner and examinee from unnecessary repetition.

Behavioral observations: The behavior of examinees during the assessment can have important implications for the validity of the findings. Brief comments on cooperativeness, energy for the tasks, work attitude, and distractibility, for example, are quite useful when the time comes to interpret the outcomes of the assessment.

Diagnostic procedures: It is important to list all of the procedures used in the assessment, even when the examiner believes that some of them failed to yield any significant information, partly to prevent repetition of the same procedures in future assessments. All procedures should be identified by their formal names; for example, reports often refer to the "Bender Gestalt," rather than the "Bender Visual–Motor Gestalt Test." The latter designation, of course, is the correct one. Using correct and precise labels makes it easier for readers to locate them and to learn more about them if necessary.

Interpretation. Some clinicians give test-by-test results, including scores, and interpretations. The decision whether to report actual test scores should be made by considering who will read the report and whether those persons can be expected to manage scores correctly. Giving test-by-test results can be useful, especially when readers might not be familiar with the tests. Some consumers may be unqualified to interpret the scores and may find this information difficult, uninteresting, or apparently irrelevant to what they want to know from the assessment. It is still true that the whole is frequently greater than the sum of its parts, so when test-by-test interpretation is done, it must be followed by a section sometimes called *Integrated Interpretation,* that is, interpretation of the collective results of the assessment. In such a section it is useful to compare performance on different tests or procedures, to identify discrepancies between history and test data or between different tests, and to call attention to reinforcement of conclusions by virtue of having similar outcomes on different tests.

Conclusions and recommendations. This is the part that people are eager to read. Just as in school settings, examiners in clinical settings must be sure that (a) the recommendations are warranted by the assessment data, (b) the examiners are sufficiently familiar with postassessment situations (treatment facilities and personnel, for example) to enable them to make sensible recommendations, and (c) the recommendations are specific enough to be followed.

Many consumers of psychological assessment reports are not familiar with DA or with the tasks that are used with it. For that reason, it is important to describe the procedures. One can do that in either of two ways: (a) by describing them in detail in the body of the report, just before reporting their results, or (b) by appending to the reports brief descriptions of the tests and procedures that have been used. I (HCH) have written a series of descriptive paragraphs on the DA tasks that I use most often and have saved it in a word processing file. When submitting a report to readers who are probably not familiar with DA, I simply select the descriptions of the tasks used in that assessment and incorporate them into an appendix at the end of the report.

Following are two case reports of clinical assessments that incorporated DA.

CASE 9.4 Tommy

Tommy, a 7-year-old boy, was examined with his mother present during the examination. They had made a long driving trip the day before the examination but had some time to rest overnight. I saw Tommy beginning at 10:00 a.m., broke for lunch at 11:30, and continued the assessment from 1:00 p.m. to 3:00 p.m. Tommy is an international adoptee, having been brought by his adoptive parents to the United States from an Eastern European country when he was about 2 years old. He seemed to adapt well to the move, acquiring English in the usual way (imitation plus using language to fulfill his needs) and socialized well with other children. As he reached school age, concerns began to arise regarding his behavior in learning and social situations. The immediate reason for this assessment was that the school was considering whether to have Tommy repeat first grade, and that decision was to be made shortly. The long-range circumstance that raises that question as well as the need for psychological and psychoeducational assessment is the fact that Tommy has not adjusted well to school in several areas, appears in many ways immature for his age, and has developed many and ingenious ways to avoid doing what others want him to do – unless it is something he wants to do.

He is a bright, friendly boy who had been well prepared for the examination: He knew my name, he was not reluctant to interact, and he responded readily, if sometimes minimally, to questions and attempts to initiate conversation. Holding Tommy's attention for more than a few seconds at a time was difficult; nevertheless, he tolerated the two long sieges of testing and cooperated sufficiently to make possible a valid estimate of his ability, his learning potential, and the non-intellective factors that need work if he is to succeed in school.

Psychological assessment procedures included the following:

Classification and Class Inclusion task (DA)
Copying of geometric figures
Plateaux (DA)
Raven's Colored Progressive Matrices
Transformation (DA)
Peabody Picture Vocabulary Test, Form III-A
Organization of Dots (DA)
Examination for sensory suppression
Complex Figure, adapted for young children (DA)
Learning samples from four *Bright Start* activities:

  Fast and Slow
  Copy Cat
  Comparison
  Classification

Overall, Tommy's performance was quite good at baseline (without any help), and improved significantly when certain pre-cognitive, self-regulatory, and cognitive strategies were mediated to him, suggesting that his unassisted performance level is about average to high average for his age and that he is capable of an even higher level of performance when his attention is focused and when he can be induced to use systematic problem-solving strategies. The various assessment procedures, and Tommy's performance on them, are discussed next.

Classification and class inclusion
This task consisted of grouping pictures of objects according to their essential similarities. I extended the task by asking Tommy to name the resulting classes, using abstract labels. For example, there were pictures of a car, a truck, a bicycle, and a bus. He quickly picked these out from many other pictures and put them in a group together. When asked what the group might be called, he indicated the concept of transportation even though he did not know that word. When "transportation" was defined for him, he adopted the word and used it later to define the group. He was similarly able to form the verbal abstractions (abstract labels) for plants, clothing, animals, musical instruments, and toys, applying those labels spontaneously. When asked to do so, he added appropriate items to each class. This task was performed rapidly, with little reflection, and with a very high degree of accuracy.

Copying of geometric figures
This task yielded Tommy's most surprising performance. From models that I drew (inexpertly!) for him, he made excellent drawings of a square, a

Figure 9.1. Tommy's copying of geometric figures.

triangle, a circle, and a Greek cross. Children of his age are only rarely able to draw the Greek cross with a pencil, especially in a continuous line (i.e., without taking up the pencil). The arms of the cross are parallel and proportional, showing a good eye for proportion and quite good fine-motor coordination for drawing. There was no sign at all of constructional dyspraxia. The square was more of a rectangle than a square, but the triangle was quite good, the circle was symmetrical and closed, and all four figures were proportional in size to each other. Figure 9.1 shows Tommy's drawings, reduced in size.

Plateaux
This is a test that was introduced by André Rey. It consists of four square plates, painted black, each with nine wooden disks ("buttons") on it. On each plate, eight of the buttons are easily detached, but one is fixed (i.e., it will not come up from the plate). The position of the fixed button is different on each of the four plates. The task is to find the fixed button on each plate and remember its position, going successively through the four plates until a criterion of three successive errorless trials is reached. The plates are then removed, and the examinee is asked to make a drawing of one of the plates, placing all nine buttons on it, and to indicate the positions of the fixed buttons on all the plates by placing numbers, 1 through 4, on the appropriate buttons to indicate the positions of the fixed buttons. Thus, a 1

is written inside the button that was fixed on the first plate, a 2 for the second plate, and so on. When this drawing has been done, the examinee is asked to look at the arrangement of the fixed buttons and to make a mental picture of it. Finally, in the examinee's view, the stack of plates is rotated 90 degrees clockwise, and the procedure is repeated to a criterion of three successive errorless trials. This is essentially a test of visual–spatial perception and spatial memory, but it yields information also on self-regulation, especially ability to inhibit impulsive responding and to use metamemory strategies. It is also a test of the ability to form a mental schema and to hold it in mind in the face of change in spatial orientation.

Tommy did this task in a minimal number of trials, although he would have done even better except for his apparent inability to keep his hands off the materials. He was disposed to explore the boards manually, touching all possible buttons in a very rapid and unsystematic manner. Mediation consisted of asking him to refrain from touching any buttons until he was "pretty sure" he knew the location of the fixed one. I also called to his attention the fact that I was keeping score – making a tally mark every time he touched a button that was not the correct one – and that part of his job was to have me make as few tally marks as possible. Both mediational strategies yielded good success. Tommy strongly dislikes being wrong or making errors, so he tried hard to limit the number of marks I made on my paper. Restraining his impulsivity required a more intensive mediation but was partially successful. Actually, he began ultimately to "self-mediate" in that he put his chin on his hands while he looked at the plates and reflected on the positions of the fixed buttons.

Tommy's scores (number of incorrect touches of buttons) on successive trials were as follows: Trial 1, 16; Trial 2, 10; Trial 3, 2. He had no errors on Trials 4, 5, and 6. This performance is remarkably good, not only for a person of Tommy's age but certainly for a clinically overactive child, which Tommy is. He made good use of the strategy of mental imagery, which he appears to do well, and of very mild verbal mediation, such as verbalizing the positions (center, top, bottom; but not right, left). Even more remarkable was his ability to gain some voluntary control over his motor behavior – at least enough to do these problems successfully. All the while, Tommy was in almost constant motion, spinning around in his desk chair, tapping on the table, changing his bodily position; nevertheless, he performed extremely well.

When asked to make a drawing of the plates and to place numbers indicating the positions of the fixed buttons, he also performed unusually well. First, he grasped quickly the notion that all four plates could be represented by a drawing of just one of them and that the numbers he would place on certain buttons would indicate the numbers of the plates on which those positions represented the fixed buttons. Second, he grasped the Y schema, that is, seeing that if the positions of the fixed buttons were connected, one would see what looked like the letter Y. Tommy subsequently used that mental image to achieve a perfect performance when the stack of plates was rotated through 90 degrees; in other words, he identified correctly the positions of all four fixed buttons, showing that his mental representation of the arrangement had not been disturbed by the rotation.

Raven's Colored Progressive Matrices
This standardized test is a combination of match-to-sample and analogical reasoning (A:B::C:?). Tommy grasped the requirements of the task quickly. He required considerable mediation, not always successful, to restrain his impulsive responding; in fact, impulsivity was the obvious source of the few errors he made. He was not even content to let me turn the pages but wanted to do so himself so he could race ahead and finish the task quickly. I worked very hard to get him to take his time, to take in the information that was present in the problems, to make a mental image of what the correct answer should be, and only then to select the correct answer from a group of possible answers. Again, I was not always successful. In spite of his constant motion and distractibility, Tommy achieved scores (number correct answers) of 9 on Set A, 10 on Set Ab, and 7 on Set B, for a total raw score of 26 (out of 36 possible). This score places him above the 90th percentile for his age group.

Transformation
This is a new dynamic assessment instrument that I have adapted from Paour's "transformation box." An example page is shown in Figure 9.2, with Tommy's marking of the answers. The material consists of pages of problems, each problem occupying one row on the page. At the top of each page are examples of transformation; for example, there is a large blue square, then a vertical red line, followed by a large red square.

There is then a large blue circle, a vertical red line, and a large red circle, and finally a large blue triangle, a vertical red line, and a large red triangle. The examinee's task is to abstract the rule that explains the function of the vertical red line, in this case, transforming color. Once the rule has been found, there are then three problems, each giving an initial figure, the vertical red line, and four possible choices. In the example given here, the initial figure is a large blue square, and after the vertical red (transforming) line, a large red triangle, large red square, large yellow circle, and large blue square. The examinee marks an X through the correct choice, in this case the large red square. On successive pages the examinee learns that color transformation occurs in more than one direction (not always from blue to red, but also from red to blue and ultimately yellow to blue, red to

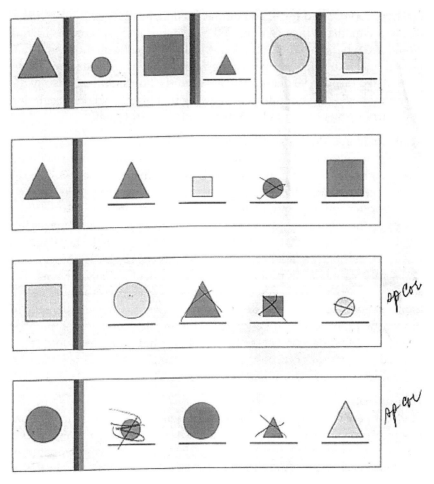

Figure 9.2. An early page of Transformation, with Tommy's marking of the answers.

yellow, yellow to red). Subsequent problems have a different color vertical (transforming) line: a blue line transforms size and nothing else; a black line transforms shape; another line transforms the nature of an animal (e.g., from pig to horse, or dog, or cat, or cow). One may also have more than one transforming line (e.g., a blue line and a black line, which together transform shape and size, so a large red triangle becomes a small red circle). This double transformation is the most complex of the problems given in this young children's series of the test. Note that examinees must abstract a transformation rule and then apply that rule appropriately to get the correct answers. Doing so requires understanding what the transforming line does and also what it does not do (e.g., a red line transforms color, from the initial color to any other color, but it does not change size or shape). This exclusivity of the transformation rule is an important aspect, because many children below age 6 or 7 find the "does not change" aspect quite difficult.

Tommy grasped the nature of this task quickly, with fairly minimal explanation, and just as quickly understood both the bi-directionality (not only large to small, but small to large, leading to the abstraction of size) and the exclusivity (the line changes size only, therefore does not change color or shape) of the rules. Working very fast, refusing to slow down and reflect as I kept trying to get him to do, he got 28 correct out of 30 problems, with the two misses being attributable to impulsive responding – he just would not slow down. In fact, he corrected those two items (marked "spontaneous correction" on the example page). There are no norms for this test, but I can say that his performance was very good indeed, and also that he required almost no mediation in order to achieve it.

Peabody picture vocabulary test (PPVT)
This is a standardized test of receptive vocabulary that is often used (usu-ally inappropriately) as an intelligence test. It can be said that the correla-tion of PPVT scores with scores on good individually administered intelli-gence tests is quite high. The examinee looks at a page of four pictures, the examiner pronounces a word (e.g., "show me 'running'"), and the exami-nee points to the one of the four pictures that illustrates the spoken word. Again, as on previous tests, Tommy was extremely active and distractible, seeming hardly to pay attention at all to the pictures or the spoken words. In spite of these problems, Tommy scored at the 90th percentile, meaning that 90% of children of his age get lower scores on this test. It would be a mistake to try to convert that performance to an IQ; indeed, the IQ does not carry much information for a child in Tommy's circumstances (i.e., a child with a high level of activity and distractibility and some well-honed habits of avoiding serious engagement with tasks). This is not a dynamic task, so no help was given.

Organization of dots
This task is part of Feuerstein's Learning Propensity Assessment Device (LPAD), adapted from Rey's Organisation de Groupes de Points. There is a model figure, followed by amorphous clouds of dots. The task is to find the model figure among the dots and then to connect the dots so as to form the model figure. It proceeds from a single simple figure, a square, to frames in which one must find two figures, often overlapping, and very often in a spatial orientation that differs from that of the model figures. The task requires use of searching strategies, the ability to visualize a connected

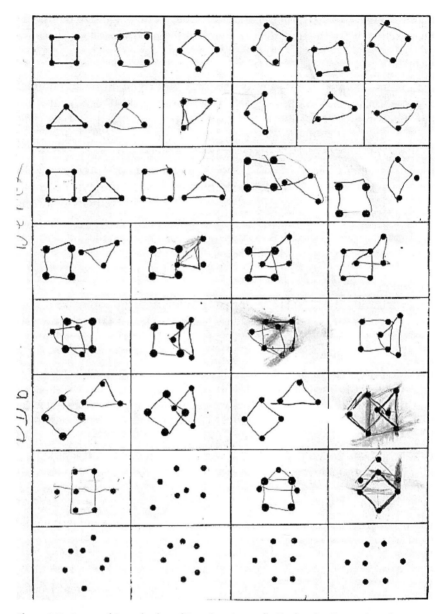

Figure 9.3. A page of Organization of Dots (see Appendix A), showing Tommy's performance.

figure before the dots are actually connected, recognition of simple geometric shapes, the ability to follow some basic rules, and sufficient motor
control to draw straight lines to connect the dots. Figure 9.3 is a scan of
Tommy's production on this task.

Tommy drew the figures in correctly (i.e., he connected the dots appropriately) in 26 of 33 problems presented to him. Of the remaining 7 problems, he did not attempt 5, so he actually made uncorrected errors on only 2 of the 28 problems that he attempted. He connected the dots rapidly but did not want to continue when he began to encounter difficulty. By the time we got to this task, Tommy was tired and becoming increasingly distractible, and he had other urgent business on his mind, such as getting back to the motel swimming pool. In spite of these problems, Tommy's productions were quite good for his age. He was not confused by differing spatial orientation of the designs, and he quickly overcame his initial reluctance (very often observed in children) to overlap figures or "crash through" lines he had already drawn. He learned and adopted the rule that each dot could be used only once (i.e., in only one of the two figures within a frame) and that all dots had to be used. My attempts to mediate inhibition of impulsivity met with utter failure: Tommy worked very fast, often started to draw lines before he had actually seen the figure or figured out where the lines would go. Although this is not a timed test, the speed with which he produced correct designs was impressive, suggesting rapid information processing and that this was an easy task for Tommy.

Children's complex figure
This task is an adaptation for young children of Rey's classic complex figure test. Only the "copy" task was used; Tommy was not required to draw the figure from memory. Figure 9.4 shows the figure itself and Tommy's two copies, one before and the other after mediation of organization, planning, precision, and structure. The figure and Tommy's drawings have been reduced in size.

Regarding sequence (second copy), Tommy drew in the major rectangle first, then the long horizontal line, followed by the two diagonal lines, then the long vertical line, the top triangle, the "nose" triangle, the antenna or cross, and finally the square at the bottom left. All the details were included, and there were no extra details. Every detail was in the correct place. Of course it would have been interesting to see how he would have made the drawing from memory, but I judged him to be too tired and distracted at that moment. This superior copying performance suggested that Tommy is good at following instructions (when he wants to do so!), can gather clear and complete information at least through the visual modality, has good fine-motor control for his age, and is capable of good organization and task sequencing.

Learning tasks from Bright Start
Self-regulation appeared to be Tommy's primary area of difficulty, so I gave him two tasks from the Self-Regulation unit of *Bright Start: Cognitive*

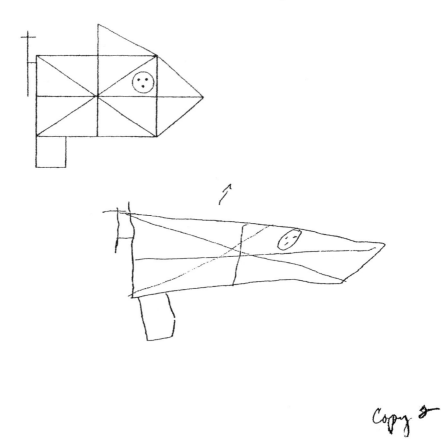

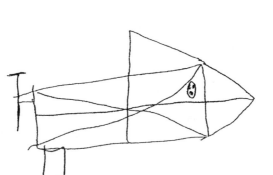

Figure 9.4. A young children version of Rey's Complex Figure, followed by Tommy's initial (premediation) copy and his subsequent (postmediation) copy. Drawings from memory were not obtained because of Tommy's fatigue.

Curriculum for Young Children: Fast and Slow, and Copy Cat. In Fast and Slow, the task is simply to grasp the rule (walk fast when the music is fast and slowly when the music is slow; stop when the teacher/examiner claps his or her hands) and follow that rule. Tommy grasped the rule instantly and followed it precisely, demonstrating that he is capable of voluntary control of his gross motor behavior and of adjusting it to the requirements of external stimuli. In the Copy Cat game, he just had to imitate the body positions shown on drawings of children, such as standing with hands on head, sitting, arms outstretched. All were done perfectly. Together, these two Self-Regulation activities suggested that he can focus his attention long enough to take in both rules and problem information and that he can conform his behavior to the requirements of external stimuli. It should be noted that these activities were designed for, and are typically used with, younger children; nevertheless, they represent criterion situations – he either can do it or he cannot. No mediation was required in these situations.

Two tasks were taken from the Comparison and Classification units of *Bright Start*. Both tasks were clearly at too elementary a level to offer any challenge at all to Tommy, who did both of them perfectly with no mediation beyond mere explanation of the tasks.

Examination for sensory suppression
A simple neurological procedure was used to examine for sensory suppression in tactile and auditory modes. With his eyes closed, Tommy had to identify, by raising his hand, which of the two hands had been touched, both when only one at a time was touched and when both were touched (without the possibility of touching both at once ever having been mentioned). Failing to identify simultaneous bilateral stimulation (touching both hands at once) would suggest the possibility of a lateral sensory suppression. Tommy had no difficulty with either unilateral or bilateral simultaneous stimulation. Similarly, with the examiner standing behind him, Tommy had to detect very soft sounds (rubbing together of thumb and one finger) unilaterally and with bilateral simultaneous stimulation. He had no difficulty at all with this task.

Behavioral Observations
Throughout the examination Tommy was quite active, being unable to sit still for more than a few seconds at a time and then usually only with urging. His attention seemed to flit from one situation to another in rapid sequence. At the same time, his performance on various tasks indicated that he had been able to focus his attention sufficiently to do a good job of problem solving. This suggests that he takes in information quite rapidly, probably in a "simultaneous" rather than a "successive" mode (although

that issue was not examined directly); that is, he grasps wholes rather than parts and gathers information somewhat in the manner of taking a photograph rather than listening to stimuli in sequence. Such a reliance on simultaneous information processing is often observed in children who have attention difficulties.

Tommy loves to succeed and also has a strong negative reaction to the possibility of failure – to the extent that he will withdraw his efforts as soon as the possibility of failure arises. This motivational characteristic limits his willingness to attempt challenging tasks and ultimately will be a major impediment to learning. If he could learn to enjoy success without dreading failure, his learning potential would be optimized, at least from a motivational standpoint.

Conclusions and Recommendations

Tommy's major problems are attentional and motivational. He does not have cognitive deficiencies that would interfere significantly with his learning of academic content. In fact, he appears to have potential for superior learning ability. His superior potential is not being realized at present, mainly because of the attentional and motivational problems.

Tommy's activity level and his level of distractibility are very high. In school, he is said to be no more active than the other children in his class, but I find that difficult to accept. His activity in the classroom may take the form of psychological distractibility (i.e., mental wandering), such that he spends a great deal of time off-task. Where he is when he is off-task is a matter of pure conjecture. When he is able to focus his attention on tasks, he does them very well indeed, sometimes at a superior level.

The only sense in which cognitive remediation is indicated is the need for Tommy to use logical and systematic thinking processes to gain self-regulation of both his motor behavior and his metacognition. By the latter term, I mean to say that he does not yet consciously and deliberately select learning and problem-solving strategies from his available repertoire and apply them systematically to learning situations. Rather, he tends to solve problems perceptually and intuitively, relying on his intelligence to produce answers rather than on systematic thinking processes. If he could be in a cognitive education class, metacognitive self-regulation could be emphasized. That is not likely to happen outside such a class because of the scant availability of teachers who have been specifically trained to use the special methods of cognitive education. If such a class should become available, Tommy has already shown that he would be very receptive. If such a class should not become available, Tommy could benefit from individual (but more from small group) cognitive education by a teacher who has been trained in the appropriate methods, such as a "mediational" teaching style.

This person could be a "pull-out" therapist (one who takes the child out of the classroom for individual work), such as a speech/language therapist, physical therapist, occupational therapist, or psychologist.

Tommy should not repeat first grade. He is cognitively ready for second-grade work. The issue is not one of immaturity but of specific obstructions from a learning disability that has attentional and associated motivational roots. I would really like to see an onsite evaluator observe him closely in the fall to see how he behaves in a classroom instructional situation: Where does it break down for him, and what can be modified about the teaching to enhance his learning? Whether he is in a first-grade or a second-grade class, the problems will be the same (or perhaps magnified if the work is too unchallenging): high activity level, distractibility, much off-task behavior, and reliance on perceptual and intuitive problem solving rather than on systematic logical thinking. In either case, he will need to be willing to slow down, address problems one part at a time, and apply systematic strategies for learning and problem solving. His excellent performances on the tasks given in this assessment should not be taken to mean that he has no need to slow down and work more reflectively. In fact, he needs to establish such habits now, while the work is relatively unchallenging, so they will be in place as schoolwork becomes more complex. It is not even a question of learning or acquiring such strategies: He already has much of what would be required. The problem is in establishing habits of applying those strategies in everyday learning situations. He has demonstrated, for example, that he can compare, classify, and form verbal abstractions. He does not do so habitually, only when asked to do it.

Given that Tommy has experienced a rather rapid decline in his math performance, he should have either one-on-one tutoring in math or a part-time resource room experience where he could get some math enrichment in a classroom setting. Both reading and math being of such a cumulative nature, he should not be permitted to fall behind at this stage of his education.

Here are some suggestions regarding his attentional and self-regulation problems:

- Model and encourage his use of task-related self-talk. This would need to be done on tasks that are challenging. The teacher (or parent) could model task solutions with self-talk and have him imitate this. This way, the frustration and challenge would be removed, and he could focus on the strategy of talking himself through difficult problems. Verbalizing what he is doing in a step-by-step fashion would help both to regulate the tempo of his problem solving and to focus his attention on his own (metacognitive) thought processes.

- Give him descriptive feedback when he becomes overactive ("You're losing it, moving around a lot. Check out where your body is. Make a picture in your mind of where you are and what you are doing so you can see yourself"). Approach this as a collaborative problem-solving process. When the problem has been identified and feedback provided, proceed to the solution: "What can we do to help you with this?" "Does this work?" "How about this?" "What do you think?"
- He already has some spontaneous strategies for inhibiting his impulsivity, as demonstrated during the testing, such as putting his chin on his hands. Use these as strategies and make him conscious of them as strategies. Give each such strategy a name and cue him when it seems appropriate for use. Example: "You're having trouble keeping your hands still. Time for chin-hands (or lap-hands)."
- Enroll him in a martial arts program of his choice to help him with self-regulation of his movements. The idea is to make him aware and self-conscious about his movements and to give him a strategy for self-regulation.
- An additional approach would be to teach him a muscle relaxation routine, possibly before going to bed so he can begin at a time when he can maximize his attention. Once he has mastered this, he can be cued to use it as a strategy when appropriate.
- He responded well when his movements were counted, as in the Plateaux task. He also demonstrated that he is a simultaneous/visual–spatial learner. The teacher and parent could chart his behavior during high-stakes activities and record the results on a graph. With time, he could learn to do his own monitoring and charting. Any behaviorally oriented psychologist can teach the teacher and/or parent to do this.
- His seating arrangement is important, especially for activities in which concentration is required. He should be in a chair that allows his feet to be flat on the floor, back against the back, if necessary, arms on the chair, no cushion. A persistent problem during the testing was the swivel chair that he occupied (because it was the only kind of chair in the room). It gave him far too much opportunity for off-task movement. He should also get preferential seating in the classroom – as direct as possible exposure to the teacher's input.
- Manipulative materials are not necessarily the best teaching materials for Tommy. His use of manipulatives should be observed and explored. Tommy has demonstrated that he is capable of solving problems at a conceptual, symbolic level, that is, in his head and not necessarily between his hands. Overactive children often get distracted by manipulative materials and fail to use them to learn the concepts.

- Tommy should also be taught a "get ready to listen" routine. This would be a good time to clear away all distracters and to do something for his motor movements such as chin on the hands, hands in his lap, or whatever he chooses that works for him. This should be worked out collaboratively with him, but then he needs to be cued and held to it.

I recommend that Tommy's pediatrician be consulted about his over-activity and distractibility. The pediatrician might wish to prescribe medication of the stimulant variety (certainly not a sedative or tranquilizer), with a view to providing internally the stimulation that Tommy now seeks externally by means of his high level of activity.

With respect to motivation, long-term reliance on contingent reinforcement systems will be counterproductive. The use of incentives and rewards that lie outside of desirable tasks should be discontinued, and task-intrinsic incentives and rewards should be systematically increased. The strongest boost to his task-intrinsic motivation will come from his success at learning and problem-solving tasks. Such success should be guaranteed in two ways: (a) adjusting the task levels to what he can do successfully, then requiring a bit more, or breaking down tasks into smaller units, and (b) giving all the help he needs and will tolerate so that failure is not possible. It is too early to expect him to work completely independently, but the guaranteed-success procedure will help to get him there.

CASE 9.5 Mr. J.

I saw Mr. J. at a community services center for people with disabilities to try to get information on his cognitive functioning and potential that might be useful in his treatment program. He was part of a services program for adults who were either classified as having developmental disabilities, chiefly mental retardation, or traumatic brain injuries. In fact, although he had suffered brain injury, he was part of the mental retardation/developmental disabilities program. His (not documented) brain injury was the result of a gang attack on him when he was a teenager, resulting in a closed head injury. Reports of his behavior and learning performance before and after that incident were not especially different, suggesting that his performance had not been higher before his injury than after. The examination lasted about 2 hours – relatively brief for the "dynamic" approach to psychoeducational assessment.

Mr. J. entered the assessment situation willingly, cheerfully, if not enthusiastically. Staff members had mentioned that he is somewhat enigmatic, appearing often to have intellectual abilities well above those of many of his peers in his day program but behaving in such ways as to avoid active learning. A question that arose in my mind quite early in our interaction was, "Is he 'dumbing down,' overachieving, or functioning in a depressed manner because of discoverable obstacles to effective learning and performance?"

Assessment procedures included a clinical interview, Rey's Plateaux Test, Haywood's Transformation Test, and Raven's Colored Progressive Matrices. This was a fairly small sample of both content and cognitive domains of functioning. This assessment will be followed later with additional work, but Mr. J. had limited time available on this occasion and in any event I did not think that I could maintain his enthusiasm for work much longer than this.

Mr. J.'s very pleasant manner of social interaction and his verbal facility and skill during individual assessment contrasted rather sharply with his lethargic, withdrawn, and minimally participatory behavior during a group testing session in which he participated later in the day. The former qualities may very well deceive people about the level of his intellectual functioning. Although I did not give a standardized intelligence test, he seemed to me to be functioning at a "dull normal" or borderline level of intelligence but to have cognitive development and skills that represented a high degree of variability.

In the clinical interview, Mr. J. was fairly readily forthcoming. I was surprised to learn that he was 31 years old, because he looks perhaps 10 years younger. He told me that "black people look younger than they are," making me wonder where he had heard that judgment. In describing his family, he said that he is the "baby boy" in a family of 11 offspring; he is the youngest of 6 boys but has younger sisters. He described his life within the family as difficult, especially with regard to the neighborhood in which he grew up. His descriptions of his family life were far too stereotypic and cloyingly positive to be true, reflecting a fantasy picture. He said he had been told that our testing would be a way to find out how to help him achieve his goals – although those goals were never specified during our session. He also said that he had graduated from high school, in a special education program. Questioned about that, he said that he had a learning disability and had always been in special classes.

On Rey's Plateaux, Mr. J. demonstrated quickly that he does not have a significant deficiency in visual–spatial perception – a question that had arisen among the staff. He does, however, have significant difficulty in visual-spatial *memory*. He rather quickly learned the positions of the four fixed buttons on the four separate plates in this task, but just as quickly lost them, so that his error scores went up after he had nearly perfect scores early in the test. He was able to discriminate the Y schema, but it did not help him to achieve a stable representation of the positions of the fixed buttons.

In fact, mediation of metacognitive strategies seemed to erect new obstacles to his performance, as if new information was distracting his attention from the main task. He thus appeared to rely primarily on perceptual learning rather than on metacognitive, analytic techniques. That is to say that he was good at taking in necessary information at a global level and processing that information as a whole but not good at working analytically and sequentially. He learned to verbalize "rules" of the activity but sometimes did not follow them unless reminded to do so. Even so, he required relatively little mediation to achieve a quite good result on the Plateaux. Strengths included a readiness to be reflective rather than impulsive, willingness to take direction, and a generally cheerful approach to his work. Problem areas included difficulty with visual–spatial memory, a nonsequential and nonanalytic approach to problem solving, and a tendency to rely on guessing. Response to mediation of metacognitive strategies, such as taking in complete information before responding, comparing, making mental images, and verbalizing rules, was overall quite good.

On the Transformation test, Mr. J. performed very well. It should be noted, however, that this task was designed for young children and can be mastered, with considerable mediation, by children aged 5 to 6 years. Mr. J. had a bit of difficulty abstracting the rules of the task, but once he had done that, he had little difficulty in applying them. His performance was reminiscent of the standard observation in cognitive research that persons who function at the low end of the "normal" range of intelligence or in the mildly retarded range are quite capable of acquiring metacognitive strategies and applying them to the solution of problems but typically do not do so unless required or prompted to do it. He required some prompting, some reminding; however, the reminding was more in the form of "Now what is the transformation rule?" or "Remember what the red line does" than actually telling him the rules. He had slightly more difficulty recognizing the exclusive nature of a transforming rule (for example, the red line changes color, so it does not change shape, size, or number – just color). He progressed quickly and automatically from recognition of a specific change, such as from yellow to black, to a generalized change, such as from black to yellow, black to red, red to blue, or yellow to any color that is not yellow. He was equally able to solve transformation problems with concrete and with abstract content: geometric shapes versus animals, for example. We progressed within the task to dual transformation problems (i.e., those having two transformation lines and therefore two simultaneous transformations). Thus, for example, a large white square followed by a red line and a blue line would become a large red triangle or circle. He required more reminding but quickly learned to deal with dual transformation rules.

Raven's Progressive Matrices test was not given in the standard way but was instead used to mediate problem-solving strategies and metacognitive operations, such as gathering clear and complete information, describing stimulus arrays before leaping to potential solutions, defining the problem, working sequentially, extracting and applying explanatory rules, making mental images of the necessary solutions, and verifying one's solutions. Getting him to master each of these strategies and operations was easy, but getting him to remember and apply all of them at once was difficult.

Throughout the assessment sessions, both individual and group, I observed occasional glimpses of well-controlled resistance and hostility. This could be circumstantial and reactive, related to his being in a (gently) regimented situation with requirements that he does not always understand (reasons for doing what he is asked to do, for example, although staff members do observably make commendable efforts to make sure that the consumers with whom they work do indeed understand why they are doing what they do), or having little personal control over his life. It is also possible that resistance and hostility arise from his cumulative experience, including growing up in a very difficult neighborhood, having been attacked and assaulted by peers, even having a large family where he could have felt lost (although there is no evidence of that). He has developed some adaptive strategies, most of which are quite appropriate, such as a pleasant demeanor, at least the appearance of cooperation, and good verbal facility. Whether he experiences psychological pain related to his identity, his existential situation, or his impaired condition is a question that should be explored with him in a psychotherapeutic relationship.

Some of Mr. J.'s ego defenses are nonadaptive, such as avoiding situations in which he might possibly fail (thus avoiding new learning), using personal charm to get through situations that require hard psychological work, and giving minimal answers.

In his treatment program, Mr. J. should be encouraged to use his good verbal facility to mediate problem solving, that is, to verbalize the nature of problems, his own resources for solving them, and probable solutions. He should be required to stick with problems until he has used effective metacognitive processes for solving them, including not only abstract classroom problems but any personal and social problems in his everyday life. Those who work with him should refuse to accept partial answers or imprecise ones. He should not be allowed to rely on perceptual problem solving or learning, but instead should always be asked to justify his solutions verbally, using explanatory rules in a sequential fashion rather than just looking at problems and hoping the solutions will jump out at him. Partial or approximate answers/solutions should not be accepted. He is able to derive considerable developmental benefit from cognitive education but will require quite a lot of mediation to get him to generalize the concepts and principles he learns there to real-life, everyday situations. Occasional bridging will not be sufficient, although he should be very good at coming up with bridging suggestions when asked to do so. A cognitive approach in psychotherapy could well be combined with supportive psychotherapy, and this would help him with generalizing thinking principles and using his intelligence to solve personal problems and make independent decisions.

Mr. J. does not exude task-intrinsic motivation. He has no vocational aspirations, explaining that he gets along very well with his disability compensation and is even able to lend money to others from time to time. Such a task-extrinsic motivational orientation can help him to avoid dissatisfaction and psychological pain, but it cannot lead to positive satisfaction with his work, his learning, or his life. His willingness to settle for the pain-avoidance rather than satisfaction-seeking strategy is an area that might well be approached in his treatment program.

The Role of DA in These Cases

DA was an important element in both Tommy's and Mr. J.'s assessments, in the sense that it revealed information that would not have been available from normative, standardized tests and that information was directly relevant to program planning for them. In Tommy's case, it was important to find out that he was able to bring his extreme distractibility under voluntary control, at least partly, and that when he did so, his performances, which were already good, improved. It was also important to discover that his planning and organizational skills, also initially good, could be improved further with mediation of essential metacognitive operations and habits. The structure of the assessment even enabled the examiner to reach useful conclusions about Tommy's motive system so that suggestions could be made for motivating him to focus his attention and efforts on learning and problem solving. Observation of his behavior also led to recommendations for helping him to gain better self-regulation.

The DA situation offered an opportunity to observe Mr. J.'s learning and problem-solving behavior under actual learning and problem-solving conditions, as well as to observe such important behavioral aspects of task persistence and different behavior patterns following success and failure. It offered as well a chance to assess the extent to which his strongly task-extrinsic motivational orientation could be diverted, at least temporarily, into productive work as its own reward, that is, to assess whether one could get this extrinsically motivated adult to behave, for a while, in an intrinsically motivated manner. The opportunity to demonstrate the absence of particular problems, in this case visual–spatial–perceptual difficulty, was important for program planning, especially given that Mr. J. participates in a day program in which many of the other participants do indeed have such difficulty. Because of that advantage, it was possible to begin a list of his assets for further work.

Developing IEPs and Service Plans

Including a dynamic approach in either clinical or educational assessment does not, in and of itself, affect the structure or intent of the plans that emerge from these activities, but dynamic assessment does have profound effects on the content of the objectives of the plans. Instead of restricting objectives to products of the individual's functioning, dynamic assessment shifts the focus onto processes. Actually, this is the effect of conducting assessments that are influenced by both neuropsychology and the dynamic model. We are no longer interested only in the ability of the student to read or complete mathematical calculations or in the ability to speak clearly or develop a plan for a budget in patients with traumatic brain injuries, but we are even more interested in the processes that relate to these skills and abilities. Moreover, our approaches to remediation will target the executive strategies and metacognitive principles that promote generalization and development of higher order mental processes.

Not all children with an attention deficit profit from the same intervention, and not all individuals with other symptoms of neurological impairment suffer from the same process deficits. We cannot make accurate far inferences from sources such as the Wechsler Block Design about the nature of either the processing deficits or the promise of specific interventions without checking these out in situ. Assessors are now being asked to recommend evidence-based recommendations for remediation. If interventions are not included in the assessment, where will this evidence come from? Research based on large groups can only propose hypotheses for what will work with an individual, and there is no realistic way to conduct research that relates to every possible remediation that may apply to every single individual in need. Evidence will have to come from $N = 1$ studies, and an efficient route to hypotheses for these studies is the dynamic model of assessment.

around educational circles for a long time; nevertheless, as a concept from which to develop a diagnostic assessment approach, this notion can indeed be viewed as antiestablishment and revolutionary. In spite of this seemingly orderly growth of the idea of learning potential, the concept is still not firmly anchored in scientific thought or buttressed empirically. Meanwhile, the practice of dynamic assessment has grown somewhat beyond the single goal of assessing learning potential into, for example, assessment of adaptive behavior (Chapter 4) and even some personality characteristics (see, e.g., Guthke & Wingenfeld, 1992, p. 72).

Guthke and Wingenfeld (1992) observed that the information derived from learning tests "should enable diagnosticians (a) to make more reliable and valid differential diagnoses . . . , (b) to make more accurate predictions about the future mental development of subjects, and (c) to derive suggestions for psychoeducational interventions from the assessment itself" (p. 64). At least the second and third goals suggest the assessment of learning potential. Budoff (1967) used the term "learning potential" to suggest that assisted performance is a better estimate of what is possible – that is, potential – than is unassisted performance. Hamers et al. (1993) have used both the concept and the term consistently to refer to their assessment procedures that involve a planned intervention. Feuerstein combines the concept of learning potential with his concept of cognitive modifiability, by which latter term he means not simply the ability to be modified by experience but ultimately the ability to modify one's own cognitive structures (in the Piagetian sense of enduring logic modes) without further need of intervention (Feuerstein, Feuerstein, Falik, & Rand, 2002).

So far so good. All theorists and practitioners who do dynamic assessment seem to use the concept of learning potential to mean that there are abilities that are not apparent in standardized testing situations. A major part of the definitional problem comes with identifying the nature of the intervention that can reveal potential (see Chapter 1). Intervention strategies range from giving clues to the correct answer to teaching metacognitive operations and rules and coaching on their application. The degree of improvement in performance that one can expect, as well as the generality and durability of such changes, depends on the nature, depth, persistence, intensity, and frequency of the intervention; yet all are grouped together under the concept of learning potential. When applied to education, what we are seeking to improve is not simply performance (scores on tests, even learning tests) but *educability* itself: the ability to derive significant benefit from opportunities to learn. We suggest that some transfer criterion would be useful for inferring learning potential. That is to say, improved performance on recalling a list of words should not be sufficient to infer learning potential; rather, one might require consequent improvement in the ability to learn subsequent lists or even to learn in other domains of content. Such a transfer criterion is seldom applied in dynamic assessment except in research, where it has been shown fairly often to occur when the intervention is focused on metacognitive and motivational aspects of problem solving. The idea is neither novel nor strange. Rumbaugh (Rumbaugh & Washburn, 2003; see especially pages 66–77) introduced a "transfer index" as a means of assessing individual differences in the intelligence of nonhuman primates, with considerable success. Harlow's (1949) "learning sets" depended on the ability to generalize training from one situation to others, allowing one to infer a "learning to learn" phenomenon. Piaget (1950, 1970) observed that there should be dual criteria, durability and generalizability, for inferring that a "structural" cognitive change had occurred. The generalizability criterion suggests a transfer requirement. Swanson (2000) has built such a transfer criterion into his probe-based approach to dynamic assessment of working memory.

DA practitioners do not assume that the performance changes that they observe following mediation are durable changes. In fact, they regard those changes as probably transient because the intensity of the intervention during assessment is assumed to be not sufficiently great, nor has it been repeated enough, to bring about lasting change. Here, then, is another angle on the concept of "potential." Having shown that improved performance is possible, given an appropriate intervention, one uses that information to infer the potential for more durable and generalizable changes given a more intense and sustained intervention of the type used during assessment. The use of a transfer criterion would strengthen the change inference as well as the notion of "potential to benefit from intervention."

It is perhaps even more important that we question the use of potential as an exclusive focus of our attention. It is unlikely that any diagnostic examiners would claim that their clients did not have greater potential than is apparent in their current level of functioning. In dynamic assessment, we would be likely to assert that any failure of a client to profit from our interventions is more a function of our failure to find suitable interventions than the inability of the client to profit from teaching. The more relevant questions are how much (degree of improvement) and how far (degree of generalization). The issues with which we are more concerned involve determination of the types of experiences needed to promote higher levels of functioning, as well as issues of estimating intensity of need for input and the nature of obstructions to higher levels of competence. Even as we acknowledge some interest in determining learning potential, we have to ask what we would do with that information. Such a concern seems to return us to dealing with questions of eligibility when we should really be paying more attention to intervention; therefore, although the roots of dynamic assessment lie within the realm of determination of learning potential, we believe that it is now time to turn our efforts toward more fruitful targets.

RELATED PROCEDURES

RTI

Potential to benefit from intervention suggests the current concept of RTI (Response to Intervention or Response to Instruction). In Chapter 1, we discussed that concept and argued that although DA is essentially RTI, RTI is not DA. RTI as currently conceived represents a significant advance in classroom assessment and remedial education for three reasons:

1. It provides continuous monitoring of classroom performance.
2. It requires use of assessment procedures that are specifically chosen for and tailored to the answering of individual questions, especially questions about how to promote improved learning.
3. It makes use of the tactic of comparing performances within a person rather than between persons, which is also consistent with DA.

We argued (Chapter 1) that, in spite of these advantages and similarities, RTI (again, as currently conceived) should not be confused with DA, for the following reasons:

1. RTI is failure-based and therefore still results in a search for deficits rather than primarily for sources of strength. This criticism is tempered by the fact that the use of curriculum-based measurement makes of it, in part, a search for successful educational strategies (What can the teacher do?).
2. The requirement that the intervention be "appropriate" and "well designed" is not sufficiently precise to be maximally useful. In the usual applications of RTI the focus of the intervention is on the curricular contents of academic learning, whereas in DA, the nature of the intervention is usually defined as one bearing on metacognitive operations, strategies, and habits, that is, on mediating tools of logical thinking and systematic learning.
3. Although some of its principal adherents insist that RTI is not primarily a classification scheme, in its everyday use it is. That is to say, it is used as a means of identifying learners who are appropriately classified as having learning disabilities (i.e., those who respond inadequately to evidence-based instruction).

It would not be difficult to reconcile the two practices by making RTI more like DA. That could be accomplished primarily by specifying metacognitive teaching as an essential part of the required intervention in RTI. In present best practice, RTI constitutes a search for successful educational practices. DA constitutes a search for qualities of learners that can be encouraged and developed so as to make them more effective learners. The goal is the same: better learning. The emphasis is different: what the teacher does in the case of RTI, what goes on in the minds of the learners (and how those events influence what the teacher does) in the case of DA. The primary concern, in our view as well as that of some of the leading proponents of RTI, is the need to use the assessment situation to identify and determine the nature of learners' needs, not to rule out all potential sources of intervention for the ultimate purpose of classification. It is not failure to profit from evidence-based intervention that should be diagnostic but use of these evidence-based interventions to build a program and array of approaches that promote success and mastery in the student. We need to find what works, not what fails to work! The several current conceptions of RTI represent an unsettled approach to assessment of students with learning disorders, one that we hope will become more useful as the model moves closer to a DA model.

TESTING THE LIMITS, TRIAL TEACHING, AND PERFORMANCE-BASED ASSESSMENT
Testing the limits, trial teaching, and performance-based assessment differ from "mainstream" DA in that they do not involve metacognitive teaching. Testing the limits usually involves a brief, limited attempt to go beyond the standard administration of norm-based items to respond to the "what if" question of how the individual would perform if, for example, provided with more time, alternative wording, or modification of mode of presentation. These explorations are very limited in time and constricted by the nature of the standardized test items to which they relate. Such explorations provide some important insight into the nature of the obstructions to learning and some leads regarding how to overcome these barriers. Testing the limits is a valuable technique, the principal value of which, in a conceptual sense, is to enable one to discover how far below the threshold of knowledge some specified information or skill might lie. In that sense, it is similar to the "graduated prompt" procedure in which examiners offer increasingly specific clues to the correct answers, the number of necessary clues being inversely related to learning potential. Testing the limits, as employed for example by Carlson and Wiedl (1992a, 1992b), lies clearly within the "changing the test situation" category of DA intervention.

Trial teaching engages learners in an interactive experience, exploring potential interventions within a specific content domain. This approach provides insights into the processes of learning; however, trial teaching tends to focus on the "what" of assessment rather than the "how." Important information regarding "what works" can be derived from this approach, but insight into "what obstructs" and how to overcome such obstructions is limited.

Performance-based assessment provides important samples of behavior in a wide variety of content domains. It is particularly relevant for the arts and athletics and is generally a useful approach for assessing skill-based learning: If you want to know how well someone sings, hear her sing; if you want to know how well someone dances, see him dance; if you want to know how well someone has mastered a science experiment, watch her perform an experiment. Performance-based assessment does not include intervention and therefore does not provide information about the responsiveness of the learners who may not yet be fully competent in the skill. It does not address issues of barriers to competence, nor does it provide significant insight into how these can be overcome. Performance-based assessment is best for determining level of mastery and as such is valuable for eligibility (for special educational services) screening.

Dynamic assessment, as we describe it, combines trial teaching and performance-based assessment with intervention. It goes well beyond testing the limits in its process focus and lack of content restraints; yet it is also possible to test the limits in dynamic assessments that use standardized or scripted interventions. Dynamic assessment is not a substitute for these alternative approaches because each has its own purpose and anticipated outcome. Again, we stress the importance of matching the assessment procedure with the questions and issues to be addressed and the decisions to be made.

APPLICATIONS OF DYNAMIC ASSESSMENT

As we pointed out in Chapter 1, DA is not for everybody. It can provide information that is not otherwise available. Getting at elusive information, especially about the specific learning processes of individuals, barriers to better learning and performance, levels of cognitive functioning and development, and responsiveness to mediated teaching, is its raison d'être. Dynamic assessment is indicated, and is useful, (a) when standardized scores lead to pessimistic predictions; (b) learning appears to be artificially constrained; (c) language and/or cultural issues may restrict performance; and (d) classification is not a primary issue in the assessment. A famous psychologist was fond of noting that the scientific enterprise starts when somebody is puzzled. The same can be said fairly of DA: One is puzzled by discrepancies, perhaps discrepancies between predictor scores and performance/achievement scores, perhaps discrepancies between performance in different behavior settings, perhaps simply discrepancies between performance and expectations.

DA works best when used to find answers to specific questions, especially questions about individuals' learning or performance potential. As we suggest repeatedly, DA cannot answer questions that have not been asked, and that leads to the assertion that it should not be a standard part of any assessment "battery" (group of tests or assessment procedures). It works best when the examiners have been well trained in the philosophy, methods, and instruments of DA (see section on training issues, this chapter). It works best when the specific procedures and assessment instruments that are used in DA have been selected by considering the questions to which one seeks answers and the form, cognitive requirements, content, and difficulty/complexity level of the instruments.

There is no evidence that DA works well when used to classify persons according to deficiencies either for special education services or for diagnostic grouping, probably because it has not been developed to serve those purposes and, so far as we know, is not used in that way. See description of Lidz and Macrine study, Chapter 7, for successful use of DA to identify gifted students. (An exception is Budoff's scheme of classifying people, on the basis of learning potential assessment, as high scorers, gainers, and non-gainers, but that scheme has not been used to track learners into, or out of, particular educational experiences.) It is not likely to work well in the hands of untrained or inadequately trained examiners. Use of DA with examinees of very limited expressive language requires particular skill and patience. One of us recently examined a group of adults with brain injuries, one of whom had unintelligible speech so she used a special communication device, much like a typewriter, to type out her responses, laboriously, letter by letter, made even slower by seriously impaired motor functions. Any attempts to do standard assessment with her would have been doomed to failure and would have resulted in inaccurate estimates of her abilities and potential. After several hours of painstaking work, the examiner was able to conclude that her essential cognitive functioning was relatively intact, that she was capable of a rather high level of abstract reasoning and problem solving, and that she could do well on untimed intellectual tasks. DA would not have worked well if the examiner had attempted to standardize the instructions, the timing, or even the interpretation of her responses. In another situation, we observed a colleague doing a dynamic assessment with a child with whom the examiner had no common language. By learning a dozen words in the child's language (and no grammar!), using signs, imitating and requesting imitation, ignoring timing expectations, and varying the manner in which instructions were presented, that examiner was able to obtain a quite useful assessment of the child's learning potential. In this case as well as in the previous one, DA would not have worked well, or perhaps even been possible, without that degree of flexibility in presentation of the tasks and acceptance of the child's different (nonstandard) modes of response. In other words, DA does not do the same job that standardized, normative tests are designed to do. It does not rank individuals with respect to the performances of others.

LIMITATIONS

Our model of DA is further limited by its heavy reliance on the mediational skill of examiners. The information that one obtains from DA comes from initial (unassisted) performance, identification of barriers to better performance, kind and amount of teaching (mediation) needed to bring about improved performance, response to teaching, and generalization of the metacognitive operations that were encouraged. At least three of those sources of DA data involve a certain amount of subjectivity on the part of examiners. If, for example, "kind and amount of mediation needed" is to be inferred from the kind and amount actually given, then the examiner must be sure to give no more than was actually needed, and that is surely a subjective judgment that rests on good training and experience. Further subjectivity is required in adjusting the instructions so as to be certain that each examinee understands the nature and requirements of the tasks. This is sometimes referred to as "control of the proximal stimulus" (what the examinee actually understands) as opposed to "control of the distal stimulus" (what the examiner says). Too much or injudicious explanation can certainly bias the interpretation of an examinee's performance. Identification of deficient cognitive and metacognitive functions is still a subjective process, based as much on observation of performance as on actual performance. With so much subjectivity, it would certainly be a mistake to try to quantify examinees' performances! We embrace this model because we value the flexibility of administration that allows for true responsiveness to the individuals being assessed, and, most important, we value the potential of this model for clinical insights and for the generation of information that promotes a real relationship between assessment and useful intervention.

DA does not meet the usual metric standards for psychological tests, for example, those developed jointly by the American Educational Research Association (AERA), the American Psychological Association (APA), and the National Council on Measurement in Education (NCME; 1999). It is not clear that it should do so, because of course DA is not a test, or even a group of tests, but rather an elaborate assessment procedure. There are, nevertheless, important issues of reliability and validity. Determining reliability is a difficult task when one sets out deliberately to change the performance of examinees. Several writers (e.g., Haywood, 1997; Haywood & Tzuriel, 2002) have suggested that the most important aspect of reliability in DA is to use tests that are themselves reliable when given in the "static" mode, that is, without intervention. The basis of that argument is the observation that with a pretest, mediation, and posttest strategy one wishes to attribute any improvement from pretest to posttest to the effects of the intervention, which can only be done if the pre- and posttest instruments have acceptable reliability; otherwise, change could be merely random or unsystematic variability in the test. Many of the tests discussed in this volume have well-established reliability when given in the static mode, but some are untested in that regard. Users should be aware of that and be prepared to submit these instruments to empirical reliability checks.

Validity is an even more difficult problem. Ideally, one would do DA, specify the conditions under which improved performance is possible, then institute those conditions and test the predictions. The huge problem is that of assuring that the specified conditions for improved performance have actually been made available. In the more usual case, one might do DA and forecast improved performance provided the examinees are given, for example, classroom cognitive education (and not if that condition is not met). There is an almost irresistible tendency then to expect the improved performance without providing the specified conditions that would make it possible to achieve.

Several investigators have actually demonstrated that DA can be a more powerful predictor of subsequent school achievement than are the usual standardized, normative predictor tests (e.g., Budoff, 1987; Guthke, 1982, 1985, 1992; Guthke & Wingenfeld, 1992; Tzuriel, 2000s). That observation bears positively on the question of the validity of DA but does not respond fully to it. The ultimate validity question in DA is, "How does DA affect clients?" Such studies are fiendishly difficult to do because of the action of a great multitude of influencing but uncontrollable variables. It is likely that individual case reports will have to bear the burden of demonstrating the validity of DA. Haywood and Menal (1992) provided one such demonstration. An adolescent girl who had been diagnosed as mentally retarded but whose psychologists thought she had greater learning potential than she was demonstrating in her behavior was given a dynamic assessment of her learning potential. That examination resulted in a recommendation for "cognitive developmental therapy" (Haywood, 2000), a combination of Instrumental Enrichment (Feuerstein et al., 1980) and supportive psychotherapy. When that recommendation was actually carried out, the girl showed both quantitative (elevated scores on the DA tests; i.e., greater benefit from mediation than was initially true) and behavioral evidence of significant psychological improvement. In the latter case, even a court of law judged her to be competent to make far-reaching life decisions. DA had thus served as a valid prescription for and evaluation of psychological treatment. Validity is more likely to be found in such large criterion variables than in psychometric criteria.

A persistent question throughout the modern development of both DA and cognitive education programs has been, "How are they related to each other?" An easy answer would be, "So far, not very closely," a judgment that would reflect the state of research on that question. Conceptually, the two should be quite closely related: One uses DA to locate the barriers to more effective learning and to suggest educational strategies, and then those specific strategies are applied to overcoming the learning barriers. More frequently, DA is given, reports are written, but all children in a given class receive the same educational intervention, even when that intervention is strongly metacognitively oriented, as in the case of classroom programs of cognitive education such as Instrumental Enrichment (Feuerstein et al., 1980), Bright Start (Haywood, Brooks, & Burns, 1992), or Philosophy for Children (Lipman, 1991; Lipman, Sharp, & Oscanyan, 1980). To make DA more individually relevant to classroom learners, one needs to have a close collaboration between the assessment person(s) and the teacher(s), such as in Cognitive Enrichment Advantage (Greenberg, 2000a, 2000b; Greenberg & Williams, 2002). The DA approaches laid out in detail in Chapters 3 and 6 show that it is quite possible, and of course highly desirable, to have that close relationship to classroom instruction, especially when DA is combined with curriculum-based measurement.

TRAINING IN DA

It should be clear that if the skill of examiners is such a vital part of DA, then training of examiners is critical. So far, training in DA has been done mostly in professional workshops of 4 to 8 days duration, with only a few graduate programs in school psychology, clinical psychology, and special education offering credit-bearing courses in DA in universities. Most trainers appear to agree that this is not ideal and that regular university courses devoted to DA, or strong DA segments of more general assessment courses, would be far preferable. The kind, quality, and intensity of DA training that one gets in professional workshops depends heavily on who is doing the training and what that person's particular theoretical orientation is, as well as how much actual experience the trainer has had in doing applied DA.

In an effort to determine whether there is agreement among DA trainers on what seemed to us to be core issues, we recently conducted an international survey of DA trainers (Haywood & Lidz, 2005). Drawing on a group of experienced trainers, we asked for their opinions on such issues

Table 10.1. Opinions of dynamic assessment (DA) trainers about DA training (from Haywood & Lidz, 2005)

Question	Response
Who should be offered training in DA?	Psychologists (86%), Special Educators (69%), Speech/language therapists (62%), Any behavioral and mental health professionals (55%)
Minimum time required	35–40 hours (37%); 70–80 hours (21%)
Optimal time for training	One academic semester (32%) 70–80 hours (27%)
Most important concepts, by rank	1. Mediation 2. Cognitive/metacognitive operations 3. Zone of proximal development 4. Concepts and development of ability 5. Social–developmental sources of poor performance
Allocation of training time, by rank	1. Techniques of application (Median = 43% of workshop time) 2. Instruments, tests, materials (32% of workshop time) 3. Theoretical concepts (30% of workshop time)
Emphasis on principles versus instruments, by rank	1. Emphasize principles, teach a few instruments (51%) 2. Teach how to make almost any test a dynamic assessment instrument (33%) 3. Emphasize repertoire, teach a variety of instruments (10%)
Importance of training on specific tests	1. Certain tests/instruments are best: those constructed for DA purposes (55%) 2. Almost any test can be used for DA with some modification, but such use destroys its normative value (45%)

as who should be offered DA training, how much time DA training should take, how that time should be allocated (e.g., among theory, methods, and instruments), and the most important concepts that should be included. We found both close agreement on some questions and great disparity on others. Table 10.1 shows some of both groups of responses.

Responses to the last two items in Table 10.1 seem to be inconsistent. On the one hand, respondents indicated that teaching principles is more important than is teaching specific tests. On the other hand, they suggested that certain tests, those constructed for use in DA, are best. It is likely that many respondents believe that both statements are true: It is important to teach principles of DA, and it is also important to recognize that some tests are more likely to yield useful data than are others.

We also asked the trainers what they considered to be the essential features of DA. They identified the following, in order from most frequently to least frequently selected. Only features chosen by at least 50% of the respondents are listed.

Mediation of cognitive/metacognitive operations
Mediation on affective/motivational variables
Removal of knowledge barriers (e.g., vocabulary, language, previous failure)
Some type of teaching intervention by the examiner
Clarification of instructions and expectations
Feedback on examinees' performance
Affective non-neutrality (examiner is clearly on examinee's side)

Even though we tried to be inclusive, that is, to enlist the participation of any and all DA trainers regardless of theoretical orientation or preferred methods of DA, it is apparent that the group of respondents was more representative of the "mediated learning" approaches than of those approaches to DA that do not require mediation of essential cognitive and metacognitive operations – witness the almost unanimous selection of "mediation of cognitive and metacognitive operations" as a feature of DA that was considered to be essential.

One startling thing that this survey suggested is that the population of persons who actually train practitioners in DA is still very small, probably no more than 50 trainers *in the world*. This is in sharp contrast to the rapidly growing number of persons who do research on or publish about DA (see www.dynamicassessment.com). Thus, training of practitioners remains a primary and difficult issue in DA. Almost all trainers agree that the optimal solution would be to have DA courses offered regularly in colleges and universities, a solution that is yet to be reached. A few trainers have worked out arrangements with universities so that academic credit can be earned for completion of workshop-based DA training, often with the addition of some other requirement such as a term paper, a period of supervised practice, or both. This is a good interim solution but ultimately only a poor substitute for semester-long credit-bearing university study and supervised practice in the professional training of school and clinical psychologists. The burgeoning literature on DA helps greatly with the training situation. After all, not everything must be taught; much can be read. To the extent that published works on DA can be combined with video-recorded demonstrations and live supervision, the training problems can be addressed satisfactorily. The key is supervised practice. One can compare DA training to the training of clinical psychologists and psychiatrists to do psychotherapy: One would not dream of trying to accomplish such training without actual supervised practice, and feedback on performance from experienced practitioners. In most graduate courses in individual intelligence testing, students are required first to observe the tests being given by an expert examiner, then to administer and submit written reports on a certain number of the tests, often under observation and with live feedback. Such supervision is at least equally important in the training of DA practitioners, and probably more so because of the many subjective elements in DA.

Just as various psychological and educational associations have established standards for psychological tests (AERA, APA, and NCME, 1999), professionals in the field of DA should consider trying to establish standards for the training of practitioners. Not intended to be restrictive, such sets of standards might be disseminated through the professional literature. An obvious such organization would be the International Association for Cognitive Education and Psychology (IACEP), the members of which encompass a large proportion of the world's DA trainers and a substantial number of DA researchers. There may be other organizations, such as the National Association of School Psychologists (in the United States) and similar groups in other countries, whose members have an active interest in assessment of individual differences in learning potential.

As we indicated at the beginning of this chapter, we have attempted to summarize our approach to dynamic assessment by discussing and highlighting some of the most important issues involved in its practice. Among the remaining challenges is for trainers to feel sufficiently competent with the model to be able to pass it on to their students. Yet another challenge is to find room in the curriculum for the inclusion of DA as an important part of the assessment repertoire. We close the book with our hope that we have contributed to making the case for dynamic assessment as a valuable member of the group of assessment procedures, one that warrants both the attention and the time of those who practice, those who train, and those who learn.

Tests Referred to in the Text That Do Not Belong to the Authors

This is a list, with descriptive information, of tests that have been referred to in the chapters of this book but cannot be presented fully (for copying, for example) because the authors of this book do not own the rights to them. Some of them are among the most useful instruments for dynamic assessment. We have tried to give sufficient information for readers to track them down, obtain the materials, and arrange for training in their use if training is required.

Test or Procedure Name	The Organizer
Author(s), if applicable	Reuven Feuerstein
Publisher	Jerusalem: ICELP Press

Obtainable from the International Centre for the Enhancement of Learning Potential. Web site: www.icelp.org; Mail address:

ICELP
47, Narkis Street
P.O. Box 7755
Jerusalem 91077
ISRAEL

LIMITS ON DISTRIBUTION Part of LPAD (Learning Propensity Assessment Device); requires training; usually comes bundled with LPAD

DESCRIPTION The Organizer is a dynamic instrument designed to assess the abilities to take in information, sequence that information, and deduce sequences of items and events from the information given in successive clues. The content of the task requires sequencing and spatial organization of items in series, according to successive clues regarding their serial position. It is cognitively complex, requiring hypothetical thinking, effective use of memory and deductive aids, and ability to manage multiple sources of information simultaneously. Items are arranged roughly in a power sequence, from simple to difficult, so the test can be terminated whenever examiners have the information they require. As is true of several of the LPAD instruments, there are forms of the test for pretest, a mediation (learning) phase, and posttest. Mediation typically includes inhibiting impulsivity and encouraging reflectivity, focusing attention on task-relevant clues, sequential problem-solving strategies, plus metacognitive operations of seriation, metamemory strategies, and verification of proposed solutions, among others (depending on examinees' performance).

Test or Procedure Name	*La Boîte à Transformation* (The Transformation Box)
Author(s), if applicable	Jean-Louis Paour
Publisher	Not published

Obtainable from Not commercially available. See description and illustration in Paour, J.-L. (1992). Induction of logic structures in the mentally retarded: An assessment and intervention instrument. In H. C. Haywood & D. Tzuriel (Eds.), *Interactive assessment* (pp. 119–166). New York: Springer-Verlag.

LIMITS ON DISTRIBUTION Used primarily in research. Not published as a separate test.

DESCRIPTION The following description is quoted from Paour (1992, pp. 131–132):

> The apparatus consists of a box . . . (50 cm × 30 cm × 20 cm) and several groups of varied objects that serve as transformation materials.
>
> The transformation box has four compartments distributed as follows:
>
> *Subject side*: (a) An opening on the top (entrance) for putting in the objects, and (b) an opening at the bottom (exit) for taking out the objects that the experimenter has substituted for those the subjects put in at the top. The bottom opening has a hinged door whose purpose is to keep the subjects' attention focused on the returned objects, at least at the beginning of the intervention.
>
> *Examiner side*: Two distinct levels: the objects that the subjects put in stay in the top level; the bottom level is for substituting the objects that the subjects then retrieve.

During practice, subjects only see their side of the box and therefore do not witness the substitution for the objects that they have put in the box.

Depending on the task, the compartments not in use are blocked by a piece of cardboard.

Subjects and examiners have identical sets of objects. Depending on the task, each set may consist of (a) small familiar objects (nails, pins, chalk); (b) little toys (beads, cars, figures); (c) cardboard forms (persons, animals); or (d) paper geometric figures.

Subjects are invited to pick up any piece from the array in front of them and place it in any open compartment at the top of the box. They are then invited to open the door at the bottom of that same compartment and take out whatever is there. In the meantime, the examiner will have made the "transformation," that is, will have defined the function of that particular compartment by placing in the bottom, from the back and unseen by the subject, the transformed object. For example, if the compartment is defined (arbitrarily) as one that transforms size, a subject might put in a small red boat, and then open the bottom door to discover a large red boat. Subjects are then asked, "What does the box do?" Over successive trials, subjects learn the functions of the different compartments, the bidirectionality of transformations (e.g., a compartment that transforms size changes objects both from large to small and from small to large), and the exclusivity of compartment functions (e.g., if it changes size it does not change shape or color). Anticipation testing is often used: "If we put this one in the top, what will come out at the bottom?" (See further description in Paour, 1992, pp. 132–135.)

Use of this test depends more on discovery than on focused mediation of metacognitive strategies; in other words, examinees learn through successive trials and their associated feedback and through judicious questioning ("What does the box do?" "What should come out at the bottom?" "Why should we expect that to come out at the bottom?" "Last time we put a big one in and a little one came out. What would happen if we put a little one in?"). The test can be made increasingly complex with the opening of a larger number of compartments, thus enabling more transformation schemes. For example, one compartment might transform only color, another only size, another shape, another thickness (of the cards on which stimuli are printed), another age (old to young, young to old).

See Transformation in the downloadable material for a full presentation of a paper-and-pencil version of this test.

Test or Procedure Name	LPAD Set Variations I and II
Author(s), if applicable	Reuven Feuerstein
Publisher	ICELP, Jerusalem

Obtainable from The International Centre for the Enhancement of Learning Potential. Web site: www.icelp.org; Mail address:

ICELP
47, Narkis Street
P.O. Box 7755
Jerusalem 91077
ISRAEL

LIMITS ON DISTRIBUTION Part of LPAD (Learning Propensity Assessment Device); requires training; comes bundled with LPAD

DESCRIPTION This test (at two levels of complexity, Set Variations (SV-I and SV-II) is a matrix test of analogical thinking that is based on certain items of Raven's Standard Progressive Matrices, especially those items that go beyond simple matching-to-sample and actually require analogical thinking. SV-I contains stimulus arrays arranged into 2 × 2 matrices, with six items from which to choose the correct answer. SV-II contains stimulus arrays arranged into 3 × 3 matrices, with eight items from which to choose the correct answer.

These instruments, part of Feuerstein's LPAD, are useful for assessing a number of metacognitive operations and habits in addition to levels of analogical thinking. These include reflective versus impulsive responding, planning, management of multiple sources of information, self-verification, rule learning and application, visual transport (mentally lifting a stimulus and "placing" it in a different place), hypothetical thinking, and part–whole relations, as well as spatial and quantitative relations and, to some extent, transitive relations.

SV-I is useful with upper elementary school children as well as adolescents and adults with developmental disabilities and brain injuries. It does not have sufficient ceiling for intensive work with competent adolescents and adults. SV-II has a much greater range, beginning at about age 12 years and reaching upward through adolescence and adulthood. Used as both a diagnostic and intervention instrument, the two levels can be applied in seriatim, provided that SV-I is mastered before beginning SV-II. In such a case, the full range of both levels is possible even with adolescents and adults who have chronic brain injuries; the upward progression is the important consideration in such cases.

Test or Procedure Name	Representational Stencil Design Test (RSDT)
Author(s), if applicable	Feuerstein, based on Grace Arthur Stencil Design Test
Publisher	ICELP, Jerusalem

Obtainable from The International Centre for the Enhancement of Learning Potential. Web site: *www.icelp.org;* Mail address:

ICELP
47, Narkis Street
P.O. Box 7755
Jerusalem 91077
ISRAEL

LIMITS ON DISTRIBUTION Part of LPAD (Learning Propensity Assessment Device); requires training; usually comes bundled with LPAD

DESCRIPTION The task is stacking stencils in the correct order to duplicate given designs. What makes it "representational" is the fact that no stencils are actually manipulated. Examinees look at pictures of solid-color squares and colored stencils, numbered, and say which ones would have to be stacked, in what sequence, in order to make designs that are just like the pictured test designs. This instrument shares with The Organizer the distinction of being the most cognitively complex of the LPAD instruments. It is useful for identifying relatively subtle obstacles to performance, following the principle that the more subtle the phenomenon one seeks to find, the more complex should be the search instrument. Cognitive and metacognitive operations and habits that are reflected in this instrument include visual transport, managing multiple sources of information, comparison, labeling, establishing sequence and pattern, representation/symbolic thinking, rule learning and application, reflective problem solving (inhibition of impulsive responding), planning, and self-verification. RSDT may be given in both individual and group modes, but in the group mode, one sacrifices the individualized mediation that characterizes individual administration. Its three separate problem sets permit a static test–mediation/learning–static posttest strategy with a sufficient number of problems to make good reliability possible. Its multiple colors and overall puzzle-like format appeal to examinees.

Test or Procedure Name	Plateaux
Author(s), if applicable	André Rey
Publisher	Not published
Obtainable from	This test is very difficult to obtain, but it is simple to make.

LIMITS ON DISTRIBUTION Not applicable.

DESCRIPTION This test is essentially a test of spatial memory, but as with most cognitive tasks, successful completion of it requires other strategies and habits as well. The material consists of four black square plates, 15 cm × 15 cm., on each of which are nine round "buttons" (≈ 2.5 cm in diameter), arranged in a 3 × 3 matrix. On each plate, eight of the buttons are removable, but the ninth button is fixed. The position of the fixed button varies from plate to plate but is always the same for a given plate. The examinees' task is to locate the fixed button on each plate and remember it, and ultimately to go through the four plates three times in a row with no errors. An error is defined as touching a button that is not the fixed one. In its use in the LPAD, the next task is for the examinees to make a drawing of one of the plates, with circles on it representing the nine buttons and then to place a numeral representing the number of the plate (1 for the first, 2 for the second, etc.) in the circle the represents the position of the fixed buttons. This is done to establish to what extent examinees have made a mental schema of the positions of the fixed buttons, which they can then use to help them remember the positions. Next, the stacked plates are rotated 90 degrees (within the examinees' sight), and the procedure is repeated, again to a criterion of three successive correct trials, to determine the relative security of the examinees' schema. The rotations may continue until the plates are returned to their original orientation.

As usual with DA tasks, impulsive responding is a major deterrent to good performance. Lack of the habit of making mental images is another obstacle that can be identified with this task, as are lack of mediating strategies (such as verbalizing the positions: top right, bottom middle), poor spatial orientation, and spatial memory. Mediation consists of searching for self-mediating strategies and use of metamemory strategies, and, of course, inhibiting impulsive responding.

Plateaux is a good exercise for opening an assessment session, for working with low-verbal examinees, and for offering an opportunity to demonstrate success. Many children, and almost all adolescents and adults, have little difficulty with it; therefore, when difficulties do arise their presence warrants further investigation.

Test or Procedure Name	Complex Figure
Author(s), if applicable	A. Rey, P. A. Osterrieth
Publisher	Complex Figure appears in many places in many contexts. The original publications are given in the next item. It has been incorporated, with elaboration, into LPAD as well as several neuropsychological assessment batteries.

Obtainable from the original publications of Rey and Osterrieth (for the figure itself). Instructions for use in dynamic assessment can be found in the Examiner Manual for the LPAD.

> Osterrieth, P. A. (1944). *Le Test de Copie d'Une Figure Complexe: Contribution à l'étude de la perception et de la mémoire* [The Complex Figure Test: Contribution to the study of perception and memory]. *Éditions des Archives de Psychologie.* Neuchâtel, Switzerland: Delachaux & Niestlé.
> Rey, A. (1941). *L'examen psychologique dans les cas d'encéphalopathie traumatique* [Psychological assessment in cases of traumatic brain injury]. *Archives de Psychologie, 28,* 112.
> Rey, A. (1959). *Test de copie et de réproduction de mémoire de figures géométriques complexes* [Test of copying and reproducing from memory of complex geometric figures]. Paris: Centre de Psychologie Appliquée.

LIMITS ON DISTRIBUTION Unknown

DESCRIPTION Complex Figure is a very widely used test, serving a variety of assessment purposes. Examinees are shown a figure constructed primarily of straight lines and asked to draw one as much like it as possible while having the model figure in front of them. They may then be asked to reproduce it from memory. In DA, a learning phase follows in which strategies of organization, sequencing, and metamemory are mediated, after which the copy and memory phases may be repeated. Here is the original figure, reduced from its usual full-page size:

Figure A.1 shows both the original complex figure of Rey and an adaptation for use with young children, made by David Tzuriel.

Test or Procedure Name	Organization of Dots
Author(s), if applicable	A. Rey, R. Feuerstein
Publisher	Original by Rey published as *Organisation de groupes de points.* Current use as part of LPAD is by ICELP Press, Jerusalem.

Obtainable from The International Centre for the Enhancement of Learning Potential as part of the LPAD. Web site: www.icelp.org; Mail address:

ICELP
47, Narkis Street
P.O. Box 7755
Jerusalem 91077
ISRAEL

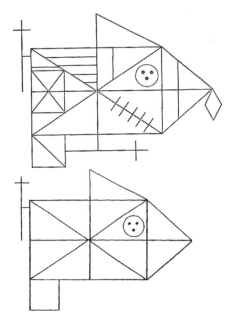

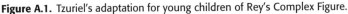

Figure A.1. Tzuriel's adaptation for young children of Rey's Complex Figure.

LIMITS ON DISTRIBUTION Part of LPAD (Learning Propensity Assessment Device); requires training; comes bundled with LPAD

DESCRIPTION This paper-and-pencil test consists of model figures that must be located in an amorphous cloud of dots and the correct dots connected to produce a figure just like the model in both shape and size (but not spatial orientation). Success requires systematic search, comparison (to model), hypothetical thinking, visual transport, inhibition of impulsivity, and rule learning and application. There are pretest, learning (mediation), and posttest forms, all of which progress from quite simple to moderately complex. This test is recommended for a wide variety of examinees representing many degrees of competence, because with appropriate mediation, even persons with substantial intellectual disability can do it. Motor incoordination presents particular difficulty.

Test or Procedure Name	The Stroop Test
Author(s), if applicable	J. Ridley Stroop
Publisher	Psychological Assessment Resources (PAR)

Obtainable from Several publishers offer the Stroop Test in different combinations of presentation and text, including some interpretation of performances. It is so well known that a Google search produces many references.

LIMITS ON DISTRIBUTION The test itself was part of a doctoral dissertation done at Peabody College in the 1930s and is probably in the public domain. Users should be careful, however, about infringing on the copyrights of authors who have published different versions and applications of the test.

DESCRIPTION The Stroop essentially presents a conflict between word reading and color naming. Word reading is more automatized. The names of colors are printed in different colors of ink, including their own (red in red, for example) and others (red in yellow, for example). The task is to read the color names, then to read by color; for example, when the word red is printed in yellow, it must be read as yellow. Resolution of this perceptual–cognitive conflict is the task. Not intended originally as a dynamic assessment task, the test can be used as such with interpolated mediation of metacognitive strategies, including rehearsal, awareness of the dual possibilities of reading the words and colors, and inhibition of the more automatic word-reading response. Such mediation in this test is a prime example of "cognitizing" functions that have become automatized. One significant problem is the use of primary colors that persons with impaired color perception – up to 12% of the male population – cannot easily distinguish. Further, when one tries to remove combinations of red and green, for example, there are not enough easily recognizable colors left to construct a parallel form for use with examinees who have impaired color perception. Nevertheless, it is highly useful and has been shown to be responsive to mediation.

Test or Procedure Name	Halstead Category Test
Author(s), if applicable	Ward Halstead, modified by Ralph M. Reitan Booklet edition by Nick A. Defilippis and Elizabeth McCampbell
Publisher	Psychological Assessment Resources (PAR)

Obtainable from The publisher

LIMITS ON DISTRIBUTION Not known; use requires some training, interpretation of performance requires specialized training in clinical neuropsychology

DESCRIPTION This is a widely used test of concept formation and recognition. It is similar to the Columbia Mental Maturity Scale in its conception: A stimulus card or picture is shown, and examinees much choose the one of four alternative displays that correctly identifies or is logically consistent with the stimulus display. In its original version, the test was presented by means of rear projection of slides onto a ground-glass screen, with a row of four toggle switches for responding. In this form, it was already a DA procedure in the sense that feedback on choice of response was given – immediately by means of a pleasant bell sound (for correct) or a somewhat raucous buzzer (for incorrect). It could be altered to eliminate the negative sound so that one could get either a "correct" signal or the withholding of the "correct" signal. There are several series of problems, yielding high reliability. The booklet form eliminates the need for the technical apparatus, which is rather cumbersome. The whole test can now be administered by means of a notebook computer that can be programmed to keep a record of the response to each item, the total score for each series of problems, and the grand total score. The test can be made more dynamic by using a test–teach–test procedure in which the teaching phase consists of mediation of essential metacognitive strategies: reflective rather than impulsive responding, careful information gathering, "internal" (mental) testing of possible responses, plus some mediation on comparison, classification, and class inclusion. Intended originally for assessment of the relative integrity of the nervous system, this remains its primary use, but as a concept formation task, it is useful as well in many other situations, especially when the question is "How much improvement in performance can the examinee make, given some teaching?"

Test or Procedure Name	Weigl-Goldstein-Scheerer Color Form Sorting Test
Author(s), if applicable	E. Weigl, K. H. Goldstein, M. Scheerer
Publisher	*The Psychological Corporation*

Obtainable from Publisher

LIMITS ON DISTRIBUTION Qualification Level B (The Psychological Corporation). Comes bundled with the Goldstein-Scheerer Tests of Abstract and Concrete Thinking

DESCRIPTION This venerable test is part of the Goldstein-Scheerer Tests of Abstract and Concrete Thinking. The Color-Form Sorting Test consists of blocks of different shape and color. Persons with brain injuries typically are attracted to color as a criterion for categorization before they are attracted to shape. Examiners ask examinees to sort the blocks according to how they go together. Having done that, they then ask the examinees to sort them again according to a different criterion. The relative ease with which examinees are able to switch criteria of categorization is said to indicate their degree of perceptual and/or conceptual flexibility versus rigidity. It was not designed as a dynamic assessment instrument but can be used as such with the addition of a mediational phase in which essential metacognitive operations are encouraged. (See Chapter 4 for an example of the use of this test in clinical dynamic neuropsychological assessment.) The test and its use in neuropsychology are described in the following publications:

Benton, A. L. (1994). Neuropsychological assessment. *Annual Review of Psychology, 45,* 1–23.

Weiss, A. A. (1964). The Weigl-Goldstein-Scheerer Color-Form Sorting Test: Classification of performance. *Journal of Clinical Psychololgy, 20,* 103–107.

APPENDIX B

Sources of Dynamic Assessment Materials

I. PROGRAMS AND MATERIALS AVAILABLE FOR PURCHASE

Test or System	*The Colabah Dynamic Assessment Method (CDA)*
Author(s)	Graham Chaffey
Language(s)	English
Address	Gchaffe3@metz.une.edu.au

Test or System	*Dynamic Assessment & Intervention: Improving Children's Narrative Abilities*
Author(s)	Lynda Miller, Ronald B. Gillam, and Elizabeth D. Peña
Language(s)	English
Publisher	ProEd, Austin, TX
Address	www.proedinc.com

Test or System	*Dynamic Assessment of Language and Reading Development*
Author(s)	Jørgen Frost
Language(s)	Danish and Norwegian
Address	www.statped.no/bredtvet

Test or System	*Dynamic Assessment of Test Accommodations*
Author(s)	Lynn Fuchs, Douglas Fuchs, Susan Eaton, and Carol Hamlett
Language(s)	English
Publisher	The Psychological Corporation, San Antonio, TX
Address	www.PsychCorp.com

Test or System	Dynamic Assessment of Young Children: *Children's Analogical Thinking Modifiability Test, with Pnina Klein* *Children's Inferential Thinking Modifiability Test* *Frame Test of Cognitive Modifiability, with Pnina Klein* *Cognitive Modifiability Battery: Assessment and Intervention* *Children's Seriational Thinking Modifiability Test*

Seria-Think Instrument Children's Conceptual and Perceptual
Analogical Modifiability Test, with E. Galinka
Author(s)   David Tzuriel
Language(s) English and Hebrew
Publisher   Author
Address   faculty.biu.ac.il/~tzuried, tzuried@mail.biu.ac.il

Test or System   Evaluacion del Potencial de Aprendizaje (EPA)
Author(s)   Fernandez-Ballesteros and Calero
Language(s)   Spanish
Address   r.fballesteros@uam.es

Test or System   IL-basis
Author(s)   J. Frost and J. C. Nielsen
Language(s)   Danish and Norwegian
Publisher   Psykologisk Forlag, Copenhagen

Test or System   Leertest voor Etnische Minderheden: Test en Hanleiding
Author(s)   J. H. M. Hamers, M. G. P. Hessels, and J. E. H. Van Luit
Language(s)   Dutch
Publisher   Swets & Zeitlinger, Lisse
Address

Test or System   L'intelligenza potenziale: Strumenti de misura e di riabilitazione
Author(s)   Rosa Angela Fabio
Language(s)   Italian
Publisher   Catholic University, Milan
Address   rosangelafabio@tiscalinet.it

Test or System   Learning Propensity Assessment Device (LPAD)
Author(s)   Reuven Feuerstein et al.
Language(s)   English, Hebrew, French, Spanish
Publisher   ICELP Press, Jerusalem
Address   www.icelp.org, lfalik@sfsu.edu

Test or System   Mindladder
Author(s)   Mogens R. Jensen
Language(s)   English
Address   www.mindladder.org

Test or System   Swanson-Cognitive Processing Test
Author(s)   H. Lee Swanson
Language(s)   English
Publisher   ProEd, Austin, TX

Address   www.proedinc.com

Test or System   *Test d'apprentissage pour les enfants étrangers en Suisse*
Author(s)   M. G. P. Hessels and C. Schlatter
Language(s)   French
Publisher   Authors, University of Geneva
Address   Marco Hessels, marco.hessels@pse.unige.ch; Christine
                  Schlatter-Hessels, christine.hessels@pse.unige.ch

Test or System   *Test d'évaluation dynamique de l'éducabilité*, 6th edition
                  Test d'évaluation dynamique de l'éducabilité adapté
Author(s)   Daniel Pasquier
Language(s)   French
Address   Daniel.pasquier@libertysurf.fr

Test or System   *Språk6-16. Test to observe language difficulties in 6–16 year olds.*
                  Static and dynamic
Author(s)   E. Ottem and J. Frost
Language(s)   Norwegian, Danish
Address   bredtvet@statped.no

Test or System   *TRAS: Early registration of children's language development*
Author(s)   U. Espenakk, J. Frost, M. K. Færevaag, H. Grove, E. Horn, E.
                  Løge, I. K. Solheim, and Å. K. H. Wagner
Language(s)   Norwegian, Dutch
Address   www.tras.org

For descriptions of most of these tests and many others that have been used in research, see Lidz and Elliott (2000), Haywood and Tzuriel (1992), and Tzuriel (2001).

II. SOME DYNAMIC ASSESSMENT RESOURCES

Web site with comprehensive list of DA publications, updates on training and conferences: www.dynamicassessment.com
    Additional Web sites with related information:

    Center for Cognitive Development and Assessment: www.bgcenter.com
    International Association for Cognitive Education and Psychology:
        www.iacep.coged.org
    International Centre for the Enhancement of Learning Potential:
        www.icelp.org
    International Center for Mediated Learning: www.mindladder.com
    Southeastern Center for the Enhancement of Learning Potential:
        www.scel.org

References

Abbott, S. P., Reed, E., Abbott, R. D., & Berninger, V. W. (1997). Year-long balanced reading/writing tutorial: A design experiment used for dynamic assessment. *Learning Disability Quarterly, 20,* 249–263.

Albrecht, J. E., O'Brien, E. J., Mason, R. A., & Myers, J. L. (1995). The role of perspective in the accessibility of goals during reading. *Journal of Experimental Psychology: Learning, Memory, & Cognition, 21*(2), 364–372.

American Educational Research Association, American Psychological Association, and the National Council on Measurement in Education. (1999). *Standards for educational and psychological testing.* Washington, DC: American Educational Research Association.

Anastasi, A. (1965). *Individual differences.* New York: Wiley.

Aranov, Z. (1999). *Validity and reliability of the ACFS Behavior Observation Scale.* (ERIC Document Reproduction Service No. ED438294; Clearinghouse Identifier: TM030602)

Ashman, A. F. (1992). Process-based instruction: Integrating assessment and instruction. In H. C. Haywood & D. Tzuriel (Eds.), *Interactive assessment* (pp. 375–396). New York: Springer-Verlag.

Bain, B. A. (1994). A framework for dynamic assessment in phonology: Stimulability revisited. *Clinical Communication Disorders, 4*(1), 12–22.

Balzac, T., & Gaines, D. M. (n.d.). *Dynamic multiple assessment: An instructional method that captures the symbiosis of assessment and instruction.* Online download: Citeseer.ist.psu.edu/295525.html.

Barrera, M. (2003). Curriculum-based dynamic assessment for new- or second-language learners with learning disabilities in secondary education settings. *Assessment for Effective Intervention, 29*(1), 69–84.

Barsalou, L. W. (1992). *Cognitive psychology: An overview for cognitive scientists.* Hillsdale, NJ: Erlbaum.

Beavers, K. F., Kratochwill, T. R., & Braden, J. P. (2004). Treatment utility of functional versus empiric assessment within consultation for reading problems. *School Psychology Quarterly, 19*(1), 29–49.

Beck, A. T. (1976). *Cognitive therapy and emotional disorders.* New York: International Universities Press.

Beck, A. T. (1991). Cognitive therapy: A 30-year retrospective. *American Psychologist, 46*, 369–375.

Bednar, M. R., & Kletzien, S. B. (1990). *Dynamic assessment for reading: A validation.* Paper presented at the National Reading Conference, Miami, FL.

Bensoussan, Y. (2002). The effectiveness of mediation on three subtests of the Application of Cognitive Functions Scale, a dynamic assessment procedure for young children. ERIC Document Reproduction Service No. 466635.

Bentley, A. M. (1980). Pattern reproduction in two cultures. *International Journal of Psychology, 15*(1), 1–9.

Berman, J. (2001). *An application of dynamic assessment to school mathematical learning.* Unpublished doctoral thesis, University of New England, Armidale (Australia).

Berman, J., & Graham, L. (2002). School counsellor use of curriculum-based dynamic assessment. *Australian Journal of Guidance and Counselling, 12*(1), 21–40.

Berninger, V. (2004). Brain-based assessment and instructional intervention. In G. Reid & A. Fawcett (Eds.), *Dyslexia in context. Research, policy, and practice* (pp. 90–119). London and Philadelphia: Whur Publishers.

Berninger, V. W., & Abbott, R. D. (1994). Redefining learning disabilities: Moving beyond aptitude-achievement discrepancies to failure to respond to validated treatment protocols. In G. R. Lyon (Ed.), *Frames of reference for the assessment of learning disabilities: New views on measurement issues* (pp. 162–182). Baltimore: P. H. Brooks.

Blachowicz, C. L. Z. (1999). Vocabulary in dynamic reading assessment: Two case studies. *Reading Psychology, 20*(3), 213–236.

Blaufarb, H. A. (1962). A demonstration of verbal abstracting ability in chronic schizophrenics under enriched stimulus and instructional conditions. *Journal of Consulting Psychology, 26*, 471–475.

Bleuler, M. (1950). *Dementia praecox or the group of schizophrenias* (Trans. H. Zenkin). New York: International Universities Press. (Original work published 1911)

Bleuler, M. (1978). *The schizophrenic disorders: Long-term patient and family studies* (Trans. S. M. Clemens). New Haven, CT: Yale University Press. (Original work published 1972)

Blewitt, P. (1994). Understanding categorical hierarchies: The earliest levels of skill. *Child Development, 65*, 1279–1298.

Bloom, B. S., & Broder, L. J. (1950). Problem-solving processes of college students. *School Review and Elementary School Journal, 73*, 1–103.

Bodrova, E., & Leong, D. J. (1996). *Tools of the mind: The Vygotskian approach to early childhood education.* Columbus, OH: Merrill.

Boring, E. G. (1950). *History of experimental psychology* (2nd ed.). New York: Appleton-Century-Crofts.

Borkowski, J. G., Chan, L. K. S., & Muthukrishna, N. (2000). A process-oriented model of metacognition: Links between motivation and executive functioning. In J. C. Impara & L. L. Murphy (Managing Ed.), *Buros-Nebraska series on measurement and testing: Issues in the measurement of metacognition* (pp. 1–41). Lincoln, NE: Buros Institute of Mental Measurement.

Borkowski, J. G., Turner, Lisa A., & Nicholson, J. (2004). Toward a research agenda on higher-level cognitive skills. *Journal of Cognitive Education and Psychology* [online], *4*, 188–198. www.iacep.coged.org/journal (Retrieved August 12, 2005).

Bortner, M., & Birch, H. G. (1969). Cognitive capacity and cognitive competence. *American Journal of Mental Deficiency, 74*, 735–744.

Bouchard T. J., Jr., & McGue, M. (1981). Familial studies of intelligence: A review. *Science, 212*, 1055–1059.

Bransford, J. D., Delclos, V. R., Vye, N. J., Burns, M. S., & Hasselbring, T. S. (1986). *Improving the quality of assessment and instruction: Roles of dynamic assessment* (Technical Report No. 1, Alternative Assessments of Handicapped Children). Nashville, TN: Kennedy Center, Vanderbilt University.

Braun, C., Rennie, B. J., & Gordon, C. J. (1987). An examination of contexts for reading assessment. *Journal of Educational Research, 89*(5), 283–289.

Bronson, M. B. (2000). *Self-regulation in early childhood: Nature and nurture.* New York: Guilford Press.

Brooks, N. D. (1997). *An exploratory study into the cognitive modifiability of pre-school children using dynamic assessment.* Unpublished master's thesis, University of Newcastle-Upon-Tyne; Newcastle, United Kingdom.

Brown, A. L., & Campione, J. C. (1986). Psychological theory and the study of learning disabilities. *American Psychologist, 14*(10), 1059–1068.

Brozo, W. G. (1990). Learning how at-risk readers learn best: A case for interactive assessment. *Journal of Reading, 33*(7), 522–527.

Budoff, M. (1967). Learning potential among institutionalized young adult retardates. *American Journal of Mental Deficiency, 72*, 404–411.

Budoff, M. (1971). *Learning potential and institutional discharge rates among adult EMRs.* RIEPrint #33. Cambridge, MA: Research Institute for Educational Problems.

Budoff, M. (1987). The validity of learning potential assessment. In C. S. Lidz (Ed.), *Dynamic assessment: An interactional approach to evaluating learning potential* (pp. 52–81). New York: Guilford Press.

Budoff, M., & Friedman, M. (1964). "Learning potential" as an assessment approach to the adolescent mentally retarded. *Journal of Consulting Psychology, 28*, 434–439.

Burns, M. S. (1980). *Preschool children's approach and performance on cognitive tasks.* Unpublished master's thesis, George Peabody College of Vanderbilt University.

Burns, M. S. (1985). *Comparison of "graduated prompt" and "mediational" dynamic assessment and static assessment with young children.* Unpublished doctoral dissertation, Vanderbilt University, Nashville, TN.

Burns, M. S., Haywood, H. C., & Delclos, V. R. (1987). Young children's problem-solving strategies: An observational study. *Journal of Applied Developmental Psychology, 8*, 113.

Butler, D. L., & Winne, P. H. (1995). Feedback and self-regulated learning: A theoretical synthesis. *Review of Educational Research, 65*, 245–281.

Butler, K. G. (1997). Dynamic assessment at the millennium: A transient tutorial for today! *Journal of Children's Communication Development, 19*(1), 43–54.

Call, R. J. (1973). *Verbal abstracting performance of low-SES children: An exploration of Jensen's theory of mental retardation.* Unpublished doctoral dissertation, George Peabody College.

Campbell, R., Donaldson, M., & Young, B. (1976). Constraints on classificatory skills in young children. *British Journal of Psychology, 67*(1), 80–100.

Campione, J. C., & Brown, A. L. (1985). *Dynamic assessment: One approach and some initial data* (Technical Report No. 361). Bethesda, MD: National Institute of Child Health and Human Development; National Institute of Education. (ERIC Document Reproduction Service No. ED269735)

Campione, J. C., & Brown, A. L. (1987). Linking dynamic assessment with school achievement. In C. S. Lidz (Ed.), *Dynamic assessment: An interactional approach to evaluating learning potential* (pp. 82–140). New York: Guilford Press.

Campione, J. C., & Brown, A. L. (1990). Guided learning and transfer: Implications for approaches to assessment. In N. Frederiksen, R. Glaser, A. Lesgold, & M. G. Shafto (Eds.), *Diagnostic monitoring of skill and knowledge acquisition* (pp. 141–172). Hillsdale, NJ: Erlbaum.

Campione, J. C., Brown, A. L., & Ferrara, R. A. (1982). Mental retardation and intelligence. In R. J. Sternberg (Ed.), *Handbook of human intelligence* (pp. 392–490). New York: Cambridge University Press.

Carlson, J. (1995, July). *Models of intelligence: Implications for cognitive education.* Presidential address, Fifth International Congress, International Association for Cognitive Education; Monticello, New York. Unpublished manuscript; Seattle, WA: University of Washington, College of Education.

Carlson, J. S., & Das, J. P. (1997). A process approach to remediating word decoding deficiencies in Chapter 1 children. *Learning Disabilities Quarterly, 20*(2), 93–102.

Carlson, J. S., & Wiedl, K. H. (1980). Applications of a dynamic testing approach in intelligence assessment: Empirical results and theoretical formulations. *Zeitschrift für Differentiele und Diagnostische Psychologie, 1*, 303–318.

Carlson, J. S., & Wiedl, K. H. (1992a). Principles of dynamic assessment: The application of a specific model. *Learning and Individual Differences, 4*(2), 153–166.

Carlson, J. S., & Wiedl, K. H. (1992b). The dynamic assessment of intelligence. In H. C. Haywood & D. Tzuriel (Eds.), *Interactive assessment* (pp. 167–186). New York: Springer-Verlag.

Carney, J. J., & Cioffi, G. (1990). Extending traditional diagnosis: The dynamic assessment of reading abilities. *Reading Psychology, 11*(3), 177–192.

Carney, J. J., & Cioffi, G. (1992). The dynamic assessment of reading abilities. *International Journal of Disability, Development, and Education, 39*(2), 107–114.

Chaiklin, S. (2003). The zone of proximal development in Vygotsky's analysis of learning and instruction. In A. Kozulin, B. Gindis, V. S. Ageyev, & S. M. Miller (Eds.), *Vygotsky's educational theory in cultural context* (pp. 39–63). New York: Cambridge University Press.

Chan, W. Y., Ashman, A. F., & Van Kraayenoord, C. E. (2000). Science and biological classification: Linking dynamic assessment to classroom curriculum. In C. S. Lidz & J. G. Elliott (Eds.), *Dynamic assessment: Prevailing models and applications* (pp. 607–639). Amsterdam: Elsevier Science.

Cherkes-Julkowski, M., & Gertner, N. (1989). *Spontaneous cognitive processes in hand-icapped children.* New York: Springer-Verlag.

Churches, M., Skuy, M., & Das, J. P. (2002). Identification and remediation of reading difficulties based on successive processing deficits and delays in general reading. *Psychological Reports, 91* (3, Pt1), 813–824.

Cioffi, G., & Carney, J. J. (1983). The dynamic assessment of reading disabilities. *Reading Teacher, 36,* 764–768.

Cohen, D. (2002). *How the child's mind develops.* New York: Taylor & Francis.

Cooper, L. A., & Regan, D. T. (1982). Attention, perception, and intelligence. In R. J. Sternberg (Ed.), *Handbook of human intelligence* (pp. 123–169). New York: Cambridge University Press.

Copple, C., Sigel, I. E., & Saunders, R. (1984). *Educating the young thinker: Classroom strategies for cognitive growth.* Hillsdale, NJ: Erlbaum.

Craig, H. K., & Evans, J. L. (1993). Pragmatics with SLI: Within-group varia-tions in discourse behaviors. *Journal of Speech & Hearing Research, 36,* 777–789.

Cronbach, L. J., & Furby, L. (1970). How we should measure change – or should we? *Psychological Bulletin, 74,* 68–80.

Das, J. P., Kar, B. C., & Parrila, R. K. (1996). *Cognitive planning: The psychological basis of intelligent behavior.* Thousand Oaks, CA: Sage.

Das, J. P., Mishra, R. K., & Pool, J. E. (1995). An experiment on cognitive remediation of word-reading difficulty. *Journal of Learning Disabilities, 28,* 66–79.

Das, J. P., & Naglieri, J. A. (1997). *Das/Naglieri: Cognitive Assessment System.* Itasca, IL: Riverside.

Das, J. P., Naglieri, J. A., & Kirby, J. R. (1994). *Assessment of cognitive processes: The PASS theory of intelligence.* Boston: Allyn & Bacon.

Delclos, V. R., Burns, M. S., & Vye, N. J. (1993). A comparison of teachers' responses to dynamic and traditional assessment reports. *Journal of Psychoeducational Assess-ment, 11*(1), 46–55.

Delclos, V. R., Vye, N. J., Burns, M. S., Bransford, J. D., & Hasslebring, T. S. (1992). In H. C. Haywood & D. Tzuriel (Eds.), *Interactive assessment* (pp. 317–331). New York: Springer-Verlag.

Delclos, V. R., Vye, N. J., Johnson, R. T., & Bransford, J. D. (1987). *Effects of dynamic assessment feedback on teacher instruction* (Technical Report No. 12, Alternative Assessments of Handicapped Children). Nashville, TN: Kennedy Center, Van-derbilt University.

DeLoache, J. S. (1991). Symbolic functioning in very young children: Understanding of pictures and models. *Child Development, 62,* 736–752.

DeLoache, J. S. (1995). Early understanding and use of symbols: The Model model. *Current Directions in Psychological Science, 4,* 109–113.

Desoete, A., Roeyers, H., Buysse, A., & De Clercq, A. (2002). Dynamic assessment of metacognitive skills in young children with mathematics learning disabilities. In G. M. Van der Aaslsvoort, W. C. M. Resing, & A. J. J. M. Ruijssenaars (Eds.), *Learning potential assessment and cognitive training: Actual research and perspectives in theory building and methodology* (pp. 307–333). Amsterdam: Elsevier Science.

Deutsch, R. (2003). Mediation from the perspective of mediated learning experience. *Journal of Cognitive Education and Psychology, 3*, 29–45. Retrieved from www.iacep.coged.org/journal October 14, 2004.

Dodge, D. T., & Colker, L. J. (1992). *The creative curriculum for early childhood* (3rd ed.). Washington, DC: Teaching Strategies.

Drahozal, E. (1997). *Validity Information for the Iowa Tests of Basic Skills (ITBS) and Iowa Tests of Educational Development (ITED)*. Itasca, IL: Riverside Publishing Co.

Ehrlenmeyer-Kimling, L., & Jarvik, L. F. (1963). Genetics and intelligence: A review. *Science, 142*, 1477–1479.

Eisenberg, N., & Harris, J. D. (1984). Social competence: A developmental perspective. *School Psychology Review, 13*(3), 267–277.

Elder, J. H., & Goodman, J. J. (1996). Social turn-taking of children with neuropsychiatric impairments and their parents. *Issues in Comprehensive Pediatric Nursing, 19*(4), 249–262.

Elliott, J. (1993). Assisted assessment: If it is "dynamic" why is it so rarely employed? *Educational and Child Psychology, 10*(4), 48–58.

Elliott, J. G. (2000). Dynamic assessment in educational contexts: Purpose and promise. In C. S. Lidz & J. G. Elliott (Eds.), *Dynamic assessment: Prevailing models and applications* (pp. 713–740). Amsterdam: Elsevier Science.

Elliott, J. (2003). Dynamic assessment in educational settings: Realising potential. *Educational Review, 55*(1), 15–32.

Elrod, G. F., & Tesolowski, D. G. (1993). Best practices in the vocational assessment of special needs learners. In H. B. Vance (Ed.), *Best practices in assessment for school and clinical settings* (pp. 69–111). Brandon, VT: Clinical Psychology Publishing.

Embretson, S. E. (1987). Toward development of a psychometric approach. In C. S. Lidz (Ed.), *Dynamic assessment: An interactional approach to evaluating learning potential* (pp. 141–170). New York: Guilford Press.

Estes, W. K. (1982). Learning, memory, and intelligence. In R. J. Sternberg (Ed.), *Handbook of human intelligence* (pp. 170–224). New York: Cambridge University Press.

Feather, N. T. (1961). The relationship of persistence at a task to expectation of success and achievement related motives. *Journal of Abnormal and Social Psychology, 63*(3), 552–561.

Fenichel, O. (1946). *The psychoanalytic theory of neurosis*. London: Kegan Paul, Trench, Trubner.

Fenwick, T. J., & Parsons, J. (1999). Using dynamic assessment in the social studies classroom. *Canadian Social Studies, 34*(1), 153–155.

Feuerstein, R., Feuerstein, R. S., Falik, L., & Rand, Y. (2002). *The dynamic assessment of cognitive modifiability*. Jerusalem: ICELP Press.

Feuerstein, R., Haywood, H. C., Rand, Y., Hoffman, M. B., & Jensen, M. (1982/1986). *Examiner manual for the Learning Potential Assessment Device*. Jerusalem: Hadassah-WIZO-Canada Research Institute and International Center for the Enhancement of Learning Potential.

Feuerstein, R., Jeannet, M., & Richelle, M. (1953). *Quelques observations du développement intellectuel chez les jeunes juifs nord-africains* [Some observations on intellectual development in North African Jewish youth]. Unpublished manuscript, Jerusalem: Hadassah-WIZO-Canada Research Institute and International Centre for the Enhancement of Learning Potential.

Feuerstein, R., Rand, Y., & Hoffman, M. B. (1979). *Dynamic assessment of retarded performers: The Learning Potential Assessment Device, theory, instruments, and techniques.* Baltimore, MD: University Park Press.

Feuerstein, R., Rand, Y., Hoffman, M. B., & Miller, R. (1980). *Instrumental enrichment.* Baltimore, MD: University Park Press.

Feuerstein, R. F., & Richelle, M. (1954). *Enfants juifs nord-africains* [North African Jewish children]. Tel Aviv: The Jewish Agency.

Flavell, J. H. (1985). *Cognitive development* (2nd ed.). Englewood Cliffs, NJ: Prentice-Hall.

Flavell, J. H., Miller, P. H., & Miller, S. A. (1993). *Cognitive development* (3rd ed.). Upper Saddle River, NJ: Prentice-Hall.

Frye, D., Zelazo, P. D., & Palfai, T. (1995). Theory of mind and rule-based reasoning. *Cognitive Development, 10,* 483–527.

Fuchs, L. S., & Fuchs, D. (1986a). Effects of systematic formative evaluation on student achievement: A meta-analysis. *Exceptional Children, 53,* 199–208.

Fuchs, L. S., & Fuchs, D. (1986b). Curriculum-based assessment of progress toward long-term and short-term goals. *Journal of Special Education, 20,* 69–81.

Fuchs, L. S., & Deno, S. L. (1994). Must instructionally useful performance assessment be based in the curriculum? *Exceptional Children, 61,* 15–24.

Fuchs, L. S., & Fuchs, D. (1996). Combining performance assessment and curriculum-based measurement to strengthen instructional planning. *Learning Disabilities Research & Practice, 11,* 183–192.

Fuchs, L. S., & Fuchs, D. (2002). Curriculum-based measurement: Describing competence, enhancing outcomes, evaluating treatment effects, and identifying treatment nonresponders. *Peabody Journal of Education, 77*(2), 64–84.

Fuchs, L. Fuchs, D., Eaton, S., & Hamlett, C. (2003). Dynamic assessment of test accommodations. Austin, TX: The Psychological Corporation.

Fuchs, D., Mock, D., Morgan, P. L., & Young, C. L. (2003). Responsiveness-to-intervention: Definitions, evidence, and implications for the learning disabilities construct. *Learning Disabilities Research and Practice, 18,* 157–171.

Gelman, S. A. (1998). Categories in young children's thinking. *Young Children, 53*(1), 20–26.

Gelman, S. A., & Coley, J. D. (1990). The importance of knowing a Dodo is a bird: Categories and inferences in 2-year-old children. *Developmental Psychology, 26*(5), 796–804.

Gerard, C. (1975, September–December). Developmental study of categorical classifications. *Enfance,* nos. 3–4, 345–372.

Gerber, M. M. (2000). Dynamic assessment for students with learning disabilities: Lessons in theory and design. In C. S. Lidz & J. G. Elliott (Eds.), *Dynamic assessment: Prevailing models and applications* (pp. 263–292). Amsterdam: Elsevier Science.

Gerber, M., Semmel, D., & Semmel, M. (1994). Computer-based dynamic assessment of multidigit multiplication. *Exceptional Children, 61*(2), 114–125.

Gettinger, M. (1984). Measuring time needed for learning to predict learning outcomes. *Exceptional Children, 51*(3), 244–248.

Gilliam, J. E., Carpenter, B. O., & Christensen, J. R. (1996). *Gifted and Talented Evaluation Scales: Examiner's manual.* Austin, TX: Pro-Ed.

Goleman, D. (1995). *Emotional intelligence: Why it can matter more than IQ.* New York: Bantam Books.

Goleman, D. (1998). *Working with emotional intelligence.* New York: Bantam Books.

Goncu, A., & Rogoff, B. (1998). Children's categorization with varying adult support. *American Research Journal, 35*(2), 333–349.

Gordon, J. E., & Haywood, H. C. (1969). Input deficit in cultural-familial retardates: Effect of stimulus enrichment. *American Journal of Mental Deficiency, 73*, 604–610.

Goswami, U. (1998). *Cognition in children.* East Sussex, England: Psychology Press/ Taylor & Francis.

Greenberg, K. H. (2000a). Inside professional practice: A collaborative, systems orientation to linking dynamic assessment and intervention. In C. S. Lidz & J. Elliott (Eds.), *Dynamic assessment: Prevailing models and applications* (pp. 489–312). Amsterdam: JAI/Elsevier Science.

Greenberg, K. H. (2000b). Attending to hidden needs: The cognitive enrichment advantage perspective. *Educational and Child Psychology: Psychological Influences upon Educational Intervention, 17*(3), 51–69.

Greenberg, K. H., & Williams, L. (2002). Reciprocity and mutuality in dynamic assessment: Asking uncomfortable questions. In G. M. Van der Aaslsvoort, W. C. M. Resing, & A. J. J. M. Ruijssenaars (Eds.), *Learning potential assessment and cognitive training: Actual research and perspectives in theory building and methodology* (pp. 91–110). Amsterdam: Elsevier Science.

Greenspan, S. I., Nover, R. A., & Scheuer, A. Q. (1987). A developmental diagnostic approach for infants, young children, and their families. *Clinical Infant Reports,* no. 3, 499–535.

Guterman, E. (2002). Toward dynamic assessment of reading: Applying metacognitive awareness guidance to reading assessment tasks. *Journal of Research in Reading, 25*(3), 283–298.

Guthke, J. (1982). The learning test concept: An alternative to the traditional static intelligence test. *German Journal of Psychology, 6*(4), 306–324.

Guthke, J. (1985). Ein neuer Ansatz für die rehabilitations-psychologisch orientierte Psychodiagnostik: das Lerntestkonzept als Alternative zum herkommlichen Intelligenztest [A new approach to rehabilitation-oriented psychodiagnosis: The learning test concept as an alternative to the traditional intelligence test.] In K. H. Wiedl (Ed.), *Rehabilitations-psychologie* [Rehabilitation psychology]. Mainz, Germany: Kohlhammer.

Guthke, J. (1992). Learning tests: The concept, main research findings, problems, and trends. In J. S. Carlson (Ed.), *Advances in cognition and educational practice* (Vol. 1A, pp. 213–233). Greenwich, CT: JAI Press.

Guthke, J., & Loffler, M. (1983). A diagnostic program (learning test) for the differential assessment of school failure in 1st grade pupils. In H. D. Rosler, J. P. Das, & I. Wald (Eds.), *Mental and language retardation* (pp. 41–50). Berlin: Deutscher Verlag der Wissenschaften.

Guthke, J., & Wingenfeld, S. (1992). The learning test concept: Origins, state of the art, and trends. In H. C. Haywood & D. Tzuriel (Eds.), *Interactive assessment* (pp. 64–93). New York: Springer-Verlag.

Guthrie, E. R. (1952). *The psychology of learning* (rev. ed.). New York: Harper & Row.

Gutierrez-Clellen, V. F., & Peña, E. (2001). Dynamic assessment of diverse children: A tutorial. *Language, Speech, and Hearing Services in Schools, 32*(4), 212–224.

Haeussermann, E. (1958). *Developmental potential of preschool children.* New York: Grune & Stratton.

Halpin, V. G. (1958). The performance of mentally retarded children on the Weigl Goldstein-Scheerer Color Form Sorting Test. *American Journal of Mental Deficiency, 62*(5), 916–919.

Halstead, W. C. (1947). *Brain and intelligence.* Chicago: University of Chicago Press.

Hamers, J., Pennings, A., & Guthke, J. (1994). Training-based assessment of school achievement. *Learning and Instruction, 4,* 347–360.

Hamers, J. H. M., Sijtsma, K., & Ruijssenaars, A. J. J. M. (Eds.). (1993). *Learning potential assessment: Theoretical, methodological, and practical issues.* Amsterdam: Swets & Zeitlinger.

Hamlin, R. M., Haywood, H. C., & Folsom, A. T. (1965). Effect of enriched input on schizophrenic abstraction. *Journal of Abnormal Psychology, 70,* 390–394.

Hansen, A. (2003). On mediation from Magne Nyborg's perspective. *Journal of Cognitive Education and Psychology, 3,* 54–70. Retrieved from www.iacep. coged.org/journal October 14, 2004.

Harlow, H. F. (1949). The formation of learning sets. *Psychological Review, 56,* 51–65.

Harvard Graduate School of Education, Educational Technology Center. (1995). *Assessing mathematical understanding and skills effectively: An interim report of the Harvard Group Balanced Assessment in Mathematics Project.* Cambridge, MA: Educational Technology Center.

Hays, D. R., III (2001). *Use of information from dynamic assessment of vocational aptitudes of persons with mental retardation by vocational rehabilitation counselors.* Unpublished doctoral dissertation proposal, Vanderbilt University, Nashville, TN.

Haywood, H. C. (1967). Experiential factors in intellectual development: The concept of dynamic intelligence. In J. Zubin & G. A. Jervis (Eds.), *Psychopathology of mental development* (pp. 69–104). New York: Grune & Stratton.

Haywood, H. C. (1968a). Introduction to clinical neuropsychology. In H. C. Haywood (Ed.), *Brain damage in school age children* (pp. 3–19). Washington, DC: Council for Exceptional Children.

Haywood, H. C. (1968b). Motivational orientation of overachieving and underachieving elementary school children. *American Journal of Mental Deficiency, 72,* 662–667.

Haywood, H. C. (1971). Individual differences in motivational orientation: A trait approach. In H. I. Day, D. E. Berlyne, & D. E. Hunt (Eds.), *Intrinsic motivation: A new direction in education* (pp. 113–127). Toronto: Holt, Rinehart, & Winston.

Haywood, H. C. (1977). Alternatives to normative assessment. In P. Mittler (Ed.), *Research to practice in mental retardation: Proceedings of the 4th Congress of IASSMD. Vol. 2, Education and training* (pp. 11–18). Baltimore: University Park Press.

Haywood, H. C. (1986). Test of Verbal Abstracting. In R. Feuerstein, H. C. Haywood, Y. Rand, M. B. Hoffman, & M. Jensen, *Examiner manual, Learning Potential Assessment Device.* Jerusalem: Hadassah-WIZO-Canada Research Institute.

Haywood, H. C. (1987/1993). A mediational teaching style. *The Thinking Teacher,* 4(1), 1–6. Also published in *International Journal of Cognitive Education and Mediated Learning,* 3(1), 27–38.

Haywood, H. C. (1988). Bridging: A special technique of mediation. *The Thinking Teacher,* 4(2), 4–5.

Haywood, H. C. (1992a). The strange and wonderful symbiosis of motivation and cognition. *International Journal of Cognitive Education and Mediated Learning,* 2(3), 186–197.

Haywood, H. C. (1992b). Interactive assessment: A special issue. *Journal of Special Education,* 26, 233–234.

Haywood, H. C. (1997). Interactive assessment. In R. L. Taylor (Ed.), *Assessment of individuals with mental retardation* (pp. 103–129). San Diego, CA: Singular.

Haywood, H. C. (2000). Cognitive developmental psychotherapy: Overview. In A. Kozulin, Y. Rand, & R. Feuerstein (Eds.), *Experience of mediated learning: An impact of Feuerstein's theory in education and psychology* (pp. 292–308). London: Pergamon.

Haywood, H. C. (2002, December). *New concepts of intelligence are needed: New methods of assessment will be required.* Paper given at the Vanderbilt Conference on the Futures of Assessment, Vanderbilt University, Nashville, TN.

Haywood, H. C. (2003a). Mediation within a neo-Piagetian framework. *Journal of Cognitive Education and Psychology,* 3, 71–81. Retrieved from www.iacep.coged.org/journal October 14, 2004.

Haywood, H. C. (2003b, November). *A transactional perspective on intellectual disability.* Keynote address, Australian Society for the Study of Intellectual Disability, Brisbane.

Haywood, H. C. (2004a). Thinking in, around, and about the curriculum: The role of cognitive education. *International Journal of Disability, Development, and Education,* 51, 231–252.

Haywood, H. C. (2004b). Theoretical bases of cognitive education: Old and new perspectives. *Cognitive Education in South Africa,* 11(2), 3–8. (Video presentation, International Association for Cognitive Education and Psychology-Southern Africa. Cape Town, South Africa, November 2004). DVD available from author.

Haywood, H. C. (2005, July). *Group dynamic assessment with adults with traumatic brain injuries: Massed versus distributed mediation.* Paper given at the 10th international conference, International Association for Cognitive Education and Psychology, Durham, UK.

Haywood, H. C. (2006). A transactional perspective on mental retardation. *International Review of Research in Mental Retardation,* 31, 289–314.

Haywood, H. C., & Bransford, J. D. (1984, April). Dynamic versus static assessment of young handicapped children. Presented at Annual Conference on Psychological Theory and Research in Mental Retardation, Gatlinburg, TN.

Haywood, H. C., Brooks, P. H., & Burns, M. S. (1992). *Bright start: Cognitive curriculum for young children*. Watertown, MA: Charlesbridge.

Haywood, H. C., & Burke, W. P. (1977). Development of individual differences in intrinsic motivation. In I. C. Uzgiris & F. Weizman (Eds.), *The structuring of experience* (pp. 235–263). New York: Plenum.

Haywood, H. C., Filler, J. W., Jr., Shifman, M. A., & Chatelanat, G. (1975). Behavioral assessment in mental retardation. In P. McReynolds (Ed.), *Advances in psychological assessment* (Vol. 3, pp. 96–136). San Francisco: Jossey-Bass.

Haywood, H. C., & Lidz, C. S. (2005). International survey of dynamic assessment trainers. *Journal of Cognitive Education and Psychology, 5*(2), 181–198. Retrieved from www.iacep.coged.org January 5, 2006.

Haywood, H. C., & Menal, C. (1992). Cognitive developmental psychotherapy: A case study. *International Journal of Cognitive Education and Mediated Learning, 2*(1), 43–54 [Version française, pp. 55–66].

Haywood, H. C., & Miller, M. B. (2003). Group dynamic assessment of adults with traumatic brain injuries. *Journal of Cognitive Education and Psychology, 3*, 37–163. Retrieved from www.iacep.coged.org/journal, November 25, 2003.

Haywood, H. C., & Miller, M. B. (2005, July). *Group dynamic assessment with adults with traumatic brain injuries: Massed versus distributed mediation.* Paper given at the 10th international conference, International Association for Cognitive Education and Psychology, Durham, UK.

Haywood, H. C., & Moelis, I. (1963). Effect of symptom change on intellectual function in schizophrenia. *Journal of Abnormal and Social Psychology, 67*, 76–78.

Haywood, H. C., & Paour, J.-L. (1992). Alfred Binet (1857–1911): Multifaceted pioneer. *Psychology, Mental Retardation and Developmental Disabilities, 18*(1), 1–4.

Haywood, H. C., & Switzky, H. N. (1974). Children's verbal abstracting: Effects of enriched input, age, and IQ. *American Journal of Mental Deficiency, 78*, 556.

Haywood, H. C., & Switzky, H. N. (1986). Intrinsic motivation and behavior effectiveness in retarded persons. *International Review of Research in Mental Retardation, 14*, 1–46.

Haywood, H. C., & Switzky, H. N. (1992). Ability and modifiability: What, how, and how much? In J. S. Carlson (Ed.), *Cognition and educational practice: An international perspective* (pp. 25–85). Greenwich, CT: JAI Press.

Haywood, H. C., & Tapp, J. T. (1966). Experience and the development of adaptive behavior. In N. R. Ellis (Ed.), *International review of research in mental retardation* (Vol. 1, pp. 109–151). New York: Academic Press.

Haywood, H. C., & Tzuriel, D. (Eds.). (1992). *Interactive assessment*. New York: Springer-Verlag.

Haywood, H. C., & Tzuriel, D. (2002). Applications and challenges in dynamic assessment. *Peabody Journal of Education, 77*(2), 40–63.

Haywood, H. C., Tzuriel, D., & Vaught, S. (1992). Psychoeducational assessment from a transactional perspective. In H. C. Haywood & D. Tzuriel (Eds.), *Interactive assessment* (pp. 38–63). New York: Springer.

Haywood, H. C., & Wachs, T. D. (1966). Size-discrimination learning as a function of motivation-hygiene orientation in adolescents. *Journal of Educational Psychology, 57,* 279–286.

Haywood, H. C., & Wachs, T. D. (1981). Intelligence, cognition, and individual differences. In M. J. Begab, H. C. Haywood, & H. Garber (Eds.), *Psychosocial influences in retarded performance.* Vol. 1, Issues and theories in development (pp. 95–126). Baltimore, MD: University Park Press.

Haywood, H. C., & Weaver, S. J. (1967). Differential effects of motivational orientation and incentive conditions on motor performance in institutionalized retardates. *American Journal of Mental Deficiency, 72,* 459–467.

Heald, J. D., & Marzolf, S. S. (1953). Abstract behavior in elementary school children as measured by the Goldstein-Scheerer Stick Test and the Weigl-Goldstein-Scheerer Color Form Sorting Test. *Journal of Clinical Psychology, 9*(1), 59–62.

Hebb, D. O. (1949). *The organization of behavior.* New York: Wiley.

Heimburger, R. F., & Reitan, R. M. (1961). Easily administered written test for lateralizing brain lesions. *Journal of Neurosurgery, 18,* 301–312.

Heinrich, J. J. (1991). *Responsiveness of adults with severe head injury to mediated learning.* Unpublished doctoral dissertation, Vanderbilt University, Nashville, TN.

Hessels, M. G. P. (2000). The Learning Potential Test for Ethnic Minorities (LEM): A tool for standardized assessment of children in kindergarten and the first years of primary school. In C. S. Lidz & J. G. Elliott (Eds.), *Dynamic assessment: Prevailing models and applications* (pp. 109–131). Amsterdam: JAI/Elsevier Science.

Hickling, A. K., & Wellman, H. M. (2000). The emergence of children's causal explanations and theories: Evidence from everyday conversation. *Developmental Psychology, 37*(5), 668–683.

Hirsch, E. D. Jr., & Holdren, J. (Eds.). (1996). *What your kindergartner needs to know.* Charlottesville, VA: Core Knowledge Foundation.

Hoover, H. D., Hieronymus, A. N., Frisbie, D. A., & Dunbar, S. B. (1993). *Iowa Tests of Basic Skills (ITBS) and Iowa Tests of Educational Development (ITED).* Itasca, IL: Riverside Publishing.

Hudson, J., & Fivush, R. (1991, April). *Planning in the preschool years. The emergence of plans from general event knowledge.* Paper presented in G. Sansone & C. Berg (Chairs). New directions in the development of planning: Cognitive, social and motivational components. Symposium presented at the meetings of the Society for Research in Child Development, Seattle.

Hunt, J. McV. (1961). *Intelligence and experience.* New York: Ronald.

Hunt, J. McV. (1963). Motivation inherent in information processing and action. In O. J. Harvey (Ed.), *Motivation and social interaction* (pp. 35–94). New York: Ronald.

Hunt, J. McV., & Cofer, C. N. (1944). Psychological deficit. In J. McV. Hunt (Ed.), *Personality and the behavior disorders* (pp. 971–1032). New York: Ronald Press.

Hupp, S. C., & Abbeduto, L. (1991). Persistence as an indicator of mastery motivation in young children with cognitive delays. *Journal of Early Intervention, 15*(3), 219–225.

Jacobs, E. L. (2001). The effects of adding dynamic assessment components to a computerized preschool language screening test. *Communication Disorders Quarterly, 22*(4), 217–226.

Jensen, A. R. (1980). *Bias in mental testing.* New York: Free Press.

Jensen, A. R. (1991). General mental ability: From psychometrics to biology. *Diagnostique, 16,* 134–144.

Jensen, A. R. (1998). *The g factor: The science of mental ability.* Westport, CT: Praeger.

Jensen, A. R. (2000). Psychometric skepticism. *Psycoloquy, 11, #39.* Retrieved from psycprints.ecs.soton.ac.uk/archive/00000039 January 19, 2005.

Jensen, E. (1998). *Teaching with the brain in mind.* Alexandria, VA: Association for Supervision and Curriculum Development.

Jepsen, R. H., & Lidz, C. S. (2000). Group dynamic assessment procedure: Reliability and validity of a cognitive assessment procedure with adolescents with developmental disabilities. *Journal of Cognitive Education and Psychology, 1*(1). Online journal of the International Association of Cognitive Education and Psychology, www.iacep.coged.org.

Jitendra, A. K., & Kameenui, E. J. (1993). An exploratory study of dynamic assessment involving two instructional strategies on experts and novices' performance in solving part-whole mathematical word problems. *Diagnostique, 18,* 305–324.

Jitendra, A. K., & Kameenui, E. J. (1996). *Experts and novices' error patterns in solving part-whole mathematical word problems: The role of dynamic assessment and instructional strategies.* Unpublished manuscript, Lehigh University, Bethlehem, PA.

Jitendra, A. K., & Rohena-Diaz, E. (1996). Language assessment of students who are linguistically diverse: Why a discrete approach is not the answer. *School Psychology Review, 25,* 40–56.

Jitendra, A. K., Rohena-Diaz, E., & Nolet, V. (1998). A dynamic curriculum-based language assessment: Planning instruction for special needs students who are linguistically diverse. *Preventing School Failure, 42*(4), 182–185.

Johnson, K., Haywood, H. C., & Hays, D. R. (1992, February). *Effects of failure within the test on subsequent subtest performance.* Paper presented at the Third International Conference of the International Association for Cognitive Education, Riverside, CA.

Kahn, R. (2000). Dynamic assessment of infants and toddlers. In C. S. Lidz & J. G. Elliott (Eds.), *Dynamic assessment: Prevailing models and applications* (pp. 229–262). Amsterdam: JAI/Elsevier Science.

Kaniel, S., & Tzuriel, D. (1992). Mediated learning experience approach in the assessment and treatment of borderline psychotic adolescents. In H. C. Haywood & D. Tzuriel (Eds.), *Interactive assessment* (pp. 399–418). New York: Springer.

Karnes, M. B., Johnson, L. J., & Beauchamp, K. D. F. (1989). Developing problem-solving skills to enhance task persistence of handicapped preschool children. *Journal of Early Intervention, 13*(1), 61–72.

Karpov, Y. V. (1982). Kriterii I metody diagnostiki umstvennogo razvitiya [Criteria and methods for the assessment of mental development]. *Vestn.MGU: Psikhologia, 3,* 18–26.

Karpov, Y. V. (2003a). Vygotsky's doctrine of scientific concepts. In A. Kozulin, B. Gindis, V. S. Ageyev, & S. M. Miller (Eds.), *Vygotsky's educational theory in cultural context* (pp. 65–82). New York: Cambridge University Press.

Karpov, Y. (2003b). Vygotsky's concept of mediation. *Journal of Cognitive Education and Psychology, 3*, 46–53. Retrieved from www.iacep.coged.org/journal, December 4, 2003.

Karpov, Y. (2005). *The neo-Vygotskian approach to child development.* New York: Cambridge University Press.

Karpov, Y., & Haywood, H. C. (1998). Two ways to elaborate Vygotsky's concept of mediation: Implications for education. *American Psychologist, 53*(1), 27–36.

Kaufman, A. S., & Kaufman, N. L. (1983). *K-ABC: Kaufman Assessment Battery for Children.* Circle Pines, MN: American Guidance Service.

Keane, K. J., Tannenbaum, A. J., & Krapf, G. F. (1992). Cognitive competence: Reality and potential in the deaf. In H. C. Haywood & D. Tzuriel (Eds.), *Interactive assessment* (pp. 300–316). New York: Springer.

Klahr, D., & Robinson, M. (1981). Formal assessment of problem-solving and planning processes in preschool children. *Cognitive Psychology, 13*, 113–148.

Kletzien, S. B., & Bednar, M. R. (1990). Dynamic assessment for at-risk readers. *Journal of Reading, 33*(7), 528–533.

Kopp, C. B. (1992). Emotional distress and control in young children. In N. Eisenberg & R. A. Fabes (Eds.), *Emotion and its regulation in early development* (pp. 41–56). New Directions for Child Development, no. 55. San Francisco: Jossey-Bass.

Korstvedt, A., Stacey, C. L., & Reynolds, W. F. (1954). Concept formation of normal and subnormal adolescents on a modification of the Weigl-Goldstein-Scheerer Color Form Sorting Test. *Journal of Clinical Psychology, 10*(1), 88–90.

Kovaleski, J. (2004). Response to instruction in the identification of learning disabilities: A guide for school teams. *NASP Communiqué, 32*, No. 5.

Kozulin, S., & Garb, E. (2002). Dynamic assessment of EFL text comprehension. *School Psychology International, 23*(1), 112–127.

Kraepelin, E. (1919). *Dementia praecox.* New York: Churchill Livingstone, Inc. (Trans. E. Barclay & S. Barclay, published 1971).

Kragler, A. (1989). *Dynamic versus static assessment; A comparison of the effects of each on the reading placement levels of Chapter 1 students.* (ERIC Document Reproduction Service No. ED327898)

Kroesbergen, E. H., VanLuit, J. E. H., & Naglieri, J. A. (2003). Mathematical learning difficulties and PASS cognitive processes. *Journal of Learning Disabilities, 36*(6), 574–582.

L'Abate, L. (1968). Screening children with cerebral dysfunction through the laboratory method. In H. C. Haywood (Ed.), *Brain damage in school age children* (pp. 128–158). Washington, DC: Council for Exceptional Children.

Lahey, M. (1988). *Language disorders and language development.* New York: Macmillan.

Laing, S. P., & Kamhi, A. (2003). Alternative assessment of language and literacy in culturally and linguistically diverse populations. *Language, Speech, & Hearing Services in Schools, 34*(1), 44–55.

Largotta, D. (2001). *Comparison of four year old children's retelling of stories in three conditions of increasing abstractness.* Unpublished master's thesis, Touro College, New York, NY.

Lee, M., Vaughn, B. E., & Kopp, C. B. (1983). Role of self-control in the performance of very young children on a delayed-response memory-for-location task. *Developmental Psychology, 19*(1), 40–44.

Levy, C. (1999). *The discriminant validity of the Application of Cognitive Functions Scale (ACFS): A performance comparison between typically developing and special needs preschool children.* Unpublished master's thesis, Touro College, New York, NY.

Lidz, C. S. (Ed.). (1987). *Dynamic assessment: An interactional approach for evaluating learning potential.* New York: Guilford Press.

Lidz, C. S. (1991). *Practitioner's guide to dynamic assessment.* New York: Guilford Press.

Lidz, C. S. (1992). Extent of incorporation of dynamic assessment in cognitive assessment courses: A national survey of school psychology trainers. *Journal of Special Education, 26,* 325–331.

Lidz, C. S. (2000). The Application of Cognitive Functions Scale (ACFS): An example of curriculum-based dynamic assessment. In C. S. Lidz & J. G. Elliott (Eds.), *Dynamic assessment: Prevailing models and applications* (pp. 407–439). Amsterdam: Elsevier Science.

Lidz, C. S. (2001). Multicultural issues and dynamic assessment. In L. A. Suzuki, J. G. Ponterotto, & P. J. Meller (Eds.), *Handbook of multicultural assessment: Clinical, psychological, and educational applications* (2nd ed., pp. 523–539). San Francisco: Jossey-Bass.

Lidz, C. S. (2003). *Early childhood assessment.* New York: Wiley.

Lidz, C. S. (2004). Successful application of a dynamic assessment procedure with deaf students between the ages of four and eight years. *Educational and Child Psychology, 21*(1), 59–73.

Lidz, C. S., & Elliott, J. G. (Eds.). (2000). *Dynamic assessment: Prevailing models and applications.* Amsterdam: JAI/Elsevier Science.

Lidz, C. S., & Gindis, B. (2003). Dynamic assessment of the evolving cognitive functions in children with typical and atypical development. In A. Kozulin, V. S. Ageyev, S. M. Miller, & B. Gindis (Eds.), *Vygotsky's theory of education in cultural context* (pp. 99–116). Cambridge, England: Cambridge University Press.

Lidz, C. S., & Greenberg, K. H. (1997). Criterion validity of a group dynamic assessment procedure with rural first grade regular education students. *Journal of Cognitive Education, 6*(2), 89–99.

Lidz, C. S., Jepsen, R. H., & Miller, M. B. (1997). Relationships between cognitive processes and academic achievement: Application of a group dynamic assessment procedure with multiply handicapped students. *Educational and Child Psychology, 14*(4), 56–67.

Lidz, C. S., & Macrine, S. L. (2001). An alternative approach to the identification of gifted culturally and linguistically diverse learners. *School Psychology International, 22*(1), 74–96.

Lidz, C. S., & Van der Aalsvoort, G. M. (2005). Usefulness of the Application of Cognitive Functions Scale with young children from The Netherlands. *Transylvanian Journal of Psychology* [special issue on dynamic assessment; Guest Ed., J. Lebeer] *1*, 82–99.

Lillard, A., & Curenton, S. (1999). Do young children understand what others feel, want, and know? *Young Children, 54*(5), 52–57.

Lipman, M. (1991). *Thinking in education*. New York: Cambridge University Press.

Lipman, M., Sharp, A. M., & Oscanyan, F. S. (1980). *Philosophy in the classroom*. Philadelphia: Temple University Press.

Lubinski, D., & Dawis, R. W. (1992). Aptitudes, skills, and proficiencies. In M. D. Dunnette & L. M. Hough (Eds.), *Handbook of industrial and organizational psychology* (Vol. 3, 2nd ed., pp. 1–59). Palo Alto, CA: Consulting Psychologists Press.

Luria, A. R. (1966). *Human brain and psychological processes* (Trans. B. Haigh). New York: Harper & Row.

Luria, A. R. (1973). *The working brain: An introduction to neuropsychology* (Trans B. Haigh). New York: Basic Books.

Luria, A. R. (1979). *The making of mind: A personal account of Soviet psychology* (Eds. Michael Cole & Sheila Cole). Cambridge, MA: Harvard University Press.

Luria, A. R. (1980). *Higher cortical functions in man* (2nd ed., Trans. B. Haigh). New York: Basic Books.

Lyon, G. R., Fletcher, J. M., Shaywitz, S. E., Shaywitz, B. A., Torgesen, J. K., Wood, F. B., et al. (2001). Rethinking learning disabilities. Washington, DC: Thomas Fordham Foundation. Retrieved January 19, 2005 from www.edexcellence.net/library/special'ed/index.html

Machleit, S. R. (2000). Working memory and writing: A comparison of two types of dynamic assessment of working memory and the relationship to sorting ability of heterogeneously grouped seventh grade students. *Dissertation Abstracts International Section A: Humanities & Social Sciences, 61*(2-A), 496.

Malowitsky, M. (2001). *Investigation of the effectiveness of the mediation portion of two subscales of the Application of Cognitive Functions Scale, a dynamic assessment procedure for young children*. (ERIC Document Reproduction Service No. 457191; Clearinghouse identifier: TM033288)

Marzano, R. J., Brandt, R. S., Hughes, C. S., Jones, B. F., Presseisen, B. Z., Rankin, S. C., & Suhor, C. (1988). *Dimensions of thinking: A framework for curriculum and instruction*. Alexandria, VA: Association for Supervision and Curriculum Development.

Mason, J. M. (Ed.). (1989). *Reading and writing connections*. Boston: Allyn & Bacon.

McFarlin, D. B. (1985). Persistence in the face of failure: The impact of self-esteem and contingency of information. *Personality & Social Psychology Bulletin, 11*(2), 153–163.

Meehl, P. E. (1954). *Clinical versus statistical prediction: A theoretical analysis and a review of the evidence*. Minneapolis, MN: University of Minnesota Press.

Meichenbaum, D. (1977). *Cognitive–behavior modification: An integrative approach.* New York: Plenum.

Meichenbaum, D. (1982). *Teaching thinking: A cognitive–behavioral approach.* Austin, TX: Society for Learning Disabilities and Remedial Education.

Meltzer, L. J. (1987). *The Surveys of Problem-Solving and Educational Skills (SPES).* Cambridge, MA: Educator's Publishing Service.

Meltzer, L. J. (1992). Strategy use in students with learning disabilities: The challenge of assessment. In L. Melzter (Ed.), *Strategy assessment and instruction of students with learning disabilities: From theory to practice* (pp. 93–135). San Antonio, TX: Pro-Ed.

Meltzer, L., & Reid, D. K. (1994). New directions in the assessment of students with special needs: The shift toward a constructivist perspective. *Journal of Special Education, 28*(3), 335–355.

Messick, S. J. (1995). Validity of psychological assessment: Validation of inferences from persons' responses and performances as scientific inquiry into score meaning. *American Psychologist, 50*(9), 741–749.

Miller, G. (1999). The magical number seven, plus or minus two: Some limits on our capacity for processing information. In R. J. Sternberg & R. K. Wagner (Eds.), *Readings in cognitive psychology* (pp. 2–18). Ft. Worth, TX: Harcourt Brace College.

Minick, N. (1987). Implications of Vygotsky's theories for dynamic assessment. In C. S. Lidz (Ed.), *Dynamic assessment: An interactional approach to evaluating learning potential* (pp. 116–140). New York: Guilford Press.

Minnaert, A. (2002). Alternative assessment of students' domain-specific learning competencies in the transition of secondary to higher education. In G. M. Van der Aaslsvoort, W. C. M. Resing, & A. J. J. M. Ruijssenaars (Eds.), *Learning potential assessment and cognitive training: Actual research and perspectives in theory building and methodology* (pp. 335–351). Amsterdam: Elsevier Science.

Naglieri, J. A. (1997). *Naglieri Nonverbal Ability Test: Multilevel technical manual.* San Antonio, TX: Psychological Corporation.

Naglieri, J. A., & Gottling, S. H. (1997). The PASS theory and mathematics instruction: A summary of initial studies. *Journal of Cognitive Education, 5,* 209–215.

Naglieri, J. A., & Johnson, D. (2000). Effectiveness of a cognitive strategy intervention in improving arithmetic computation based upon the PASS theory. *Journal of Learning Disabilities, 33*(6), 591–597.

Nguyen, S. P., & Murphy, G. L. (2003). An apple is more than just a fruit: Cross-classification in children's concepts. *Child Development, 74*(6), 1783–1806.

Nigam, R. (2001). Dynamic assessment of graphic symbol combinations by children with autism. *Focus on Autism & Other Developmental Disabilities, 16*(3), 190–197.

Olswang, L. B., Bain, B. A., & Johnson, G. A. (1992). Using dynamic assessment with children with language disorders. In S. F. Warren & J. E. Reichle (Eds.), *Causes and effects in communication and language intervention* (pp. 187–215). Baltimore: P.H. Brookes.

Osterrieth, P. A. (1944). *Le Test de Copie d'Une Figure Complex : Contribution à l'étude de la perception et de la mémoire* [The Complex Figure Test: Contribution to the study of perception and memory]. *Éditions des Archives de Psychologie.* Neuchâtel, Switzerland: Delachaux & Niestlé.

Otto, S. P. (2001). Intelligence, genetics of: Heritability and causation. *International Encyclopedia of the Social and Behavioral Sciences* (pp. 7651–7658). Amsterdam: Elsevier.

Owings, S., & Siefker, J. M. (1991). Criterion-referenced scoring versus norming: A critical discussion. *Vocational Evaluation and Work Adjustment Bulletin, 24*(3), 109–111.

Palinscar, A. S., & Brown, A. L. (1984). Reciprocal teaching of comprehension-fostering and monitoring activities. *Cognition and Instruction, 1*(2), 117–175.

Palisin, H. (1986). Preschool temperament and performance on achievement tests. *Developmental Psychology, 22,* 766–770.

Paour, J.-L. (1988). Retard mental et aides cognitives [Mental retardation and cognitive aides]. In J.-P. Caverni, C. Bastien, P. Mendelsohn, & G. Tiberghien (Eds.), *Psychologie cognitive: modèles et méthodes [Models and methods in cognitive psychology]* (pp. 191–216). Grenoble, France: Presses Universitaires de Grenoble.

Parrila, R. K., Kendrick, M. E., Papapoulis, T. C., & Kirby, J. R. (1999). Efficacy of a cognitive reading remediation program for at-risk children in grade 1. *Developmental Disabilities Bulletin, 27*(2), 1–31.

Peña, E. (2000). Measurement of modifiability in children from culturally and linguistically diverse backgrounds. *Communication Disorders Quarterly, 2*(2), 87–97.

Peña, E. (2001). Assessment of semantic knowledge: Use of feedback and clinical interviewing. *Seminars in Speech and Language, 22,* 51–64.

Peña, E. D., & Gillam, R. B. (2000). Dynamic assessment of children referred for speech and language evaluations. In C. S. Lidz & J. G. Elliott (Eds.), *Dynamic assessment: Prevailing models and applications* (pp. 543–575). Amsterdam: JAI Elsevier Science.

Peña, E., Iglesias, A., & Lidz, C. S. (2001). Reducing test bias through dynamic assessment of children's word learning ability. *American Journal of Speech Language Pathology, 10,* 138–154.

Peña, E., Miller, L., & Gillam, R. (1999). Dynamic assessment of narratives in children from diverse backgrounds. *California Speech-Language-Hearing Association Magazine, 28*(2), 12–13, 18.

Peña, E., Quinn, R., & Iglesias, A. (1992). Application of dynamic methods of language assessment: A nonbiased approach. *Journal of Special Education, 26,* 269–280.

Peña, E., & Valles, L. (1995). Language assessment and instructional programming for linguistically different learners: Proactive classroom processes. In H. Kayser (Ed.), *Bilingual speech-language pathology: An hispanic focus* (pp. 129–152). San Diego, CA: Singular.

Peña, L. (1993). *Dynamic assessment: A non-biased approach for assessing the language of young children.* Unpublished doctoral dissertation, Temple University, Philadelphia, PA.

Peverly, S. T., & Kitzen, K. R. (1998). Curriculum-based assessment of reading skills: Consideration and caveats for school psychologists. *Psychology in the Schools, 35,* 29–47.

Piaget, J. (1950). *Introduction à l'épistemologie génétique* [Introduction to developmental epistemology]. Paris: Presses Universitaires de France.

Piaget, J. (1952). *The origins of intelligence in children*. New York and Paris: International Universities Press.

Piaget, J. (1970). *Le structuralisme* [Structuralism]. Paris: Presses Universitaires de France (*Que sais-je?*, No. 1311).

Piaget, J., & Inhelder, B. (1969). *The psychology of the child*. New York: Basic Books.

Poehner, M. E., & Lantolf, J. P. (2003, October). *Dynamic assessment of L2 development: Bringing the past into the future* (CALPER Working Papers, No. 1). University Park: Pennsylvania State University, Center for Advanced Language Proficiency Education and Research. Retrieved from calper.la.psu.edu/downloads/download.php?3, November 23, 2005.

Reed, H. B. C., Jr. (1968). The use of psychological tests in diagnosing brain damage in school children. In H. C. Haywood (Ed.), *Brain damage in school age children* (pp. 109–127). Washington, DC: Council for Exceptional Children.

Reinharth, B. M. (1989). *Cognitive modifiability in developmentally delayed children*. Unpublished doctoral dissertation, Ferkauf Graduate School of Psychology, Yeshiva University, New York.

Reitan, R. M. (1962). Psychological deficit. *Annual Review of Psychology, 13*, 415–444.

Reitan, R. M., & Wolfson, D. (1985). *The Halstead-Reitan Neuropsychological Test Battery: Theory and clinical interpretation*. Tucson, AZ: Neuropsychology Press.

Renzulli, J. S., & Westberg, K. L. (1991). Scale for rating students' participation in the local gifted education program. In S. L. Hunsaker, M. M. Frasier, E. Frank, V. Finley, & P. Klekotka (1995). *Performance of economically disadvantaged students placed in gifted programs through the Research-Based Assessment Plan* (No. RM95208; p. 45). Storrs, CT: National Research Center on the Gifted and Talented.

Reschly, D. J. (1987). Assessing educational handicaps. In I. B. Weiner, A. K. Hess, & K. Allen (Eds.), *Handbook of forensic psychology* (pp. 155–187). New York: Wiley.

Reschly, D. J. (1997). Diagnostic and treatment utility of intelligence tests. In D. P. Flanagan, J. L. Genschaft, & P. L. Harrison (Eds.), *Contemporary intellectual assessment: Theories, tests, and issues* (pp. 437–456). New York: Guilford Press.

Resing, W. C. M. (2000). Assessing the learning potential for inductive reasoning (LIR) in young children. In C. S. Lidz & J. G. Elliott (Eds.), *Dynamic assessment: Prevailing models and applications* (pp. 229–262). Amsterdam: JAI/Elsevier Science.

Rey, A. (1941). L'examen psychologique dans les cas d'encéphalopathie traumatique [Psychological assessment in cases of traumatic brain injury]. *Archives de Psychologie, 28*, 112.

Rey, A. (1959). *Test de copie et de réproduction de mémoire de figures géométriques complexes* [Test of copying and reproducing from memory of complex geometric figures]. Paris: Centre de Psychologie Appliquée.

Richards, R., Berninger, V., Nagy, W., Parsons, A., Field, K., & Richards, A. (2004). Dynamic assessment of child dyslexics' brain response to alternative spelling treatments. *Education and Child Psychology, 22*(2), 62–80.

Rosch, E. (1999). Principles of categorization. In R. J. Sternberg & R. K. Wagner (Eds.), *Readings in cognitive psychology* (pp. 225–241). Ft. Worth, TX: Harcourt Brace College.

Roseberry, C. A., & Connell, P. J. (1991). The use of an invented language rule in the differentiation of normal and language-impaired Spanish-speaking children. *Journal of Speech and Hearing Research, 34,* 596–603.

Rosenfield, S. (1987). *Instructional consultation.* Hillsdale, NJ: Erlbaum.

Rumbaugh, D. M., & Washburn, D. A. (2003). *Intelligence of apes and other rational beings.* New Haven, CT: Yale University Press.

Saldaña, D. (2004). Dynamic Master Mind: Interactive use of a game for testing metacognition. *School Psychology International, 25*(4), 422–438.

Salvia, J., & Ysseldyke, J. E. (1991). *Assessment* (5th ed.). Boston: Houghton-Mifflin.

Sattler, J. M. (1988). *Assessment of children* (3rd ed.). San Diego, CA: Author.

Scarr-Salapatek, S. (1975). Genetics and the development of intelligence. In F. D. Horowitz, M. Hetherington, S. Scarr-Salapatek, & G. Siegel (Eds.), *Review of child development research* (Vol. 4, pp. 1–57). Chicago: University of Chicago Press.

Sclan, S. G. (1986). *Dynamic assessment and thought disorder in paranoid and nonparanoid schizophrenic patients.* Unpublished doctoral dissertation, Vanderbilt University, Nashville, TN.

Schlatter, C., & Büchel, F. P. (2000). Detecting reasoning abilities of persons with moderate mental retardation: The Analogical Reasoning Learning Test (ARLT). In C. S. Lidz & J. G. Elliott (Eds.), *Dynamic assessment: Prevailing models and applications* (pp. 155–186). Amsterdam: JAI/Elsevier Science.

Schloss, P. J., Smith, M. A., Hoover, T., & Wolford, J. (1987). Dynamic criterion-referenced vocational assessment: An alternative strategy for handicapped youth. *Diagnostique, 12*(2), 74–86.

Schneider, E., & Ganshow, L. (2000). Dynamic assessment and instructional strategies for learners who struggle to learn foreign language. *Dyslexia, 6,* 72–82.

Schwebel, A. I. (1966). Effects of impulsivity on performance of verbal tasks in middle- and lower-class children. *American Journal of Orthopsychiatry, 36,* 13–21.

Shurin, R. (1998). *Validity and reliability of the Application of Cognitive Functions Scale with preschool children with disabilities.* (ERIC Document Reproduction Services No. ED435681; Clearinghouse Identifier: TM030312)

Siegler, R. S. (1998). *Children's thinking* (3rd ed.). Upper Saddle River, NJ: Prentice Hall.

Snow, R. E., & Yalow, E. (1982). Education and intelligence. In R. J. Sternberg (Ed.), *Handbook of human intelligence* (pp. 493–585). New York: Cambridge University Press.

Spector, J. E. (1992). Predicting progress in beginning reading: Dynamic assessment of phonemic awareness. *Journal of Educational Psychology, 84,* 353–363.

Steiner, J. (1993). *Psychic retreats: Pathological organizations in psychotic, neurotic, and borderline patients.* London: Routledge.

Sternberg, R. J. (1982). Reasoning, problem solving, and intelligence. In R. J. Sternberg (Ed.), *Handbook of human intelligence* (pp. 225–307). New York: Cambridge University Press.

Sternberg, R. J., & Grigorenko, E. L. (2002). *Dynamic testing: The nature and measurement of learning potential.* New York: Cambridge University Press.

Swanson, H. L. (1992). Generality and modifiability of working memory among skilled and less skilled readers. *Journal of Educational Psychology, 84,* 473–488.

Swanson, H. L. (1995). Effects of dynamic assessment on the classification of learning disabilities: The predictive and discriminant validity of the Swanson-Cognitive Processing Test (S-CPT). *Journal of Psychoeducational Assessment, 13,* 204–229.

Swanson, H. L. (2000). Swanson-Cognitive Processing Test: Review and applications. In C. S. Lidz & J. G. Elliott (Eds.), *Dynamic assessment: Prevailing models and applications* (pp. 71–107). Amsterdam: JAI/Elsevier Science.

Swanson, H. L., & Alexander, J. E. (1997). Cognitive processes as predictors of word recognition and reading comprehension in learning-disabled and skilled readers. Revisiting the specificity hypothesis. *Journal of Educational Psychology, 89,* 128–158.

Switzky, H. N., & Haywood, H. C. (1974). Motivational orientation and the relative efficacy of self-monitored and externally imposed reinforcement systems in children. *Journal of Personality and Social Psychology, 30,* 360–366.

Szymula, G. (1990). Vocational assessment. In C. Schiro-Geist (Ed.), *Vocational counseling for special populations* (pp. 65–97). Springfield, IL: Charles C Thomas.

Tanner, H., & Jones, S. (2002). Assessment of children's mathematical thinking in practical modeling situations. *Teaching Mathematics and Its Applications, 21*(4), 145–159.

Tatik, T. (2000). *A concurrent validity study between the Application of Cognitive Functions Scale and the Leiter-Revised International Performance Test.* (ERIC Document Reproduction Service No. ED445033; Clearinghouse Identifier TM031638.)

Tawney, J. W., & Gast, D. L. (1984). *Single subject research in special education.* Columbus, OH: Merrill.

Teo, A., Carlson, E., Mathieu, P. J., Egeland, B., & Sroufe, L. A. (1996). A prospective longitudinal study of psychosocial predictors of achievement. *Journal of School Psychology, 34*(3), 285–306.

Tissink, J., Hamers, J. H. M., & Van Luit, J. E. H. (1993). Learning potential tests with domain-general and domain-specific tasks. In J. H. M. Hamers, K. Sijtsma, & A. J. J. M. Ruijssenaars (Eds.), *Learning potential assessment: Theoretical, methodological and practical issues* (pp. 243–266). Amsterdam: Swets & Zeitlinger.

Tymchuk, A. (1973). Effects of verbal concept training versus stimulus enhancement on verbal abstracting in institutionalized retarded delinquent boys. *American Journal of Mental Deficiency, 77,* 551–555.

Tzuriel, D. (2000). The Cognitive Modifiability Battery (CMG): Assessment and intervention. In C. S. Lidz & J. G. Elliott (Eds.), *Dynamic assessment: Prevailing models and applications* (pp. 375–406). Amsterdam: JAI/Elsevier.

Tzuriel, D. (2001). *Dynamic assessment of young children.* New York: Kluwer Academic/Plenum.

Tzuriel, D., & Haywood, H. C. (1984). Exploratory behavior as a function of motivational orientation and task conditions. *Personality and Individual Differences, 5*(1), 67–76.

Tzuriel, D., & Haywood, H. C. (1985). Locus of control and child-rearing practices in intrinsically motivated and extrinsically motivated children. *Psychological Reports, 57*, 887–894.

Tzuriel, D., & Klein, P. S. (1985). Analogical thinking modifiability in disadvantaged, regular, special education, and mentally retarded children. *Journal of Abnormal Child Psychology, 13*, 539–552.

Tzuriel, D., & Samuels, M. T. (2000). Dynamic assessment of learning potential: Inter-rater reliability of deficient cognitive functions, type of mediation, and non-intellective factors. *Journal of Cognitive Education and Psychology, 1*, 41–64. Retrieved March 3, 2005 from www.iacep.coged.org/journal.

Tzuriel, D., & Schanck, T. (1994, July). *Assessment of learning potential and reflectivity-impulsivity dimension*. Paper presented at the 23rd International Congress of Applied Psychology, Madrid, Spain.

Utley, C. A., Haywood, H. C., & Masters, J. C. (1992). Policy implications of psychological assessment of minority children. In H. C. Haywood & D. Tzuriel (Eds.), *Interactive assessment* (pp. 445–469). New York: Springer.

Valencia, S. W., Campione, J. C., Weiner, S., & Bazzi, S. (1990, December). *Dynamic assessment of reading achievement*. Paper presented at the National Reading Conference, Miami, FL.

Van der Aalsvoort, G. M., & Lidz, C. S. (2002). Reciprocity in dynamic assessment in classrooms: Taking contextual influences on individual learning into account. In G. M. Van der Aaslsvoort, W. C. M. Resing, & A. J. J. M. Ruijssenaars (Eds.), *Learning potential assessment and cognitive training: Actual research and perspectives in theory building and methodology* (pp. 111–144). Amsterdam: Elsevier Science.

Van der Aalsvoort, G. M., & Lidz, C. S. (in press). A cross-cultural validation study of the Application of Cognitive Functions Scale: A dynamic assessment procedure, with Dutch first grade students from regular primary schools. *Journal of Applied School Psychology, 24*(1).

Vaughn, B. E., Kopp, C. B., & Krakow, J. B. (1984). The emergence and consolidation of self-control from eighteen to thirty months of age: Normative trends and individual differences. *Child Development, 55*(3), 990–1004.

Vye, N. J., Burns, M. S., Delclos, V. R., & Bransford, J. D. (1987). A comprehensive approach to assessing intellectually handicapped children. In C. S. Lidz (Ed.), *Dynamic assessment: An interactional approach to evaluating learning potential* (pp. 327–359). New York: Guilford Press.

Vygotsky, L. S. (1929). The problem of the cultural development of the child. *Journal of Genetic Psychology, 36*, 415–434.

Vygotsky, L. S. (1978). *Mind in society: The development of higher psychological processes.* Cambridge, MA: Harvard University Press.

Vygotsky, L. S. (1986). *Thought and language.* Cambridge, MA: MIT Press. (Original work published 1934)

Warren, A. (2002). *MATHPLAN: A Diagnostic and Prescriptive Task Collection: A trip to the toystore.* Cambridge, MA: Balanced Assessment in Mathematics Project, Harvard University, Educational Technology Center.

Warren, A. (2003, July). *MATHPLAN: A Diagnostic and Prescriptive Task Collection: A Trip to the Toystore: A plan for evaluating the validity and reliability of a new dynamic assessment instrument.* Unpublished paper presented at the International Association for Cognitive Education and Psychology Conference, Seattle, WA.

Warren, A. R. (2006). *Evaluating the evaluator: An examination of two new methods for evaluating the skills of the teacher as dynamic assessor.* Unpublished doctoral dissertation. Cambridge, MA: Harvard University.

Weiss, A. A. (1964). The Weigl-Goldstein-Scheerer Color-Form Sorting Test: Classification of performance. *Journal of Clinical Psychology, 20,* 103–107.

Wellman, H. M., Ritter, K., & Flavell, J. (1975). Deliberate memory development in the delayed reactions of very young children. *Developmental Psychology, 11,* 780–787. (ERIC Document Reproduction Service No. ED445033; Clearinghouse Identifier TM031638)

Wheeler, L., & Reitan, R. M. (1962). The presence and laterality of brain-damage predicted from responses to a short aphasia screening test. *Perceptual and Motor Skills, 15,* 783–799.

Wiedl, K. H. (1999). Cognitive modifiability as a measure of readiness for rehabilitation. *Psychiatric Services, 50*(11), 1411–1413.

Wiedl, K. H. (2003). Dynamic testing: A comprehensive model and current fields of application. *Journal of Cognitive Education and Psychology, 3,* 93–119. Retrieved from www.iacep.coged.org/journal, December 3, 2003.

Wiedl, K. H., & Schottke, H. (2002). Vorhersage des Erfolgs schizophrener Patienten in Einem psychedukativen Behandlungsprogramm durch indikatoren des Veranderungspotentials im Wisconsin Card Sorting Test. *Verhaltenstherapie, 12*(2), 90–96.

Wiedl, K. H., Schottke, H., Garcia, M., Calero, D. (2001). Dynamic assessment of cognitive rehabilitation potential in schizophrenic persons and in elderly persons with and without dementia. *European Journal of Psychological Assessment 17*(2), 112–119.

Wiedl, K. H., Schottke, H., Green, M. F., & Nuechterlein, K. H. (2004). Dynamic testing in schizophrenia: Does training change the construct validity of a test? *Schizophrenia Bulletin, 30*(4), 703–711.

Wiedl, K. H., Wienobst, J., Schottke, H. H., Green, M. F., & Nuechterlein, K. H. (2001). Attentional characteristics of schizophrenia patients differing in learning proficiency on the Wisconsin Card Sorting Test. *Schizophrenia Bulletin, 27*(4), 687–696.

Wigfield, A., Eccles, J. S., & Rodriguez, D. (1998). The development of children's motivation in school contexts. In P. D. Pearson & A. Iran-Nigad (Eds.), *Review of research in education* (Vol. 23). Washington, DC: American Educational Research Association.

Williams, R. H., & Zimmerman, D. W. (1996). Are simple gain scores obsolete? *Applied Psychological Measurement, 20*(1), 59–69.

Wood, D. (1988). *How children think and learn: The social contexts of cognitive development.* Oxford, U.K.: Blackwell.

Woodcock, R. W. (2002). New looks in the assessment of cognitive ability. *Peabody Journal of Education, 77*(2), 6–22.

Zelazo, P. D., Müller, U., Frye, D., & Marcovitch, S. (2003). The development of executive function in early childhood. *Monographs of the Society for Research in Child Development, 68,* Serial No. 274.

Zigler, E., Abelson, W. D., & Seitz, V. (1973). Motivational factors in the performance of economically disadvantaged children on the Peabody Picture Vocabulary Test. *Child Development, 44*, 294–303.

Zigler, E., & Butterfield, E. C. (1968). Motivational aspects of changes in IQ test performance of culturally deprived nursery school children. *Child Development, 39*, 1–14.

Zimmerman, B. J. (1990). Self-regulated learning and academic achievement: An overview. *Educational Psychologist, 25*(1), 3–17.

Author Index

Subject Index

Tests and Testing Materials Index